UNSW

A PORTRAIT

PATRICK O'FARRELL

UNSW
A PORTRAIT

THE UNIVERSITY OF NEW SOUTH WALES
1949–1999

PUBLISHED ON BEHALF OF
THE UNIVERSITY OF NEW SOUTH WALES

A UNSW Press book

Published by
University of New South Wales Press Ltd
University of New South Wales
Sydney 2052 Australia

© Patrick O'Farrell 1999
First published in 1999

National Library of Australia
Cataloguing-in-Publication entry:

Patrick O'Farrell.
   UNSW A portrait:
   The University of New South Wales 1949–1999
   Includes bibliography, index.

   1. University of New South Wales—History.
   2. New South Wales University of Technology—History.
   3. Universities and Colleges—New South Wales—
   Sydney—History. I. Title.

   Hardback ISBN 0 86840 417 9
   Boxed numbered edition ISBN 0 86840 617 1

   378.9441

Editing Roderic Campbell
Design Di Quick & Dana Lundmark
Cover illustration Simon Fieldhouse
Printer South China Printing, Hong Kong

CONTENTS

Dream and Destinations

1998

FOREWORD

by The Honourable Gordon Samuels AC
Governor of New South Wales

Professor O'Farrell has written a vigorous and enthralling account of how UNSW got to be where it is now; how the Sydney Technical College became one of Australia's leading universities in what must be regarded as very much under the ordinary time for the course.

He has called this history a portrait, which may mislead some who think of portraiture as a static medium. But this book is nothing if not a wholly dynamic realisation of an academic society whose achievements over its brief span of years have been immense. What made this possible?

Professor O'Farrell describes UNSW as unusual, unorthodox, lively and informal. It certainly has been, and still is, all of these. But above all, it was hungry; it was the epitome of the hungry fighter seeking success and recognition.

Those who taught at Sydney Technical College, or who held its diplomas, had a good conceit of themselves, and made an aggressive assessment of their own capabilities. They were far from cowed by Sydney University's (or should I say the University of Sydney's) condescension, but stung to a kind of intellectual swagger which, as Professor O'Farrell points out, led them (along with powerful allies) to insist upon University rather than Institute as the title of their new (and to its opponents unthinkable) technical educational establishment.

What was perceived to be the practical technological ethos of STC persisted well into the university's early years, and perhaps found its refined character in the blend of principle and pragmatism, which has always characterised UNSW. At the farewell dinner in honour of my predecessor, Robert Webster, a senior metallurgist (not

Rupert Myers) took me aside and said: 'I hope you're not going to try and turn this place into a college of liberal arts!' I do not think that UNSW has ever become a college of liberal arts, although it has flourished in all the respects necessary to achieve that status. Baxter and Myers, who were the firm supporters of UNSW's statutory bias towards science and technology, were by no means opposed to flirtations with the arts; or, indeed, to more serious affaires. Michael Birt was a serious supporter of liberal cultivation.

The book portrays the university largely (but not merely) in terms of its vice-chancellors, a treatment that I think works well. The development of UNSW can indeed be illuminated by the conviction of Baxter, Myers and Birt; and its future may perhaps be seen in John Niland's perception of the university's destiny.

Professor O'Farrell's narrative omits nothing of importance; and his judgements are fair, penetrating and sensitive. UNSW's first fifty years have found a worthy chronicler.

PREFACE

ooking back is a vital part of best seeing forward. To be hard-headed about it, history is an investment in the future. No mere nostalgia-romp for fun. As TS Eliot has it, 'A people without history is not redeemed from time, for history is a pattern of timeless moments'. Such as now. And Eliot, again, in *Little Gidding,* in verse which has central relevance to the search and discovery which lies at the heart of the university enquiry:

> We shall not cease from exploration
> And the end of all our exploring
> Will be to arrive at where we started
> And know the place for the first time.

For the University of New South Wales to review its history is not an indulgent luxury for it, but an incumbent necessity. Particularly at this time. Not only is it appropriate and convenient to make an appraisal to commemorate fifty years of life, 1949 to 1999, but it is timely also in regard to the major processes of change which have questioned, throughout Australia, the traditional notions of university life and character. Pragmatic public utility? Self-sustaining corporation? Degree factory? Such questions pose fundamental challenges — and threats — to the intellectual life and freedoms which universities embody and represent. This book, and the University of New South Wales, of which it tells the story, affirm the values of the modern university — ideals tempered by realism. This balance has been the

4

university's trademark; its weights and symmetry varying over the years, its components reflecting time and circumstance, but never an ivory tower, some remote position of lofty seclusion. No. The key to the University of New South Wales has been, and is, its friendly and close involvement with the society that sustains it, a society which deserves and expects the best of what it can get, by way of scholarship, research and teaching.

How to begin? Modestly, like the university itself: from rags to riches, log cabin to White House. Or, to be specific, from nothing in 1949 (if its grounding in the Sydney Technical College be discounted) to be one of Australia's premier universities in 1999 — in fact, earlier than that. ONE of the premier universities? Some would say THE. But let the smaller, less pretentious claim prevail: the University of New South Wales bids to share the description of intellectual excellence, research achievement, world-class university stature. And size? From nothing in 1949 to a stable level in the mid 1990s of just over 30,000 students and just over 2400 academic staff in a total of 5000. What follows is the story of this institution.

It goes without saying (yet let it be said) that the growth and maintenance of the University of New South Wales has been the achievement of an extraordinary, and extraordinarily diverse, group of people. This book cannot do justice to such a large company; nor does it try, in the sense of inclusion of individuals. Nor, sadly, particular schools, even faculties. To have attempted to do so — there are at present seventy-nine schools, ten faculties — would have overloaded the text to the degree of unreadability. The sheer size, diversity and complexity of the institution defeat any attempt to exhaustively depict or contain its parts. Readers with particular circumscribed interests will be disappointed, as will those searching for their own names — or, as the colourful image has it, those looking for a prop for the short leg of their billiard table. Some university histories make very heavy reading, almost impossible to lift physically, let alone uplift the spirit. In such august company, perhaps it is cheeky to aspire to be readable; but, given that the book, as art form, seeks to communicate and presumes an audience, it is pointless — a waste of trees — unless some interested human contact is established. Moreover, in such a various enterprise the interested, personal involvement of one participant is the tedium, incomprehension, and irksome irrelevance of another. It is not an illustration of the old dictum about the impossibility of pleasing everybody, but a running of the risk of pleasing nobody. There will never be space enough in such a compilation to do proper justice to those included, never — whatever the protestations — enough to justify omissions. This is a problem which cannot be addressed, let alone remedied, at the level of general history. Sadly, many people will inevitably be left out. It falls to faculties and schools to do individuals and their contributions to university life some measure of justice. Nor is that function of due personal recognition the only useful and beneficent product of history at that intimate level: it locates and enables faculties and schools to assess their character, appraise the past with a clear and informed eye to the future. In any intellectual and scholarly endeavour, perspective is imperative: setting present work and planned initiatives on firm, known foundations. An obvious procedure — think about it. One hopes that one lesson of this overview is that faculties and schools should do the same within their particular orbits. Even the students' Guild. Although the effort has been made to include students here, much is to be learned from a view from the bottom up, of how the audience sees the actors. Whatever the problems of span and continuity, the students' Guild might also see its life and times clearer in the context of things past.

Forget the disclaimers. What is attempted? What does this book seek to do? Provide a general overview, organise the past into intelligible coherence, try to make some sense of it all, attempt to spell out its meaning. Its purpose is, within the society of its time and the resolutions of its nature, to explain how we got to where we are, how and why things came to pass.

The Baxter Years revisited —

AH Willis, the author, presents a copy of

his book to Sir Philip Baxter, then aged 78

November 1983

This is an ambitious aim — as are all essays in the interpretation of complex human affairs, especially those involving highly intelligent people. It is bound to encounter unsolved mysteries and provoke disagreement, and that on serious grounds involving neglect, or contentious facts, or personal view. On the latter I can only plead involvement with the university for forty of its fifty years — and affectionate, if at times irked and critical, gratitude for being among its company. On the former I can only offer the limitations and shortcomings of all human endeavour, even those guided by professional standards and commitment.

There may be those hurt or offended by what they find here: universities are notoriously plagued by politicking and in-fighting, and that at a high level of abstruse complication. My remarks are less directed at them — they are big boys and girls, able to look after themselves — than at those who find this book a deal too candid, and who, timidly, prefer their history sanitised, the surface account of bland appearances. They recoil into make-believe from a past which offers challenge and engagement. To them I offer the observation by the head of that most sensitive, indeed secretive of institutions — the Roman Catholic Church. As I pointed out in one of my earliest books: 'It was Pius XII's hope, as expressed to the Tenth International Congress of Historical Sciences, that historians would "make past history a lesson for the present and the future". Nothing of historical worth is to be learnt from sanctimonious self-praise, pious inventions, edifying fables or comfortable forgetfulness — or from blind partisanship. I hope that none of these faults, whatever others, have crept in here.' These are sentiments I echo now, in response to any critics of the openness and candour with which I have coated love: that love is not passion or romance, but its essence — commitment. Love builds on justice, on appraisal, on criticism as well as praise. On such a stance, I have tried to position what I have written here.

Enough of intellectual sentiment: its practical consequences in regard to this work? When, in 1994, the UNSW Fiftieth Anniversary History was begun, my understanding with the vice-chancellor was that I have complete freedom in pursuing that task, and be designated sole author and holder of copyright. The university provided generous funds for research assistance and for some teaching relief for myself, over the four-year period. This book is the property of the university and any profits go to it. This agreement has been scrupulously honoured. Senior members of the university, from the vice-chancellor down, have read this in draft and made helpful comments but no one has attempted, even mildly, any kind of intervention. I am most grateful for, and honoured by that trust — though wryly, as it leaves me carrying the can.

Sources. The factual framework has been constructed from the orthodox public materials and university documentation cited in the bibliography. However, the book is without footnotes or end notes. This because it is very substantially based on, and interlarded with, material derived from recollections and impressions supplied on the understanding of confidentiality. The project has conducted interviews with over fifty people associated with the history of the university, at all levels and in diverse fields. Such interviews have been of one to two hours' duration, recorded, and with a transcript sent to the interviewee for checking or amendment. The basic understanding of this information- and opinion-gathering has been confidentiality, no attribution to precise source. The same condition applies to the Oral History collection — about a hundred interviews — assembled over the years since the 1980s, by the University Archives — which I have also used extensively. I regret that the confidentiality provision will frustrate those seeking chapter and verse and gospel authors, but I can offer no remedy other than to assure them that all transcripts that have been listed in the bibliography have been lodged with the University Archives, and are available there — provided that the enquirer has the permission of the interviewee. This personalised approach to the gathering of source material has had the immense advantage of imparting lived reality and vibrant humanity to what otherwise might be a dull chronicle.

I am conscious of being a member of the Faculty of Arts, that is, of having a view naturally conditioned by my own subjective experience in a university conceived in, and having distinguished public eminence in science and technology. A strong, conscious effort has been made to balance treatment (to a degree which in fact may do Arts itself some injustice!). But it should be noted, ruefully, in relation to a book of 100,000 words, that whatever the disciplinary perspective taken will seem less than adequate to some — if not also the other!

I am also sensitive to the needs of those who might want a detailed factual chronology rather than the discursive interpretative essay I have written. Accordingly, each chapter is preceded by a list of important university events in the chapter period. These sections do not purport to be exhaustive or to extend downwards into minutiae, however individually significant that may be. Those who do not require such treatments will skip them.

Style. In 1983 Emeritus Professor Al Willis published *The University of New South Wales. The Baxter Years*, which covers the earlier years of the university with JP Baxter as vice-chancellor, in a straightforward, structured way — formal reportage. This is not such a book, though I am obliged to Professor Willis for his valuable work, and his ready cooperation with this project.

I trust I have not written anything needlessly quirky, but it is certainly idiosyncratic and personal. Particularly, perhaps, in the way in which I have sought to use anecdotes and personal experience to analyse and illuminate serious and important points in university life: amusing stories are often more implicitly revealing of their subjects than pages of prosaic prose.

In my view, best historical practice calls for the style to be appropriate to the nature of the subject, in this case, UNSW — unusual, not traditional, unorthodox, lively, informal. It would not be true to the university to adopt the style of the traditional presentation of university histories: this is not such a place, and I will not, in my approach, do it the injustice of pretending that it is other than unique. It is what it is and has been. I hope that my style reflects the character of its integrity. Mirrors, too, the sense and flavour of those many candid interviews on which I have so heavily relied. Ten people, from vice-chancellor to former students have read the book in earlier drafts. Their unanimously enthusiastic response, however they might differ in matters of interpretation, convinces me that at least the treatment here lives.

While I have sought to offer some coverage of all the main elements within the university's evolution, the emphases have not been determined by any laws of equal treatment, but rather by a wish to illuminate, to pounce on vital elements of character and change. Perhaps some may opine that a casualty of this strategy has been some spatial underrating of the ordinary rank and file, those unspectacular foot-sloggers whose energies, dedication, and resolve carried forward the work, and reputation of the university. It would take a stern and fanatical egalitarian to so argue — and one dismissive of, not only the coverage throughout of these foot-sloggers, but of the sympathies and identifications generated by my own career within the university. I joined it as the most junior of lecturers in April 1959, my doctorate incomplete, and I have occupied here each of the steps on the academic ladder. I joined the Staff Association in 1959, and retain — if not always happily — membership still. I have known, if not all that closely, all four vice-chancellors. My personal judgement is that the university has been extremely well-served by its vice-chancellors. Each has played a vital role in his own phase of institutional development, embodying it, employing it, and giving his own individual positive response to the demands of the worlds the university inhabited.

In my view, things work in this way. Inevitably the generals get the press and publicity. This book recognises that fact as inescapable, connives in it to the extent that these generals — vice-chancellors — determined policy, and, to an extent, events. They were responsible and should be held so. Hence the attention paid to them: they were the central element in the university environment. The fact that many students — and staff — never sighted them, and took their acquaintance and governance from those much further down the hierarchical chain was immaterial. It was the vice-chancellors who ruled the roost — in so far as anybody could: universities were open to the dictates of politicians and the forces of the economy, to social change and the fluxing atmosphere of the intellect.

So it is that the organisation of this book is not merely a reflection of controlling personalities. It stresses the ideas behind its development, its emergence as a University of Technology, the dominance of Baxter, the multiple challenges of the 1960s and 1970s, its achievement of steady state in the 1970s and 1980s, the transformations inflicted by Labor and Liberal constrictions, and the bid, in the 1990s, to occupy world stage. Always the conflict between ideal and reality, the war between dreams and resources, between science and technology and the rest, pressures from outside impacting on plans for a quiet life within. Always, too, business as usual, the ordinary daily life of teaching and research. But always, too (I hope), the pursuit of the life and vocation of the academic intellect.

Now, read on!

The University of New South Wales — |>

an aerial view looking out towards the sea

1995

ACKNOWLEDGEMENTS

The University of New South Wales provided money to me to employ research assistance and for teaching relief. The School of History, first under Professor Martyn Lyons, then under Professor Roger Bell, provided facilitation and a welcoming and cooperative environment. My colleagues, and the school secretaries, Jenni Granger and Sonja Wilkinson, helped and encouraged, in a wide variety of ways. Dr Damien McCoy and Dr Karen Hutchings gave me research assistance and interview techniques of a kind which could not have been bettered. Both, in their different ways, provided highly intelligent and alert, unstinting research work, and wordprocessing skills, to the highest level of academic competence. Their energetic and youthful help made pleasure of an arduous task, which is in their debt in basic ways. I am particularly grateful to Karen Hutchings for her help in the final stages of the work, which was, as all such books are, exacting and variously demanding.

A number of people read early and later drafts and commented on them in detail. In this regard I am particularly grateful to Beverley Kingston, Ian Black and John Ingleson in the School of History; John Niland, vice-chancellor, Chris Fell, deputy vice-chancellor, and Jane Morrison, pro-vice-chancellor; Robin Derricourt of UNSW Press; Justin O'Farrell of Freehill, Hollingdale and Page; Virginia O'Farrell of Westpac; Laurie Dillon, university archivist; and Emeritus Professor John Thornton. John Thornton, reading both first and final drafts to their significant improvement, went beyond the considerable investments of time and expertise and generosity these readings represented by all those I have thanked.

Without the collection, and ready cooperation of the University Archives this book could not have been written. I am most grateful to Laurie Dillon, the archivist, and his staff, particularly Karin Brennan, and to Julia Horne, for their constant help. That also extends to the photographs, of which the University Archives has a collection in excess of 80,000. The book is illustrated mainly from that collection but I also acknowledge Richard O'Farrell, the *Sydney Morning Herald*, the *Australian*, and the photographic resources of the university's Publishing and Printing Services, namely Tony Potter and Rosemary Allan. For kind permission to use cartoons, I thank George Molnar, and Phil Schofield of this university's School of Biochemistry.

Then there are many people within the university who took the time and trouble to make themselves and their recollections and observations available for interview to myself and by my research assistants Damien McCoy and Karen Hutchings. Their names are writ in the book of university life and their honour will be renowned for evermore. They are too numerous to be mentioned in this space and, as primary sources, they are properly listed in full in the bibliography. However, it should be noted here, as it is in the bibliography, that such interviews were given on the basis of confidentiality and transcripts are available only with the permission of the interviewee.

In addition, many people have helped in a variety of ways. Amongst these were the following: Belinda Allen, Michael and Jenny Birt, Peter Boadle, Fr John Bosman, RG Burdon, Andrew Coombs, Peter Cranewell, Valerie Craven, Graham Croker, Stanley Croker, Allan Egan, Chris Fell, Melanie Harris, Gernot Herser, Pat Howard, Keith Jordan, Bruce Kaye, Muhamed Kazim, Vanessa King, Andrew Krane, Valerie McCallum, Fred Orr, Ben Robinson, members of the students' Guild, Ellis Swinbourne, Richard Willgoss, University Regiment. I should also wish to thank those many university officers, especially in the media and publications sections, who were generous with their help and cooperation. My apologies to those many people whom we did not interview, who might have made contributions. Over the previous four years we have appealed on four occasions in *Uniken* for such people to come forward but we appreciate that many may not have seen our requests, or were too busy — or modest! — to come forward. My regrets.

Plus the obvious, the Almighty's permission, brokered up to now by doctors associated with the Royal North Shore Hospital — Associate Professor Ross Smith, Ian Fevre, John Gunning, and Tony Hathaway. In this, and every other context, my wife as always has been of inestimable help. Her association with the university parallels my own since 1959 and her recollection of various incidents is often better than mine. Another family matter. All our five children have been students at the university. Their interviews are listed in the bibliography, but I should record here the fact that their experiences have significantly widened and deepened my own experience of, and encounter with, the university.

My debt to the University of New South Wales Press, to Robin Derricourt and his staff — particularly Di Quick — is very great. And to my editor, Roderic Campbell, whose meticulous and sensitive work has enabled me to say much better what I mean.

May I, finally, thank the subject. It has been a challenging and very worthwhile research topic, which I have enjoyed immensely, pushing my capacities and capabilities to their limits. I hope I have not failed to do my own university some semblance of historical justice.

Patrick O'Farrell
Professor of History
July 1998

1

THE IDEA OF THE UNIVERSITY: TO 1949

1878

1878

Sydney Mechanics' School of Arts Working Men's College is formed — later known as the Sydney Technical College.

1883

1883

New South Wales government takes financial responsibility for the college but leaves administration to a voluntary Board of Technical Education, with 19 appointed members.

1887

1887

Norman Selfe, acting president of the Board of Technical Education, expresses a hope that Sydney Technical College might become a second tertiary education institution in New South Wales.

1889

1889

1 NOVEMBER Board of Technical Education dissolved by the minister of Public Instruction, its responsibilities transferred to the Technical Education Branch of the Department of Public Instruction.

1891

1891

9 MARCH Sydney Technical College's first building opens at Ultimo campus.

1933

1933

Sydney Technical College's Council of Studies sets up a committee to prepare draft legislation to found a technical university.

SELECTED EVENTS

Turner Hall, Sydney Technical College
1912

Engineering building, Sydney
Technical College

1936

1936

Sydney Technical College
appoints first principal,
HJ Swain, and first deputy
principal, A Denning.
• Sydney Technical
College Advisory Council
established.

1940

1940

DH Drummond's Technical
Education Act (unproclaimed)
refers to the foundation of an
Institute of Technology.

1946

1946

JUNE Australian National
University, Canberra, founded.
9 JULY The proposal by RJ
Heffron, the New South
Wales minister for Education,
for the creation of an
'institute of technology'
accepted by government.

1947

1947

8 JULY Establishment of the
Developmental Council
approved by New South
Wales government, and
members appointed.
27 AUGUST Developmental
Council holds its first
meeting.

1948

1948

1 MARCH First degree
courses established: in civil,
electrical and mining
engineering; 46 students
enrol.
MAY Sydney University sets
up a chair of Coal-mining.
JUNE Developmental
Council recommends
a change of name from
Institute of Technology to
New South Wales University
of Technology.
27 JULY New South Wales
government makes clear its
intention to establish a
university, rather than an
institute, of technology.
SEPTEMBER Professor
Le Fèvre (of Sydney
University) resigns from the
Developmental Council over
the name-change proposal.

SELECTED EVENTS

∧

Facade and much more —

the Mary Ann St frontage

to the Sydney Technical College

Central Building, to which adjoining

buildings were related

ca late 1940s

Origins? The received version is this: the crisis demands of the Second World War drew urgent attention to the national importance of science and technology, to Australia's radical deficiencies therein, and to the centrality of diploma holders of Sydney Technical College (formed from 1878 to deal with technical education, and located at Ultimo in central Sydney) in responding to that challenge. The post-war Labor government of New South Wales — with RJ Heffron as minister for Education, and Wallace Wurth, wartime director-general of Manpower, as chairman of the Public Service Board — was acutely aware of this. It was convinced of the need, in converting an agricultural society into a modern, industrial one, to train high quality engineers and technologists in numbers beyond the capacities and characteristics of the existing University of Sydney. This led to the acceptance in principle by the government, on 9 July 1946, of the proposal that an Institute of Technology be created. This issued, a year later, on 27 August 1947, in the first meeting of a Developmental Council of nineteen members, representing the government, professions, industry, higher education, and trade unions, under the chairmanship of the minister for Education. High-powered stuff, whose calibre was such as to lead some to date the university's foundation from that time.

The Developmental Council was authorised to advise, recommend and liaise on practical steps to be taken to set up the institute, a first step which led on by stages, but with a natural momentum and logic, to the establishment of a university.

This is the essence of Vice-Chancellor JP Baxter's account in 'A Short History of the University of New South Wales to 1964', published in the *Australian University*, May 1965. All true enough, if on the bland and aseptic side. And given that Baxter had arrived in Australia in January 1950, after the foundation of the university, and well after the discussions, debates, and disputes that had preceded it. And also given that he was writing not so much a history as a public relations exercise. But for the professional historian — Baxter was a chemical engineer — truth is a territory, a locale in which the centre is always elusive, unattainable. The terrain, while remaining itself, presents appearances which differ with altitude. Baxter's view is from far above, in which distance blurs all but major features. On the ground things may seem — may be — different.

But the historian is not to be placed on oath. Do you swear by almighty God that the evidence you shall give will be the truth, the whole truth and nothing but the truth? So help me God. Yes, but with the proviso that the whole truth can never be known, and the recounting of the evidence will be the best that can be done within the limits imposed by the discipline and the constrictions of time and money. And there is quarrel here, contradiction even, with those simpletons of factology who would declare that there was no mystery about these men who played a certain part in history. And there is no evasion of the central mystery at the heart of these academic things, the mystery at the heart of matters of the mind. What of the humble joy to be taken in the mere company of excellence? For all the politics and jostling, ambition and competition, the usual human shortcomings, there are also those still moments of recognition of intellect at full stretch, of delight and admiration of gifts being exercised at the furthest boundaries of the mind's capacity. For what is being born and reborn here is no dull and dutiful corporation. Here is a constant adventure in discovery, with its tediums and hard work, long journeys into the ordinary, yet also its fleeting arrivals at the seeming centre of things; instantly lost, superseded but so exhilaratingly gained.

Enough of the egregious poetry of things. Where stand we now in the matter of origins? With historical climates far and near. In his book on social change and analysis in Australia in the 1950s (*Governing Prosperity* 1995) Nicholas Brown makes it clear that the University of Technology sat very uneasily in the intellectual and university climate of the Australia of its day. Much more to the point of the debates of those times was the foundation of the Australian National University (ANU) in June 1946. In introducing its establishing Bill into federal parliament, JJ Dedman, minister for Post-War Reconstruction, suggested that 'in the social sciences more than any other field of learning, Australia has an outstanding contribution to make. It could once again lead the world as a social laboratory.' When Marcus Oliphant came to direct the Research School of Physical Sciences in 1949, he was soon to remark that the physical sciences had been a virtual afterthought to a university previously defined around the social sciences. The ANU represented the focal point for Australian thinking and controversy at that level, and that was in matters of government, economics, political science and social policy. As Oliphant observed, science came last to the minds of that day.

There is a strong case that this balance of intellectual concern worked to the University of Technology's advantage: had the priorities been otherwise, it seems unlikely that the establishment of a marvellously well-endowed Australian National University with a science ethos would have left room for a poor scientific cousin in Sydney. But, as things were, there was such room — mental space which the proponents of the scientific might occupy, and in which they might establish an institution of their own which might grow.

Against this were the consequences of the weight of the non-scientific intellectual consensus, at best apathetic, unenthusiastic or out of sympathy, at worst vehemently opposed. It was all very well that the university should promote itself as the appropriate culminating outgrowth of a technical education, needed as never before to ensure the development of an industrial nation. Point conceded: no argument. But to a sceptical mind this had to do with the need for better and more extensive technical education; nothing to do with universities. To call the technical institution in Sydney a university was preposterous, not only absurd but insufferably uppish: even its planners had debated the matter of whether it should be termed 'institute' as more appropriate, initially adopting that title. They dropped it on the declared grounds that the public did not understand its significance and that only the name 'university' carried meaning in the popular concept of higher education; and that staff recruitment was greatly facilitated in Britain by identifying the new entity as 'university': prospective staff were reluctant to join a foreign-sounding and unfamiliar 'institute'. Disgraceful pragmatism this seemed to those outsiders who based their definition of university on principle and precedent. They had a point; the new 'university' had been created as a label to suit what existed — a demand for the teaching of science and technology at the highest level of technical excellence, an uncomprehending public, and a status-seeking staff. And such critics would have had more of a point if they had realised — perhaps they did — the sheer effrontery of the whole operation, and its personal vanities. It suited Heffron's ego to be promoting a dignified and heavy university rather than a glorified tech college. And Wurth in Britain, sussing out institute staff in 1946, was much happier to have a 'university' within his gift. Over all was a Labor cabinet not to be intimidated by the ponderous and selfish voices of establishment and tradition. If it wanted a university then that is what it would have, whatever the term meant, and be damned to all the stuck-ups and Jeremiahs. Very quickly, virtually overnight, the language changed. For 'institute' read 'university': the arguments and justifications changed not at all. What had changed was the government's outlook. It was sick of deferring to, and trying to accommodate, the old frustrative order. It would go its own way, have its own will.

All this seemed arrant presumption, galling, to those critics who looked down on the technical as of inferior status. On all grounds — intellectual, social, cultural — the 'university' of technology was found wanting, lesser. Take the matter of student origins and background. The chancellor of the University of New South Wales adverted in 1961, in a publicity brochure, to 'young people from families who previously would not have thought of going to a university' as being part of the university's clientele. The university seldom referred to such sensitive matters, open to contention and misinterpretation, particularly at a time and in an environment in which it was the first in a new wave of university expansion. However merited and creditable as an extension of educational democracy, any claim of serving some underclass was likely to be resented by those of that class who acknowledged no inferiority.

But the social fact was that the university's students tended to come from the wrong side of the tracks, from western and southern suburbs of Sydney, migrant and ethnic groups, and with worker parental occupations viewed as inferior by the populations of the more affluent suburban homelands of the traditional university suppliers. To this was added other dimensions of outsiderism — the bureaucracy of the university derived from the public service and was reputedly the home of Roman Catholics, its banking was with the Rural Bank (now the Colonial State), its staff was mainly technical college or English provincial university. Traditionalists viewed askance the pretensions of such persons to claim equality: they should know, and keep, their place. That this should be, and remain, a common view, generated and sustained in University of New South Wales sensitivities, was a kind of embarrassing triumphalism and its opposite, uneasy deference. The stigma of inferiority was also attached to part-time study, the education mode of those not rich or exceptionally talented enough to afford full-time studentship — and the University of Technology was initially composed of such persons, indeed designed for them. Unsurprisingly, the university made a virtue of this, trumpeted its uniqueness in providing full-time courses for evening students, and in serving industry and commerce — that is, those functions of society regarded as subordinate by those who saw themselves as occupying the higher orders. As for weaving a requirement for practical experience in employment into university education, the same prejudice applied, though there it rested on more rational principles. It was taken as axiomatic in traditional university circles that the practical had no more than a tiny place in an institution properly governed by contemplation, matters of the intellect and wide principle. The whole notion of 'applied' knowledge was anathema.

What came across to Sydney Technical College and those who held its diplomas, however, was Sydney University's unyielding and contentious opposition, to which, not unnaturally, the friends of Sydney Technical College reacted with increasing hostility. An early, distinguished diplomate, NA Whiffen, who was to have important scientific positions in the United States of America, saw the position as one in which everything was done to conciliate the University of Sydney — in vain, no compromise. That university adhered to the classic definition of a club — a body united for keeping people out. Worse, its professors, when overseas, went to considerable trouble to denigrate the initial institute and subsequent university, internationally. (Nor did Sydney University hostility quickly die: it became known, or at least reputed, that a long-serving Sydney registrar would never recruit anyone from the University of New South Wales to administration staff.) Sensitivity to Sydney's status and actions had mixed outcomes: initially, a competitive dynamic — encouraging a career of being not-Sydney, the energetic and successful underdog. Catching up and surpassing had their dangers — cockiness and visions of infallibility.

To give those matters of hostility their due, there was more to them than snobbery and pretension, though that was a very large element. What was also at stake was the idea of the university itself, its intrinsic nature. To an orthodox mind, whatever the new educational institution in Sydney was, by simple definition university it was certainly not. Its claim to be one was a nonsense which might be either viewed with a politic tolerance through to seeing it a joke, dismissing it with contempt, or opposed with rage.

There was also its relationship to the domain of politics proper. There had long been tension in Australia between governments and universities: many academics thought that politicians, particularly in Labor governments, sought to bring universities under their control, to the diminution of academic independence. The University of Technology sinned against such canons of academic conformity. It was, in all the stages of its developments, essentially the creation of the Labor government of New South Wales, and it made no secret of its debt. Its very existence cut across the prevailing academic beliefs about government intentions, and its origins and its alignment won it no friends among anti-Labor elements in the establishment, most powerfully the *Sydney Morning Herald*. What was standing proof of this subservience to government, and evidence of it at its intrusive worst, was its administration as virtually a public service department until 1954 — all amounting to what the *Herald* saw, looking back from 1954, as a victory for those 'in government circles who really do not understand the purpose of a university education'. The University of Technology was testimony to the ignorance, smallmindedness, and thuggish determination of a cabal of Labor politicians and public servants. Or, as the 1949 parliamentary debates more politely put it, it could not be a university because it was government-controlled and -financed, and could not be independent, being part of the public service. The essence of a university was freedom. This institution was not free, but a reversion to centralised, government-dominated education. It was no effective riposte to put such criticism down to envy — the resentment of a favoured few when faced by education for the ordinary man or woman; the charge that in refusing to recognise diploma students of Sydney Technical College the University of Sydney was simply unfair. To Sydney University, being fair or unfair was not the issue. Nor was this necessarily merely a simple matter of small-minded selfishness. Dr CG (later Sir Charles) McDonald, was a member of the Senate of the University of Sydney. He was also a high-minded and principled man. His public objection to what he saw as a state university, controlled by the public service, was reasoned, temperate, and motivated by real concerns for freedom from political domination.

There was ample seeding ground here to place the worst possible construction on what befell the new university: from 1951 resignations of professorial staff (citing constriction by public service regulations, and lack of 'spiritual progress'), questionable selection procedures, and an abysmal student record — high failure rates, poor facilities, inadequate and incompetent staff. Nothing the University of Technology could say in its early days in denial or defence availed — that it was too early in its history and too impoverished; that its deficiencies were small in relation to its attraction of research funds, its graduate teaching, and its service to science and industry.

The multiplicity of discontents focussed on the University of Technology had one major dynamic. University funding was seen as a zero-sum game: what went to Technology was money which did not go to the University of Sydney. On the occasion of the centenary of the University of Sydney in 1952 the *Sydney Morning Herald* took the Labor government to task for getting its priorities wrong. This 'misnamed newcomer has a useful job to do', but the government had lost the balance between 'skills to earn a better living, and culture to make living better'. The *Herald* line was couched in terms of skills versus culture, but the basic realities of hostility were much less high-flown. The supporters of the University of Sydney saw Technology as existing at their university's expense. Funds rightfully theirs had been devoted to this crude and inferior imitation. This was galling, unjust, and insufferable. Who, or what, was to blame? Social change: technology represented the path to the future. But the University of Sydney also had itself to blame, for its failure to discern, its ignoring of opportunity, its obstructionism, and its haughty refusal to change or compromise. The minutes of the Developmental Council of the New South Wales Institute of Technology (August 1947–May 1949) make these things abundantly clear, even down to the piddling objection to the usage, in informal discussion, of the term 'Sydney University'. The placing of the geographic reference in front detracted from the name of an educational establishment: it was 'The University of Sydney'. Dignity can be a ludicrous standing ground.

In November 1947 the Developmental Council committee charged with considering this, agreed that the title of the new institution be 'The New South Wales

Institute of Technology', but that title soon gave way in public usage, to 'the technical university'. Heffron made the point in June 1948 that this was how he referred to it since people were confused as to what an institute signified: technical university they could readily comprehend. The committee decided to consider such a title change: it came up with 'New South Wales University of Technology' only to be confronted by the objections of 'certain members' that this should be referred to the Senate of the University of Sydney for approval — the implication being that this was unlikely to be forthcoming. Wurth countered this with a motion that the title be adopted and referred to Cabinet, which could, if it wished, seek the views of the University of Sydney. Being thoroughly out of patience with the University of Sydney's evident unwillingness to budge, the Cabinet chose not to consult in a matter of foregone conclusion, and in August 1948 came out unanimously in favour of technical university. Immediately Sir Charles Bickerton Blackburn, chancellor of the University of Sydney, approached the minister to object: 'institute' was the appropriate description. The chancellor was on a hiding to nothing. The minister was Heffron, known advocate of the 'university' appellation, member of the unanimous Cabinet, who must have known that when the *Herald* and its ilk sneered about those in the government who did not know what a university was, they had him principally in mind. As chairman of the Developmental Council he had heard all Bickerton Blackburn's arguments before. Ad nauseam.

There was no Cabinet concession. It had determined on 'university' and that was that. Sydney continued to ride high horse in vain. The Developmental Committee was mildly discomfited in that several members had supported 'university' on condition that Sydney agreed: one resigned. The committee was anxious to avoid alienating Sydney, for instance in the underlying implication of the new university's very existence that sufficient technologists had not been forthcoming in the past, but that was extremely difficult if not impossible to do. Placating Sydney with soft words and evasions about different functions and approaches could not be allowed to result in self-diminishment.

This unwillingness to accept a secondary and subordinate future role was evident in the matter of determining a site. So an area at Darlington occupied in part by the Institute for the Deaf, Dumb and Blind was rejected. Perhaps some members also saw the possibility of hostile jokery inherent in inheriting that location. But it was initially preferred because it was convenient to public transport and to both Sydney University and Sydney Technical College. Its proximity to the university was an advantage as considered within a subordinate mind-frame; seen within the ambit of a separate ambition with independence and equality as mainsprings, it was a major liability. According to Baxter's later account, Wallace Wurth's practical vision was the key to sensible big thinking. Darlington was initially larger, but expansion through resumption would be prohibitively costly. A small site at Kensington was on a section of Crown land, and Wurth had no doubt of his manoeuvring ability to acquire the lot.

Obviously, the national and local academic environment was hostile, or at least unreceptive, to the idea of a university of technology of New South Wales.

Powerful forces. But even more powerful forces favoured it, internationally, nationally, and some specific to Sydney. Those influences which were international were not so much British as European and those of the United States, and were political as well as technological. Specific to Sydney was the push from Sydney Technical College.

As in so much else Australian, Britain led the way, but it was a Britain within the Cold War and in the wake of close-run victory in 1945; a Britain, too, within the context of the belief that it had lost the leadership of the new industrial and technical world, indeed had been losing it since the 1850s. The great discoveries of the new scientific age had been made in Great Britain, but applied and developed elsewhere — America and Europe — down to the present: radar, jet flight, atomic power. A growing current of British opinion, political, and within the provincial universities, was critical of the Cambridge and Oxford models of university education: there must be universities of applied science, vocationally oriented and tied in with the workshop; in the same way as doctors, grounded in the university, were to move into hospital clinical training and experience. This telling analogy was used by Marcus Oliphant in an article for the *Universities Quarterly* in 1949. He was then director of the Department of Physics, University of Birmingham; soon to take the directorship of the School of Physical Sciences at the Australian National University in Canberra. And he was representative of those academics in scientific Britain who were unhappy with the traditional universities. And not only academics. The physicist and influential novelist, CP Snow, to be identified from the late 1950s with the concept of 'the two cultures' — the 'gulf of mutual incomprehension' between scientist and literary intellectual — was a friend of Oliphant from Cambridge days. Many scientists in Britain were of Oliphant's view: he was to act as referee for several of the early senior appointees of the New South Wales University of Technology.

But it was not only a wave of younger British scientists who were impatient with the old university order, taking the position with Oliphant that 'A university is not a static foundation' but rather an evolutionary entity reacting to the demand of the times, as well as reflecting the timeless. Even more important, in terms of practicalities, were the lessons British politicians took from the war — that Britain, in a position of crisis had a dire lack of skilled technologists, which was overcome only with American aid. The very existence of Britain in the face of the prospect of defeat, then as its continuance as a leading industrial nation, was endangered by failure to secure the application of science to industry, a failure partly due to deficiencies in education: such was the disturbing conclusion in 1945 of the Percy Report on Higher Technical Education, followed by the Barlow Report on Scientific Manpower in 1946. The British reaction was from a position of acknowledging major shortcoming, but the new superpower reached the same conclusion, in the Bush Report to the American president in 1945, 'Science — the Endless Frontier'.

Heffron himself, at the laying of the foundation stone of the first major university building on 25 February 1950, made specific reference of indebtedness to Dr Karl Compton, president of the Massachusetts Institute of Technology, who had visited Australia in 1946. Heffron and other supporters of the technology lobby had discussions with him, as a result of which 'we were able to crystallise our ideas in regard to the type of university we should establish'. (He also might have thanked the director of Technical Education, Arthur Denning, and Harold Brown, to be appointed foundation professor of Electrical Engineering. They sat on advisers' chairs in the parliament when Heffron was due to speak on this matter, and fed him, via the passing of notes, answers to questions.) Obviously, American example, set in the context of the whole Cold War outlook, was crucial in determining New South Wales political attitudes so important for the university's foundation and future. The then government saw itself as acting in the national interest. It was representing the leading Australian industrial state, which would give a lead to all others in providing an education which would meet 'the inevitable demand for technical manpower': it saw itself as providing for a new Australia. The deprivation of traditional sources of supply, inflicted by the war, had also been a liberation. Australia had proved its ability to be self-sufficient and innovative, permeated by a 'give it a go', 'can do' philosophy rather than crippled by deferential conservatism. War had been both warning and proof — proof that Australians could rise to the demands of a new industrial scene. The government was in no mood to defer to traditionalist objections. Besides, far-sightedness would win votes. Advances in cinema, radio, and (soon) television had created popular consumer demand impinging on the services of technology, and voters would support a government of the future which gave them this. Indeed, the government rode on a wave of buoyant euphoria of self-congratulation as forward-looking, adventurous, courageous. Here was a Labor administration far from doctrinaire, but whose roots were far from the orthodox university world. It would have its university, now, practical, down to earth, for people like themselves — gifted, ordinary inhabitants of the real world, enthusiasts, pioneers, untrammelled by hindrance from precedent and past.

This was all very edifying, but the fact was that the previous State government, a United Australia Party–Country Party coalition, with DH Drummond as Education minister, had, in 1940 passed a sweeping reform of technical education, which established, among other things, an Institute of Technology. Before this Act could be proclaimed, a newly elected Labor government nullified it. Odd? No, Labor's major objection to the 1940 Act was that it would, it was believed, advantage Broken Hill Proprietary (BHP) and turn technical education, particularly in Newcastle, into a servile company instrumentality. No self-respecting Labor politician could countenance anything that might help that epitome of Australian capitalism with its long, strike-ridden history of repression and exploitation. It tainted the image of technical education — but only under non-Labor governments. Labor was very different, and, by 1945, no government could ignore the transformation of the Australian economy nor the centrality of Sydney Technical College diploma holders to that extraordinary metamorphosis. Sharper still, and more urgent, were the demands of the Commonwealth Reconstruction Training Scheme designed and funded by the federal Labor government to meet the needs of returned servicemen to acquire tertiary qualifications. The scheme placed enormous strain on existing resources. One university in Sydney was simply not enough — a fact the University of Sydney seems not to have recognised.

Such was the immediate political context. It was backed by the long-germinating, and by then very powerful interests of the Sydney Technical College and its diploma holders. Here were people who had long believed that their qualifications were the equal of university degrees and who strongly resented the refusal of the University of Sydney to so recognise them. That resentment stretched back to the 1880s, surfacing first as an aspiration, then increasingly as a frustration. The University of Sydney opposed equality on two declared grounds: first, that entrance to diploma courses was below university matriculation level; second, that courses lacked intellectual depth. When, in the 1940s, diploma entrance and matriculation were made identical, the university fell back on the teaching objection, in a manner offensive to college staff and the students they taught. Besides, many of the college staff taught part-time at the university: in May 1948 two had been appointed to the university full-time. As diploma holders enhanced their status (such as by gaining equivalence to degrees in the eyes of overseas professional bodies), the more the University of Sydney attitude seemed absurd and odious. It seemed an unmistakable and unwarranted assertion of noxious pseudo-superiority.

RG Robertson/UNSW Archives collection

Electrical Engineering students at Ultimo

late 1950s

It was these excluded diploma holders who were at the core of the New South Wales industrial development under wartime pressure, who represented Australia overseas in Allied scientific and industrial initiatives, particularly in the United States. Convinced they had proved themselves, they were not of any mind to accept petty and unjustifiable treatment by the University of Sydney. The notion of an 'Industrial University', in the air since the 1880s, they took up readily and actively. Back in 1883 WC Windeyer, president of the Sydney Mechanics School of Arts (precursor to Sydney Technical College), had foreseen the ill-effects of having a divided 'national school of learning'. He wanted 'no opportunity for the accusation that the student of one university was pursuing an undergraduateship of dreamy impracticality and genteel idleness, while the other, in the acquisition of useful knowledge, was preparing himself for the work of the world'. He foresaw 'contemptuous retort' on 'the low ideal and vulgar aims' of those who sought knowledge merely because it paid. His was a keen perception of what might happen, and of course happen it did.

Not that Sydney explicitly sought this. Fundamentally, its mind was selfishly elsewhere. It feared that the establishment of a second university would diminish government funding when it saw its own situation as being that of imminent bankruptcy. The Institute of Technology was determined that it would be independent and that it would confer degrees: if it came to the threat of a punch-up, it would stand its ground. And it did. Tempers simmered over the institute belief that there was a deliberate University of Sydney campaign to denigrate it. The institute saw its efforts to recruit overseas staff as being undermined by informal academic correspondence from Sydney, dismissing it as 'only a technical college', not up to university standards. But what really set the cat among the pigeons was the University of Sydney's establishment, in May 1948, of a chair in Coal-mining. So much for the 'friendly rivalry' predicted by unworldly idealists: this betokened competition set on subordination and annihilation. The institute regarded this as clear encroachment on its agreed territory — a sally by Sydney, built around a department thought stagnant, to deprive the technological university of its students and industrial base. Within the Developmental Council Dr RK Murphy, principal of Sydney Technical College, put this hostile interpretation to open test. Murphy was an extraordinary galvanic — and confrontationist — figure in the college's history, from the time he joined it as a brash young American in 1915, to begin a long and distinguished career. By 1948 he had long been championing the technical college as the equal of all other educational institutions and was not in any awe of the British educational tradition. It seems highly likely that the American and European influences obvious in the university's beginnings derive, at least in part, from Murphy. Personally, Murphy was an amazing phenomenon. An excellent teacher, he had once attracted students' attention as he entered the lecture hall, by throwing sausages at them. Being frozen in liquid nitrogen, they exploded when they hit the floor. He also pioneered one of the devices whereby Government Stores could be persuaded to authorise the purchase of necessary scientific apparatus. When a refrigerator was needed for the Industrial Chemistry laboratory, his requisition was refused as unnecessary. He then ordered a 'negative hot plate', which was approved. This was an ordering procedure much used in the early university to cope with the scientific innocence of Government Stores staff. As for Murphy, his contribution to the university was honoured from 1957 in the annual RK Murphy Memorial Lecture given in the School of Chemistry. For long the impatient victim of the University of Sydney's assertions of superior exclusionism, he was not beyond hurling exploding sausages in their direction. At a 1948 Developmental Council meeting he enquired whether the university reserved the right to enter every field devised by the institute, to claim a share. To which Sydney representatives stated that they could not say, but the university would not be restricted from entering any field it wished. Or, essentially, they would do what they pleased.

Ah, but would they? Their candour seems to have been the last straw for Cabinet. Two months later, on 27 July 1948, the government made clear its intention to establish a UNIVERSITY of Technology, to the rage and fierce objection of elements of the University of Sydney. Fortunately this did not include the vice-chancellor, Sir Stephen Roberts, moderate and realist. He had himself nominated as Sydney representative on the new university's council, rendering singular service by not attending meetings — and by thus ensuring that Sydney's combative, frustrative elements were excluded. As to the University of Technology, its attitude towards Sydney was conciliatory. Toes were occasionally trodden on, gaucheries committed and minor snubs endured, but generally relations were cordial enough. Underneath, Sydney's attitudes had not changed. In 1961 a demarcation dispute arose over the field of metallurgy, revealing that Sydney still thought itself superior in attracting future staff in terms of 'the opportunities offered by a traditional university with a long history of scholarship'. That popular guru of the Sydney Philosophy department, John Anderson, was not above composing, in 1961, a song ('Philosophical Blues') which satirised the formation and character of the technical university:

From the Railway end of Broadway
Came a burst of mournful song
Throbbing through the aspirations
Of the proletarian throng
Was a pioneer of Western culture
But swapped it for a mechanical sepulture
And as I punch the Bundy
Every blessed Monday
Sing these Philosophical Blues

Oh, the streets were choc-a-block with adolescent BScs
And the trams were running over with incipient BEs
But the voice came sadly wailing
'Take away those dungarees!'

And so on, through 'Being useful drives me silly' 'horny-handed erudition' and the like. Even by 1961 many at the University of New South Wales found that decidedly unfunny, but the Rugby Club's proud self-mockery was equal to the Andersonian mockery:

> From the halls of smoky Ultimo
> To the sands of Kensington
> We'll transfer the old degree shop
> When Big Brother turns it on
>
> Ruination of the nation
> Everything we try it fails
> With a slide rule and a grease pot
> We are all from New South Wales!

Was this kerfuffle appropriate, proportionate, true to the projected size of what was envisaged? Not initially so. Seen in the light of today's actualities, yes, but then, at the time, no. Visiting the university as governor-general in the early 1950s, Sir William McKell made it clear repeatedly, in conversations at which the registrar GL Macauley was present, that when McKell was premier of New South Wales during the gestation and establishment of the university, the institution had been conceived as small, selective and devoted substantially to research. As to a large place, that, according to Sir William, was not the idea at all — which was why the university was given little site space, and why he regarded the rumour that the university had designs on the whole of Kensington Racecourse as ludicrous. Had its opponents at Sydney University been aware of these limited ambitions, their reactions and tactics may have been different. Keeping a possible threat to tiny intended size was one thing; confronting a major competitor was quite another. Certainly, McKell's expectations proved wrong, but they were the initial reality.

All of the aforesaid leads to the conclusion that the university was in some way inevitable — except that nothing ever is. Certainly, it was a development with the grain, an outgrowth and expression of powerful new currents of the age, reflection of the rise and dominance in the world of new concepts of science and technology, sign of a general social impatience with the old and restrictive, portent of a crude and clamorous egalitarianism, very much the child of its time. Quite so. Yet the clichéd perceptions echo comfortably after the event because it fits in, seems appropriate from a distance, succeeds. What is unique — its particular immediate formative dynamic? None of the above which formed its setting. No. It was the decisions of the New South Wales Labor Party, and the insight and energies of two men — Heffron and Wurth — which made things happen, how and when they did.

The Main Building, with Tom Bass sculpture ▷

1955

2

UNIVERSITY OF TECHNOLOGY 1949–58

1949

1949

117 enrolments • Society of Students formed.

7 MARCH First enrolments in applied chemistry, chemical engineering, architecture, and postgraduate course in electronic engineering.

22 MARCH Bill to establish the new University of Technology introduced.

APRIL The Technical Education and New South Wales University of Technology Act (NSW), 1949, passed—the university's establishing Act.

26 MAY Developmental Council's final meeting.

1 JULY The Technical Education and New South Wales University of Technology Act (pt III) proclaimed, by which the university is incorporated

APPOINTMENTS A Denning, as first director of the university; HJ Brown, as foundation professor of Electrical Engineering; JC Webb, as first Registrar; FEA Towndrow, as foundation professor of Architecture.

5 JULY University Council [hereafter Council] appointed.

6 JULY Council's first meeting: Wallace Wurth elected president.

12 AUGUST DW Phillips

appointed foundation professor of Mining Engineering.

12 SEPTEMBER Council affirms undergraduate courses will have a practical experience in industry component and a compulsory humanities component • First steps taken towards establishing University of Technology branches at regional centres: engineering courses at Newcastle planned to start in 1950.

20 OCTOBER Kensington decided on as site for the new university campus • Construction of Main Building begun.

10 NOVEMBER Dr AE Alexander appointed foundation professor of Applied Chemistry.

1950

1950

University Wives' Group forms.

JANUARY • APPOINTMENTS Major RK Wilthew, as Student Amenities officer; GL Macauley, as registrar; Dr JP Baxter, as foundation professor of Chemical Engineering (16 January); NF Astbury, as foundation professor of Applied Physics (26 January).

1 FEBRUARY Professorial Committee first meets, under the university's director, A Denning.

25 FEBRUARY First foundation stone set — for Main Building, by the New South Wales governor, Lt-General Sir John Northcott • Lord Nuffield endows a Nuffield research chair in Mechanical Engineering.

6 MARCH Conversion courses for science and engineering inaugurated (diploma holders to proceed to degree status).

APRIL Postgraduate course in television commenced.

8 MAY First faculties established: Architecture, Engineering, Science.

7 JUNE First faculty meeting: in the Faculty of Science.

16 JUNE RM Hartwell appointed foundation professor of Economic History.

25 JUNE Korean War begins.

4 JULY Professorial Board first meets.

15 SEPTEMBER Equipment and Supplies Committee of the university first meets.

14 NOVEMBER New South Wales University of Technology is admitted to Association of Universities of the British Commonwealth.

1951

1951

Wool Technology degree introduced — the first university course in the world devoted specifically to the application of science to wool production.

1 JANUARY
ASSOCIATE PROFESSORS APPOINTED PR McMahon (Wool Technology), CH Munro (Civil Engineering), AH Willis and JFD Wood (Mechanical Engineering), G Bosson (Maths).

FEBRUARY Council takes responsibility for the conduct and administration of all State Dept of Technical Education's diploma courses, acquiring extra staff and students from Sydney Technical College, Newcastle, Wollongong, Lithgow and Broken Hill • Newcastle University College established.

JUNE Professor Astbury resigns (to take effect from 28 September) • Professors Alexander, Hartwell, Phillips, and Towndrow sign a 'Prayer to Council'.

JULY University regiment approved; recruitment begun.

9 JULY RH Myers appointed foundation professor of Metallurgy (but takes up duties on 3 May 1952).

12 SEPTEMBER Cricket Club formed.

12 NOVEMBER APPOINTMENTS AS PROFESSORS PR McMahon (Wool Technology) and G Bosson (Mathematics) • Mining Society and Chemical Society constitutions approved • Degree of PhD approved.

3 DECEMBER Newcastle University College, Tighes Hill, opens and R Basden appointed warden.

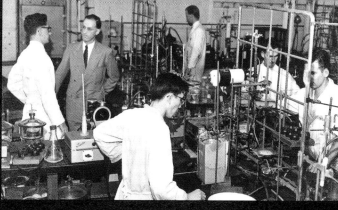

The Old Tote, Kensington
1948

Organic research lab, Ultimo
1956

5 DECEMBER The New South Wales University of Technology (Construction) Act passed (allows for buildings to be erected on Kensington site and provides funds for this purpose).

1952

11 Colombo Plan students enrolled in university • Engineering Yearbook produced by the Mining Society, with the help of the Society of Students — the first major student publication. • University of Technology Students' Union succeeds the Society of Students, JD Smith being elected its first president.

4 FEBRUARY Professor Baxter appointed deputy director of the university • JI Carroll research laboratory opened at Ultimo (later moved to Kensington), containing a Geiger counter X-ray spectrometer, the first of its kind in Australia.

15 FEBRUARY Professor HJ Brown (Electrical Engineering) resigns.

MARCH University regiment begins operation as University of Technology Regiment, Royal Australian Electrical and Mechanical Engineers: Lt-Col. WR Blunden, first commanding officer.

10 MARCH APPOINTMENTS AH Willis, Nuffield Research professor of Mechanical Engineering; CJ Milner, professor of Applied Physics.

15 MARCH First graduation ceremony (held at Great Hall, University of Sydney): 34 degrees awarded, in engineering and science — June Griffith, the first female graduate, among these.

12 MAY Provision made for study leave for academic staff.

19 MAY University arms and motto received from the College of Heralds, London.

8 SEPTEMBER Students' Union officially recognised, with membership becoming compulsory for all registered students.

3 DECEMBER 24.5 ha of land at Kensington transferred to the university.

8 DECEMBER Council votes on directorship of university, the vote going in JP Baxter's favour. • University Sports Association founded, membership becoming compulsory for all registered students.

1953

Korean War ends • 32 Colombo Plan students at the university • Prefab aluminium buildings, Union Hall and Common Room, installed on Ultimo campus to house student and staff amenities • New library building completed on Ultimo's Thomas St frontage • Students produce the first *Orientation Handbook*.

1 JANUARY JP Baxter appointed director of the university.

FEBRUARY First university activity on the new site: School of Chemical Engineering moves to temporary buildings on Kensington campus; first planting of lawns and shrubs and system of roads, footpaths and car parks begun. • Student hostel opens.

MARCH *Tharunka* publishes its first issue, under joint editorship of Sid Dunk and Harold Spies.

6 MARCH Dr Roy Harman resigns as vice-president of the university, and from Council.

17 MARCH Hon. JSJ Clancy, Supreme Court justice, elected vice-president.

16 MAY First graduation ceremony for Newcastle University College.

JULY Civil Engineering Society begins.

AUGUST GH Aylward appointed first warden of student hostel.

DECEMBER School of Metallurgy moves into four 'light-framed', temporary buildings at Kensington.

1954

First degree course in optometrical science in Australia offered • Establishment of hydraulics lab at Manly Vale approved, for School of Civil Engineering.

JANUARY Student hostel alterations increase accommodation to 218 single rooms • Sydney Technical College Students' Union dissolved (1 January), its affairs being transferred to University of Technology Students' Union. • Newcastle University College provides arts courses as part of an arrangement with the University of New England.

FEBRUARY Part-time degree courses in the faculties of Science and Engineering are offered • University regiment reorganised as an infantry battalion.

4 FEBRUARY HRH Duke of Edinburgh, on a visit to Sydney University, meets members of the Council of the University of Technology; the University of Technology Regiment forms a guard of honour along his route.

SELECTED EVENTS

Chemical Exposition, Sydney Town Hall
1950

Graduation Ball
1954

6 APRIL JOA Bourke appointed bursar.

10 MAY Institute of Nuclear Engineering established.

11 MAY New accommodation at Kensington opened for the Schools of Metallurgy and Chemical Engineering.

17 JUNE Newcastle University College Advisory Council first meets.

18 JUNE 1.2 ha of railway land transferred to university.

23 JUNE 1.2 ha of land on western side of Anzac Parade transferred to university.

JULY Establishment of the School of Applied Psychology approved. • University regiment moves from Ultimo to the Old Tote building, High St, Kensington.

1 JULY 'Appointed Day': full control of the university is vested in Council. It now has authority and responsibility for the employment of staff, for building work, and other functions previously discharged by the Public Service Board.

12 JULY Faculty of Humanities and Social Sciences approved.

31 AUGUST–1 SEPTEMBER Symposium 'Atomic Energy in Australia' held at the university.

SEPTEMBER Constitutions approved for Newcastle University College Students' Association, University of Technology Students' Union and the University of Technology Sports Association.

14 SEPTEMBER Royal Australian Chemical Institute approves the degrees of BSc and MSc in Applied Chemistry and Chemical Engineering.

22 NOVEMBER Council decides to increase undergraduate course fees by as much as 100 per cent. • New full-time food technology course approved.

1955

Colloid Research Unit created with CSIRO grant. • First presentation of sports Blues. • Land at Kingsford acquired for sporting activities.

8 FEBRUARY Heinz Harant and Roger Beattie, University of Technology Students' Union president, stage protest meeting in Sydney Town Hall against undergraduate fee increases.

4 MARCH University titles of president, vice-president, and director are changed to chancellor, deputy chancellor, and vice-chancellor, respectively. • Council membership increased from 30 to 39.

14 MARCH Overseas Students' Association constitution approved. • Rifle Club granted permission to build clubhouse at Liverpool Rifle Range.

16 APRIL Main Building officially opened by the New South Wales governor, Lt-General Sir John Northcott; Applied Physics, Mining Engineering, Applied Geology, Humanities and Social Sciences, and university Administration move into it. • First graduation ceremony on Kensington campus: 112 students graduate.

27 APRIL Faculty of Humanities and Social Sciences holds inaugural meeting.

26 MAY Buildings for Food Science, Food Technology, and Petroleum Engineering Centre commenced.

SEPTEMBER Building G2 commenced. • G Caiger appointed Public Relations Officer.

NOVEMBER Professor DW Phillips appointed first pro-vice-chancellor. • Professor RM Hartwell appointed first dean of the Faculty of Humanities and Social Sciences. • Dr M Chaikin appointed foundation professor of Textile Technology.

DECEMBER Dalton building begun.

1956

First issue of *Science Yearbook*, published by students in the Faculty of Science • School of Biological Sciences established — the first in Australia.

13 FEBRUARY Major Wilthew redesignated Student Amenities supervisor, and manager of student hostel.

MAY Traffic engineering course approved.

14 MAY RM Hartwell resigns (to take effect from 30 October).

27 MAY Building G2 officially opened (completed in February).

10 JUNE Storm damage to roof of Main Building.

29 JUNE Faculty of Technology created — Professor DW Phillips is its first dean.

AUGUST Dr SB Hatfield appointed foundation professor of Hospital Administration. • The university's first digital computer arrives from England (later known as UTECOM).

20 AUGUST WR Blunden appointed foundation professor of Traffic Engineering.

SEPTEMBER Students' Union affiliates with the National Union of Australian

SELECTED EVENTS

Main Building, University of Technology
1955

Fire in the Main Building
1957

University Students • New part-time and full-time courses in commerce approved and a four-year textile technology degree.

11 SEPTEMBER At the opening of the university symposium 'Automation and Australia', the university's new computer is formally named by the New South Wales premier, JJ Cahill.

31 OCTOBER The Central and South Food Science and Food Technology buildings and the Petroleum Engineering Centre completed.

NOVEMBER New courses approved: industrial engineering; hospital administration; at Newcastle University College, full-time and part-time BComm.

18 NOVEMBER AE Alexander resigns.

29 NOVEMBER HRH Duke of Edinburgh visits Kensington campus.

1957

Nuclear reactor simulator constructed. • University of Technology Arts Society formed. • University Co-operative bookshop begins operation.

FEBRUARY Classroom block completed.

27 MARCH Committee of deans set up by Baxter to meet weekly.

8 APRIL Emergency Operations Centre (originally built as caretaker's residence) established.

13 APRIL Honorary degrees conferred on: A Denning (first university director), Dr RK Murphy (Sydney Technical College principal and Council member) and WG Kett (Developmental Council and University Council member). • Open Day: 2000 visitors attend.

15 APRIL Dr DF Orchard appointed foundation professor of Highway Engineering.

MAY Council approves establishment of Examinations and Students Records Branch and a Purchasing Branch.

20–25 MAY For the first time university clubs host intervarsity competitions: the Athletics, Rugby Union, and Rifle clubs.

5 JUNE Faculty of Commerce established.

15 JULY Construction of Parade Theatre begun.

19 JULY Food Science and Food Technology North building begun.

AUGUST Construction of student residential college (Basser) begun.

SEPTEMBER Murray Report on Australian universities presented to federal government. • University of Technology becomes a member of the recently formed Australian Institute of Nuclear Science and Engineering.

5 OCTOBER Fire in Main Building destroys JI Carroll research laboratory and its X-ray spectrometer.

21 OCTOBER Honorary DSc conferred on Rt Hon. RG Menzies, the prime minister.

NOVEMBER NEW DEGREES MComm and Master of Technology.

15 NOVEMBER Parade Theatre completed.

30 DECEMBER Dalton building completed (but officially opened on 28 August 1958).

1958

Library finds temporary accommodation in new Dalton building. • NEW DEGREES: full-time, in Industrial Arts; part-time, in Industrial Engineering.

JANUARY Emergency Operations Centre completed.

1 FEBRUARY Dr MS Brown appointed foundation professor of Sociology.

25 FEBRUARY Food Science and Food Technology North building completed (opened officially on 29 May).

MARCH New building completed to house Schools of Wool Technology, Traffic Engineering, Hospital Administration, and the Department of Industrial Arts.

APRIL Honorary DSc conferred on Cobden Parkes (government architect).

JULY Draft memo and articles of association for the National Institute of Dramatic Art (NIDA) approved by Council. • Committee for the establishment of an autonomous University of Newcastle formed.

SEPTEMBER Vice-chancellor Baxter and Professor MS Brown appointed as university representatives on NIDA board.

OCTOBER School of Business Administration established, within the Faculty of Commerce.

7 OCTOBER The University of New South Wales Act (NSW), 1958, passed — under which the university's name is changed to the University of New South Wales and also its interests are extended to include Medicine and the Arts.

NOVEMBER Foundation chairs created in Medicine, Surgery, Pathology, Anatomy and Physiology.

usty decorum on the face of it; something new, and revolutionary, within. The first meeting of the Council of the University of Technology, set up under the Technical Education and New South Wales University of Technology Act of April 1949, took place on 6 July 1949 in the Executive Chamber of the Chief Secretary's Department in Bridge Street, Sydney. The setting looked sternly back to an overbearing, nineteenth century offi-cialdom; dark panelling, gilt-framed portraits and landscapes, vases ornate and vast, heavy furnishings. The council members posed for the obligatory founding photo-graph, solemn, formal, clones of respectability, in three-piece suits, or that fashion of the professions which still lingers in the dress of some older academic scientists — ties tucked into jumpers under suit coats. Dowdy relics of some bygone age?

Nothing of the kind — formidable men, hard, certain of themselves. Whatever the appearances, here were future-mongers. The council knew what it was about: the provision at university level of training and research in applied science and technol-ogy to provide scientists and technologists for the industrial and commercial devel-opment essential to State and nation. It saw its context as being that of post-war urgencies and insecurities and its intellectual emphasis as being vigorously practical rather than theoretical. While new and independent, it would be a departure grounded within the existing technical education system and public service of the State of New South Wales. Embryonic degree courses in civil, electrical, mechanical and mining engineering, and architecture had been established already in March 1948 — the industrial heavyweights.

It was an initial preponderance which always marked the balance of the institu-tion, proliferating into a multiplicity of specialist departments but never losing that centrality. After all, engineering as a discipline encapsulated the essence of what the university was basically on about: it, in all its forms, was the place where 'respectable' science and commerce/management met. The setting was rough, tough territory — the gradual civilising of an environment in which the accommodation (No. 1 Mews St in Ultimo) was a derelict warehouse, air-raid shelters and a set of terrace houses which reputedly had formerly been brothels, and with a staff of about fifty part-timers, some not sighted for several years, each teaching their own syllabus: only John Wood of Mechanical Engineering knew all their names. Engineering had been formerly under the control of Crawford Munro, who had joined the British Army as an officer in Burma. He returned in 1947, twice as large as life — he mixed being impossible with magnetic social skills, any residue of rows during the working day being wiped away with pub conviviality — injected new life into Civil Engineering, though not without constant abrasion later with JP Baxter as vice-chancellor. By the early 1950s, the engineering names of the new university were in place — John Wood, Stan Hall, Crawford Munro, Rupert Vallentine, Harold Brown, Al Willis, many others. All men of resource in primitive conditions. No furniture? Pinch some-one else's. No theodolites? Get a friendly army officer to declare his surplus to requirements. Academic buccaneers, improvisers, reared in the streetfighters' catch-as-catch-can world of Sydney Tech. It was not until 1966 that Civil Engineering moved to Kensington. Meanwhile, it preserved its own distinctive ethos of making do, and of pushing for practicality and high standards. Other schools feared they might appear inferior.

In March 1949 followed, into that engineering-dominated pioneering, Applied Chemistry, Chemical Engineering and a postgraduate course, Electronic Engineering. In traditional terms, all this was all new; but even more innovative was the requirement that each course embody a specified and substantial period of practical training in industry. Even more unprecedented was the inclusion of compulsory instruction in the humanities. So, for all that the new institution bore the face of sombre tradition and the structures of academic familiarity, it was in fact strikingly different from anything that had appeared before on the Australian university scene.

Old structures: the Act set out a university within the traditional framework of governance — council, professorial board, faculties with deans, schools or departments with heads. But some different names, and certainly different faces. A president — Wallace Wurth, chairman of the New South Wales Public Service Board. A director — Arthur Denning, director of the Department of Technical Education.

Government Printer/UNSW Archives collection

∧

The first meeting of the governing Council

of the University of Technology

6 July 1949

A council replete with industrialists and public servants. And the key foundation professors — JP Baxter (Chemical Engineering), AE Alexander (Applied Chemistry), NF Astbury (Applied Physics); FE Towndrow (Architecture), HJ Brown (Electrical Engineering), DW Phillips (Mining Engineering). These were the core people — an assemblage of public servants, Sydney Technical College men, founding academics, mainly from British provincial red-brick universities. It was this unlikely mixture that concocted the new entity. Plus, of course, that maverick oddity on the fringe — the humanities.

Who thought this up? Heffron as minister for Education introducing the Bill in March 1949, referred briefly to the matter in the context of a long speech. Graduates would not be merely technical experts but with a broad understanding of human affairs — 'compulsory courses in language, literature, history, economics, and psychology. Such courses will avoid the handicaps which result from

A Physical Chemistry III class conducted by Dr David Lark,

Old Sheds, cnr Thomas and Harris Streets Ultimo

1956

narrow specialisation and will help the graduate to take a leading place in the community for which he is otherwise qualified.' Generally, the assumption that the new university have a humanities dimension was floating easily around in the parliamentary debates that preceded the 1949 Act. Some parliamentarians argued against the new institution having the humanities, which should stay at the University of Sydney: ridding Sydney of technological subjects by creating a new technical university would allow Sydney to blossom culturally, fulfil its true functions as a university, not be a super technical college. Others argued that humanities were imperative in the new enterprise. Massachusetts Institute of Technology, Cal Tech (California Institute of Technology, Pasadena) and the Berlin University of Technology were seen as legitimating and pioneering the path to be followed by the New South Wales University of Technology.

The Developmental Council, which had fashioned the institute idea in 1947–48,

UNSW Archives

∧

Crawford Munro (extreme left) and friends

at a Broadway pub

1961

had decided unanimously on including a compulsory humanities element. The Department of Preparatory Studies at Sydney Technical College had been deputed to come up with a basic subject structure. There followed, on the Developmental Council, lively conflict to aims, principles, content, and what proportion of degree time had to be so devoted, coming up with 6 per cent. The new University Council acted promptly on implementing this. No one quite knew what this meant or entailed, other than that it was generally a good thing and 'generally agreed to be a desirable trend in educational practice'. It was assumed by these founding fathers that it would include English language and literature, economics, history, and psychology, and it would amount to 6–10 per cent of the total curriculum, but no one had thought through what this meant in practice or detail. The first person to hold a chair in the Humanities school, in Economic History, was an Australian living in Britain, RM Hartwell, of Nuffield College. He was given leave to visit institutions on the Continent and in America before taking up duty. (One of Hartwell's research topics in 1951 was 'Officialese'. Long after his leaving, into the 1960s, the jargon-ridden aspect of the university's persona remained a joke: staff were 'officers'.) When Hartwell arrived in 1950, he found the humanities courses, then being taught by Sydney Technical College staff from Preparatory Studies, of integrated and cross-disciplinary type. In 1952 he changed this to English and history in first year, history and philosophy in second, electives in economics, psychology or government in third and fourth, a structure which prevailed for a decade. In that time, Humanities became a faculty (1955) and Applied Psychology and Economics were split off, and the staff grew to twenty-four, including three in a new elective, sociology. When Hartwell left, he was succeeded

After the first meeting of the Professorial Board: 4 July 1950.

<| (from left to right) RM Hartwell, AE Alexander, G Bosson, CH Munro, FEA Towndrow, R Basden and PR McMahon.

▽ G Bosson and RH Myers.

CJ Milner/UNSW Archives collection

CJ Milner/UNSW Archives collection

eventually by JB Thornton as acting head, in 1957; then, in 1958, by Morven Brown — 'Amorphous Brown' as the wits had it. Brown was Baxter's choice. Baxter continued to be decisively involved in the professorial selection processes to the degree of appointing people cordially (or otherwise) detested by deans and other senior staff. By the 1960s his earlier capacities, to be perceptively right, were deserting him. But the earlier university, in common with all others at the time, had 'god-professor' appointment procedures, in which those so favoured could be offered jobs without interview. It was an Australian practice accepted as usual. Baxter's actions were not seen as untoward — nor his intervention against candidates he did not want.

As to lecturing staff, generally throughout the university most came from existing staff at the Sydney Technical College — and physically remained there, some for many years, as the university was initially almost completely dependent on the college's accommodation and facilities at Ultimo in central Sydney, gradually building its own campus in Kensington. Some came from Sydney Teachers' College. Research and technical staff were also local appointees. So, to a very great extent, the early university was an outgrowth and an elevation of the college, and a realisation of the college's professional ambitions to become more than the University of Sydney would allow. Those college origins, and their continuance in the form of the staff employed, constituted problems of quality and applicability in the early years of the university. The case of mathematics illustrates the difficulty. In the college it was assumed that only an engineer could teach engineering mathematics. The result was that three of the small maths staff had no general maths qualifications and things that needed to be taught they had never learned themselves. This problem could be solved only with the effluxion of time, and the employment of specific maths specialists, trained, for example, in statistics.

Students? Initially forty-six enrolments. The first had commenced in Engineering in March 1948 via Sydney Technical College diplomas, opened in

STUDENTS'

"SIX MUNCE AGO
I CUTNT EVN
SPEL
METULERJIST
—AN NOW
I ARE ONE"

◁

The need

for general studies

late 1950s

1950 to conversion courses to degrees. The basic annual requirement for students was six months at the university and five months in practical experience in industry. This, together with the substantial presence of senior industrialists on the University Council, produced a close collaboration with a wide, and ever-widening, range of industries: initially the giants, such as BHP, ICI, the Joint Coal Board (a major factor in the push for a university to train staff for its top positions), CSR, Lysaghts, Commonwealth Steel, Kirbys; soon others. The outcome of this linkage was profound in relating the new university to power, wealth, and influence in the wider community. More immediately, it produced scholarships and benefactions as industry used the university to train its expert and managerial classes. It also imparted to the university — although this industrial context was congenial already, given the background of professorial staff — a good deal of their attitudes and values:

<|

David Brewster — one of the first

University of Technology students,

at Ultimo

late 1940s

Note the surplus stores/services

demob jacket.

UNSW Archives

hierarchical, strict, moral. These were times in which divorce also entailed resignation from positions of responsibility: if you cannot manage your own affairs you certainly cannot manage this company's. Hats were required wearing by persons moving on company business. Forms of address were formal: even into the 1960s some professors required their staff to call them 'Sir' if not 'Professor'. The mores of the large company and government department — hierarchical, distant, rule- and regulation-ridden, socially conservative, respectable to the degree of scruple — permeated the atmosphere of the early university. In that day, though, this was nothing other than what was generally anticipated in the general professional community, unnoted.

The main source of finance, and thus sharing pre-eminence of influence, was the State of New South Wales. A quarter of the members of the first University Council were leading public servants. The Public Service Act 1902 applied to the university until 1 July 1954, giving government control over staff appointments. Even then university autonomy was exercised within a close public service relationship. And over all reigned, from foundation president in 1949 to his death as chancellor in September 1960, Wallace Wurth, power eminence extraordinary of New South Wales public affairs.

GK Cranny/UNSW Archives collection

First committee of Society of Students (forerunner to Students' Union)

1951

In one of those sonorous, clichéd aphorisms beloved of the day, it was said of Wurth in 1960, in relation to the university, that 'an institution is the lengthened shadow of one man'. His successor as chairman of the Public Service Board called him a genius. Certainly he was a man of remarkable capacity and vision. University folklore conceded his stature in terms of power but misconstrued its nature. No dull or suppressive bureaucrat, Wurth despised red tape and the worship of precedent which marked the caricature public servant. Integrity, strict discipline, hard work, rules were Wurth's invariable yardsticks, which brought him disfavour with those

UNSW Archives

∧

Occupying armies. The old Kensington Racecourse was the site of a succession of military encampments in times of war. Shown here, the Bushman's Contingent at their racecourse camp in 1900, during the Boer War. Only fifteen years later troops would again be camped on the racecourse, this time before leaving for Anzac Cove.

who took a slacker view. He was the ideal founding chancellor, commanding the widest community respect and protecting the university from dismissive criticism.

Both his character and experience fitted him for that position. His role during the Second World War, as director-general of Manpower, brought him into intimate association with industry and the complexities of government — and bore in on him the vital importance to Australia of scientists and engineers, and the need to train them for the future. He had been, with RJ Heffron, minister for Education, the planner and foundation member, from 1947, of the Developmental Council. During a visit to England in 1946 he sought to look, not only at university financial management, but at potential senior founding staff, only to find that the prospect of joining an 'institute' — as the university was then envisaged and titled — was unattractive: it conveyed neither prestige nor significance. Immediately upon his return to Sydney he ensured that the government change this title to university. Wallace Wurth's advocacy and advice remained of this energetic, practical kind. It was mainly his influence and insistence which ensured the rejection of the first site offered the university — constricted, close to the University of Sydney — and led to the establishment on the present site. And he smoothed the path to securing adjoining land.

Wurth's centrality to the public service, government, and Department of Technical Education, advantaged the new university's operation in a myriad of ways, from day-to-day access to Government Stores to the high politics of the Loans Council and Premiers' Conference. Wurth was also an enthusiast for the university, not only involved in its public and political promotion and formal business but also in its social life, including that of students. He believed in the national importance of its mission and gave himself to that. His mild, bespectacled appearance generated the myth, beloved of later critics, of grey nonentity — the secret, faceless man. The reality was iron will, a dominant personality, a superb administrative intellect, a man of rigid principles and high ideals, a decider, loyal to a vision of serving a new technological Australia. Yet without cant or pretence: wounded as a stretcher-bearer on the Western Front in 1917, he had risen from the ranks in the public service as in the army and never forgot his origins in reality. Nor did rhetoric carry any weight with him. Mere traditionalists and Jeremiahs he deemed irrelevant. Difficulties were meant to be overcome by devising the best means to solve them — in the university's case by getting money or buildings, or land, or materials, from those who could provide. And by choosing the right men to lead, like-minded, practical. Determine on the right course of action: then get on with it. His was a mind-frame of immense value in the university's origins and early years: he gave Baxter his head, something of enormous consequence. That, the position he occupied, and the power and influence he commanded, gave the university, in the words of a contemporary, 'a fifty years' start'.

Certainly, the mood of the first public appearance of the university in 1949 was that of an institution already running — and running confidently and fast. It developed innovations even beyond those evident in its core subjects' structures: a very popular postgraduate course in the then new area of television for instance; new courses in matters basic to the economy — wool technology, food technology, metallurgy. Practicalities pervaded its view of education responsibilities, an approach in

42

which the university took great pride. Council took the view that it was a unique and distinctive enterprise, operating, as it reported in 1952, 'outside the ordinary fields of University activity', that it had a 'special function' in pioneering new paths. This conviction sprang from a mixture of visionary exhilaration, with simple belief in the importance of technology, and pride in the virtues of the practical intellect. As they saw it, these people — industrialists, public utility heads, bureaucrats — occupied and controlled the real world, and ought to have a greater role than they were conceded by the University of Sydney. There is, in their energy, assertiveness and addiction to the new, something of the outsiders' determination to be in, to prove they were top persons, beyond the exclusions of the establishment's old brigades.

As to realism and practicality, the council practised what it preached. It came to an immediate arrangement with the Department of Technical Education in 1949–50 to accept responsibility for its relevant diploma students who had long been anxious to achieve degree recognition. It was this, however, impelled by the logic of the technical education imperatives of the institution, which, in one move — or rather, giant leap — placed the university on its feet, running. By this single act the university, with 46 students enrolled in 1948, accessed an extra 3544 diploma students, a vast inflation which brought with it a commensurate increase in staff, direct transfers from Sydney Technical College. Thus relations between university and college were

cemented and intertwined from the beginning, in terms of staff, but also, necessarily, in sharing the existing college buildings at Ultimo. And in all this the university proclaimed great pride, and stressed its frugality to the accountants of government: the cost to the university budget was offset by the savings in technical education, so the total State outlay would be the same — an attractive proposition but false, as the university must have known, and intended. As to the impact on students, their enthusiasm was such that, given the acceptance of their studies as potentially of degree status, they appear to have had no demur about consequences — some courses were of five-year duration, others six. In that day such extended time-frames were unquestioned, partly because the studies were interwoven with employment and advancement therein, and partly because such dimensions of instruction were a given social aspect of part-time tertiary education. Life held little leisure for students working — in all senses — towards a degree. Work 9–5, classes 6–9, assignments on the weekend, for five or six years. Or longer. By 1952 there were fifty-six postgraduate students, fourteen of them enrolled for PhDs: most were employees in industry. But recollection has it that the students of this time were extraordinarily determined and grateful, especially those who had come through the war. Regimented — and even downtrodden — but utterly dedicated to getting as much as possible from the courses they undertook.

Government Printer/UNSW Archives collection

<|

Panoramic view of lower campus before the

university was built — note the drainage problems,

forming what was later christened Lake Bourke

1949

∧

This early view of lower campus shows the

migrant hostel, which became student hostel

accommodation, and the racecourse grandstand

1950

Yet student life was vigorous. Students had established a student society in 1949. There were student sporting teams competing locally — rugby, tennis, golf, basketball, swimming, even ice-skating. There was a camera club, drama and opera. As to student sport, it was to grow and diversify with the university itself, to an extent and scale beyond brief description. In 1951 there were fourteen sporting clubs, from athletics to weight-lifting, and nine recreational activities, from bushwalking to photography. From January 1950 the university supported this with an Amenities Service, arranging amenities, booking grounds, organising the Students' Annual Ball, the Graduation Ball, the first Engineering faculty *Year Book* (1951–52), much else sporting and social. Remarkably soon, student sports-persons featured in State, and then Australian teams. Initiatives of all kinds were to abound. And in all directions. Eventually even to overseas links. This sports involvement and commitment was something which the university itself backed strongly from its beginnings. Particularly was this so in the development of space on campus — tennis courts, the Village Green for cricket; eventually, in 1971, a sports and recreation centre, for squash, gymnasium and indoor swimming — but also in the acquisition and development over the years of parcels of land in adjoining suburbs for sporting purposes. In this the university was responding to, fostering, evident student enthusiasm and need, but such was the level of achievement that it drew attention to the university and its name in the general sporting world was an image-enhancing factor.

Rugby and cricket were the sports in which the university was to achieve greatest prominence, in some individual cases up to international level. The cricket club was formed on 12 September 1951, its ground being various sites on the campus until it settled on the present Village Green in 1968, and, in 1989, moved to its permanent pavilion, to be eventually named after the sports-furthering university Amenities officer, Sam Cracknell. That oval was subject in the 1960s to major flooding. By the 1970s the club had become a force in Sydney grade cricket and by the 1980s had produced optometry student, Geoff ('Henry') Lawson as its first Australian representative, by no means the last. Sport, and concomitant socialising, was an early thread to be woven across time into a strong and colourful fabric.

To return to the 1950s. However much the university might see itself as physically dependent well into the future on continuing use of the facilities of Sydney Technical College, its council acted quickly to begin a building program on its own site: the first major brick building was commenced on the old Kensington Racecourse in October 1949. Immediately erected also were prefabricated buildings, seen as of 'pleasing design' and long-term function. Whatever the adventurous disposition of its confrontation of its tasks, this did not extend to the visual. To take pleasure in prefabrication, and to award an honorary degree in 1958 to the government architect, Cobden Parkes, for buildings baldly functional and uninspiring, betokened the lack of any aesthetic sense. Parkes himself later explained that when he was commissioned, with Harold Brown, to draw up plans for what is now the old Main Building, they had no experience in university building. Their main experience was in designing hospitals, so they adapted a set of hospital plans. Thus, the Main Building emerged like a hospital, with enormous corridors, wide enough for two

The first building under construction

(Main Building), seen from Anzac Parade

1950

beds to be wheeled past one another. It was only under the pressures of the early 1980s that these vast corridors were absorbed by renovation into teaching and office space. This hospital-like look misled some early critics of the university. They took it that the design was in order to permit easy conversion to a hospital if and when the university enterprise failed; malevolence sees plots and conspiracies everywhere; silly simplicity escapes it. Certainly, cost factors were central, but a professor of Architecture, FE Towndrow, was among its foundation chairs and the campus was to continue, apparently without protest, to house itself in the most indifferently depressing public service-style accommodation; monuments to the industry of the State Brickworks. Towndrow is recalled by his staff as 'a delightfully simple soul', a better architectural publicist and journalist than designer of buildings. A man of charm and good will; if the vote went against his wishes in faculty he would just say, 'Oh well, we won't count that vote', outrageous behaviour which escaped censure.

GL Macauley, the registrar

ca 1960s

As to students, they had superior practical know-how but lacked the assurance and polish of the University of Sydney product. Certainly, Baxter was working within constraints other than his own, though his home environment — unfashionable Enfield (the first registrar, GL Macauley, lived in Wentworthville) — might suggest indifference to style and false pretension. It was a matter of most building for least money, and acceptance of that atmosphere of post-rationing austerity dominant generally in the 1950s; anything grand would have been publicly unacceptable. That buildings should look like hospitals or factories was par for those times, and harmonised with Baxter's industrial background. So, not an academic factory in any derogatory sense, but, perhaps in a housing context, a factory for academics. The Kensington campus had begun as what a student of the time described as 'one great, large, sand paddock', on which the early buildings rose like oases, gradually reclaiming a desert wilderness, with long, sand-blasted treks for the traveller between. This did not trouble Baxter. Peter Spooner, first professor of Landscape Architecture (in Australia) recalls that Baxter was not a believer in a master plan, or any consistency of architecture. Hence the campus grew like Topsy, buildings sited wherever land was available, designed by different architects from outside the university.

From the beginning there was a dynamic for expansion, a vista beyond Kensington. Given the university's industrial orientation, outreaches to Newcastle, Broken Hill, and Wollongong were obvious initiatives. Broken Hill offered few parenting problems, Wollongong's move to independence was mainly smooth and affable, but Newcastle was another matter. The University of Technology opened a college at Newcastle, within the premises of the local technical college, on 3 December 1951. The impulse was neither imperial nor expansionist, but one of obligatory decentralisation as laid down in the 1949 establishing Act. The university sought to bring its classes and degrees to areas of need in regional New South Wales: obviously Newcastle, a city based on heavy industry, was a first choice, particularly as there was, in Kensington's perception, an 'apparent public demand for university facilities'. But, on opening, it was found that the number of students presenting was tiny; insufficient to justify anything beyond evening courses: in 1952 there were only 5 day students, with 27 doing conversion courses and 330, the diploma. What Kensington did not appreciate was that what Newcastle wanted was its own facilities, not Sydney hand-me-downs. Furthermore, as the University of Technology was soon to discover, Newcastle wanted a 'real' university of the traditional kind, not what it saw as a truncated and inferior technical variant. There was about the early University of Technology a beguiling innocence, an unthinking assumption that others, whatever their differences, would bear it no ill will, but enter into its youthful spirit, share its enthusiasms, grow in common cause. It was to find otherwise; but it was to encounter the mean-spirited, the reactionary, and the narrowly selfish and intolerant, with constant surprise and to deal with them with a degree of reluctance and disbelief.

By the late 1950s experience had rid Baxter of much of his naivety, but he was never to fully comprehend the extent and depth of the hostility harboured by the University of Sydney. Students and staff, however, felt this keenly. The dismissive jibe

'Kenso Tech' stung, and clung in the mind and memory: the University Foundation in the 1990s was to fund 'Kenso' scholarships in defiant affirmation of its origins. Sporting and debating contests in the 1950s and 1960s were marked by polite — and not so polite — assumptions of Sydney superiority. Baxter's was a case in which duplicity interacted with the wish to gain acceptance to produce illusion. But, so what? The university assumed that it would be welcomed, and when it was not, it still happily went about its own business. That business was increasingly bustling, novel, unique. For instance, in 1952 the university acquired a Geiger counter X-ray spectrometer, the first in Australia. Degree enrolments, full and part-time, sped up, doubled. Courses proliferated: most in subjects carrying the preface 'Applied', but also in fields unusual or unique — Leather Chemistry, Food Technology. Take, for example, Food Technology, a subject entirely innovative in Australia. The first

In the first Food Technology laboratory are

(from left to right) Sher Ahmed Khan (Pakistan),

Soemartono (Indonesia), Poernomo (Indonesia),

Siddiqui (Pakistan), and Malik Khan (Pakistan)

1953

UNSW Archives

professor, FH Reuter, cash-strapped and without facilities, found himself dependent on the generosity of food-processing manufacturers for equipment, which was often not suitable for teaching and research. It was not until 1953 that the Colombo Plan (that Commonwealth initiative of 1950, aimed at alleviating South-East Asian poverty, by training Ceylonese students in Australia) provided adequate specialised resources.

The explosion in demand and supply confirmed the University Council in its confidence that the university was filling a very important public demand in tertiary education. Special graduate courses were being welcomed by industry and the professions, and, most satisfying, paying for themselves, and more: the university, if only in limited areas, was on its way to making profits, the road of the future. Special research was being undertaken at industry's behest, special services made available for laboratory testing, as in Wool Technology — again a path to be well-trodden by future industry. Students, including those under the Colombo Plan, were beginning to pour in, useful things were being done; the technical professions were happy and so was industry, as was evident from the growing number of scholarships provided by major firms. A little money was being made, to add to the intangible gains to the economy and to society from educational investment.

All this was immensely gratifying. If self-doubt had been entertained, it had never surfaced, and by 1953 all indicators were positive. At least those within its own purview. The full strength of traditionalism, reaction, regionalism, radical politics was yet to emerge and discomfort: the university was as yet deemed by critics too negligible an entity to merit serious attention. So, in so far as such an atmosphere can escape the air of stilted banality that surrounds such documents, the Council Report of 1953 exudes a breathless optimism: all was well in the best of possible worlds. Men (and of course all were men) of a certain kind, new men, men of the scientific culture depicted in the novels of CP Snow and representative of one side of the polarity expressed in his notion of the two cultures, had at last found their niche in New South Wales, indeed in Australia, proclaiming in a university their achievements, their success, their ambitions, their rightful place. Their orientation is evident in those they honoured.

Three honorary degrees were awarded at its first graduation ceremony in March 1952. Viscount Nuffield, giant of British industry, had been present at the laying of the foundation stone of the first university building on 25 February 1950. He was a substantial donor to the university through providing scholarships and endowing the Nuffield research professorship in Mechanical Engineering. Professor Marcus Oliphant, leading nuclear scientist, and director of the School of Physical Sciences at the newly established Australian National University (ANU) was also honoured. He symbolised new directions in Australian science and technology, recognition of their national importance, the specific direction of their growth in a nuclear age. Moreover, Oliphant was of a disposition akin to Baxter's — authoritarian, believer in the 'god-professor', elitist, convinced of his own superiority and the absolute rectitude of his own judgement. He and Baxter were of a pair — men of power, awe-inspiring. And, a third to be honoured was Lieutenant-Colonel Sir Charles Bickerton Blackburn,

Λ

University Director A Denning reads the messages received from overseas at the ceremony for the laying of the foundation stone for the first building at Kensington 25 February 1950

chancellor of the University of Sydney, epitome of the Australian academic tradition: the very new was anxious to make its obeisance to the old. The gesture was not merely politic. Baxter was always to believe that Blackburn was well-disposed to the university. But the prevailing atmosphere at the University of Sydney was undoubtedly hostile. How a man as astute as Baxter could underestimate this might be ascribed to the wiles of convenience or his absence from the discussions that predated the university's foundation. It was obvious in the parliamentary debates preceding the university's establishing Act that issues and matters of relative status related to the University of Sydney were centrally involved, both for and against, openly and as undercurrents. A government member referred to the University of Sydney's relations with Newcastle. Sydney delegations agreed to offer help when in Newcastle, but effectively denied it on return. Jealousy of its own preserves was evident, and lay behind arguments that the new university would be state-controlled, unfree, and by definition not a university. Hearnshaw, member for Ryde offered a passage from *Through the Looking-Glass*:

Government Printer/UNSW Archives collection

<|

Ladies at the foundation

stone-laying ceremony

25 February 1950

∧

Wurth's Circus in the making

— the scene on the former Kensington Racecourse

at the foundation stone-laying

25 February 1950

"'When *I* use a word," Humpty Dumpty said in rather a scornful tone, "it means just what I choose it to mean — neither more nor less."
"The question is," said Alice, "whether you can make words mean different things."
"The question is," said Humpty Dumpty, "which is the master — that's all.'"

He had a point, indeed two. One related to the description of the new institution — university? The other is that the government was master, and it wanted a university and it applied this word to what had been devised, University of Sydney objections and fuming notwithstanding. There were class tensions too. This university would be for 'the ordinary man and woman', 'the average Australian lad', children of the 'middle-class and working-class'; not the domain of a 'favoured few'. A government member barbed his contrast with a quotation from Henry Lawson:

> You grope for Truth in a language dead
> In the dust 'neath tower and steeple!
> What do you know of the tracks we tread,
> And what of the living people?

Surely Baxter must have been aware of how things stood with Sydney. Whatever, and howsoever the politics of such recognition, it was the mark of youth. The architects of the university were young in heart and wise only in the ways of hope and limited experience, experience which was small indeed. Some of the University Council lacked university degrees. Most who had them had Sydney's and simply assumed that their alma mater could only wish them well. The young, the enthusiasts, the gifted and confident new could think only in terms of what marvellous things they had to offer, and in that they rejoiced, brash upstarts, blind to how they might seem to others, and utterly sure in their self-importance.

But change was on the march in the early 1950s. And something of a palace revolution had taken place in 1951, the dominant power of the public service and technical college interests had given way to control which was increasingly academic and independent. In September 1951 the university's chief executive, its director, Arthur Denning BSc (Sydney), Dip.Ed, ASTC, director of New South Wales Technical Education, left for six months' study leave. His place was taken, as acting director, by John Philip Baxter, OBE, BSc, PhD (Birmingham), MI ChemE, professor of Chemical Engineering. Baxter had a background ideally suited to the character of the new university. Although highly qualified academically in chemical engineering, he came to New South Wales (in January 1950), not from a university academic post, but from a senior research and managerial position in the Imperial Chemical Industries (ICI) laboratories at Widnes on Merseyside. From there he had been seconded in 1944 to the American Manhattan Project at Oak Ridge, Tennessee, to assist in the production of the first atom bomb. After the war he returned, to be centrally involved in the British atomic energy program. On his American experience, he was fond of a story regarding his first meeting at Oak Ridge to discuss his future plans and requirements. On

Government Printer/UNSW Archives collection

<|

Baxter emergent

ca 1955

leaving the meeting late in the evening, he found a huge bulldozer, under floodlights, excavating a nearby site. It was to be his future laboratory. This 'get up and go' determination delighted him. It was his own style, written in his future. Coming from private industry with managerial administrative dimensions, with no academic experience, Baxter saw forward opportunities while others looked back to tradition.

Why Australia and the New South Wales University? Push, pull, push? ICI was withdrawing from nuclear energy research. With four young children, Baxter was unhappy about the politics and economics of post-war Britain. So, neither the workplace nor general environment were as welcoming as before. Pull? He said, much later (in 1982), it was to settle down to a quiet academic life, but it was said in irony, by way of contrast with actuality. More revealing is a comment he made to a colleague in the 1950s that he had always wanted to build a new university and this was his chance to do so. Behind the dynamic energy and great ability was a determined, even harsh, ambition. Denning was no match for this, or Baxter's academic status and extraordinary work experience. Besides, Denning's protracted absence had the effect of a bloodless coup. In Denning's absence Baxter presided over a crucial stage in university development — a study leave scheme, staff housing arrangements, conversion courses by evening study, arrangement with defence forces to establish a university regiment, negotiations with the government to minimise disruption of student programs by National Service requirements, and a host of lesser matters.

The university regiment, formed in 1952, was very much the creation of this time, encouraged both by the then dominant community values — loyalty to the Crown, service, patriotism, acceptance of authority and defence preparation — and the university's desire to emulate the University of Sydney in having its own prestigious regiment: it was strongly supported by Baxter, who provided it with a building on campus. From the army's viewpoint, the university regiment offered the advantage of contact with an institution which had strong technological and engineering dimensions — of which the army was chronically short. As the honorary colonel put it in his message prefacing the 1977 history of the regiment, 'At Kensington Campus Academus and Campus Martius co-exist in harmony, albeit divided by an optimum cordon of suburbia'. In harmony? Indeed, as the university called on the regiment for guards of honour on various public occasions, and its administrators participated in regimental dinners. With the emergent student radical movement its reputation was predictably different. The army's short-back-and-sides, its whole ethos — all this was

$\overline{\text{V}}$

Sir John Northcott, the governor, inspecting the University of Technology Regiment

at the opening of the Main Building

1955

repugnant to the long-haired, anti-Vietnam generation. Agitation in the 1970s took one form in the daubing of anti-war slogans on the regiment's drill hall at Kensington. However, that war had little effect on membership. The government's changing of the tax law for army reservists did. From a peak membership of 646 in 1957: it declined to present stability — 285 in 1998.

On his return from leave Denning was massively out of touch. On 8 December 1952 council met to determine the matter of who should be director. Both Denning and Baxter had applied. A ballot was held, which Baxter won. Not surprisingly — such is the way of palace revolutions — Denning was most unhappy, and council's expression of 'deep appreciation' did little to salve the deep wound inflicted by his overthrow. He was to accept an honorary degree, and his portrait hangs in the Council Chamber, but his feelings, it seems, were those of injustice and ingratitude suffered. No building carries his name. He resigned a few weeks later, declaredly to devote his full time to the Department of Technical Education. Baxter took his place as director.

Only one matter clouded the horizon in 1953. Certainly, there had been earlier problems with staff dissatisfaction, coming to a head with the resignation of NF Astbury as professor of Applied Physics in 1951 and a 'Prayer to Council' from those professors who wanted more autonomy for the university, better salaries, and a housing scheme. The council regarded all this as an annoyance rather than a challenge, given that it saw itself as moving in the same direction as the petitioners, only at a slower, more realistic pace. Problems in teaching were another, and very immediate matter going to the heart of the university's functioning. Wurth summoned a conference. By 1953 the high rate of student wastage in diploma courses had become evident. Requirements were too onerous for students attempting to combine full-time employment with attendance at lectures. Accordingly, the university revised course structures, modifying requirements and helping students with additional tutorials and increased laboratory instruction. Whatever complexion might be placed on it, this was capitulation to reality: the move was not merely a matter of retaining numbers, but of conciliating industry, on which the university relied. It was a victory of practice over theory. The university had conceded its ideal intellectual ground to the demands of the world of work, the first of such movements which were to characterise the university's acute apprehension of its role. It was not necessarily a diminution of standards (though some were to think so), but rather alertness to immediate pressures and threats, of being alive to the need to see itself in relation to its educational context. Whereas other universities tended to hand down their courses as Holy Writ, determined by masters *in vacuo*, the University of Technology saw itself, necessarily, as interactive, a stance which was to hold it in good stead increasingly in an anti-authoritarian, democratic future. This attitude was not merely a convenience, but a way of seeing itself as flexible, open to the flux of the world, no ivory tower.

This distinctive approach was also embodied in the humanities and social sciences program. There were no Australian precedents to consider. By 1953 it was moving, with additional staff, into offering students a great range of courses, which introduced them to wide social and cultural questions of contemporary significance.

In humanities also, experience was reacting back on courses. Two years of teaching had taught staff what needed modification. They were teaching across a wider range and had begun personal research programs. All this fed into that air of confidence that permeated the whole university enterprise. Student impatience with what some saw as an additional burden was to come later, but for that golden moment the humanities dimension was one in which the whole institution felt that here was an extra, very positive element in the university persona, something in which the whole entity could take merited pride and from which derive satisfaction. Again it was something pioneering, novel, worthwhile — a major injection into that motivational inflation which carried along the ballooning ego of confidence which pervaded the institution.

MJ Dunphy/UNSW Archives collection

∧

Overseas Student Association's

Orientation Week welcome to new

students: the personal touch

(unnamed students)

1954

I can myself remember being initiated into humanities lecturing in 1959 through ordeal by concrete mixer. My lecture room (Nineteenth century British history, I think: hardly a subject to capture students' fascination) was adjacent to the concrete materials laboratory. Competing with a bank of six mixers at once was a make-or-break challenge. So too was the problem of adapting material to the capacities of the audience. The story is told (one of many such) of the English lecturer whose speciality was seventeenth and eighteenth century French and English poetry. He had been lecturing (his first) a class of engineers, when a student in the front row turned to a student behind him and asked in a very loud voice, 'Hey Joe, what's this bastard talking about?'.

Even the composition of the student body pointed the way to the future — a significant Asian element. ('Arabs' as affectionate student labelling had it.) In February 1953 a hostel accommodating eighty students was opened: sixty were Asians, most under the Colombo Plan. They interacted well, giving each other talks on 'My Country' and reacting well to the foibles of the ex-army major who ran it: charming and sociable in the mornings, gossip had it that his habits led him to spend each afternoon in bed. The 'hostel' envisaged 300 students: it was in fact mainly former migrant accommodation, timber and fibro huts on Anzac Parade.

And, generally, students were showing increasing interest in their own affairs, with clubs of all kinds — sporting, social, cultural and religious — to be recognised formally by the university in

September 1952: membership of the Students' Union was made compulsory.

And another sign of happy times. Beginnings were made on some beautification — lawns, flowers, trees, plus an artesian bore to water them. Fences? Chain wire but ornamental gates. The university had come to stay. But was it to be so simple — untroubled growth, the difficulties just those natural to a new enterprise? No: tension and conflict between public service and academic power and expectations had been built into the foundations of the university. They had flared up in mid-1951 with Professor Astbury's resignation and the 'Prayer to Council' signed by Alexander, Hartwell, Phillips, and Towndrow, urging immediate academic autonomy; a virtual revolt by foundation professors against what they regarded as intolerable public service rule. Their claim was that Technology was not a 'real' university and this claim was made in confrontationist language deeply shocking to those imbued with the quietist public service tradition. As Bruce Kaye has pointed out, a section of the 'Prayer' complaint related to the matter of 'university atmosphere' and there the four professors who protested invoked the authority of Cardinal Newman (*The Idea of the University*) to contend that the institution had failed to create a proper university ethos. It was a criticism which was hardly intelligible to a pragmatic governing body: they simply did not speak such language. Although movement was to be made in directions — suggested? demanded? — in the 'Prayer', the tension was not resolved until the 1960s. Requirements of signing on and off for academic attendance lingered until then — and so too did the protracted and public repercussions of the Russel Ward case, which erupted initially in

Max Franklin/UNSW Archives collection

∧

Basic simplicities

— dormitory accommodation for early students

August 1963

1956. The Staff Association, comprising many of those with the trade union dispositions they had inherited from Sydney Technical College, was by no means supine or compliant. Its members were particularly irked by the requirement to 'punch the bundy', a demeaning practice not imposed by other universities and therefore signifying in staff minds an inbuilt concession of inferiority. Agitation on this, and other status issues, drew packed meetings of staff into the 1960s. The university's Staff Association had sought an industrial award, the first such in Australia. Such dissatisfaction, initially less with salaries than with what they saw as humiliating conditions, had a positive effect within the staff body in that it was drawn together by dissatisfactions which transcended faculties and schools, made leading and vocal personalities known, and provided common cause. Usually, against the administration. Coupled with the enthusiasm and optimism were feelings of frustration and annoyance: Baxter held together an unstable amalgam.

If the focal and fashionable intellectual notion of the late 1940s was that of the rise of science and technology, that of the mid 1950s was nuclear power. In both, the leading Australian exponents were the modern foundations of the University of Technology and the ANU; but the ANU, being devoted solely to research, lacked the mass teaching dimension that the University of Technology was building. By 1954 and 1955 what had been fluid or problematical had consolidated: the University of Technology had taken clear form and confident direction. The day of 1 July 1954 had been declared the 'appointed day', on which complete authority under the 1949 Act was taken from the Public Service Board and vested in the university's own council: it acted quickly and energetically to assert its independent powers, its first act being to reorganise its own administrative structures, to deal with day-to-day matters. It made appropriate noises of gratitude to the Public Service Board, but, particularly in view of the frustrated professorial demands for autonomy evident in the 1951 'Prayer', there is no doubt of its relief to be standing on its own

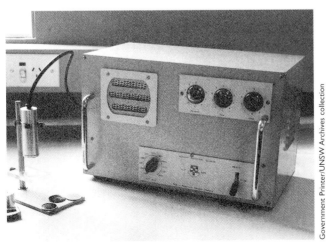

Nuclear radiation counter

used in radiation chemistry

1959

Government Printer/UNSW Archives collection

unhobbled feet. Yet much remained of the public service linkage, of necessity in that the university still needed to depend on its facilitation for a range of practical matters, but also by choice and habits of mind. The bonds of respect and shared tactical disposition between Baxter and Wurth were only the highest point of personal contacts and interactions which kept the university within an — albeit diminishing — public service orbit. That orbit could be annoyingly petty. In the old (then new) Main Building the key to the ladies' toilet was kept by the senior lady clerk. She had to be asked for it by others, who regarded this as demeaning and believed she was keeping a record. The bursar made individual keys available. Or another demeaning oddity. Furniture, however solid and weighty it might be, was made in the workshops of Long Bay Prison. And both furniture and staff room size were governed by strict public service regulation. The legacy of these marched on, into the 1980s and beyond, in the *Blue Book*, a compendium of rules and procedures covering all aspects of day-to-day university operation.

On 31 August and 1 September 1954 the university hosted a symposium 'Atomic Energy in Australia', with nuclear power for industry its focus. The high point was the announcement by the New South Wales premier, JJ Cahill, of a grant of £125,000 to support a Research Institute of Nuclear Engineering within the university, a very large sum at the time. Paper-givers came from all over Australia, headed by Marcus Oliphant; not only academics, but also scientists and bureaucrats, such as the Secretary of the Department of National Development. The emphasis of the symposium was that Australia's concerns lay in the technological field rather than that of the fundamental sciences, a position whose implication was to put the university at the head of moves towards national development, and the heart of future policy. This was a blatantly political initiative engineered by Baxter (with the support of Metallurgy Professor Rupert Myers), designed to assert the university's unique character, pressing its claims to a central role in the national endeavour — and carrying the latent demand that it be resourced to discharge this. Baxter's position on the Australian Atomic Energy Commission (AAEC), formed to advise the government in 1949, enabled him to write in its 1953 report that the 'atomic age has opened up to mankind new prospects of technological and social progress', in which 'Australia can play a part fully commensurate with her status as a nation' and could be confident that the tasks that lay ahead were 'being undertaken with practical vision and a full realisation of their importance'. Perhaps. But Baxter himself, according to one of his assistants in the area, had what would now be regarded as a casual attitude to things nuclear, bred of familiarity, no doubt. More so in the Chemistry school itself. According to Stanley Livingstone, historian of the School of Chemistry:

In 1957 a lecturer asked a member of the laboratory staff to transport a radioactive material by public transport to another part of the metropolitan area. Adequate precautions were not taken and the laboratory staff member was admitted to hospital with suspected radiation damage. Fortunately he was not seriously affected. In consequence of this incident, it was decided to set up a radiation laboratory under the control of James Green, who had been appointed Lecturer in the Department of Physical Chemistry in 1956.

Baxter's high-flown nuclear verbiage, with its references to mankind and vistas of progress, was in a context of the centrality of Australian uranium ore to British and American planning, to which he was, apparently, privy. It reflects his faith and zeal, but was to involve him with a range of security organisations and agents to the degree of prompting charges of improper behaviour. These reached their extreme in 1970 with the book *Without Hardware* by Catherine Dalton, widow of Clifford Dalton, director of the Lucas Heights reactor, who had died in 1961. Dalton was to allege that her husband had in fact been murdered and that Baxter had been involved. Dalton also suggested some degree of involvement in the still unsolved Bogle-Chandler murder case of 1963, Bogle being a laser scientist employed by the CSIRO. These were absurd allegations, but they point to the world of high scientific and governmental politics, of security and secrecy and heady idealism in which Baxter moved. And in which he continued to move. Following his retirement from the university in 1969, his chairmanship of the Australian Atomic Energy Commission took him into what was increasingly contentious territory — the domain of the anti-nuclear protest. Public enthusiasm for this source of energy had, by the 1970s turned into its opposite. In 1975 he felt compelled, in a reply in *Search*, journal of the Australian and New Zealand Association for the Advancement of Science, to reject 'out of hand' criticism of the AAEC he regarded as 'unfounded and defamatory'. This intense controversy, and others like it in the nuclear area, fortunately for the university fell beyond Baxter's vice-chancellorship. However, it reveals his distrust of politicians and 'open government' in matters technological — his distrust of the notion 'that everybody should have the right to know all about everything'. A senior subordinate in his vice-chancellorship has remarked that Baxter 'knew everything about everything', an attitude which permeated his whole management style.

The declaration of nuclear intentions was not the only university manoeuvre to bid for attention. Initiatives were taken in 1954–55 in a range of novel directions. But first the university placed itself on a nomenclature par with all others. On 4 March 1955 the establishing Act was amended to change the executive titles of president, vice-president, and director to chancellor, deputy chancellor, and vice-chancellor — Wurth, Mr Justice Clancy, and Baxter. The University Council was increased significantly in size, from thirty to thirty-nine, so as to include agricultural, pastoral,

JOA Bourke, the bursar, in caricature (nd)

Pugnacity outfaced:

a bulldog slinks away

from confrontation

with JOA Bourke

1962

and rural interests, and graduate representation. And in 1955, to formalise the move to university independence, 518 members of the staff working at the university but formally employed by the Department of Technical Education were invited to join the university: all but three accepted.

By 1954 changes had already been made in administration, to strengthen the centralisation of bureaucracy by establishing a Personnel Division, under a bursar, James Ormond Aloysius (Joe) Bourke, a personality who soon became, and remained until his death in 1965, a colourful legend. Bourke had appropriated the title of 'bursar' from Oxford, where it denotes a powerful college official, a term with financial controlling overtones and centrality to decision-making which admirably suited his view of himself — and the actuality. His signature conveyed to academics what they wished to know — and much they did not — about the day-to-day operations of the place: rules and regulations, requirements, limitations, the whole public service apparatus. He was a great admirer of Wurth. Bluff and hearty in a deadpan Irish-Australian way, Bourke was both liked and respected while exercising a tough and unyielding authority. Strange harmony: the lovable complete bureaucrat. And the university 'character', a hero to many, gregarious and sociable, given to hosting regular Friday night drinks in his office, at which he held court, seeing the university world as divided into 'goodies' and 'baddies'. No gentleman wears a brown suit: so the sartorial dictum goes. Cads and bounders only. What then is to be made of the reminiscence of Joe Bourke walking across the road on Wednesdays to Randwick races, attired in brown suit, brown bowler hat, with furled umbrella? But, of course, there was much more to him than that: he was very well-connected 'downtown', that is, his Public Service Board connections gave him access to places of power vital to the operation of the university. It gave him power and influence above that of Registrar Macauley, who eyed this with wary envy. (On my first day at the university in April 1959 Bede Nairn of History took me to see Joe. It was after five. The bursar produced several bottles of porphyry from the vice-chancellor's cellar — a mark of civilisation now sadly vanished. He plied me — then having no experience with wine — with porphyry, to dire effect: I have not sampled porphyry, a sweet dessert wine, since.)

Students saw Bourke as the university's human — if stern — face. In the 1950s Randwick's drainage problems meant major stormwater flooding of low-lying areas. (As late as the 1970s I recall a student actually swimming across the Alison Road-Anzac Parade intersections in order to deliver a plastic-wrapped, thus waterproofed honours thesis to me before the deadline.) These conditions, after heavy rain, meant deep and frequent flooding of the university site now occupied by the Village Green cricket oval. Students put this to good use for water sports and general wet hooliganism (the ultimate prank was the introduction of a baby crocodile, purloined from Taronga Zoo), and christened it Lake Bourke. They entered this on street signs, which Bourke had scrubbed out as soon as he heard. Win some, lose some. In 1957, or was it 1958, Basser College had no hot water for a fortnight. Their pleas unavailing, the students phoned television news stations, and then marched, in towels, down Anzac Parade to shower in the hostel there. The students there repelled them with fire hoses, in the process drenching the public passing in the old toast-rack trams. Watched by Bourke and Macauley. And all on television. The hot water was fixed immediately. An early example of student power and administration humiliation. There were other incidents, less happy, of Bourke's toughness. In some university rowdiness, one of his 'henchmen' punched a student, knocking him down. Protest was met by Bourke with hard dismissal: this did not endear him to students.

The opening of the first permanent building on the Kensington site, on 16 April 1955, was both a concrete (and red Australian brick) achievement, and an affirmation of ideals. It coincided with the first conferring of degrees at Kensington, in the open air of that pioneering space. The building — unadventurous brick box, practical and adaptable — proclaimed the spirit of the university's dreams on its facade: Tom Bass's copper mural 'The Falconer' (being the technologist as construed by Bass, following the symbolism of the pretentiously indifferent poem by Sir Herbert Read, 'The Falcon and the Dove'). It rose 42 feet (almost 13 m), facing the building's entrance, seeking to symbolise the idea that all technologists should bear in mind the aesthetic aspects of their professional work. Baxter opined that every graduate should become to some extent an artist, a view which prompted cruder members of staff to supply the usual Australian coarse definition of where such artistry might lie. Certainly the notion was high-flown and problematical.

Much more down to earth and enduring than the sculpture, whose style has not

worn well, were other artistic initiatives taken at this time. The university began its collection of paintings, representative of contemporary Australian achievement, with a nucleus of eighteen works by prominent artists such as John Passmore, Rupert Bunny, Donald Friend, Margaret Olley. The initiative was Baxter's, widening his long and participating interest in drama and the stage into the full range of cultural and artistic endeavour. And the trappings of the civilised academic life. Baxter sought also to involve the whole university community in his musical enthusiasms. The Science Theatre, opened in 1960, enabled him to combine the resources of technology, in a superb sound system, with the latest recording achievements, a young Joan Sutherland, at the height of her *bel canto* powers, introduced by him personally from the stage, to an invited audience of staff, to their wonderment and joy. Works of art, music to the ear, things of beauty, the life of culture and refinement, the wider world of soul and spirit: the University of Technology was to be, in the Baxter vision, expansive, all-engaging, human and humane.

But ever-present was technological ambition and expansionism, and hard-headed realism: the books must balance and someone must pay the bills. So, for 1955, student fees were simply doubled — from £30 to £60. This sparked widespread student anger culminating in a meeting of protest, organised by Heinz Harant of the Students' Union, at the Sydney Town Hall and the resolution not to pay the increases. What happened? Essentially nothing, and the Students' Union went back to debating the issue of whether the separate Sports Association should be under its authority.

At least the university did not push its students too far in its drive for funds: perhaps their reaction made their resistance amply clear. (Or did it? The performance was repeated in 1957.) New directions were backed by major benefactions, a euphemism for the pushy negotiations which were behind the establishment of chairs in Traffic Engineering and Highway Engineering by the Australian Automobile Association and the New South Wales Department of Main Roads, and various agricultural projects funded by the Rural and Commonwealth Banks. Highway Engineering was a British Commonwealth first, reflecting not so much Baxter's vision, as his wish to have as many separate schools as possible, an inflation designed to make the university seem bigger and more impressive: thus, also, the proliferation into both Traffic and Highway Engineering, when their functions could have been subsumed under Civil Engineering — a judgement made by Traffic Engineering's

Hugh Hyland/UNSW Archives collection

<

Students' tug of war in Lake Bourke

1963

Note the Kenso Cakes and Sponges

building in Barker St (on left).

first professor, Ross Blunden. There was, as well, the Hydraulics Laboratory at Manly Vale, supported by the Metropolitan Water Board and several government departments. And, of course, since 1954, substantial inflow of funds came from the Australian Atomic Energy Commission, which, given Baxter's key role in the AAEC, was Baxter supporting Baxter. There was also an incestuous element in the university's entry into the computer age in 1955. The largest of the four computer projects launched in that year was tied in with nuclear engineering and the British Atomic Energy Authority, again Baxter's home ground.

But most was innovation and the operations of the brilliant entrepreneurial spirit. By the late 1950s, the university had related itself to an enormous range of enterprises, government and private. Not only was it the tertiary arm of heavy industry — coal, iron, steel, power — but of light industry. Household names were involved: Felt and Textile carpets, Arnott's and Weston's biscuits, Taubman's paints, Bond, Bradmill, Cottee's jams, the whole complex of Australian manufacturing was reflected in research projects, scholarships and benefactions; the university was woven into the fabric of productive Australia. And more was being constantly acquired — other contacts, other initiatives, expanding real estate. The outreach was extraordinary, the vision remarkable, the time and energy required staggering, the pace breathtaking. With Baxter as prime mover, explosive force: though to help him in September 1955 a public relations officer had been appointed — George Caiger.

Meanwhile, there was activity in television, publications (the symposium 'Wool Technology'), a swing towards the problems of primary industry, agricultural engineering and water research: a symposium on water resources was held in 1955. Initiatives outside the basic parameters were added in 1956 — Schools of Textile Technology and Hospital Administration. A reorganisation of faculties produced a separate Faculty of Technology in that year. And in 1956, in the first of its Open Days, in conjunction with its graduation ceremony, the university put itself on public show: over 2000 took the grand tour of inspection. *Tharunka* — the student newspaper (its name, Aboriginal message stick) — had begun in 1953.

Amid the push towards extending into what was new, care was taken to foster what was, in the university's brief historical span, old. Notably, building student numbers, still overwhelmingly part-time, to 5309 by 1956. But also the Newcastle problem. Efforts had been made to curb Newcastle unrest, by applying convoluted devices designed to remedy the university's legislative inability to offer arts formally. Arrangements had been made, effective from 1954, with the University of New England in Armidale, whereby it examined and conferred degrees at Newcastle, the teaching being done by the University of Technology's School of Humanities and Social Sciences: ninety-five students enrolled under this scheme. Staff were appointed to Newcastle to deal with this, notably that Irish paragon of academic ambition, historian JJ Auchmuty. The British Foreign Office had circulated Commonwealth universities to advocate the cause of British academics ousted by Nasser's national revolution in Egypt. Auchmuty, from Alexandria, had attracted Hartwell, and his aspirations rapidly took him up the university ladder. His appointment to Newcastle in 1955 energised and focussed a movement towards autonomy, building on an

RJ Heffron speaking at the first graduation

advisory committee of local citizens: student enrolments had reached nearly fifty by 1954. But at unknowable Kensington cost. It is said that the Newcastle experience hardened Baxter against arts, or, rather, added to a disposition also fostered by Hartwell and the Ward case. In Newcastle a determined anti-University of Technology push was led by the local Workers' Education Association (WEA) tutor Harry Eddy, who wanted an arts university, and to whom technology was the end of civilisation as we know it: the University of Technology represented everything he hated. With the powerful support of the Anglican bishop of Newcastle, the Eddy campaign gave Baxter a very hard time, and generated in him understandable resentment.

At Kensington building activity continued, enabling further movement from the Broadway site. In 1955 land at Kingsford was acquired for sport, in which there was substantial and growing interest. Hostel accommodation was expanded and upgraded, dining facilities enhanced, dormitories divided into single rooms — a comment on the Spartan nature of previous student conditions and on rising expectations. Academic activity in 1956 had blossomed not just into Hospital Administration, under the sponsorship of the Kellogg Foundation, but also the beginnings of Accounting and Economics and the Commerce degree. All seemed to augur well in the brightest of expanding worlds.

By 1956 university income had risen to £1,296,555. This included, after University Council representations to the New South Wales government, a supplementary State grant of £53,000 to meet salary requirements. Putting it thus, in this bland matter-of-fact fashion, disguises the reality of this extraordinary situation. What would have happened to staff salaries had the money not been forthcoming? What kind of financial management allowed this to happen? What kind of drift, irresponsibility, and casual presumption, were at work in university administration? Surely these were the hallmarks of brazen extravagance and budgetary brinkmanship?

In responding to the request for supplementation, the government made clear (what was patently and painfully obvious already) that the university's budget was in deficit and it could not expect to match this in 1957. Indeed, it could assume no more than £1,100,000, a drop of almost £200,000 on 1956. In the face of this situation, the university was given notice by the State that it should consider its position and look to its own resources to deal therewith. Given the university's bad financial behaviour, the State Treasury made no bones about spelling out to the university its clear obligations and obvious options — immediate economies, increasing fees, and seeking outside, non-government, money. The admonishment was polite, but nevertheless amounted to pointing out the elementary lessons of book balancing to those who should have known them.

The golden age when the university's expansion was limited only by its own ingenuity and energy had been brought to an abrupt end. In a mere five years, staff salaries had climbed from an initial £36,000 to nearly £1,500,000 in 1955–56, a progression certain to attract Treasury attention. A halt had been called by the holders of the purse-strings, those whose responsibility was to balance the State's books. They were impervious to, and uncomprehending of arguments urging scientific and technological values in the national interest.

In any case, no one was fielding such arguments: the university response was meek. Given the university's efforts to fund its expanding initiatives from outside sources, private, semi-governmental and departmental, the possession of a cavalier attitude to financing seems improbable. More likely seems the possibility that the university was testing the State to see how far it might go in committing the State to new initiatives and their associated expense.

A halt being called, and notice of limits given, the university braked instantly. Heavy staffing cuts were imposed. Vacancies were not filled. A substantial proportion of part-time staff was stood down in third term. Spending on classroom materials and plant replacement was slashed. Not that equipment had been lavish before. The contrary. Dr RG Burdon recalls his initial experience in the early 1950s as lecturer in Mining Engineering, a school advantaged by its support from the Joint Coal Board:

> When I held my first laboratory classes the only equipment that I had for Mineral Processing was a panning dish and large galvanised tub purchased from Anthony Horderns, and for Coal Preparation a beaker and tea strainer to illustrate Heavy Media Separation Process. Obtaining equipment presented many difficulties since many items were not available from Australian manufacturers and import licences were required. As I was principally in charge of requisitioning I spent many hours with Purchasing Officer, Mr Jack Best, preparing applications for import licences and attending interviews at the Customs Department.

He was fortunate. FH Reuter in Food Technology recalls subsisting on donations — jacketed steam pans and a canning retort from CSR which eventually failed to get its annual inspection certificate but had to be used nevertheless, a can-closer from Heinz, a small retort from Holbrook's. Beg, borrow, stopping short of steal — so was vital equipment acquired. And diligent perusal of the Government Stores list: much needed stainless-steel-topped tables could be found under the heading of 'Mortuary Tables'. It was only Commonwealth financing in relation to Colombo Plan students which changed poverty into affluence. Minor carpentry and wall-painting the staff did themselves.

The purchasing point represents the common experience of many of the technology-based schools — massive time-wasting imposed by external bureaucracy, government regulations, and red tape, in order to acquire basic equipment. Even within local resources, absurd shortcomings obtruded. The professor of Mining Engineering, DW Phillips, moved into his room in the old Main Building, to find it well-furnished — except for a desk. Staff rallied to construct one, from packing cases and an unused door. The stringency meant that existing staff were required to do more and their research was thus curtailed. The University Council insisted that the university, as a concept, was still incomplete in its realisation, and that areas had been entered without regard to funding consequence — 'the demands of the new technologies which cannot be resisted have yet to be estimated in terms of cost'. The rhetoric had a Baxter flavour — 'cannot be resisted' — and the lesson was Baxteresque: all were stuck with what had been embarked upon — staff and State — and would have to wear it, work harder, find the money. In what was billed as an emergency, the university sought to ingratiate itself to the State, seeking talks and advice on the university's predicament, from Treasury and the Education ministry, a stratagem both flattering and necessary, in pursuit of a repentant common cause. Increasingly both the premier and minister for Education — Cahill and Heffron — already university supporters, were to be seen at university events, dinners.

So, from 1957, all fees were increased by 50 per cent, estimated to raise an additional £45,000, but still placing fee levels beneath that of other universities. How this would impact on students who had had their fees doubled only two years before was not considered, mainly because most were in work, or covered by scholarships. It was put to the Commonwealth that its payments for various university services were less than appropriate — a popular argument in State Treasury circles, on this occasion conceded by the federal authorities. And the university itself conceded that its building program, then running at a lavish £650,000 per annum, would have to be hard pruned.

All this cutting and cheese-paring (even paper was rationed) set a pattern of priorities which was to be maintained in the recurring boom–bust of university finances. Arts and humanities, always lean, squeezed first and hardest, and the budget balances always distorted and skewed in favour of science and technology. Not that commerce, and indeed engineering, saw themselves as doing much better. Even engineers, the initial and continuing backbone of the university, felt themselves neglected in comparison with what they saw as the 'exotica' of Applied Science — wool, textiles, food processing, mining, the like. They believed that vice-chancellors, the ultimate font of money, were swayed by the fashionable, those activities that attracted commercial support, the new and publicly interesting, while the old fundamentals went begging. From the arts perspective, the Machiavellianism of this seemed obvious. What was less obvious was the selflessness that permeated the university's core. A striking aspect of early appointments was their extraordinary personal and professional quality. Most were true and dedicated believers in their mission, in themselves, and in the institution they were creating. They saw it as embodying the future of mankind and as thus placing on them demands for their best, and on the institution a necessary hierarchy of subordination in situations of limited resources. That an arts perspective might construe this as unfair and arrogant is hardly surprising, but any appraisal of these early years could hardly gainsay the remarkable devotion, professional pre-eminence, and sheer (dare it be said?) nobility of those who had decided to join it. Their calibre is humbling — Baxter himself, Phillips, Willis, Milner, Myers, Vowels, Mellor, others — commanded respect, however they might differ, or their goals be questioned or rejected. And they were willing to carry personally the consequences of entry into uncharted scientific waters. Here was a university where all staff, top to bottom, were expected to carry the burdens of decisions which looked forward to a shared technological common good, determined by internal masters above. This was not an institution for the fainthearted or work-shy. Loads were often excessive in comparison with other, more established, leisurely places. That the staff were not overly resistant to this derives, in part, from the spirit of commitment that permeated the adventure which the university was. In part. But, to be realistic, also in part from the fact that many staff had backgrounds in the Sydney Technical College, where they had been used to heavy teaching loads and slim resources — and were glad to be in a university environment. There was also one unique staff perk, offered by no other Australian university — free, feeless, tuition for the children of staff. The university's largesse in this was prompted no doubt by the notion that staff progeny were likely to prove better students, and to raise the standards of student intake. Whatever of this, the concession was attractive to staff in those days of larger families. Some did not avail themselves of it, but it was there as an attraction, or future one, for those with young children. It was to cease in the Whitlam years, when, from 1974, general abolition of fees made it meaningless. It was not revived.

Despite the financial stringency, and the need and willingness to confront it with frugality and discipline — those on site, staff and students would carry the can — the university persevered in its determination to expand and diversify: such was its ordained mission as seen by its power elite. Thus were introduced, in 1957, several courses new to Australian education — extra expenditure, promoted as 'amply justified ... in view of the university's responsibility to develop facilities for tertiary education in fields outside the traditional disciplines'. Or — to dispense with the official sermonising (though that was part of the performance) — the university had an apostolic vision of itself, serving the worldwide cause of science and technology. This heavy duty and great adventure were not to be obstructed by mere lack of money. Excitement was the mood of that time, the lift that came with involvement in the hopes and dreams of a new scientific mankind. Inchoate, barely understood beyond its simplicities even by its proponents, a world revolution worth making real sacrifices for, to maintain that sense of limitless possibilities within grasp, dazzling achievements foreseen.

So, new courses. More students were moved from Broadway. Numbers increased in 1957 — 5634 at Kensington, 694 at Newcastle. Cooperation with industry and government departments was expanded. The university's computing facilities were increasingly drawn upon by outside organisations. More staff were employed at senior levels — associate professors. University Council widened its membership to include commerce, trade unions and the university's own staff. Commerce attracted an accelerating number of students. Newcastle grew. A ten-year building program was accepted in principle. Nuclear business was as usual: Baxter was senior Australian technical representative at the inaugural conference of the International Atomic Energy Agency in New York in September 1956. And computer activities expanded with the arrival from England in August 1956 of the English Electric electronic digital computer, known locally as UTECOM. This was the first such computer to work in Australia. Operated by Electrical Engineering, it was also an initiative of the School of Mathematics, under Geoffrey Bosson: high-level research required the speediest possible number-crunching, although most early maths students were engineers doing maths as a required course. Students lived in awe and reverence of UTECOM, but as a valve-driven device it operated best when working continuously. Switching off for the weekend produced a crop of troubles when it was re-started, leading the engineers who serviced it to propose that its name was an acronym for 'unable to exactly compute on Mondays'.

The following month the New South Wales premier opened a high-powered symposium on 'Automation and Australia': heavy speakers, forward-thinking subjects.

Stringency? Yes, but the conviction, and practical conclusion, was that this must be temporary. Nothing could succeed like success. The dynamic was unstoppable.

But not quite. Hiccups. Or were they major upsets? In October 1956 RM Hartwell, professor of Economic History since 1950, dean of the Faculty of Humanities and Social Sciences, resigned. The council reported this as 'to take up appointment as Reader in Recent Social and Economic History at the University of Oxford', and made the usual formal noises of regret, thanks, and good wishes. The actual situation was nothing so simple or pleasant. Hartwell had resigned in protest against the university's refusal to proceed with a decision to appoint Dr Russel Ward as a lecturer in history. These decisions raised, or appeared to raise, questions of the university's internal governance, independence from external interference, and ideological disposition, given Ward's former membership of the Communist Party, and given the widespread assumption, though this was never proven, that this was the basis for the university hierarchy's declining to proceed with his appointment against the recommendation of its own selection committee. The obvious conclusion was not necessarily the correct one, given the diversity of Ward's prior career, and the closed and mysterious nature of decision-making, which shrouded what had

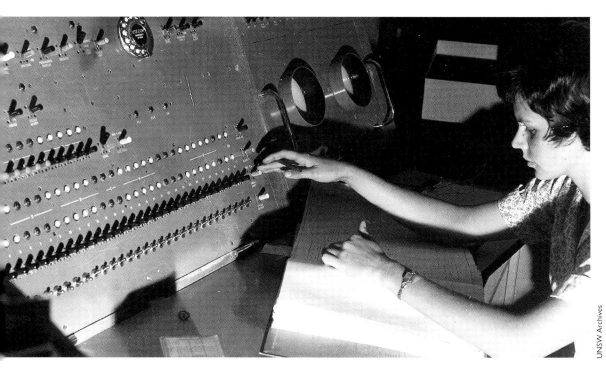

UNSW Archives

UTECOM, the university's first computer

1960

occurred. Indeed, granting Baxter and Wurth a measure of decency and sense, it seems that there was more to the matter than meets the jaundiced eye. Baxter was to imply such. Few attended to this. The dominant prevailing fact was that rumours of security interferences abounded at this Cold War time, throughout the whole Australian university scene. There had been noises of suspicion in various places, the University of Sydney included, but there it was believed, by those so disposed, that security intervention had occurred early enough to prevent suspect candidates from being considered. Or so the story went.

Whatever, the Ward case took on a life of its own, reviving in the early 1960s. It came to be seen by libertarian and ideologically ill-disposed eyes, as exhibiting Baxter at his authoritarian worst — secretive, presumptuous, scornful of, or neglecting contrary opinion, and devious and inept when compelled to deal with it. And resentful. He appears not to have forgiven arts (as embodied by Hartwell) for trouble-making, and to have distrusted the arts disposition, its failure to be of one mind with him, thereafter, to the continuing disadvantage of that area. However guiltless, it was to pay for Hartwell's sins as Baxter saw them. Or so the hostile story and interpretation went: given the confidential nature of selection procedures, Baxter was not in a position to combat or deny these harsh and impassioned charges. As to Hartwell, the Ward case seems to have brought to the surface buried tensions, the ambivalence he felt in regard to the differing rewards, demands, and atmospheres of Australian and British academic environments. As is usual in such circumstances of dispute, no one emerged from it with much credit, save in their own eyes and those of their partisan supporters.

But to take the essentials of the conflict at face and public value, the context of the university's foundation and early days were those of the Cold War from 1947, the Korean War in 1950–53, and the overwhelming public perception of communist external threat and internal subversion in Australia. The pervasive belief was that there were immensely powerful socialist, Marxist, Russian forces poised without, and insidious enemies operating within, which must be combated. The prevailing atmosphere was one of conviction of communist menace, suspicion of radicalism, fear of betrayal, faith in ASIO (the Australian Security Intelligence Organisation), and the need to be alert to infiltration in all areas of public power and influence. This university was part of that arena, particularly in view of it being seen as a battleground for ideas — and in its atomic research dimensions. Though its formation and outlook were devoid of any overtly political allegiance, there is no doubting the university's overall conservative disposition and sensitivity to security matters: it saw its scientific and technological orientation as entwined with the national well-being — and that of 'the free world'. Besides, its operations in both teaching and research, and funding, were intimately tied in with government and its agencies and defence-orientated projects and industries. As was the background of senior staff, many from British red-brick universities, and previous defence employment there.

Hartwell's origins, milieu, and intellectual outlook and disposition were very different. An Australian, he had been in Oxford on a scholarship — in arts not science. This was the Oxford which, together with Cambridge, produced disquieting facts, and a legacy of classic espionage fiction headed by John le Carré; the world of MI5, agents, spies and counter-spies, moles and ideologies, ferment about values which seethed throughout the Cold War and beyond. Hartwell was no radical, but neither was he an unthinking empire loyalist. He was a man who respected freedom and diversity and had an 'arts' view of a university environment — his world being that of the broad interplay of ideas rather than that of more narrow, professional excellences. And it seems highly likely that his stand on the Ward case was purely one of principle. He was to confide, in the 1990s, that he had no liking for Ward the man, and liked his politics even less. It was indicative of his openness, as against the bizarre and disturbing world of security police, that it should have been one of Hartwell's first appointees — JB Thornton — who was detained and questioned (presumably as a security risk), in 1950, by French police. Thornton had agreed to represent the New South Wales Teachers' Federation at international conferences of the teaching profession, first in Malta, then in France, and had argued at the Malta conference for the Teachers' Federation's right to be affiliated with the New South Wales Trades and Labor Council and, more generally, to engage, if it chose to, in political action — a view strongly denounced by most other delegates as no more than Marxist propaganda. Hartwell would have disagreed with it too. When he returned to Sydney, and to Ultimo, Hartwell steadfastly refused to join the university Staff Association, because of its trade union leanings and affiliations with the Teachers' Federation; although most of the university staff, including the present author, were members: the fact that the federation leadership included communist elements did not deter those who wanted to take advantage of its discount shopping facilities or the fact that it offered trade union representation to university staff. Jack Thornton was no red, but, as Hartwell discerned, an exciting appointment of potential excellence, to be amply demonstrated — as the university was to find to its profit — over the next thirty years.

Oh if the university were to be so fortunate in finding a successor to match Hartwell's own success as dean of Humanities and Social Sciences. He was followed by JJ Auchmuty, no intellectual, rather the man of ambition whose destiny was to lie with Newcastle, and with national tertiary education politics. It was he, so it was said, who as vice-chancellor made the University of Newcastle develop a British Protestant temper to a degree and in a way, different from other Australian universities. And after his translation came Morven Brown, good if rushed at his job, giving the impression of a worried, unhappy man, running his hands through his hair. Or was it that he was simply whimsical and irascible? Baxter appointed Brown, apparently after having been immensely impressed by a speech Brown had given at Baxter's son's school. Tony Vinson tells a story which encapsulates 'Morv'. Talking with Brown, Vinson, then a very junior lecturer, became increasingly concerned as time wandered past the appointed lecture hour. Said Morven: 'My boy, am I to judge from your agitation that you imagine your presence in their classroom could be of some benefit to the students? The good ones', he said, 'will get there without you, and the others you can do nothing for.' A marvellous piece of Wildean wisdom whose truth both revealed and transcended the unconventional 'Morv'.

Government Printer/UNSW Archives collection

RM Hartwell at a University Council meeting

14 November 1955

Under this stimulus Vinson designed a social work degree: Brown was under the duress of having publicly promised such a course, and with a parent threatening legal action unless the university provided it. The story, apocryphal or not, of Brown's appointment is typical of Baxter's modus operandi — absolute judgemental self-trust and authoritarian rule within his own orbit. And that orbit, from 1958, depended on giving increased power to deans. As to Morven Brown, a man of great presence, it is in a way surprising — even given his great contribution to the Arts faculty — that he should have the honour of having a university building named after him. Not only did Brown not have much love for engineers and technologists, but, with a Sydney University background, he transmitted the intangible sense of being different. He formed a natural friendly alliance with that other outsider dean, Bryan Smyth. They both endured, perforce, a financial diet of crumbs from the table of the university's scientific rich.

Contribution to the Arts faculty? Certainly, but Brown's contribution to the university was to prove much more than that. It was he who introduced those dimensions of sociology and social work — the social sciences — which were in the future so much an important public part of the university's achievement and reputation.

In 1958 Brown joined the university from the University of Sydney to be professor of Sociology and first dean of Arts. Sadly, not for long: he died in 1965. But by then Sociology was firmly established, and led to Australian and international importance by his successor, Sol Encel. As professor, teacher, and author of important books on Australian society, Encel advanced the field to be a distinguishing — and distinguished — aspect of the university's persona, however much it came under criticism, as a joke and a soft option, by scholarly traditionalists.

Brown, recognising his own courses' shortcomings in regard to social work, imported from Sydney his former colleague, Norma Parker, to oversee and teach that area in 1966, an appointment which quickly led on to the establishment of a chair. John Lawrence became the first professor of Social Work in any Australian university in 1968. Social Work was central to the Faculty of Professional Studies set up in 1973, but it, together with Education, Librarianship, Health Administration, and Industrial Arts — the vocational studies — were accorded fringe and inadequate accommodation in all senses, despite the public prominence and importance of their work. On Lawrence's retirement in 1996, the Department of Social Security, the university's own Social Policy Research Centre formed in 1978, and the Australian Institute of Criminology were among many who paid lyrical tribute to his centrality in government operations and initiatives. As community and welfare programs grew and diversified in a changing society in the 1970s and 1980s, so did Social Work. Lawrence, a mild-mannered, helpful man, convinced of the need for a moral and ethical basis for any social work programs, a true professional, tended to find himself and his subject at something of a remove in a vigorously hardnosed, utilitarian university environment. His successor as head of school in 1983, Tony Vinson, was no less professional, particularly in relation to prison work, where he had a high-profile reputation, but perhaps a little more combative within the politics of the university until he fell out with it over the matter of the St George campus closure in 1996. Both were hampered by the relative newness and 'soft' reputation of their area — encouraging a dismissive inattention in the university though Social Work was financed well enough. Besides, the very nature of the subject meant that it was focussed elsewhere, out in the concerns of the general community, family, children and the like, particularly its social problem areas. There, its influence and impact were very great — considered, progressive, benign, a true if distant legacy, with Sociology, of Morven Brown's vision.

The September 1957 report to the federal government of the Murray Committee on Australian universities was a turning point for the tertiary system, but none was more favourably affected than the University of Technology, both in its character — it became the University of New South Wales — and its financing. The Murray Committee expressed the acceptance by the Menzies government of responsibility for the university system and its financing. The outcome was a University Grants Committee to assess needs and advise the Commonwealth on financial requirements. This worked to the university's particular advantage. While it was acknowledged that all universities were under-resourced, particularly given the predicted explosion of student numbers in the wake of the post-war baby boom, the committee saw science and technology as especially deprived. It recommended inter-university cooperation in high-cost areas — wishful thinking in situations of jealousy and selfishness. More practically, the effects of its financial emphases were such as to amount to a generous rescue of the university from its spending brinkmanship. It came just at the right time and to the appropriate degree to disperse the element of risk-taking that had been embarked upon. It made possible extra staff and increased salaries. How much further the university might have teetered along its dangerous path of course-creation, extravagance and staff pressure, without either damage to morale or insolvency, was, happily, to remain an unasked and unanswered question. The Murray Committee magic changed rags — and living beyond means — if not to riches, to at least good living and reasonable indulgence of expansionist ambitions. Was it foreseen by astute risk-takers? Indeed part of the risk?

The report also proposed that this university's functions be widened to include arts and medical studies and that its name be changed to the University of New South Wales. The University Council accepted this with alacrity and pleasure, a reaction partly impelled by its delighted willingness to do whatever the marvellously generous Murray Committee suggested. But it also saw this development as broadening the scope in which it might pursue its scientific and technological essentials: the original aims would be all the better pursued. Not all staff saw things that way. A significant number took the view that such was a retrograde step: technology should stand at university level in its own right. It should pursue the logic and integrity of its own novel establishment and internal dynamic and not be seduced away into diversions inevitable in the traditional paths of arts and medicine. Having achieved separate university status, some of the technological idealists were reluctant to concede what they saw as a relinquishing of it, a dilution of the purity of their achievement, a sell-out to the old regime of tradition. The actual polarity was hardly this. Certainly, the change represented reality, the way to get money, the price that had to be paid and the language that had to be spoken to sustain technological expansion. Besides, as envisaged by the more pragmatic and hard-headed of the idealists — Baxter for instance — in the changed institution technology would remain dominant, advantaged and well-funded. Less attentive to such intentions, more taken by appearances, the university's Arts staff received this new name with unalloyed pleasure: their inferiority of reputation in the Australian university scene would disappear. Menzies received an honorary degree in 1957.

Long afterwards, towards the end of his life, Baxter revealed publicly the convictions which drove him and the university he led. He wrote in *Search,* in 1975, in a reply to criticism there:

> Our technological civilisation produces a continuing stream of problems of a most complex technical character. Only a small proportion of the population is capable of understanding issues of this sort. The experts must in the end be trusted. To submit such matters to the ballot box, the street demonstration, or the politician who has a divine conviction that he understands technical problems, can only lead to trouble and possible disaster.

Or crudely, this was a technical world and scientists must rule it. More grandly, the university was positioned in the vanguard of the leaders of civilisation. Those who controlled it were responsible for extending technology's parameters and discharging its trust. This imposed onerous professional duties and serious moral responsibilities.

On the personal level and a lighter note, Valerie McCallum, key person in the day-to-day administration of the university, learnt to drive a car in seven lessons. Registrar Macauley took forty-five, and spent the rest of his life discussing every gear change. Bursar Joe Bourke failed the test and never learnt to drive. Val McCallum's own story illustrates Baxter's extraordinary ability to spot talent — and get it. A very young personal assistant to the assistant director of Sydney Technical College, she was asked by Baxter in 1949 to join the university. Her mother told her that she needed a safe job, not at a university which might fold. Baxter assured her that he did not found universities which would fold. How to get to Kensington? She got bus-sick and tram-sick. Baxter told her to get a car. She was expected to join the Drama Club. Each week Lady Baxter, with son and daughter, came to her office to help with typing so that she could attend rehearsals. McCallum controlled appointments, personnel, the Staff Development Unit.

The Turner Hall of Sydney Technical College boasted an early dishwasher, used by the Wives' Group: 'our helpful engineering husbands tried to work it with the result that the machine broke down completely'. The Wives were banned from using it in future. So much, some thought, for the University of Technology. Baxter's belief in the primacy of the technological informed even Baxter's enthusiasm for the theatre. His own three-act play 'The Day the Sun Rose in the West' was a futurist piece of science-fiction, set in a world of politics, religion, science, academics, defence issues — a popularist extravaganza featuring the common scientific assumptions of his time.

This disposition did not go without contradiction in his own university, given other intellectual enthusiasms of that time. The Drama Club, beloved by Baxter, performed, in August 1956 TS Eliot's darkly religious *Sweeney Agonistes*. And it was a period of strong intellectual religion among students: Student Christian Movement (SCM), Evangelical Union (EU), Newman Society — and they were confronting the meaning of their immediate environment. In 1956 the Newman Society held a seminar on 'Technology and Theology' and in June 1957 on 'Technology and Human Happiness'. The Newman Society in particular had close links with staff. This was a day when denominational religion and what was later reduced to farce — the question of the meaning of life — were seen as seriously important, and the university was viewed by the traditional Catholic hierarchy — in the person of Cardinal Gilroy — as animated by insidious threats to faith and morals. Catholic students and staff had this as background environment, however irrelevant to happy personal experience. They also felt the duty, in that time of 'Catholic action' — the papally approved evangelism of the era — to be active in a university apostolate. Hence the vigour of their intellectual concerns in a university context. Many had read Newman, and Bruce Truscott's *Red Brick University* (1951). There was strong staff/student feelings on the need for commonality. Religion transcended barriers and distances within and between universities: relations with Sydney University Catholics were frequent and easy. The same went for the SCM and EU: strong links locally, nationally and internationally, with those of similar religious conviction.

Nor is it surprising that Baxter's exalted view of the pre-eminence of scientists in his schema for mankind should meet other, more secular, resistance. Some, both inside and outside the university, saw him as the advocate of an autocracy of scientists and technocrats; indeed, he was seen by some, incredibly, as an evil man, herald of the tyranny of the archetypal mad scientist of fiction. Yet, beneath the pettiness of such criticism when it served its own agendas, and the serious misgivings of substantial contrary opinions, lay a buried element of deeply instinctive distrust and disquiet, recognition of a powerful threat to the known world. The university embodied this in its scientific triumphalism. Its ambition was to pioneer a civilisation which would extend its frontiers ever further into the scientific and technological unknown. On that basis, the change in name from University of Technology to University of New South Wales was a step along the road to a wider world — more than mere verbiage, or recognition of progress, or bow to tradition. No. Beneath lay the ultimate arrogance, the belief that science and technology, and their practitioners, were at the heart of, and carried the keys to, the brave new world.

3

BAXTER FLOREAT
1958–69

1959

The first Rhodes scholarship awarded to a UNSW student — JP Kennedy. • BJ Ralph appointed foundation professor of Biochemistry • Sydney Technical College Associateship (ASTC) diploma courses (offered since 1951) to be gradually replaced by part-time courses such as BSc (Tech) • University regiment moves to Day Ave, Kensington, and is renamed University of New South Wales Regiment • NEW DEGREES/DIPLOMAS Master of Technology, in — Chemical Engineering, Nuclear Engineering; Bachelor of Building. Graduate diplomas in Food Technology, Wool Technology, Librarianship; Diploma of Sociology • Newcastle University College: Union, Engineering, and Science buildings begun.

FEBRUARY Unisearch established.
2 FEBRUARY J Metcalfe appointed university librarian.
MARCH Plans approved for erection of first permanent buildings at Wollongong.
2 APRIL Dr MG Mackay appointed master of Basser College.
MAY Broken Hill School of Mines renamed the Broken Hill Division of the University of New South Wales • Compulsory £5 library fee for students approved • Meetings of some faculties can now be presided over by an elected chairman, following Council's decision (previously the dean presided).
21 MAY New Metallurgy building begun.
JULY PhD regulations extended to the Faculty of Commerce; degree of DSc approved • At Broken Hill new Associateships approved in Minerals Technology, Mechanical Engineering and Metalliferous Mining Engineering.
1 JULY University's Tenth Anniversary: Governor-General Sir William Slim receives honorary DSc as part of celebrations. •
J Lederer appointed Associate Professor in the School of Optometry • Basser College (which was completed in May) opens, with accommodation for 200 students.

2 JULY School of Civil Engineering's hydraulics lab at Manly Vale opens. Upper campus (10.1 ha) acquired following Randwick Council's resumption of golf course and oval — to become site for medical school.
SEPTEMBER Academic year changed to three ten-week terms (formerly three twelve-week terms).
16 SEPTEMBER University Union building begun.
12 OCTOBER Robert Heffron building begun.
NOVEMBER Faculty of Humanities and Social Sciences terminated (effective from 1 January 1960).
9 NOVEMBER JB Thornton appointed professor of Philosophy.

1960

Institute of Administration established • School of Applied Physics renamed School of Physics • Faculties of Medicine (23 July) and Arts, and Board of Vocational Studies hold their inaugural meetings • 'Show Cause' regulations approved (taking effect from January 1962, but retrospectively) • First summer school for high-school chemistry teachers • University regiment forms a brass band, with Warrant Officer WE McGuiness as bandmaster • Newcastle University College: Professor JJ Auchmuty appointed warden.
NEW DEGREES/DIPLOMAS Master of Technology, in — Control Engineering, Communications Engineering, Public Health Engineering. Graduate diplomas in Industrial Engineering, Food and Drug Analysis •
CAMPUS IMPROVEMENTS Central Store and Workshop, and Electrical Engineering building begun.

A changing campus — viewed by Dupain, *ca* 1959

Bacchus Ball, early 1960s

1961

1 JANUARY Faculty of Arts established, Professor MS Brown being appointed dean • HJ Oliver appointed professor of English.

MARCH Fees raised to be commensurate with Sydney University's.

8 APRIL BA degrees conferred at Newcastle University College for first time by UNSW (previously conferred by University of New England).

27 APRIL Vice-Chancellor's Advisory Committee (VCAC) first meets.

29 APRIL Science Theatre opens.

JULY Preliminary outline medical course approved. • Institute of Highway and Traffic Engineering research funded (from 1 July) for a four-year period by New South Wales government.

3 JULY Mechanical and Industrial Engineering building begun.

18 JULY AT Cuningham appointed warden, University Union.

4 AUGUST Foundation stone laid for medical school.

6 SEPTEMBER Metallurgy building opens.

16 SEPTEMBER Wallace Wurth, the chancellor, dies.

NOVEMBER Hon. JSJ Clancy becomes chancellor and RJ Webster, deputy chancellor • Council decides to name new medical school building after Wallace Wurth.

1961

Faculty of Medicine: first enrolments — 75 students; animal house constructed at Little Bay, to service the faculty and teaching hospitals • Radiation Protection Service established • Common first year introduced for Faculties of Applied Science, Engineering, Medicine, and Science • Department of Postgraduate and Extension Studies established, under Professor D Broadbent • Student Counselling Unit established, with GA Gray as its head • Educational Research Unit established, with Dr LN Short as director • First Foundation Day float procession • Gradual withdrawal of ASTC diploma courses from Wollongong and Broken Hill begins. NEW DEGREES Master's in Machine Design, Nuclear Engineering, Building; PhD regulations extended to the Faculty of Arts • CAMPUS IMPROVEMENTS solar furnace completed (commissioned 1962), for the School of Physics — the only one of its kind in the Commonwealth; Central Store and Workshop completed.

1962

1 JANUARY JH Salmon appointed professor of History.

FEBRUARY Last Sydney tram runs along Anzac Parade.

MAY JJ Thompson appointed foundation professor of Nuclear Engineering and School of Nuclear Engineering established • UNSW's radio station VL2UV begins transmission • Wollongong University College formally constituted; Advisory Committee established, and Professor CAM Gray appointed warden.

5 JULY University Union board first meets; Professor B Smyth becomes first president.

27 JULY University Union building — later known as the Roundhouse — officially opened (having been completed on 31 May).

NOVEMBER Council decides to institute selection process (under an admissions committee, and effective from 1962) to limit student enrolment in popular courses, such as architecture and medicine — for the first time qualified applicants can be refused admission to courses.

4 DECEMBER The University of New South Wales Act (NSW), 1961, passed — under which representation of professions on Council is increased from four to five, and it is permitted to carry-over unspent balances on recurrent grants.

22 DECEMBER University of New South Wales Press Ltd incorporated.

1962

Library accommodation extends to include top floor of Robert Heffron Chemistry building (as well as in Dalton building) • School of Chemistry transfers from Ultimo. • Institute of Highway and Traffic Engineering moves into King Street, Randwick premises (officially opened on 10 May 1963) • Wollongong University College: buildings completed; staff and students transfer from technical college quarters before the beginning of the academic year.

SELECTED EVENTS

Students on Library Road, by Dupain
1967

Dupain view of the emerging Commerce
courtyard, late 1960s

JANUARY First summer school for secondary school mathematics teachers.

MARCH Newcastle University College Council established, and members appointed.

1 MARCH Wollongong University College buildings officially opened.

12 MARCH Degree of Doctor of Medicine approved.

MAY Master of Administration (with first enrolments occurring in 1963) and postgraduate course in Business Administration approved.

16 MAY Robert Heffron building opened, by Premier Heffron (although not completed until 9 August).

28 JUNE 'TV Ballroom' incident in the Roundhouse, involving Michael McDermott and other students.

10 JULY Professor DW Phillips, pro-vice-chancellor and head of Mining Engineering and Applied Geology, dies. The university's Daceyville playing-fields named after him.

SEPTEMBER New full-time course, leading to a BSc, approved in Applied Psychology.

OCTOBER Student Health Unit established.

NOVEMBER All graduate diplomas in Faculty of Applied Science to be uniformly awarded as DipApplSc.

12 NOVEMBER Professor JF Clark, dean of Faculty of Science, appointed pro-vice-chancellor. • Council agrees to the university setting up a joint fund with Prince Henry and Prince of Wales hospitals for medical research and postgraduate instruction • The Post-Graduate Committee in Medical Education of the University of NSW established.

DECEMBER Student Loan Fund approved — for deferment of fees or cash loans to students in need.

6 DECEMBER BHP chairman, Dr Colin Syme, presents the university with a ceremonial mace, to be used for academic processions — Dr Cobden Parkes appointed official mace-bearer.

1963

1963

Old Tote Theatre Company founded • Council recommends that humanities programs be placed under a Board of Studies. This is appointed and a Department of General Studies created • School of Western European Languages established • Contentious issue of the Orientation Handbook produced by Michael McDermott • Student Affairs Committee set up: Professor Vowels is first chairman and Heinz Harant is a member • New technology: the university installs closed-circuit television (CCTV); the School of Nuclear Engineering acquires a PACE TR-48 analogue computer and the School of Highway Engineering, an IBM 1620 digital one. • U Ball Committee (later called U Committee) formed • Monomeeth Association formed. • NEW DEGREES Master of Surveying and Master of Librarianship.

1 FEBRUARY HN Barber appointed foundation professor of Botany.

17 FEBRUARY JO Robinson, appointed Professor of French and Head of School of Western European Languages.

4 MARCH The buildings for the Wallace Wurth School of Medicine and the School of Biological Sciences officially opened by HRH Queen Elizabeth II.

13 MARCH University acquires the former golf clubhouse, cnr Botany and High Streets.

29 MARCH Wollongong University College holds its first graduation ceremony.

14 AUGUST U Ball Committee first meets.

13 SEPTEMBER Mechanical and Industrial Engineering buildings opened (having been completed on 16 July).

22 OCTOBER Electrical Engineering building opened.

27 OCTOBER UNSW Regiment presented with the queen's colours and regimental colours by the governor.

29 OCTOBER First graduates of the university — of 1952 and 1953 — hold their Ten Year Reunion, with dinner and campus tour.

9 NOVEMBER Philip Goldstein, Goldstein College benefactor, dies.

11 NOVEMBER Lillian Livingstone appointed warden of women students.

SELECTED EVENTS

Sir Robert Menzies opening the
Menzies Library 1966

Alison Leigh — Miss UNSW 1964

16 DECEMBER APPOINTMENTS
Dr PVA Leppan as foundation
professor of Surveying;
Professor JFD Wood (of
Mechanical Engineering) as
foundation professor of
General Education and head
of the Department of General
Studies.

1964

1964

The Australian Universities
Commission allocates for the
first time large amounts of
money to universities specifi-
cally for research purposes •
Dr GWK Cavill, Organic
Chemistry, awarded first per-
sonal chair at UNSW •
Graduate School of
Engineering established •
Department of History and
Philosophy of Science created
within School of Philosophy •
First Doctor of Science
degree awarded—to
Professor S Angyal • 600
acres (ca 243 ha) at
Wellington obtained for rural
research (opens 1966) •
NEW DEGREES/DIPLOMAS
Master of Surgery; full-time
Bachelor of Social Work; part-
time Bachelor of Building.
Graduate diplomas in
Corrosion Technology,
Landscape Design, Civic Design,
Biochemical Engineering •
CAMPUS IMPROVEMENTS: MENZIES
LIBRARY building begun. • H
Flugelman's sculpture unveiled
in Goldstein College court-
yard.

MARCH Dr GA Wheen
appointed master of
Kensington Colleges.
27 APRIL Construction of
Central Lecture Block begun.
26 JUNE First U Ball held.
30 JUNE Goldstein College
opens • Women's Hall is
first college accommodation
for women.
JULY New South Wales
University Press moves from
Ultimo to King Street,
Randwick, premises.
1 JULY As a Foundation Day
prank, students kidnap a live
crocodile from Taronga Zoo
and deposit it in Lake Bourke.
17 AUGUST John Goodsell
building begun.
28 AUGUST Inaugural
Wallace Wurth lecture delivered by Sir Robert Menzies.
SEPTEMBER Undergraduate
diploma in Hospital
Administration approved. •
Master's residence, Basser
College, begun.
23 SEPTEMBER Chancellery
building begun.
NOVEMBER Civil
Engineering building begun.
1 NOVEMBER 'Gas Lash' by
Martin Sharp appears in
Tharunka: Vice Squad called in
to report on its allegedly
obscene character.
16 NOVEMBER Arts-
Mathematics (later called
Morven Brown) building
begun.
14 DECEMBER
Construction of Union stage
II begun.

1965

1965

Second National Service
Scheme — entailing conscription for 20-year-olds — introduced by the federal
government, to build up army
reserves (in the light of conflict in Vietnam) • Goldstein
Hall wins Sir John Sulman
medal for Architectural excellence • Dr MW Allen
appointed foundation professor of Electronic
Computation and director of
Digital Computing Laboratory
• Chairs of Education and
Geography established •
Departments of German and
Spanish established in School
of Western Languages •
Diploma in Sociology discon-
tinued. • Australian School
of Nuclear Technology
opened by D Fairbairn, minister for National Development
• CAMPUS IMPROVEMENTS
Library building (first stage),
and Union stage II completed
• Broken Hill Division
acquires 'Zinc Barracks' for
use as office accommodation
and first residential space for
students.

1 JANUARY Newcastle
University College gains
autonomy to become the
University of Newcastle,
under Vice-Chancellor JJ
Auchmuty.
4 FEBRUARY Metallurgy
Process building begun.
23 FEBRUARY Inaugural
Dunrossil Lecture delivered
by HRH Duke of Edinburgh.
26 FEBRUARY Psychiatric
teaching unit at Prince Henry
Hospital opened.
5 MARCH Central Lecture
Block completed.
APRIL Master's residence,
Basser College, completed.
24 APRIL Anzac Memorial
(later to be incorporated into
Anzac Parade gateway)
unveiled by Sir Ivan Mackay.
JUNE JP Baxter receives a
knighthood in queen's birth-
day honours.
18 JUNE FC Hollows
appointed associate professor
of Ophthalmology.
JULY UNSW Drama
Foundation established.
9 OCTOBER Professor MS
Brown, dean of Arts Faculty,
dies.
1 NOVEMBER Senior
Common Room Club found-
ing committee first meets.
11 NOVEMBER JOA
Bourke, the bursar, dies.

SELECTED EVENTS

The Subiaco columns

1966

Harold Holt, the prime minister, announces that national servicemen will be sent to fight in Vietnam. • Jane Street theatre opened • A Horton appointed university librarian. • New chairs approved: in Human Genetics, Marketing, Pure Maths, Mechanical Engineering, Russian • First undergraduate courses in Spanish and German offered • Union stage II (later known as the Blockhouse) opened. • Development of Biological Science and Fuel Technology laboratories at King Street, Randwick. • Senior Common Room Club formed • NEW DEGREES DLitt and Master of Education, in Faculty of Arts; Bachelor of Town Planning • CAMPUS IMPROVEMENTS Lake Bourke drained, as a result of connection to off-site stormwater drainage. Subiaco columns erected on lower campus; Metallurgy Process building completed; Architecture building begun (January).

1 JANUARY Fowler's Gap leased to university for initial 10-year period, as arid zone research centre.
24 JANUARY Institute of Languages established.
5 APRIL Last occasion on which the University of New South Wales confers degrees at a ceremony in Newcastle.
15 APRIL Wollongong University College: first two women graduate.
JUNE Broken Hill University College holds its first graduation ceremony.
25 JUNE Morven Brown building (completed on 29 March) opened.
29 JUNE An old bowling alley on Anzac Parade is converted into premises for Unisearch and, later in 1966, is first used as an examination centre.
JULY Chancellery building completed.
12 JULY Smith's Lake, northern New South Wales, made available by the government for the study and preservation of native flora and fauna, for School of Zoology.
25 AUGUST School of Civil Engineering moves to Kensington to its new building (completed on 8 April), opened by the governor-general, Lord Casey.
30 AUGUST Wellington Field Station officially opened.
2 SEPTEMBER Roger Covell appointed senior lecturer in Music.
7 SEPTEMBER Library building opened by Sir Robert Menzies.

28 SEPTEMBER Land acquired on which Pindari, the vice-chancellor's residence, is later built (1972).
14 OCTOBER Philip Baxter College opened (having been completed on 6 March); Professor EP George appointed warden.
1 NOVEMBER S Encel appointed professor of Sociology • UTECOM replaced by IBM 360/50.
7 NOVEMBER John Goodsell (Commerce) building opened by the New South Wales premier, RW Askin (having been completed on 14 August 1965).

1967

First Higher School Certificate (HSC) exam • Grainger Singers formed • Chair of Medical Microbiology created, and separate Department of Medical Microbiology • St George Hospital, Kogarah, and St Vincent's Hospital, Darlinghurst, affiliate with UNSW as teaching hospitals • School of History begins teaching East Asian history in BA courses • Charges introduced for parking cars on campus • Students' Union starts Casual and Vacation Employment Service. • Hockey club becomes first university club to win a first division competition • NEW DEGREE Master of Applied Science (MApplSc) • CAMPUS IMPROVEMENTS Library's air-conditioning installation begun. Substantial building program begun on Prince of Wales site.

SELECTED EVENTS

Central Lecture Block 1965

Engineering plaza fountain

JANUARY Hon. JSJ Clancy, the chancellor, receives a knighthood in the New Year's honours. • Construction of Basser Steps begun.
FEBRUARY Architecture building completed.
10 FEBRUARY First medical students graduate — a woman, Bronwyn Jones, achieving the highest mark.
MARCH The MBBS degree of UNSW recognised by the United Kingdom General Medical Council • School of Human Genetics established.
4 MAY Construction of International House begun.
5 JUNE Professor JF Clark, pro-vice-chancellor and head of School of Applied Psychology, dies.
6 JUNE Basser Steps completed.
1 JULY Unisearch Ltd recognised as an approved research organisation by the Australian Industrial Research Development Grants Board.
7 JULY JOA Bourke Memorial Fountain dedicated.
10 JULY AH Willis and RE Vowels appointed pro-vice-chancellors.
20 JULY Broken Hill Division's WS & LB Robinson University College officially opened.
2 AUGUST Monomeeth Gates officially handed over to the university.

1 OCTOBER Sir Leslie Martin appointed professor of Physics and dean of the new Faculty of Military Studies, set up jointly by UNSW and Royal Military College, Duntroon.
1 NOVEMBER Professor T Cizova takes up her position as head of School of Russian.
6 DECEMBER Alumni Association formed.

1968

1968

University of New South Wales Act (NSW), 1968, passed. • Entry to university of first students to complete a 6th year at secondary school. • Australia's only dual gold medallist in 1968 Olympic Games is UNSW BComm student, Michael Wenden (receives an MBE in New Year's honours). • University of New South Wales Opera's first production staged — Britten's *Turn of the Screw*. • J Lawrence appointed foundation professor of Social Work. • Chair of Librarianship established. • Faculty of Biological Sciences established. • Institute of Marine Sciences established. • Institute of Languages opened by Japanese ambassador. • Students' Union opens secondhand book exchange. • New graduate diploma (part-time) in Industrial Design.

FEBRUARY Department of Finance created, within Faculty of Commerce.
23–27 APRIL U Committee holds its first book fair — raising $10,000.
29 APRIL Degree of BSc(Mil) or BA(Mil) introduced at new Faculty of Military Studies, Royal Military College, Duntroon.
3 JUNE The Institute of Languages commences teaching — courses in Russian, Japanese and French.
14 JUNE International House opened by Sir Roden Cutler, the New South Wales governor (the first students having moved in on 27 May); Professor AH Willis appointed warden.
20 JUNE Faculty of Military Studies first meets.
9 SEPTEMBER The Educational Research Unit becomes the Tertiary Education Research Centre (TERC).
11 NOVEMBER Graduate School of Business created within the Faculty of Commerce, to replace the School of Business Administration.
29 NOVEMBER Institute of Administration opened at its Little Bay premises.

SELECTED EVENTS

'The best-laid schemes o' mice an' men/Gang aft agley' — bardic wisdom which would have been contemptuously lost on Baxter triumphant, particularly given its drunken Celtic source. But they do. Scientific utopia soon became casualty to Baxter's other empire-building ambitions, to say nothing of its own inbuilt banality. Like so many of the otherwise distinguished and brilliantly gifted scientists and technocrats of his day, Baxter was addicted to what would now be regarded as the superficial promotion of science as snake oil. For all his formidable and passionate dedication, his philosophic stance was a belief at the popular level, that of HG Wells, CEM Joad, Lancelot Hogben's *Science for the Citizen* — the cultists of progress, the vulgarians of public science. Here, on an uninformed, critical view, was a man who chose to live in the better part of the once-fashionable but then déclassé suburb of Enfield, had a large model train layout in his house, and sent his four children, on egalitarian principle, to state schools. Or was it that there was the family man, confronted with a Sydney housing shortage, buying a house which he could get, and meet the mortgage for, its dilapidation a challenge to his considerable do-it-yourself skills. Sending his children to state schools, as private were beyond his means, and, in his view, educationally no better. Collecting trains — fun for his children and himself; expandable as means allowed. Money, family, housing, the familiar human basics. How easy it is in looking at the big picture, the lineaments of career, professional development, the play of politics and power, to forget the driving forces on which all rested — the personal day to day, and the household economics. The sheer power of Baxter's public persona, his personality and position, banished from the mind the fact that he too was subject to the daily grind — of mortgages and bills. In days when vice-chancellors' salaries were not lavish, Baxter, if comfortable, needed to bear in mind the law of life, living within one's income. Besides, his upbringing gave him the habit of economy: he always spent carefully. When, later, other responsibilities came his way, the Australian Atomic Energy Commission for instance, snide questions of his personal financial circumstances were asked by enemies; they held no real bite: Baxter was patently abstemious and honest in such matters.

There was a strong and strange contrast between public and private personas. The happy family man, playing trains with his children, devotee, with his wife, of theatricals, down to that very English parlour game charades (recollected as crawling under a carpet, to illustrate visually the waves of the sea). Baxter under a carpet in such a context of cavorting was simply beyond the imagination of those who encountered only the public persona. Or Baxter, directing a member of the Drama Club in a scene which required him to act poisoned, illustrated by rolling around on his office floor, moaning and screaming. Or appearing in some student prank film, apparently endorsing some breakfast cereal supposed to give tremendous energy. The before scene showing lethargy and slow work, then the packet of gritty granules, and he comes to exuberant life. That power, authority, seriousness, iron-willed self-confidence, were not donned as some sort of mask. They were an integral part of the formidable complexity which was Baxter, that part which effected

Baxter floreat

1963

in the public arena the objects of his university ambition. Asked the recipe for success, he replied, 'Easy: just make your job your hobby'.

It was the vehicle which he had built to carry his own technological ambition which took him away from it. The new-born University of New South Wales, enacted on 7 October 1958, had its own logic and dynamics, of which science was a shrinking part. There was to be medicine, with tensions and conflicts of its own, and something external — well outside Baxter's ideological orbit, and University Council's own cautious preferences, if within Wurth's horizons: he had been thinking of it since 1955; thus Hospital Administration. Even more alien was arts, despite the high-flown commitment of 1949 to humanities. Arts, with its apparent lack of discipline, forever talking and arguing, following weird paths of its own, notoriously misbehaving sexually — all things repugnant to Baxter's notion of how his university should be. Yet even his own loves had energies which galloped out of control when he gave them their head. Amateur theatricals on the English provincial model, in which both he and his wife had been involved, were one thing: the National Institute of Dramatic Art (NIDA) quite another.

Story has it of NIDA that the proposal, emanating from theatrical circles and the Australian Broadcasting Commission (ABC), went first to the University of Melbourne, whose vice-chancellor put it to the professorial board, which rejected it as being out of keeping with that university's character. Hearing of this, Baxter made it known that he would accept it and would not consult his board. It was neither the first nor last time the university was to profit from such small-minded decisions made by others and of course it reflected not only Baxter's personal enthusiasm but his autocratic style and dominance of university structures. It also demonstrated his perception. He appreciated, as many other academics did not, the need of the acting profession and those who taught them, for substantial independence, not to be constrained by the normal expectations and procedures of university bureaucracy. Later, in the 1980s, this was to become a disputed issue, as some members of NIDA's controlling board sought to bring it much more closely under university authority and regulation, but their efforts failed and autonomy and flexibility continued as before. Baxter had seen clearly the distinction between the academic, and the creative life. NIDA was given a welcoming and facilitating home, and was constituted as a private company with a board of directors, on which the university had representation: a happy situation for it. Baxter got a pet interest realised on the grand scale, and the marvellous public advertisement that NIDA's association gave the university. It was a relatively small cost to have to put up with the unruly antics of the students, who tended to be among the leaders of campus agitations. The whole thing brought light and colour into a world made less drab. This, from 1958, with the added bonus of involvement with the other major national players — the ABC and the Elizabethan Theatre Trust. The aim was to offer instruction in the theatre arts and encourage their appreciation. It also (as ever-practical and forward-looking Baxter discerned) met a present urgent need — that of a new, emergent television industry for trained people in all aspects of theatrical presentation. It proved quickly to be an initiative of immense importance,

(top left)
Baxter directing a
university play
1950s

(top right)
NIDA students in
rehearsal
ca 1960s

Drama students outside
the Old Tote Theatre
May 1969

central to the future of Australian drama and acting, its influence not only national, but through its graduate actors, international as well. Central, too, was the School of Drama, with Robert Quentin in the first chair of Drama in Australia, and the Old Tote Theatre Company, on campus, and then the first resident theatre company at the Opera House. In that wide world of the performing arts, achievements indeed.

What of those schemes of mice and men? Of the great need to serve science? Or was Baxter aware that ambition carries those who pursue it where it will? Did he put growth — under his leadership — before ideal? Did his success in achieving his scientific goals give him a taste for striding the wider fields of power: follow the paths of growth wherever unscientific they might lead? Did the dream of science ruling all give way to the demands and interplay of ambition, iron will, and the intoxication of success? No, they did not: he wanted both, believed he could have both, and proclamations of the primacy of the science objective kept echoing down a future increasingly devoted (the word is wrong, 'given over' better) to other things. The tensions and inconsistencies did not become inescapable until the vice-chancellorships of Birt and Niland. But the introduction of Arts — and Medicine and Law — created, within the university's character, a central element of creative tension of a confusing and contradictory kind. Science ruled the roost, and was seen as the modern, progressive element in the hatchery. Yet, in fact, it was potentially authoritarian, conservative in its attitude to knowledge and student disposition. Arts meant, it seemed, the introduction of the traditional, the backward-looking. As it turned out, it was the liberalising and humanising dynamic which gradually percolated, and conditioned the university atmosphere. This through its staff — young, at a changing society's cutting edge, oddball, convention breakers.

"See you here again when our health breaks down through lack of exercise."

George Molnar

Sydney Morning Herald

1959

George Molnar

PUBLIC NOTICE
RANDWICK GOLF LINKS WILL NOT
BE AVAILABLE TO THE PUBLIC AFTER
SUNDAY, 13TH MARCH, 1960, WHEN WORK
WILL COMMENCE ON THE ERECTION
OF UNIVERSITY BUILDINGS ON THE SITE.
R.T. LATHAM

∧
Par for the course

1959

And through its students — minor rebels, not laboratory bound, addicted to strange habits and practices. It was the votaries of science who espoused conservatism, even reaction, remaining devoted to their pullovers and ties. Who then at New South Wales was 'modern'? In different ways, the whole amalgam.

So, from 1958, the university broadened, radically and rapidly, with medicine and arts. It also remained more of the same. It established, to operate from early 1959, its own research and development limited liability company, Unisearch. Unisearch, an Australian university first, much imitated, but never very successfully. This was to market to industry the university's services, its charges seen as an increasingly valuable, independent source of revenue, which was indeed to prove the case. All kinds of technology sprouted, the university being particularly proud of diversity in industrial engineering — ceramics, paint, plastics, rubber: you think of it, we had a course in it. Then there was, at something of a tangent, a major new direction for the future, a School of Business Administration.

By 1960 the swing to arts and medicine was well under way. Teaching towards an arts degree began in that year, distinctive to the university in that all students were obliged to do two courses from a group of science subjects (to which was

Current issues
1. Staff availability
2. R+T.C's programme 1975 — staff develop.t
   — intercountry
   — national
   — faculty
3. I.H. workshop
4. On-site activities in Papua New Guinea

∧

Professor FF Rundle

1975

added a special subject on the history and philosophy of science). This was the reverse application of science students' requirements to do elements of humanities. Arts staff were obliged to teach the humanities requirement. In both cases this situation met resistance so strong and continuing as to lead eventually to special arrangements and staff to deal with 'general studies', as this requirement became known for non-arts students: eventually the science requirement for arts was ended.

Planning for a second medical school in New South Wales had begun in 1957, generating all kinds of protest, both professional and regional, factionalism and animus, much of it loudly public, most directed against the university as being thought, for one reason or another, not a fit location for such a school. These problems could hardly be said to have been resolved by the time the government made a decision to base it at the university: after it had placated the medical school at the University of Sydney, foundation chairs were advertised worldwide for occupiers in 1960, though FF Rundle in Surgery came in October 1959. First on offer was a distant site near Prince Henry Hospital, 5 miles (*ca* 8 km) south. Then, after much finagling, the State government resumed the adjacent Randwick Park, home to a public golf course and thus much defended by Randwick Council and in the media. Unavailing. Buildings were being negotiated for a medical course to begin in 1961.

Faced with these major new commitments — Arts and Medicine — the University Council was at pains to affirm in 1960 that, nevertheless, the university remained its essentially unchanged self. 'While these new developments will inevitably bring about a change in the character of the university, the original conception of the university as a body primarily devoted to scientific and technological studies remains the dominant theme of our activities.'

Whistling for a wind. A change which is no change. The council's protestations were so much afflatus. The old order was in retreat, none too gracefully. What had once been a comfortable monopoly of interest and outlook was becoming now a question of preponderance, in which science and technology still ruled, but under increasing internal siege.

Still, rule they did. More students, almost 7000 by 1959, paying more (a £5 library fee); more courses, more independence as the old technical college diploma courses were withdrawn; more building, various applied sciences, the more interesting, circular Union Roundhouse, and Metallurgy were in progress, and Basser College, aided by a gift of £40,000 from Sir Adolf Basser, was opened. Basser, a Polish migrant success story, listed himself in *Who's Who* as a philanthropist and race-horse owner, director of the jeweller's firm of Angus and Coote: trained as an optometrist, he had been a highly successful salesman. His reputation as philanthropist was well-merited, with major benefactions to the University of Sydney and to various research projects as well as charitable causes. The gift was a significant slice of Basser College's £310,000 cost, the rest being borne by the State government. The college opened as part of the university's tenth anniversary celebrations on

▽

The first students at UNSW's medical school

ca 1961

Basser College

1963

Basser Steps

Late 1960s

1 July 1959, with promotion which linked it back to the first Oxford college in 1249. It was for male students only, a sign of the times beautifully caught in relation to the opening ceremony itself. 'In view of the limited accommodation available [in the Main Building] it was not possible to include ladies in this luncheon. Lady Slim [wife of the governor-general] has therefore been invited to lunch at the Oceanic Hotel Coogee with the wives of those attending the official luncheon. Cars will be arranged to take the ladies to the Oceanic Hotel ...'.

Basser College, and other colleges that followed, were important providers of accommodation. They failed, however, to live up to the ideals preached at their opening. Their effect tended to be divisive of the student body — college students and non-college — and to persist in carrying out degrading fresher initiation rituals, totally bewildering especially to overseas students: the point of being dumped in the central city in underpants and with no money escaped them. Alcohol abuse remained a continuing problem, as with college students everywhere, and the university doctor did not see it as his responsibility to campaign against it. Aping of Sydney University was a dominant impulse, helped by the fact that the first warden, Malcolm Mackay, a Moderator of the Presbyterian Church and television presenter, had little interest in Basser. The early students were a happy lot, with college life great fun, even down to the student construction, from old railway sleepers, of the first Basser steps, which saved them a circuitous route to lower campus. Basser was the university's first residential college so claimed (which ignored the first Anzac Parade huts used as a student hostel).

The University College at Wollongong was growing, with some aid from BHP money. Newcastle was being reorganised towards independence with a Board of Studies and a warden, a sort of vice-chancellor — who else but JJ Auchmuty, unkindly dubbed 'The Great Auk'. As for the building boom, it was better, or at least more expansive, than usual, thanks to the massive injections of Commonwealth money.

<|

Western campus

huts

ca 1950s and

thereafter

Government Printer/UNSW Archives collection

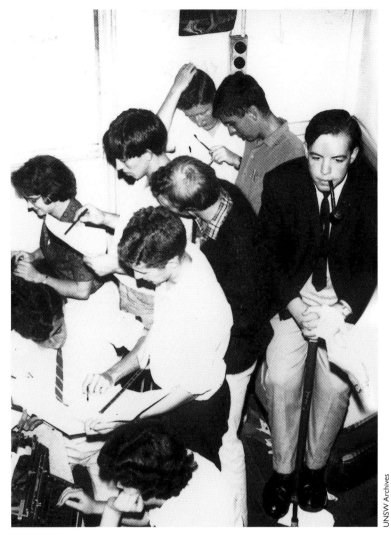

Tharunka staff

early 1960s

UNSW Archives

Better even for Arts, in Science hand-me-downs, as scientists moved to new quarters. As an occupant of the Main Building in 1959–60, I recall the exciting sense of commonality instilled by low partitioning of large floor areas into rooms, allowing all staff to converse happily at once and to enter rooms readily, to borrow books and so on, by climbing the dividers. This was much more conducive to a collective spirit than the previous Arts/Humanities accommodation, tiny rooms in the remote army/migrant (or were they Department of Transport?) huts on the western side of Anzac Parade. Yet even these had unintended atmospheric ambience. They abutted the backyards of the Greek and Italian families that had moved into Kensington, with their vivid, outdoor life of constant loud exchanges and rowing. The positioning of the Arts (and Commerce) staff made them an adjunct to this clamour. If entertainingly exuberant, this warred against quiet or thought, so fostering the present writer's preference for home study — albeit in dressing gown and two pairs of football socks, on a plank across metallic tubs in a bleak fibro wash-house in Brookvale.

The 1960s, swinging and otherwise, burst into the university's relatively placid world, demanding attention. Up to then, the university lived largely within itself, if not indrawn, facing outward from a position of self-absorption. The 1960s ended that. Those years insisted that the university pay attention to the local reflections of international events and transformation in politics, society, and culture. It was compelled to cope with things outside itself, outside its control, new, and often repellent currents in the wider world. A few oddballs, Marxist cranks, and unpleasant bohemians could be grudgingly tolerated, but what when the university became in effect one of the leaders of the worldwide sexual revolution? In 1961 *Tharunka* pushed open sexuality beyond horizons previously encountered and publicly thinkable, not only locally, or parochially, but in wider fields. In his autobiography *Hippie Hippie Shake* (1995) Richard Neville, then a part-time Commerce student, details how bawdy apprenticeship in *Tharunka* led to the foundation of *OZ* and its moving to London and the famous, corrupting public morals trial (involving the legal talents of John Mortimer and Geoffrey Robertson) at the Old Bailey in 1971. Sexual exhibitionism was only one aspect of the attack mounted by *Tharunka* against all kinds of established and traditional authority. It demanded a royal commission into the university, and the vice-chancellor's resignation.

Baxter was already under fierce attack. The Ward case had surfaced again, very publicly, in 1960, drawing wide media coverage to the issue of academic freedom. The influential fortnightly magazines *Nation* and *Observer*, launched in 1958, seem to have singled out the university for special critical attention, which Baxter greeted with disdain merited, as he saw it, by venom, suppression and distortion. His response to this multiform challenge — from students, staff, general public — was authoritarian. Fitting treatment, he thought, for a prodigious waste of time and energy: treat it with ignore, or heavy-handed denials — no give and take, no humour. He regarded all this as high-sounding bilge and mere kerfuffle, not proper business for the university to be engaged in.

Worse, in September 1960 Wallace Wurth died, aged sixty-four. He was succeeded as chancellor by Supreme Court Justice JSJ (later Sir John) Clancy. Wurth, man of like mind, confidante, prop; Baxter described Wurth's death as 'a desolation' to the university — he meant also to himself, and the word is no exaggeration — supportive, a leader in corridors of power. And Wurth's leadership was of Baxter's kind: private, achieved by negotiation with key men, conscious of technology's vital social role. He was the archetypal, behind the scenes thinker–doer; not so much an enemy of the principle of 'academic freedom' but impatient of what he saw as academic ingratitude, privilege, and unreality: he had no time for those apparently unaware of the demands of public policy, the need to pilot things through time and place. Wurth was what now would be described as an operator, though a very proper and upright one, who insinuated, most skilfully, his own aims and will into the decision-making process, storing useful things away. For instance, he had long had in mind the old Kensington Racecourse as a site on which an idea might be made actual. Nor was he averse to gamble and bluff, even misinformation, to gain worthwhile ends. (In his commemorative address, written with Joe

Bourke, Baxter confessed: 'I was lured to these sunny shores by the promises of a quiet life of research and fifteen hundred pounds a year' — or so he liked to believe.) Wurth had contacts everywhere — Nuffield, Carroll, BHP, Basser, Goldstein, men of wealth and power. Manipulating, persuading, bullying, cajoling, 'seducing', as his panegyric had it — and misleading, as he did with the financing of the proposed institute which led on to the university, in selling the government the idea that, by moving people and resources around, it would cost, essentially, nothing. A compelling argument, in that it was efficacious if largely fallacious. As to his role in founding that university, Baxter's panegyric reached unaccustomed heights (or depths) of verbal extravagance: 'He literally took this venture in his nervous active hands and led it intrepidly onwards'. Wurth's central role was recognised by critics in the jibe of the time: the University of Technology was dismissed as 'Wurth's Circus', that being a play on the name of one of the popular circus companies. He not only made possible bricks and mortar but injected them with true university spirit. In speaking of Wurth, Baxter was, of course, also preaching of himself. Here, in Wurth, was a man creating an order in which constructive freedom could prevail. Academic freedom was not licence, nor pursuit of selfish ends. Overall, order must prevail for the common good. Wurth was, as Baxter put it, 'our friend, faithful and just to us'.

Which he was — on the larger view that saw big things made possible, achieved: money in millions, people in thousands, buildings in bulk. But in terms of its

George Molnar's views of the University of Technology
Sydney Morning Herald
1954

George Molnar

"And now five hours 53 minutes for the cultivation of the liberal spirit."

bearing on individuals and particularities, the Wurth system seemed open to other judgements. His world was that of the public service, not the university. Staff found the traditional bureaucracy irksome and demeaning and rebelled against it: it is appropriate to reiterate the Staff Association meetings of 1959–60 were large and vigorous in protest, particularly against 'punching the bundy'—signing on and off at the university. It was not merely the inconvenience of this, and its inapplicability to research and writing programs, but, most of all, its implication that university staff were mere public servants: they thought themselves a considerable cut above that, and no other university had such petty measures of accountability. And all staff shared, to some degree, the grievances set out by professors in the 'Prayer to Council' of 1951: frustrative proceedings inimical to action and wasteful of time, obsession with precedent (and for university needs there often was none), intrusive hierarchy, 'proper channels' — the whole bondage of classic red tape. In the common university mind Wurth became the symbol and font of these impositions. He was, but he saw them otherwise, as part of a necessary order and accountability. So, true; but only truth of a relatively minor order. The big truth was, as Baxter put it, that it is hard to conceive of the university coming into existence without him. Or Baxter. Much of Baxter's eulogy of Wurth could be applied to himself. Or to them both together. With Wurth's death something in Baxter died too.

Under attack, his friend taken from him, Baxter and his regime soldiered into the 1960s. But it had lost something of the zest of earlier days. It was a little harder in edge, more remote, more about the 'proper business' of a university, which was, as Baxter conceived it, not talking, or arguing, or criticising, but expansive development. Total student numbers in 1960 were 7884 — and there were whispers of restricting enrolments if pressure became more intense. Certainly, the totality of the university enterprise was accelerating at a rate which could not be sustained: income — £3,971,550 for 1959 — had shot up to £5,261,124 for 1960. Building was filling the campus — all completed was Building F, the Science Theatre with its accommodation for nearly 1000, Metallurgy; the Union, almost so. The first building for the Wallace Wurth School of Medicine was under way on the resumed golf course on the hill overlooking the original site. Both Wollongong and Newcastle were expanding. From 1961 a new degree of Bachelor of Technology displaced the diploma, and, major innovation, a common first year was introduced for the Faculties of Applied Science, Engineering, Science, and Medicine, an astonishing common recognition of the need for rationalisation, a sharing of the conviction that a common grounding was needed in the basic sciences. Arts lecturing commenced in 1960 with an enrolment of fifty, mostly in English and History. Total academic staff reached 500. Donations ranged from very large to small: the Chick Sexers Association of New South Wales donated 23 guineas to optometry research. All helped.

But if comfort and satisfaction were there to be taken, they were also to be denied. A harsh, outside world kept breaking in, nasty unwelcome intruder, most notably in relation to a public revival, between 1960 and 1962, of the controversy surrounding the resignation in 1956 of Professor RM Hartwell in protest against the university's refusal, on what Hartwell believed were security grounds, to appoint Dr Russel Ward as lecturer. In 1960 Hartwell revived this matter in a book review, quoting his letter of resignation to the effect that it had been, on principle, a protest against a political test. Baxter replied that Hartwell's charge was 'untrue and not in accordance with facts' but later declined to specify the facts, as unjust to candidates and possibly open to litigation. Hartwell's revival of the case suited the then agenda of the Federal Council of the Federation of Australian University Staff Associations (FAUSA). In 1958 it had written to all Australian universities on the matter of political discrimination. It found Baxter's reply unsatisfactory. Standing on his most haughty dignity (hardly a conciliatory or sensible posture), he in effect told FAUSA it was impertinent to enquire. Not surprisingly, FAUSA came up with a hostile finding, convicting the university of prolonged discrimination. Perhaps conflict was inevitable — FAUSA was an organisation of the intellectual left, Baxter a man of the authoritarian right. FAUSA's journal *Vestes* pounced on the Hartwell opportunity; Hartwell wrote an article for it. Thereafter the case became everybody's property. Ward, hitherto unnamed, revealed that he, as a former member of the Communist Party, was the person in question. The *Times* in London took the matter up, as did, of course, the university's old enemy, the *Sydney Morning Herald*. Prime Minister Menzies was compelled by the House of Representatives to look into the case: he issued a denial of security involvement. The university had hit the headlines in the worst of possible ways. Why had it taken so long to reach this point? A range of factors and accidents — and personal matters. Baxter had provoked FAUSA and did not like Hartwell — nor Hartwell him. Besides, back in 1956, Baxter had behaved less than creditably or sensibly. He was always uneasy about how he had acted, as late as 1982 trying to rewrite history in his favour, shifting responsibility away from himself. And there was also the matter of the allegation that Hartwell knew of the Oxford job before resigning, a charge which Hartwell deeply resented. There is something about the handling of the whole affair by Baxter which rings less than true. Perhaps it was his reaction to an action which he saw as disloyal to his beloved — and the emphasis is also on *his* — university. If so, it was short-sighted and selfish. If Hartwell believed, and he patently did, that a matter of high and important principle was at stake, he — and that principle — deserved very different treatment. Perhaps it is understandable that Hartwell should harbour deep resentment, that he was extremely bitter, sufficient as to wish to cause that university damage. He described himself — his word — as an 'exile' compelled by principle to leave his own country.

In an attempt to stem the damage, in December 1960 Clancy and Baxter issued a public statement denying security or any other political or religious test. Instead of quieting the controversy, this exacerbated it. In that situation any statement was bound to be critically scrutinised by those disposed to be hostile and the problem was also that older staff knew and accepted that prospective employees had in the past been vetted by the New South Wales Public Service Board. One such incident took place in 1955 or 1956 in the Registrar's Division, when an appointee was not approved, he having been an active member of the Labor Club when a student at Sydney University. In this case, after staff protest the decision was reversed and the appointment made. Why the need for vetting? Nobody seems to have adverted to the possibility that this was to ensure that such persons were 'of good character' —

whatever that meant in a subjective, judgemental world. Perhaps it was such an assumption that his view reflected a common norm that lay behind Baxter's denials. Meanwhile, Hartwell had approached the Australian Vice-Chancellors' Committee to institute an enquiry. It refused. But, in January 1961, *Nation* took up the matter in an extended article, which included a section from Hartwell. The rest, unsigned, was an unbridled attack on the university, and on Baxter in particular, going far beyond the issues raised by the Ward case.

Thereafter, rational discussion was impossible. Opposing camps vigorously asserted their positions. Personalities became paramount issues. Charges of lies, lack of integrity, that Baxter had terrorised others, including vice-chancellors, that an unprincipled plot existed to denigrate the university — all this was in the electric air. From the University of Sydney Professor AE Alexander, of 'Prayer to Council' fame, joined the fray in support of Hartwell. Alexander, when in Chemistry, had found Baxter's authoritarian style — and the supine performance of the Professorial Board when confronted by it — not at all to his liking, indeed to his intense frustration, and had left for the University of Sydney. Alexander was on poor terms with his own Chemistry staff, being himself authoritarian and arbitrary, courting in at least one case, a vice-chancellorial overruling in favour of staff. It is unlikely he had much love for Baxter. In his case it seems that his enemy's embarrassment provided his own opportunity. University Council decided not to respond. And *Vestes* reviewed the situation, critical of the university, but temperately enough.

Here the matter might have rested, or at least simmered down, had it not been for what appears as a further piece of ill-judgement on Baxter's part. He seems not to have been willing to leave well enough alone, but to have wanted everybody to feel warm and to love one another as if this nastiness had never been. A commendable aim. Early in 1961 his 'Letter to Graduates' reproduced the university's December 1960 denial of interference in a modified form, open to construction as reflecting on Hartwell and others. Immediately the old antagonists were at it again. And Ward revealed that Baxter had misrepresented and inflated Ward's courtesy in thanking him for lunch following an address Ward had given to the university's Socratic Society. The incident revealed a Baxter who seems open to the charge of being devious and — what was politically much worse — inept. As to Ward, the future was to reveal that he had developed an obsessive dislike of the university. Many years later, long after Baxter was gone, Ward, then a prominent name in Australian history as a profession, accepted an invitation from the University of New South Wales School of History to lecture. His unease in the staff room was palpable and disconcerting. The harm done the university by the whole imbroglio was immense.

At long last, the heated controversy died down, at least in the public view, in mid 1962. The most sensible summation came from Professor JB Thornton, president of the Staff Association, in a letter to *Tharunka* on 7 September 1961. This took the carefully reasoned position that the case, by its nature, was beyond proof or settlement. The individual and verbal nature of the evidence, the death of Wurth, the nature of security systems, the involvement of other issues, of personalities, interests and emotions, taken together rendered any final conclusion inaccessible. That was enough. Thornton did not consider what may have been in the nature of things: that was not his brief. Yet at all points conflict and decision seem cast in a science versus arts mould, differing ways of seeing the world and priorities within it, differing modes of encountering and responding to reality. In essence, Baxter was a security-conscious, war-shaped research scientist; Hartwell, an intellectual academic.

The Ward case was to dog the university's reputation for many years. The allegation that it applied a political test became, and remained, the main distinguishing feature of the university thereafter, particularly among left-wing publicists. It broadened from there into widely held general impressions of intolerance and authoritarian oppression among those ignorant of any detail. Baxter mismanaged the whole affair. Neither he nor Wurth were used to being questioned, let alone being called to account, and did not recognise, let alone brook, the validity of certain areas and kinds of activity being open to legitimate academic challenge. Baxter, moreover, enjoyed exercising power and took pleasure in control, a dangerous indulgence. The case should have taught him that firm leadership can easily stray into tyranny, or be experienced as such. It should also have been a demonstration of his limitations: not easy with people, devoid of charm, lacking what would now be called people skills, a poor judge of how best to proceed when in a position of defence and disadvantage. Did he learn? In 1963, together with the Irish ambassador, I approached the vice-chancellor for a slight anticipation of study leave due. We were rebuffed, in line with regulations, but in such a style as to leave both the ambassador and myself recoiling in dismay: the shock — it was nothing less — of encountering an iron will, implacable, needlessly exerted in a matter of minor import, was totally disconcerting. Yet there is ample private evidence, in a case involving the psychological breakdown of an Arts lecturer over the period 1960–66, of patience, compassion, and willingness to talk to and advise the staff member concerned, and to extend, not bureaucratic solutions, but humane consideration. Acknowledge his authority — and he oversaw every detail of his realm — and real need would be recognised. Contest it? Ah, then. As to students, in that weird way that some university administrators have, Baxter evidenced little interest in them on the human level. His son, a student in the early 1960s, was often in a difficult position with his fellows, given his father's remoteness from the student body. They knew of Baxter well enough, from the photographs that appeared frequently in the press, but his emanations were those of unapproachability: he did not mix with students and was thus deemed a distant and unfriendly eminence. It was Macauley, the registrar, who represented to students the administration case, and was willing to stay into the wee small hours to listen and help.

Much more to Baxter's taste was the commencement of the new Faculty of Medicine, with an initial enrolment of seventy-five students. The background to this major initiative is sketched generally and very politely in that faculty's as yet unpublished, exhaustive history. That history does not relate or convey the atmosphere of University of Sydney selfishness, and bitter medical profession in-fighting that beset

∧

The official party — at the opening of the Wallace Wurth medical school building and the Biological Sciences building 4 March 1963

∨

Queen Elizabeth II, with Professor BJ Ralph, inspects equipment in the Biological Sciences building, following the opening 4 March 1963 the efforts to meet the patent and urgent need for a second medical school, and then over its location with the University of New South Wales. The faculty was born in the midst of fierce private, and public, controversy — a cracked-brain plan said the *Sydney Morning Herald*. The faculty's history locates the first moves towards a medical school as coming from Sydney Hospital but these foundered on that Hospital Board's unwillingness to cooperate with the university. Wurth had a medical school in mind before these discussions took place in 1957, when the university's position was that it would act if the State government provided the finance — which it would not. But the Murray Committee Report of that year urged medicine as a priority, and that it be under the university's aegis. With that, vigorous public controversy erupted, particularly over where pre-clinical and clinical facilities might be located. At the same time the State government, following some maverick agenda of its own, appointed its own committee of advice. All this was too much for the doctors' organisation, the BMA (the Australian branch of the British Medical Association), which denounced the government's committee as unrepresentative. WF Sheahan, the fiery minister for Health, retorted that the BMA was not the government of New South Wales. His government was, and would do what it would do. The *Sydney Morning Herald* was already in a paroxysm of rage over the university's involvement and the Kensington location proposals. Conservative doctors trumpeted about 'the standards of the profession'. In the midst of all this brouhaha the university proclaimed its independence — and willingness to proceed, given money. In November 1958 five foundation chairs were approved. When appointments were made, Professor Frank Rundle of Surgery proved the most dynamic and his ideas were the most formative, though his leadership style was experienced by some as abrasive.

The commencement of medicine in 1961 was, of course, a major extension of the university's persona. But it was not until its actual establishment that the university fully realised how costly it was, particularly in relation to teaching hospitals, and this in a university already, because of its scientific and technological nature, a high cost academic environment. The initial teaching hospitals were Prince Henry at Little Bay and Prince of Wales at Randwick, with specialised arrangements with some other metropolitan hospitals. For the first time in Australia clinical professors in the university medical school were directors of the clinical departments in the teaching hospitals. At every point in this enterprise there was criticism and contention, professional and public. The queen's opening of the first building, in 1963, went forward with due pomp and apparent tranquillity, but in fact it was not until 1967 that the university itself felt relatively easy about its medical financing and teaching hospital provision.

Even by 1965 Medicine had gained an attractive reputation amongst those students not constrained by family traditions dictating continuance at the University of Sydney. And it offered advantages in other ways. If you took Maths as an option, and decided doctoring was not for you, you could transfer to Science, even Engineering at the end of first year. University of New South Wales courses were acquiring a superior reputation among informed parents by the 1970s. To a student reminiscing of entering in 1965 (won over by the Open Day comparisons), Sydney seemed entrenched in tradition, behind the scientific times. The University of New South

Wales seemed new, with excellent teachers, much better equipment, and much more 'modern' in its attitude towards the science of the time. Experience in the medical school confirmed this. And also an atmosphere of happy harmony between students — male and female; impressionistically one-third Jewish, one-third 'average Australians', one-third Asian — with a staff significantly Catholic. Or so it was believed, though precise actualities suggest perhaps otherwise. Is it also apocryphal that at the Roundhouse medical ball in 1964 a professor stripped naked and danced around on the table? As in all medical matters, stories abound. As also in matters of students living very hard, experimenting with drugs, magic mushrooms, and the like. What seems to be the case, however, is a certain degree of pro-doctor prejudice among staff, who tended to anticipate in students a medical family background and a private school education. Correctly, by and large, in that many of the students were doctors' sons who could not get into Sydney.

So what? Medical students at the University of New South Wales were well aware of their superior facilities — for instance, four to a cadaver as against around thirty at Sydney, where facilities were 'grim'. Those in a position to compare — in micro-biology for instance — found a much closer relationship between students and tutors: in practical classes each tutor had ten or twelve students; at Sydney, thirty, with no chance to get to know students. And at the University of New South Wales the emphasis was on modern teaching methods — defining goals and what to know to get there. Set against this was the faculty's policy for choosing the better students from first year Science at the cost of excluding their own bottom students, a practice which raised some vigorous parental objection. Even among staff there were those who protested, to the point of resignation, against the severity of standards. Indeed they were severe: anatomy and obstetrics held weekly examinations; other subjects demanded large 'holiday' tasks, physiology for instance. At the University of New South Wales determination to be equal to the best sometimes took it too far. The government was to intervene to allow more students to progress — leading to staff protest. And internal rumpus — the first professor of Physiology resigning in conflict with the dean, Rundle. Of the 117 who enrolled in the second intake in Medicine, 26 reached the finals in December 1967. Over 75 per cent of the Class of 1968 were in specialty positions thirty years later. The student costs at university amounted to fatigue and some feeling of deprivation that there was not sufficient time to grow and enjoy university life. In fact, in the clinical years the system and requirements of the course meant living in, in a variety of hospitals — little time or opportunity for 'university life'.

There was some professional resistance to this new wave of intensive training. The 1950s and 1960s were dominated by anecdotal as against evidence-based medicine. Thus, there was some antipathy to academic, science-oriented medicine among general practitioners and hospitals — and it was there that the emphasis of the teaching of medicine at the University of New South Wales lay. However, the faculty had the initial advantage of hard men in charge, first-rate men of great ability and reputation, but, above all, deciders, autocrats with it — master builders of a new, complex, medical edifice. Within the rules of the institution, though.

Evolved from public service and Sydney Technical College backgrounds was a rigid teaching hourage requirement: at the top, tutors around sixteen hours a week; graduating down to professors at four to six hours, with allowance for evening classes. Strict adherence to this was the basic requirement for any argument for additional staff. Medicine was no exception to this rule. The university's reputation for hard-working teachers in all faculties sprang in part from youth and commitment but also from this simple measure of coercion.

As to Medicine, a major influence was the relationship (if that is the right word) with Sydney University: dead hostile initially to the University of New South Wales medical school; then anger, resentment, regret, and finally acceptance — though not without using its old boys' network to secure the new Westmead Hospital in the 1970s, and attempting to outstrip the University of New South Wales in its decision to introduce the five-year degree in 1973–74 (the six-year course came back in 1988). Medical politics tended to be petty, competitive, and nasty: in no area did the University of Sydney–University of New South Wales rivalry last longer, or be as intense, as in medicine. Meanwhile, John Hickey and Doug Tracey were putting St Vincent's ahead on the medical map. And major developments focussed on Prince of Wales, to make it the major hospital it is today.

V

Then prime minister, RJL Hawke, congratulates the author at the book launch of *The Irish in Australia,* in University Roundhouse, as Allan Horton, the university librarian, and Mrs Deirdre O'Farrell look on

1986

Patrick O'Farrell collection

At the University of New South Wales were lateral-thinking, teaching doctors, destined to be leaders in their fields: Penny, Dwyer, Hollows, Beveridge, McCloskey, and so on — men who did not wish to stay with the establishment, but to create and mould a new medical world of their own. As human beings. Their attitude to patients — listen, talk — was very different from the superiority affected by Sydney. At that early stage, entry was not determined by an astronomical, competitive Tertiary Entrance Rank (TER) performance, a situation of requirement which many medical staff were to deplore: students offering no people skills, indeed anything beyond being good at getting marks.

Part of the initial opposition to the medical school had been local, given that its establishment involved resumption of the golf course, a deprivation bemoaned by the *Herald*. It did indeed begin the university's territorial expansionism, an imperative which concerned the university's neighbours. At the same time as the medical school was acquiring a site at the expense of golfers, the university was acquiring 15 acres (*ca* 6 ha) at Daceyville for playing fields and other facilities, pavilion, clubhouse; and 2 acres (*ca* 0.8 ha) at King Street, Randwick, for highway and traffic research. Thus began a program of purchase, extending to single dwellings, which involved the university with local interests, particularly Randwick Council. Acute street parking difficulties were to lie in the future, but the university's expansionist tendencies became at times matters of deep local resentment and suspicion. The university's largest and most powerful neighbour, the Australian Jockey Club (AJC), saw itself as particularly vulnerable, inhabiting a racecourse, a site of the same kind as that which the university now occupied, and believing that the university had had little difficulty in persuading the government to resume the Randwick golf course: all open land seemed under threat. Eventually, the AJC took action to defend what it saw as its exposed periphery by fronting upper High Street with stables and jockeys' quarters. Some ratepayers profited directly by providing student accommodation, and many indirectly through increased trading; but many also were hostile in the face of an increasing student invasion, which introduced outsiders, indeed many from outside Australia, into a formerly conservative, traditionalist, suburban environment.

Medicine was the major new development of 1961. But the magnitude of this innovation dwarfed others significant in their own right. A radio station was begun, VL2UV under Associate Professor Derek Broadbent, designed to provide extension courses to students unable to attend lectures. Its range (the metropolitan area) and equipment (specially adapted receivers) combined to make this a restricted initiative. Not so (but only eventually) the New South Wales University Press, founded in the same year. Initially the press was hardly more than the taking over, from the Sydney Technical College, of sales of stationery and text books together with a printery for prescribed student notes — they being a teaching aid then much in vogue. Its first book, properly so called, seems to have been in 1963 — predictably, on the principles of accounting.

It was not until 1974 with the advent of DS Howie as general manager (subsequently managing-director) that the press gradually launched itself into the national — and international — publishing arena, with quality books on an enormous range of subjects, from horticulture to history, from fauna and wild flowers to contemporary affairs. Its policy was that of ensuring these met scholarly standards of content, and the highest requirements of design and distribution. Aside from established texts and reference books, the press had a number of national — and international — best-sellers. David Oldroyd's *Arch of Knowledge* and Patrick O'Farrell's *The Irish in Australia* come to mind as works by University of New South Wales authors, although the press did not restrict itself to that writing source. Such books took the name and image of the university to the world. Strangely — or is it strangely, given the curious continuing conservative deference to others exhibited by academics? —

the press found it difficult to get suitable manuscripts, those combining scholarly status with commercial viability. University staff still preferred 'outside' publishers to their own, thus denying their own press access to the increasing excellence of university achievement. The press built where it could, but it was not until into the 1980s that it became a formidable and respected force within the public domain. Curiously, too, successive vice-chancellors were less than enthusiastic: the press received no financial backing from the university; it was left to fend for itself. As it proved in the long run, this was no bad thing, as the need to survive pushed the press into commercial policies which protected it from the mistakes and indulgences which brought other, institutionally backed, university presses crashing in the 1980s. In fact, the needs and energies of the press eventually were to find a further outlet in its takeover, from the University Co-operative Bookshop chain, begun in 1957, of book-selling on campus. This occurred in 1997, not without conflict — indeed litigation — but to the satisfaction of staff who viewed the Co-op's vision of a university bookshop's role as depressingly limited and inadequate. As to the lukewarm vice-chancellorial attitudes, these probably flowed from their scientific backgrounds and cultural dispositions: theirs was a world of journals, research papers, equipment, not primarily a world of books.

UNSW Archives

∧

First woman graduate

June Griffith

1952

Staff tepidity? The press experience is but one aspect of the operation of an infe-riority complex — to press a crude label on something much more complex. Many staff, particularly at the sub-professorial level, were conscious of origins in inferior-ity — of being a second university, deriving from a technical college, with makeshift buildings and an unlovely site, public service attitudes, second-rate students, and a contentious history of which to be ashamed: the wider repercussions of the Ward case gravely damaged internal morale.

Were the students of the 1950s 'second-rate'? Certainly they were different from those who had traditionally attended university, thus open to dismissive criti-cism. A questionnaire survey of a large sample of 1950s students, conducted in the 1990s, revealed the consciousness and characteristics of that time. Obviously they were aware of their university's depiction in the press as 'Kenso Tech' and the 'Poor Man's University', and of the haughty dominance asserted by the University of Sydney. But they well knew, or at least believed, that people of working-class back-ground, as they mainly were, were not welcome at Sydney University, as out of place. Their reaction was a sense of pride in the University of Technology, new, exciting, with a young and committed staff. And a staff which, Baxter apart, was not remote, but involved and friendly. John Kennedy recalls the Students' Union and the Professorial Board getting together around 1956 for a sing-song. Al Willis, pro-vice-chancellor, and an excellent pianist, played, while all got together in Noel Coward songs. Besides, it offered access to a degree, which they otherwise would not have. And, of course there were those who came because the university offered unique subjects, in wool technology and food technology for instance. And because it was believed that many employers preferred graduates with industrial experience — central to the university's whole approach to its teaching operations. And, above all, because it permitted, indeed expected, part-time enrolment. One could be in the workforce — and get a degree.

Who were these students? Almost all men, many older, studying conversion courses. Women were a few curious oddities, brave in their entry into a male profes-sional world (and in their willingness to brave Ultimo, at that time a notorious red-light district and home to criminality). Into the 1960s strict formality prevailed. An adventurous female student in Applied Science who took to wearing shorts was qui-etly taken aside and told to desist. The 1950s saw the university as virtually a male pre-serve, though the first female graduate, June Griffith, in Chemistry, took her degree in 1952 and went on in 1966 to be a pioneer woman member of staff — with Ruth Atkins of Political Science, and Norma Parker in Social Work. June Griffith was an enthusiastic and personable lady, whose directorship of first year Chemistry from 1968 made her well-liked by students. The 1960s saw that imbalance changing rapidly in the student intake, particularly with the commencement of the Arts faculty. Equality was established there in the 1970s, but even in Civil Engineering in 1961 there were enough females to field a 'Miss Civil Engineering' contest, in keeping with the beauty contests, Miss Australia and the like, popular at the time. Civil Engineering's contest had the mark of avuncular patronage exercised by that warm character, Professor Crawford Munro, whose harmless hugs of contestants would be unacceptable in later days. Most students lived at home with their parents, even some who were married. They relaxed, with staff, at favourite Broadway pubs, the Clare and the Duke of Cornwall. They were, as their contemptuous critics discerned, from the working or lower-middle classes. On the way up? Yes, and in more than educational ways. Those on the Kensington campus had, as their most favoured sport, tennis — that genteel, upper-middle class pastime, the domain of clubs and private courts. Of course, the 1950s were the days in which Australia ruled the tennis world. Next in popularity came a sport which has virtually vanished — ice skating at the Sydney Glaciarium. This was a sport whose social setting was more akin to the dance hall, a place where young gentlemen might meet, and have fun with, young ladies.

How did the gradual female percolation — evident, too, in staff and administration — affect the character of the institution? Undoubtedly, in a balancing, civilising way, altering the tone and refinement of university life. Booze-ups, crudities, men's power games—all became less acceptable and less common. This is not to gainsay the defection of some women to men's behavioural camps and the growth of instances of unhappy sexual liaisons in circumstances of propinquity and greater opportunity. But, overall, the university atmosphere informally reflected a greater gentility, and, from 1984, formal Equal Opportunity structures. Equality was building towards female preponderance in some subjects, particularly in Arts — even, in the 1990s, in a reverse of the 1950s situation, to female preserves. What had changed by the 1990s also was the 'ethnic' origins of these female students. Those of 'Anglo-Saxon' parentage were a minority: a range of European derivations, mainly Mediterranean — marked the female intake. As yet, few Asians, at least in Arts. But the question to be asked of the late 1990s stood the old question on its head — why were there so few men? Statistics for the whole university tell a striking gender story: in 1981, 32 per cent female students; fifteen years later, in 1995, 45 per cent, and climbing — and the day was soon to come when, across the whole university, there would be more female students than male.

The staff situation of the 1950s and 1960s was more vulnerable. Their own misgivings and lack of confidence were worsened by community and, particularly, university expectations: New South Wales University staff were expected to concede their inferiority, to acknowledge their lesser status, to live in some posture of permanent apology for their poor cousinage. Many did, and deferred to those who styled themselves superior. Not to do so was to risk hostility and insistent demand that one knew one's place — often, but not always, conveyed politely, and by emanation of atmosphere. This made for difficult relations with other universities, notably the University of Sydney, given this expectation and given the fact that people, for instance on syllabus committees, knew each other personally and were familiar with the rules of accepted behaviour. Used to monopoly, the University of Sydney did not react well to outsiders foisted upon committees by government departmental or other hierarchical decrees. Nor was this kind of disposition restricted to academics. My own brash intrusion into Sydney Catholic intellectual circles encountered such resistance. Perseverance in the face of such unwelcoming and grudging acceptance was sometimes difficult and uncomfortable. Easier to opt out or take a subservient role. Easier, too, for senior academics, protected by acknowledged status and professional pre-eminence, who did not experience the exclusions meted out to their junior colleagues. Such is the tenacity of negative imagery that it was to continue well past the reality of achievement of equality, into the 1980s. Indeed, such is the lag and conservatism in the public mind that not until the wide promotion in 1996 of the university as 'best in Australia' was this realisation made actual — whatever 'best' might signify in general consciousness.

The year 1961 was also the one in which the university acknowledged some major internal problems. Following the Murray Committee Report, a committee was set up in 1958, to investigate student failure and wastage, to find, in Baxter's words, whether this resulted from 'institutional murder, group suicide or natural death'. It reported in 1961, and this led to the establishment of two new units: the Educational Research Unit (later the Tertiary Education Research Centre), and the Student Counselling and Research Unit. Their very titles indicate that the report — much discussed in the university but little publicised outside it — found problems both in teaching and student response. Baxter had sought to pre-empt in this way the obvious areas of hostile criticism to which the university's enemies would resort — that incompetent teachers were lecturing to low-quality students. He also moved

V

Crawford Munro warmly congratulates Miss Civil Engineering,

with other entrants looking on

1961

in another significant direction. It was found that part-time evening students — the major element in the university's base — completed their courses (if they in fact ever did so) substantially more slowly, on a realistic comparison, than full-time students did, unproductively tying up rooms, resources and staff. In an effort to remedy this, and to improve student conditions and performance, Baxter wrote to employers, asking them to increase allowance for day-time attendance. It was this mind-frame also which led, in 1968, to the establishment of an Institute of Languages. Initially it taught English to European migrants, then increasingly, to Asians. But, given that its domain was simply language facilitation, it was seen by the university — and felt itself — very much the poor cousin, indeed an inferior relative, there on sufferance. Inadequately resourced, later housed in an off-campus, broken-down foundry, not permitted to offer its full-time staff more than one-year contracts, it saw itself as shabbily and unjustly treated, and developed deep resentments. Whatever the merits of the arguments involved on both sides, the Institute did not prove to be the happiest of the university's initiatives.

The other major internal problem of 1961 was an explosion of student numbers in Arts. The initial policy, in line with the university's determination to preserve its traditional character, is summed up in the official adage, 'Few, but good'. Whatever of the 'good', the 'few' came under immediate contradiction. The first intake in 1960, of thirty-three students had rocketed in a year to ninety-eight, putting it fourth in faculty enrolments for 1961. Commerce was first, with 152. Only then followed Engineering (129) and Science (126). The problem lay not so much in catering for these numbers as in accommodating this to the university's mentality. The 'few but good' mind-frame continued to dominate university thinking — and internal allocation of resources and financing. What amounted to a belief in moral superiority and necessary continuance maintained the science and technology establishment — in all senses of that word — unchanged and unmoved despite what amounted to a tidal wave in Arts. University decision-makers continued to subscribe to, and act on, their own vision, which was being increasingly questioned in its applicability by the sheer weight of numbers. There were other related reasons for downgrading Arts and its needs — the common view that it harboured scruffy troublemakers, lazy and undisciplined: these were students who had too much time to think and talk; long laboratory sessions stopped this dangerous sort of thing. So — keep Arts poor.

The 'few but good' ethos also conditioned the university's — read Baxter's — reaction to the establishment of Macquarie University in 1964. Arising from government concern in 1960 over an anticipated explosion in university enrolments, Macquarie was to meet this in arts, science and economics. Macauley and Myers were involved in the initial discussions and committees and were immediately aware that it offered no threat, to engineering, for instance, and the University of New South Wales domain generally. Indeed it would, it was believed, siphon off demand in arts. Baxter thought a third university in Sydney was inevitable. That it should take the unwelcome arts elements (Baxter liked the applied arts, such as the theatre; not its intellectual dimensions) was all to the good. True, Macquarie's site was much larger and more salubrious, and Baxter respected and liked the first vice-chancellor, AG Mitchell, as a down-to-earth arts person. The matter of Macquarie's establishment was, therefore, a matter of no concern to New South Wales University's higher echelons, and relations were initially, and thereafter cordial.

So much for the university's higher ups. To the lower orders, at least in Arts, things appeared rather differently. Macquarie was seen as very much the progeny of the University of Sydney, in staff selection disposed to favour its own. To the extent that this was so, New South Wales University academics could blame their own administration for its lack of interest. It was the submissions of the Senate and Professorial Board of the University of Sydney which were, uncontested, the most decisive and influential in the formulation and character of Macquarie. The other element which gave New South Wales University academics pause was Macquarie's emanation of the odour of evangelical Christianity, an atmosphere very different, if

Roundhouse on completion

1961

intangibly so, from the highly secular ethos of their university. This was not productive of hostility, more a belief that Macquarie was not for them. It was their administration's attitude, writ small and for other reasons.

The arts tide from 1961 was driven to some extent by the attractions of a fashionable, educated, hippie lifestyle, but more practically by pressure to train teachers to staff a vastly expanded school system. At the University of New South Wales arts students were met by a less than adequate comprehension and recognition of their needs, in terms of space, staff, and library. Moreover, they were entirely full-time students, at variance with — however Baxter might be conscious of excessive failure rates — the traditional university ethos. In fact, the Arts requirement of full-time study was precursor to a trend right across this university. The university as a whole was losing its part-time character to a point in the mid 1960s when there were more full-time students than part-time. The change is more than of statistical interest: it produced a radical, though gradual change of university ethos and disposition. The campus became more focussed on student interests and activity. Where before student involvement was relatively slight, given that it consisted of attendance in the evening at the end of a work day, and university was a tiring (and often tiresome) adjunct to a job and career-oriented life elsewhere, it was now becoming a major and enjoyable activity, an interesting part of life rather than a small footnote to it. The impact on the university totality was considerable as more students became active participants in determining their environment, both social and academic.

The Union, an adventurous building, carefully designed and furnished, was opened in 1961, catering to a variety of needs of students and staff. The staff wish for a separate social venue was met by a staff club in November 1965. It was not granted a liquor licence until 1970 and was beset by problems of relations with the Union, employed staff, and premises: it was the manageress, Mrs McMonigal, who, on miserable wages, long held the enterprise together. Its members tended to be a committed, convivial few, not a staff majority, and the question of its continued viability eventually became urgent in 1998 — a comment on the lesser sociability and eating habits of a busy, sandwich-eating staff.

As to the Roundhouse, it was the setting for a famous (or infamous) incident of student protest in 1962. The ABC had hired the large floor area for its program 'Television Ballroom'. While this was being televised nationally, rolls of toilet paper were hurled down from the balcony upon the dancers, and a long conga-line of students entered, completely disrupting the show in the name of student assertion of rights to possession. This negative publicity further worsened the Union's image in the eyes of university administrators. The first warden of the Union, AT Cuningham was to complain, not only of disruptive student radicalism (or, rather, the activities of 'rent-a-crowd'), but also of a high degree of unreality in expectations of the Union — everything cheaper than elsewhere. (He was also to treasure the memory of Alf Van der Poorten, president of the Union, exercising brilliant and informed chairmanship of meetings, while reading a science-fiction novel under the table.)

In 1961 a start was made on a range of major new buildings: £3 million of the annual £7 million budget devoted to them. And as before, Newcastle and

Wollongong were growing: the university took pride in its geographic spread —
Kensington, Ultimo, Newcastle, Wollongong, Broken Hill.

But the internal problems of 1961, large as they were, were as nothing to the
external pressures mounting: the baby boomers had arrived — but not the money
to teach them. In 1961 enrolments had blown out by 12 per cent over the previous
year: an increase of 1000 students, to make a total of nearly 9000. This was in the
overall context of Australia-wide problems of student growth and pressures placed
on resources to meet those demands. It was not Arts alone that faced these demands.
In 1962 University Council acknowledged that recruitment of staff was less than
that necessary to cope and new building was falling fast behind. This, however, bit
deepest on Arts. It had at last been realised what were the consequences of the university's not having a long history of book acquisition. Books were now being purchased, but where to put them? Temporary quarters were overflowing long before
completion of the new building was due. That came as a huge relief in 1965–66,
housing 280,000 books, almost double the number in 1960: it is now 2 million. The
then height of library technology, the building was fully, indeed luxuriously (ideal
for 'sit-ins') carpeted and appropriately furnished. Sprayed asbestos ceilings reduced
noise. (So much for the triumphs and fallibilities of science and technology. Research
eventually revealed asbestos as hazardous to health. The ceilings had to be removed
in the 1990s at enormous expense and disruptive cost.)

All the time there existed a delicate balancing act. Money, on the one side; on
the other, the university's character and environment. That character was subject, as
must be all the affairs of men, to things human. David Phillips died suddenly in July
1962. Welsh, pioneer in Mining Engineering, pro-vice-chancellor and first chairman
of the Professorial Board (1953–59), much loved — Phillips was pivotal in the university's formative years. (Joe Bourke and Morven Brown were to die in 1965: the
old university was to be inevitably eroded by the passing of the old guard.) But that
old university was determined to preserve its technological character, not from selfishness, it claimed, but because it saw itself as pursuing objects of national importance. In 1961 the form this took was determination to resist quotas and restrictions
on student intake, save in two areas: architecture (because of acute shortage of drawing accommodation) and medicine (because of insufficient assurance that clinical
facilities required would be available when students reached that stage of their
course). Somehow the university would hold science's besieged fort. Indeed, continue and extend its forays. Unisearch thrived, undertaking more than 600 investi-
gations for industry in 1962. Textile Technology came up with a new money-saving
way of scouring wool. Chemical Engineering invented a new hydraulic system of
transporting bulk coal and ores. Biological Science had been engaged in extracting
alginates from seaweed. In 1963 an Institute of Highway and Traffic Engineering
with federal and State government backing joined the Schools of Highway
Engineering and Traffic Engineering. There was vigorous expansion in postgraduate study. And there was a raft of new buildings, pulling Ultimo activity into
Kensington, ending that Ultimo feeling of being outside the mainstream of university life, and heartening Kensington dwellers with physical evidence of their own

Civil Engineering building

ca 1960s

The Library

ca 1966

confident progress, and the supremacy of science. Within the university there were signs of integration: a Board of Studies in General Education was set up in 1963 to provide non-arts students with humanities and social science subjects. But the main heartening developments lay outside. The university was increasingly taken up with summer schools, and school prizes, with Mathematics and Chemistry to the fore. Mathematics was particularly active in its outreach to school students and teachers. Its lectures (roneoed and given to each student) were very popular and, with a school journal *Parabola*, encouraged many students to come to the University of New South Wales. Students felt they knew the staff already. Summer schools were flourishing by 1960. In that year Chemistry (then Physics) followed this example. Mathematics even had its own student cadetships.

The 1963 university symposium saw the minister of National Development, Sir William Spooner, in complete accord with Baxter's proposition that the threat to the energy needs of a power-based civilisation, posed by the ultimate exhausting of fossil fuels, had been obviated by nuclear power: Australia must have its own reactor. Such was the conclusion of both government and university in declarations on the grand scale, in which concepts such as 'mankind' and the progress of the human race, were the accepted phraseology. The Baxter vision could hardly have hoped for clearer government endorsement.

And, in the main, the government paid up. True, in 1963 fees were increased by 20 per cent, bringing them into line with Sydney University's. (Perhaps the introduction of a student loan fund the previous year had this massive hike in mind, but most fees were paid for by scholarship providers or employers.) But the Murray Committee Report had led to joint federal–State funding and a massive increase in available finance — and to triennial budgets, which allowed universities long-term planning over a three-year period.

Very satisfactory; except for one basic thing — the money was never enough to match the ambition. A large ambition indeed. The English view of optimum university size was 10,000 students. The University of New South Wales made it known in 1963 that its target, following American example, particularly UCLA, was 25,000. This was in accordance with modern needs and best current thinking on how universities should develop to fill their proper role in a modern industrial society — or so went the fashionable jargon of the day. It was thinking of a kind and scale way beyond the usual Australian parameters. It was both product of, and generated, impatient ambition: it seemed directed towards achieving that target very quickly; no long-term goal, but immediate objective. With no self-doubts as to its stature. In words given to the queen for her opening of the medical school on 4 March 1963, 'It is already taking its place with the older universities in the world'. (She presented the university with a signed photograph of herself and Prince Phillip. It was nice, and the university made grovelling noises. Money would have been nicer. But then monarchs don't give money: better to have name-thirsty politicians. The photograph used to hang in the old Council Room but did not survive the move to the new: it reposes in the Archives. In the new setting the icons were chancellors and vice-chancellors.)

As befitted this large conglomerate of international aspirations, considerable thought was being given to the setting — lawns, gardens, trees, major walkways, for instance the one from the covered entrance at Anzac Parade through to the Dalton building. Trees were carefully chosen — Port Jackson figs and *Ficus hillii*, coral trees and plants, the quick-growing to be removed when the large had developed. There was landscaping and some statuary, fountains, a plaque identifying the site as a camp for the First Infantry Brigade prior to its leaving with the First AIF for Gallipoli in 1915. Only one aspect of the landscape went untamed, and that the most permanent in student recollection — the bitter, cutting winds that swept in from south and west in winter, and still do, indeed channelled, in some cases, by building shape and casts of shade.

All this, outside and in, on sunny, hard-boned days, found their record in the 1960s and 1970s through the lens of that pre-eminent technician of Australian photography, Max Dupain. The choice of Dupain reflected Baxter's taste for the clarity of technically pure excellence: no softness, no fogs or mysteries of light diffused. Unpeopled, or with a dwarfed tiny few, Dupain's photographs were confrontingly stark, austere, hard lines and angles, harsh, bright and dark. Brilliantly executed, lonely structures inhabit desert places. Monoliths rise on earth's emptiness. Did he capture the essence of these seemingly soulless constructions, which, in a harsh view, lacked love?

Yet, rather than alienating occupants, was it perhaps this neutrality, this nothingness, repose, that contributed to, allowed, the generally happy relations that prevailed among staff? These stemmed from many factors, not least a sense of commonality in building a successful enterprise from nothing, but also perhaps reflecting the lack of competing demands for attention from the housing itself; utilitarian boxes, receptacles without anxiety or involving tension. When the university felt itself able to move beyond the urgency of needing simple and thrifty containers in which to do its job, its choice was to avoid ornament or pretence. The official view is laid down in describing Goldstein Hall, opened in June 1964. 'The walls are of clinker brick, and no veneers, claddings, rendered or painted surfaces have been used externally. This is in the tradition of the "truthful" approach to architecture derived from Mies van der Rohe and Le Corbusier, who believe that materials should be used "honestly" — that the essential characteristics of the materials, the grain of the timber, the texture of the brick, should not be disguised or hidden under paint or plaster.' And it won acclaim. It was what it was. Goldstein Hall won the Sulman Medal for Architecture in 1965. There was nothing sham or

Max Dupain/UNSW Archives collection

∧

The Invisible Man as contrived by

Max Dupain at Goldstein College

1964

mere show about the University of New South Wales. It was what it was, take it or leave it, its excellence and eminence in the quality of its teaching and research. Save for a small bow in the direction of that from which all universities claim derivation — the middle ages. In commenting on the Goldstein dining hall, University Council remarked 'In effect it is a combination of the medieval and the modern — the medieval in the austere, monastic atmosphere, and the modern in the use of materials and techniques'. It was an observation which, in a curious, atmospheric way, through echoes of task and style, held truth in regard to Baxter himself, and the university over which he ruled. But there was more to such consciousness of a linkage to the monastic than these wry perceptions. Coming to direct a play in the Clancy Auditorium, Sir Tyrone Guthrie found it hateful. He is reputed to have described it as 'the stunted pyramid of an idiot Pharaoh'.

Escalation continued in 1964, enrolment increasing by 11 per cent on the previous year to 11,000. An exultant council felt compelled to explain that numbers would drop — temporarily — as a result of Newcastle autonomy, proclaimed for January 1965. In so far as considerations of imperial prestige were concerned, the loss of Newcastle — hardly unbearable, given its long and troublesome agitation for independence — was balanced by territorial domain elsewhere. In 1967 it gained 600

Field stations — Fowler's Gap

ca 1970s

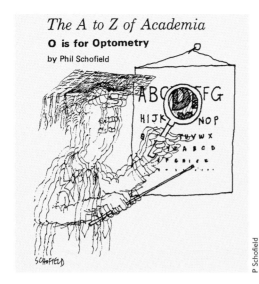

The A to Z of Academia

O is for Optometry

by Phil Schofield

P Schofield

Phil Schofield caricature series

Uniken 20 October 1979

acres (*ca* 240 ha) near Wellington, western New South Wales, to be known as the Wellington Station, to add to its holdings at Parkes and Forbes, and to its major holding of 100,000 acres (*ca* 40,500 ha) at Fowler's Gap, 112 miles (*ca* 180 km) north of Broken Hill. No resident students, but arid zone research facilities, field work on marsupials, the adaptation of sheep and land and water use, to hot, dry conditions.

The University Council's word for the building program in 1964 best describes it — spectacular. On the upper campus, the Library, Chancellery, Arts–Maths and Commerce buildings were all under way: after 1967 accommodation problems should be over (save for hospital capacity for Medicine). Or so the council then said. But by 1967 it had changed its tune, radically. It then declared that only about half its building program had been completed and it would be 'necessary to maintain substantial construction programs for several more triennia'. Several more triennia? The 'think big' mentality was starting to overreach itself. Or become disordered and contradictory and unsure. In 1967 the predicted student optimum had dropped from 25,000 to 15,000; that, council declared, would meet student demand into the 1980s. But the optimum was virtually reached (14,706) in 1968, with 2000 more students than in 1967. Council seemed to be faltering in its grasp of the realities of its own domain. Who was in control of the basic elements of the situation, knew what was happening? Baxter perhaps, but the 1960s have an air of things getting out of hand, of surrender to the unplanned exigencies of the unpredictable and bizarre. In their minor and major ways, things fall apart, the centre does not hold. Even the triumphing of Baxter's will.

Opticians had formerly been trained at Sydney Technical College, a process to which the university fell heir. By the mid 1960s the matter of their training and competence had become a contentious issue, with opticians (who had begun to call themselves optometrists) pressing for greater decisive power in the treatment of disease, and the use of medication — a demand strenuously resisted by the new Faculty of Medicine. Baxter sided with the opticians in what became an intense dispute, worsening when the optometrists proclaimed themselves an independent clinical science, neither medical nor paramedical, but having sole responsibility for their patients. Baxter saw the resolution of conflict in the appointment of a new head of the department of Ophthalmology, who, he assumed, would implement the vice-chancellor's wishes. These were the circumstances in which the eye surgeon

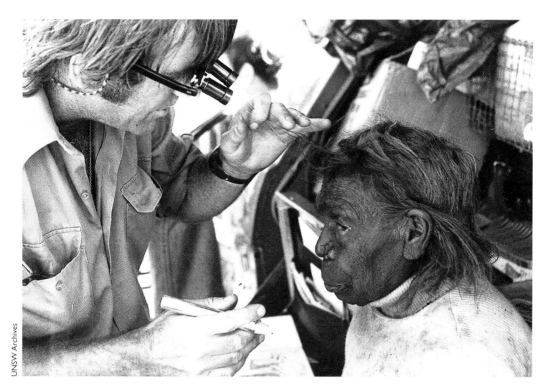

∧

Professor Fred Hollows

1978

Fred Hollows arrived to take up the position in 1965. The roughest of diamonds, with the vocabulary and disposition of the colonial New Zealander, Hollows, on grounds of professional principle, refused to accept the optometrists' demands — and Baxter's wishes. The outcome was an even fiercer storm Hollows—his tenure on the line—in his own term, 'weathered'. A clash with Baxter, even for a personality as ebullient and confident as Hollows, was something to be endured, not enjoyed. But Baxter had lost, and the story circulated, in hushed tones, around the staff of the day. Few took any pleasure from it. More like reverential awe. Nor was it much seen to Baxter's diminishment. An aberration. As to Hollows, a stormy career, arrested for protesting against apartheid at a Springbok match at the Sydney Cricket Ground, other things.

So what of 'Baxter's empire on which the concrete never sets'? The realisation of plans into structures was prodigious. Yet not even in the translation of his own discipline into buildings did Baxter have unfettered say. The Dalton building, occupied from 1958, was named after John Dalton, the English schoolmaster who did so much to develop atomic theory. When it came to a new building, Baxter was constrained by costs to lop off six feet from the width, but wanted it named after the Russian chemist Mendeleeff. But the head of school, David Mellor, and the

Molnar on the

problems of

technology

Sydney Morning

Herald

1967

"We apologise. Due to an unavoidable technical hitch . . ."

MOLNAR
6. 4. 67

George Molnar

entire staff wanted Lavoisier. University Council decided that from now on buildings be named after foundation members of council. Thus the Heffron building, on 16 May 1962. Baxter could be overruled. A major defeat? Hardly. With two buildings and adequate space, Chemistry was conspicuously advantaged. But not all was success: given the proliferation of ideas, it is not surprising that some were bad ones. The Commerce–Arts complex held facilities for closed-circuit television, a teaching mode which the university had pioneered, but which was, thankfully, not to develop in the extensive, international ways envisaged by its enthusiasts. In fact, the whole matter of technology in the workplace, given the bias of the university, turned out to be of surprisingly small importance. As in all institutions, the typewriter gave way to the wordprocessor, and faxes, e-mail, the internet, and the like, became the dominant modes. But what particularly distinguished this pre-eminently technological institution? Virtually nothing out of the ordinary. Technology has not transformed teaching. Paperwork and meetings have proliferated on the back of technology, rather than being transformed by it. So passed the television lecture into the de-personalised oblivion it merited. Some ideas originally thought bad proved good. Initially greeted with derision, a chair of Marketing proved enormously successful from 1964.

Then there were the mixed fortunes of halls of residence. The opening of Philip Goldstein College, with its dining room capable of seating over 400, all made possible by a benefaction of £40,000, was a major positive achievement. Anglican and Catholic churches had agreed to build affiliated colleges: the Catholic response, in the form of the introduction of the Opus Dei organisation, was to cause protest and trouble. And one high ideal was to fall, well not flat, but flattish. By 1964 the university had approximately 1000 overseas students. Planning had begun for

UNSW Archives

∧

The courtyard at Goldstein College with the Herbert Flugelman sculpture,
irreverently dubbed the Professorial Board; walking by is Harry Reed, whose association
with the campus began in the days when he rode winners on the Kensington Racecourse

1964

International House, with the involvement of the Sydney Rotary Club. The concept was that this would serve, beyond its accommodation, as a meeting place for Australian and overseas students. High ideal, disappointing realisation. Early, in the days of the Colombo Plan and small numbers, relations between overseas and Australian students had been close and easy. Growth meant that overseas students developed their own separate national communities, speaking their own languages and led their own social lives. The effect was corrosive of the earlier sense of commonality and integration, despite attempts, such as International House, to foster it. Moreover, as far as academic performance was concerned, the university itself acknowledged 'some difficulties', a polite way of referring to the higher failure rate of overseas students. These 'difficulties' centred on lack of command of English. This was to be reduced only by the growth in the late 1960s of the practice of overseas students attending secondary schools and doing the Higher School Certificate prior to presenting themselves at university. It is worth noting that at this time the university attitude to overseas students was not that of providing them with a service, but rather the reverse. Their presence made a valuable contribution to the general education of Australian students, and it was on this self-centred ground that they were welcomed. In the 1980s student experience of International House was of the world — minus Asia. Students from Australia, Europe, America and Japan

The beginnings of outreach to Asia, and beyond

1963

got on famously together, but students from South-East Asia — the International House majority — did not mix and clung to their own racial groupings.

The most important development of 1964 for the university's future was the request, by both Bar Association and Law Society, for the university to establish a law school. This was a major recognition of the university's significance and status. So, too, was the choice by Menzies of the Wallace Wurth inaugural lecture to set out the federal government's university policy. Menzies made it clear that pressure for new universities involved much more than bricks and mortar. It entailed the availability of highly qualified staff. The time when that could be met from overseas had passed: it would have to be met from within the Australian system — a declaration which made newspaper headlines. Nor was it inapplicable to the university in which he spoke: it, too, was guilty of the cringe of that time towards the imported product. Menzies, however, also delivered a judgement highly palatable to his hosts. In the immediate aftermath of the Ward case, he defined academic freedom as no different from nor greater than freedom for other citizens. So much for special pleading, the claim of some academics to something particular and large.

Some consolation. But the golden Menzies days were over, and the university found itself confronted by financial appropriations for the 1967–69 triennium, which were not at all to its liking. Saying so altered nothing.

K Doig/UNSW Archives

∧

International House residents in the courtyard of the college

1982

By the mid 1960s the university was becoming increasingly a public institution, venue of a wide range of specialised conferences, and cultural centre, particularly in drama. The Old Tote theatre, founded by NIDA in 1963 had been immensely successful publicly as well as innovative. In July 1965 the University Drama Foundation had been established to oversee and coordinate the university's drama undertakings: there was NIDA, founded in 1958; the Department of Drama established in 1960 as an uneasy part of the School of English and separate in 1963; and the Old Tote. The whole dramatic enterprise, training school and production company, was a major encounter with, and contribution to, public awareness of the university, not least by making it acceptable in newspaper social pages. First nights, formal wear, the big society names, all made for a university which was part of the glittering social scene.

The university's authorities were keenly aware of the 'sharpening of the university's image in the public mind'. Equally important, again in the realm of intangibles, was the reflected product of this — 'an enrichment of the spirit of the university', an internal growth of staff and student pride and confidence, as the university's reputation spread and deepened.

It handled this well. The request to establish a new law school was an immense compliment but it was taken not as flattery, but as a proposal meriting the greatest caution. First, was there indeed a demand, as the profession claimed? Independent enquiries confirmed this, but there was a subsequent basic question. What form of legal education should be offered? The conclusion was cautious: appoint a chair who would advise University Council on the best course to take — or rather, courses, to use the word academically — which would meet student needs, professional standards, and public requirements. This sounds like clichéd academic piety, but in fact it was a balancing act of no mean vision and skill. Yet, that would be a superficial view. Sensitivity to public considerations and the predicted needs of the society of the day had been ingrained into the history of the university since its beginnings. Its experience within the ambit of science had been of this kind — a good teacher.

So, too, dealing with the problems of the medical school — its lack of adequate, clinical teaching facilities — produced reasoned pugnacity. The university put its position to the government in 1965: the medical school, built, equipped, and staffed at public expense had been operating far below capacity for want of hospital facilities, with a resulting loss to the State. Here was the right style and approach in argument.

Sensitivity to the public, too. The university was very much aware of the uncertainty and misgivings, centred around matriculation, arising from the changed system of secondary education, the Higher School Certificate, due for introduction for 1967. The Professorial Board of 1965 was keeping its mind open to public criticism, directed against New South Wales universities in general, given their cooperation in the development of a common matriculation requirement. It was also conscious of the difficulties created for matriculating students by faculty prerequisites. Gone were the days when simple matriculation was enough to secure admission. Confronted by a vast increase in numbers and growing failure rates, staff had sought protection for themselves and their subjects in a number of ways, direct protest unavailing. One was to demand guarantees of proven or, at least, likely student suitability. An enormous investment of faculty time went into wrangling over what schooling backgrounds were imperative for this course or that. Prerequisites sprouted everywhere in an effort to control student numbers and decrease wasteful failures: self-protection.

So much for the immediate context of public openness. The university was also acutely aware of a wider public context; the world, particularly that of Asia. Its 1965 symposium 'Population, Food, and Australia — the Next Twenty Years' was technical enough, but its message went far beyond modes of production. To educate was crucial and logical. Constant handouts could not solve the problems of shortages in developing countries. That could only come from within. Teaching the local providers should be the university's role and duty. That urging of role and duty also drew on foundational visions. In the inaugural Dunrossil Memorial Lecture, established by the Institute of Radio and Electronic Engineers, given in February 1965, the Duke of Edinburgh referred to the urgent need of the 'two cultures' to grow and work together. 'The outlook for humanity is very bleak unless the engineers of humanity and the engineers of technology get together to design the sort of world in which mankind and all God's creatures can exist together.' At this stage the university saw its redemptive mission as extending to Africa as well as Asia, but it was, in its thinking, moving outside its Australian setting to its obligations on the world stage.

〜〜〜

Of course, the immediate remained the prime concern. The late 1960s saw an explosive increase in enrolments: 1966 saw them at 13,336, up over 18 per cent on the previous year, well above estimates for the triennium. Of these enrolments, 65 per cent were full-time, and for the first time the number of higher degree students was over a thousand. Wollongong was even more remarkable, up nearly a third in a year, to 881 enrolments. The number of women students at the University of New South Wales (2243, or 17 per cent of all students) was large enough to merit University Council notice. Overseas students, mainly from Malaysia and Hong Kong, constituted about 10 per cent of total enrolments. The university had undertaken to the Universities Commission in 1964 to accept all qualified students. Accept them it did. At a cost. The astonishing building program meant there was room for the influx, though timetabling became increasingly difficult. The greater burden fell on staff. Increasingly as the 1960s progressed, it was they who paid for the university's refusal to impose quotas as being not in the public interest: more teaching hours, larger classes, more marking, particularly in that faculty least able to bear it — Arts. More pressure from students also, for individual attention, continuous assessment, advice on personal problems, complaints, protests against hitherto normal procedures. The old discipline and role expectations showed signs of disintegration. Traditional formalities — the use of titles and surnames in staff–student interchange, gave way to the use of given names, in part a reflection of the youth of new staff, not much older than their students, but also an anti-authoritarian affirmation.

But boom was in the very air, and the excitement of success. The university was host or venue to a myriad of public lectures, conferences, symposia. Public awareness of the university, its staff's participation in all kinds of outside activity — all were growing exponentially. Big numbers, vigorous activity, boom town; the campus was an exciting place, university life lived full and wide, to the margins of possibilities. When Tony Wicken (deputy vice-chancellor 1992–98) arrived from England in 1967 as a senior lecturer in Microbiology '… it was still very young and raw in 1967 and there was something about the energy and aspirations of the place I liked. It also looked after me in terms of the research I was doing …'. This was a common experience and self-perpetuating — indeed self-extending as like attracted like. Dynamism attracted the dynamic.

Into this efflorescence came, inevitably, flatteners. The 1966 Report of the Committee on Tertiary Education put the view to the federal government that universities should restrict their interests to their own students and opt out of community involvement. That, as the University Council put it, in a cliché it seems to have just discovered, would be to withdraw into an ivory tower. Which the council declined to do: it declared its belief that part of the university's value depended on its being part of the community. True — and particularly true of the University of New South Wales. Its very history lay in response to phases of public need. The university was never an abstract affirmation, but always a child of its times — from science, arts, medicine, commerce, law, management — product of a changing society, often ahead of it, never behind. That is, in matters academic. In matters moral or behavioural, things were different, conservative. Under a progression of vice-chancellors the university maintained, genuinely, its respectable face. The Arts faculty in particular, but not only it, generated problems of aberrant behaviour endemic in changing times, especially problems of lax sexual morality and marital breakdown, and even liaisons with students. These met the firm disapproval of vice-chancellors as damaging to the reputation of the university.

The overall change in social climate was one of the reasons the University Council felt compelled in the late 1960s to stress the university's original character and purpose — education of engineers. Trumpeting Engineering's achievements, which were very large (claimed to be one of the world's foremost schools of Engineering) occupied a large part of the council's 1967 report, which amounted to a promotional blurb for that field. What council's apologia does not reveal, though it amounts to an attempted justification, was the skewing of the university's financial resources, not so much in favour of Engineering, as to the detriment — and resentment — of other areas. The Faculty of Applied Science was particularly favoured, given the prior disposition of vice-chancellors, and its exploitation by astute politicking. In fact, engineers believed that they were not being given anything like a fair financial deal, in spite of the council's honeyed words. They were in the process of turning out graduates who would one day lead a host of other major industrial enterprises; a proud future which those who taught engineering could see, but those who determined the university's financial priorities apparently could not.

The Arts faculty saw itself, yet again, as the main victim of this internal funding imbalance. There, cynicism about its deprivations and the inequity of resourcing went back to the days of Humanities in the 1940s and 1950s but the growth of other elements, notably Commerce, outside the charmed Science circle meant that the matter became a more widespread source of resentment, and some threat to its morale. (Nevertheless, it was not until the 1980s that it was rectified, by the tying of funding to faculty student populations.)

In fact, by 1968 Arts was, by far, the largest full-time faculty and almost (with 2166 students) the largest of all, pipped by the substantially part-time Commerce by a handful. Engineering came third, with 2141: there was no doubt where the student numbers lay — in Arts and Commerce. At long last the university was compelled to act to control the flow which threatened to overwhelm it — and its traditional character. It had long made a virtue of its willingness to take all-comers: holier than thou. But, by the end of 1968, survival was at issue. Quotas would be necessary in Architecture, Arts, Commerce, and Social Work, as well as Medicine. But not Engineering or Science. Put thus, it sounds like selfishness. It was — Engineering and Science might have taken cuts or lesser growth to accommodate the crisis elsewhere. But it also reflected reality, a swing in public interest and belief away from faith in technology as the saviour of mankind, away from the mythology of unending progress that had informed the university's beginnings. Students were not forthcoming in sufficient numbers to keep the Engineers happy. They were turning to other fields of interest — ideas and principles, the nature of society and its discontents, history, poetry, and where best to earn a living.

As a true believer, this shift in the public mind must have been deeply disappointing to Baxter, though he was never to abandon his personal certainties. There had been success after success, but not in the direction he most desired. Those best-laid schemes. What he had built with enormous verve, ability, determination and good fortune was following paths other than what his mind expected or his heart desired.

<|

The beginnings of ADFA

— Royal Military College,

Duntroon

1976

The years 1966 and 1967 saw the first steps towards the Faculty of Military Studies, then the University College within the Australian Defence Force Academy (ADFA), entailing agreements made with the federal departments of army, navy and air force. The aim was to enable the services 'to cope with the rapid advances being made in all branches of knowledge', but obviously this was seen in technological terms, and thus in harmony with the university's traditional nature and preferred emphasis: as in the history of the university itself, the growth — as was to occur — of a significant arts element was hardly envisaged. With the army the arrangement was directed towards the making of the Royal Military College (dated from 1911) at Duntroon, just outside Canberra, into a merged, autonomous, degree-granting institute. With the navy, a first year was to be completed at the navy's college, Jervis Bay, the university teaching the rest of a degree; the arrangement with the air force at Point Cook was initially similar.

These dealings were made not without initial criticism and subsequent difficulties. Critics, outside the university and within, rejected the whole notion of military

Geoff Swinburn/UNSW Archives

∧

Seminar in progress

— the School of Political Science common room

1977

organisations having any part in the basic concept of a university and as foreign to its nature. This argument seems to have been particularly strong in Canberra academe, where geographic proximity pointed to the Australian National University as the logical university connection for the military. Some elements in the army, with their own snobbery and parochialism, were unhappy to be associated with the University of New South Wales, given its downmarket reputation with the old establishment. At the other remove, anti-war and left-wing elements in the university objected to the connection as politically motivated, and indicative of the university's subservience to a conservative, militarist, and America-sympathising government. This criticism, highly sensitive to American involvement in Asia, intensified with Australia's military involvement from 1965 in the Vietnam War, which not only stimulated intense student protest but deeply agitated and divided public opinion generally. It was not a propitious time to embark on such a venture, already contentious in principle. Could a military academy become a faculty of a university? The question of whether the University of New South Wales was a 'real' university surfaced again, and 1966–68 were not good years in which to raise it.

The wonder is that there was relatively so little controversy, or damage done. As the relationships developed, the predictable, and previously experienced difficulties arose — those associated with distance and the resentment shown by subordinates. However frequently and sympathetically staff from Kensington might visit, the outpost had its own life. And there was also a more fundamental matter. The essence of the military approach was, necessarily, discipline, command, obedience, and hierarchy. Ideally — if not always in practice — the university rested upon freedom and debate. The ethos of each was very different and divergent and they did not sit easily together. Their tension impinged on the daily life of cadets, and troubled senior military command, which saw the university dimension as erosive of morale and authority. Nor did some university staff relate well to the demands of the military environment. The university–military amalgam was to work, and continue to do so, but not without extending the limits of give-and-take. Indeed, thirty years later, in October 1997, when the ADFA was costing a million dollars a year to run, some academic inventors of the Duntroon wheel announced startling new discoveries, that the campus was devoid of the usual sights and sounds of a university, such as 'music at lunchtime, lovers, spruikers, stalls, megaphoned information, argument, laughter and a diversity of clothing styles'. These critics seem not to have been aware that this ground had been traversed at the college's formation, at much more fundamental levels than disparities of appearance. However, they offered new ground in likening cadets to 'juvenile street gangs'. The 1997 critique spoke its volumes about deficiencies in the realism and sense of some of its academic staff, rather than of the inevitable nature of the institution.

The year 1968 was also to see a glimpse of the university's future in the topic of the annual symposium: 'Australia: A Part of Asia?'. As always the university was in the vanguard of public concerns, but that forefrontery had its dangers to the functioning of the university as a social appraiser and critic. Its leadership tended to be that of seizing an idea and pushing it further, to be a distant mirror to latent but beckoning social trends. This was at a cost to duties of contemplation, the responsibility of appraising fundamental questions of meaning and direction. Too often it accepted, without much thinking, advanced elements in the status quo, in order to galvanise and hurry them — which it did with spectacular success. Yet, what Australian university was there which ever called some halt, which said, let us pause, take stock? Part of the symposium on the Asian connection did just that: History Professor FK Crowley spoke on 'Australia: Outpost of Europe'. Did the 'spirited discussion' reported of symposium matters 'both philosophical and practical' attend to that? Doubtful. The university's bent was to favour the practical.

And to favour the respectable, or at least the appearances thereof. The 1968 University Council report noted, as a first item among 'Student Achievements': 'One result of the extra year at high school required by students under the Wyndham Scheme was noted in this year's Orientation Week function, for the prospective students were visibly more mature than hitherto both in respect of dress and general demeanour'. Such signs of maturity evaporated quickly in favour of uni-sex jeans and t-shirts, but the comment reveals the criteria of judgement prevalent in the university's upper echelons and relevant to more than appraisal of the student population. It confirmed, above the surface, the negative, dismissive image held of the Arts faculty. Its staff had increasingly adopted the informal, not to say scruffy dress modes of the 1960s anti-establishment. Obviously, the way these people presented themselves, garnished with long hair and beards, invited dismissal of themselves and their opinions. The fact that council should advert openly to matters of dress and demeanour indicated the degree to which departure from traditional orthodoxy affronted members of the university government. The compliment on improvement testified to years of unspoken disapproval.

▷

Bryan Smyth
conducts a
seminar in
Commerce
May 1966

Staff were expected to know better. Hartwell's grey Oxford bags and tweed jackets were deviant, but tolerable as coming from a familiar British university tradition; but open-neck shirts, or worse — such as the garb of psychology lecturer Alex Carey, who disguised his considerable intellectual attainments with his thongs and brief tattered shorts which would do a hobo discredit — were viewed from above with distaste and contempt. Short-back-and-sides sniffed at long hair. Even before Baxter left (the 1970s were to see these distinctions confirmed) the university was inhabited by two tribes distinguishable by costume. Suits were the vesture of administrators and senior academics; informality, usually drab, even dirty or suggesting it, prevailed elsewhere. The explanation lies not only in fashion but age and generation. Staff were recruited younger and saw no need to dress other than as they had at the university they had just left as students. They saw the wearing of suits as distancing themselves: often they did not possess suits or feel comfortable in their psyches wearing them. There was also that element which used dress as a symbol of protest against authority. Towards them the hostility of suit-wearers was appropriately directed. These challenged all that the suit represented — uniformity, conformism, power, success, bourgeois values. As to females, informality was asserting itself there too. The compulsory white gloves for graduation had gone by the late 1960s. (A few male students in these rebellious times were challenging the graduation ritual by wearing their gowns over shorts and t-shirts.) Beverley Kingston recalls that in 1969 she and Heather Radi demolished Frank Crowley's rule against female staff wearing trousers. The matter of dress generally had one negative outcome. It led to younger staff absenting themselves from graduation ceremonies. Lacking the dress, formal or academic, to attend, they often resorted to regarding such ceremonies as irrelevant and meaningless rituals, not a view held widely amongst graduands and their families. Staff absences diminished such university occasions.

The staff ethos was changing in other ways too, not only in relation to general cultural change. In part the change was a consequence of staff numbers — in 1964, 803; in 1996, 2055. The university of the 1950s and 1960s offered some possibility of faculty members knowing each other or at least knowing who people were, outside their own schools. Indeed, some faculties shared close accommodation with others in the early university, where buildings were few — a common feature among all Australian universities at this stage. Even sharing, if they were lucky, in days of sandwiches brought from home, common Common Rooms. The mix was socially and intellectually productive. I came to know the foundation professor of Accounting, and dean of the Faculty of Commerce, Bryan Smyth, in that way: Arts staff knew Commerce staff well in the 1960s. A distinguished member of the accounting profession and author of several standard texts, Smyth had a wide view of a commerce education. But he was not a man, as the cliché has it, to suffer fools gladly. And, given that he had not a university education — his very high qualifications were in accountancy — he tended to be very impatient with academic blah and pretence, politicking and delay. Fools did not suffer down-to-earth Bryan gladly. His forceful practicality was alien to bull artists. He got things done. Organising the University Union and its Roundhouse in 1961, for instance, are examples of his wider contributions to university life. Less happy were the tensions between the School of Accounting and the School of Economics. Smyth tended to be one of the 'crash through or crash' practitioners so important in the university's early days. Later people met different demands, gentler and more complex. But under him Commerce diversified: Business Administration with Neville Wills (a tense relationship), Marketing with Roger Layton, Finance with Rex Olsson, Dexter Dunphy in Behavioural Science, John Nevile in Economics. Yet this was in spite of, rather than because of, university trends and character. Bryan Smyth used to get 'as mad as hell' with a university willing to buy wasteful unused science equipment at the same time as denying him staff. And to add insult to that kind of injury by refusing book purchases: 'Accountants don't read books, do they?'.

Commerce sported the largest and most active student society on campus in the 1960s and 1970s. Evolving from the 1957–58 Accountancy Diploma Association, the society had a packed social agenda, a journal, offered prizes and held visiting lectures. In 1968 it organised no less than four Bacchus Balls, all packed — on 6, 7, 8 and 9 December. Legend has it that the society perished on its own alcoholic sword. It is said that a society function in Centrepoint Tower in the city resulted in spectacular $10,000 worth of damage to function rooms, damaging public relations for the university, and leading to the society's disbanding by the then dean, John Niland, who has no recollection of the incident. Such university intervention seems inherently unlikely, but the story itself is not out of character with the spirit and practice of the society's lively social persona and (damage aside) not out of keeping with the work hard, play hard ethos of Bryan Smyth.

A Catholic but no religious intellectual, Bryan had unwisely agreed to give a speech of welcome, to Sydney, in 1960 to the new apostolic delegate, Cardinal Maximilian de Furstenberg. In last-minute panic, unable to think of anything to say, he turned to me for help. I had just acquired the German theologian Karl Rahner's *Free Speech in the Church*, a revolutionary tract in its day. Mischief led me to summarise it and provide it to Bryan. The delegate sat back to hear the usual pious platitudes, only to be electrified by Smyth's clarion call to liberty, uttered, of course, in complete incomprehension of its content or context. It is tempting to speculate on the delegate's concerned diplomatic report to Rome, the astonished reaction of some Vatican bureaucrat to this evidence of galloping subversion preached by this unknown professor in this university at the end of the earth, to the 'please explain' which no doubt went to Cardinal Gilroy, within whose bailiwick lay this apparent further threat to an embattled papacy. Is the University of New South Wales the subject of some worried Vatican archive? The Vatican connection? The very question sounds like the title of some airport bookstore spy thriller. There wasn't one: the university was a rigorously secular institution, but its openness to Catholics of ability, and its connections with the New South Wales public service, convinced some — unused to encountering Catholics in universities that the university was in thrall to an Irish Catholic 'ocker in-group', not gentlemen, but the 'naked ocker at his very worst, posing as an academic'. Smyth and Bourke were seen as the high priests of this 'in-group', which collected at the Regent — that 'dreadful hotel on Anzac Parade' — to drink and socialise 'in that awful ocker way'. Even within Smyth's own faculty there were those who viewed this with distant contempt, this 'Catholic-Irish, Catholic-tech-college in-group', despite that group's persistent efforts to try to include them! Fortunately, the university had few of this superior — and sectarian — complexion. Most of those not of the alleged Bourke-Smyth nexus enjoyed the colour and conviviality they offered as an entertaining spectacle. Were these high priests aware of the tiny element of hostility and contempt they attracted? Ocker they may have been, but they were too subtle and astute for much to pass them by. But it was not their style to advert openly to it.

I remained blissfully ignorant for over thirty years of the sensitivities aroused by my own appointment, as a Catholic, in 1959. One historian whom I was to know pleasantly enough in his later incarnation as chairman of the Australian Vice-Chancellors' Committee, had an Irish Protestant background, which disposed him to be suspicious of Catholics. Following his own appointment he had approached Hartwell, it was said, to complain that some of his Catholic colleagues were proselytising, and demanded that he do something about it. Hartwell (who had been approached to join by the masons at Sydney Technical College) declined to act in any way. This was a time of the assertive, aggressive Catholicism associated with BA Santamaria's Movement in which some anti- (or at least, non-) Catholics felt concerned and threatened. (Coming from tranquil New Zealand, I thought everybody was mad.) At any rate, on the selection committee considering my application, that historian argued strongly that O'Farrell should go back to Greymouth (his birthplace). Indeed, anywhere but Kensington: it was a close-run thing. Or so the story goes. Perhaps, as I responded to this tale, I was thick, but I was not aware of the operation of such prejudices in my regard, though I knew of the masonic-versus-Catholic tensions that had existed in the old Sydney Technical College. The university had none of that; it was a happily open situation some ascribe to Arthur Denning's influence. He was no Catholic, but fostered that environment of tolerant broad-mindedness which became the hallmark of the new university.

Or was it simply a far less high-minded, secular latitudinarianism? Baxter, a nothing religiously, could not have cared less. And Bourke was essentially a caricature Catholic, non-practising, almost all of his friends not Catholics. There were no influential masons: efforts by a few employees to set up a university lodge came to nothing. In fact, the unanimous testimony of retired or long-serving members of the university is that there were no ideologies, no fanatics, few personality clashes and the only abrasive division was that between administration and academics. Not quite the only division. In earliest days, the teaching staff inherited from Sydney Technical College looked down on research and researcher. And the staff of 'pure' science had contempt for industrial applied scientists.

Sir Philip Baxter retired, as from 30 June 1969. His world of suit-wearers was to continue uninterrupted. His successor, Professor Rupert Myers, was even better dressed, dapper, and with the same essentially authoritarian style. He made the big decisions. But in a different way: open, warm if with an edge, friendly but distant, the complete family man with clear integrity — one conscious of a changing world, within and without, to which he must relate. A hazardous trick of giving Baxter's values and vision of a nation a new face and a different life, something he

UNSW Archives

∧

Professor Rupert Myers (left) receives the

School of Metallurgy Seat of Learning Award, as JP Baxter looks on

1960

did with great success, superb skill and — what Baxter lacked — smooth style: the vice-chancellor as professional art form.

Baxter's achievement in reaching this point had been prodigious. No sensible person would deny his greatness, his extraordinary vision, his remarkable power. These qualities took him beyond the university to points outside it, national and international, but his primary commitment was the university he led for twenty years. He used to wander around the campus alone, isolated by office and personality. When he had lunch guests, he took them to eat in the Roundhouse, queuing up with all others. The extraordinary capacities he had shown in building a university from virtually nothing to an educational institution of major significance and greater future had their cost. One could not do what he had done and with such speed and confidence, without attracting some anger and criticism, often from lesser men, and without making some mistakes or exhibiting some shortcomings. The word most used by his detractors was 'ruthless'. Be it so. The authoritarian style, the centring of power and decision-making in the one person and him not gregarious or sociable, hid the hours of anguishing and compassion that went into decisions about people — this being the testament of Rupert Myers, who worked closest to him; indeed, in the early days they shared an office. A visionary manager, he would yet turn his mind to those staff in turmoil or trouble. A punctilious adherent to the canons of proper managerial behaviour, he remained silent in the face of misunderstanding and roguery when he knew the facts otherwise. There were not many academic scoundrels but there were a few: there were things you could not reveal but things you knew. A superficial reputation for arrogance, for off-putting reserve were as nothing measured against the dimensions of the man, against the excitement of his bravura performance, against the achieved greatness of his vision. So what if it was an unattractive campus, so what if it was ruled hierarchically. Even that was something of a canard. Myers saw him as 'a great devolver of authority', compared to, for instance, Sir Stephen Roberts, who, as vice-chancellor, ran the University of Sydney in every particular. Anyhow, so what? Baxter's university was very much and very powerfully THERE.

His judgement did not fail him in his time of leaving. Decision-making was becoming no longer the prerogative of small groups of men who knew each other and spoke the same language. The changing university environment was becoming less congenial to his manner and taste and the direction of his real interests: retirement from the university allowed him to become full-time chairman of the Australian Atomic Energy Commission. Time to leave the university's problems to others — and they were problems indeed.

Max Dupain/UNSW Archives

∧

The overpass between the Robert Heffron building

and the Dalton building

ca 1967

4

CHALLENGES
1969–75

1969

University of New South Wales Opera mounts the first Sydney performance of Britten's *Albert Herring* and first Australian performance of Monteverdi's *Coronation of Poppaea* • First student from Papua New Guinea sponsored by Students' Union and Public Service Association (Port Moresby) • Land acquired at Tarban Creek, Gladesville, to build university boatshed • Wollongong University College Advisory Committee replaced by Wollongong College Council; Board of Studies also set up. • NEW DEGREES/DIPLOMAS Master in Marketing; graduate diplomas in Transport, Health Administration • CAMPUS IMPROVEMENTS Air-conditioning installed in the Science Theatre and Unisearch House

13 JANUARY Construction of Sir John Clancy Auditorium begun.
10 FEBRUARY Electrical Engineering building final stage begun (adding an extra floor for Senior Common Room Club).
21 FEBRUARY Construction of Warrane College begun.
8 MARCH Sam Cracknell sports pavilion opened (named after IR Cracknell, former supervisor, Student Amenities).
1 APRIL Ian Channell takes up appointment as 'Gandalf, the Wizard of Oz'.
MAY Construction of Newton building begun.
8 MAY Parade Theatre opened.
28 JUNE Radiotherapy Department and new Polyclinic at Prince of Wales Hospital opened.
30 JUNE JP Baxter retires as vice-chancellor. • New facilities at Hay Field Station completed.
JULY Chancellery's south wing extension completed.
1 JULY Professor RH Myers appointed vice-chancellor; also has his investiture as Rupert, Prince of New South Wales.

14 JULY Professor JB Thornton appointed pro-vice-chancellor.
19 JULY House at Pooh Corner, the Students' Union child-minding centre, completed.
13 SEPTEMBER Applied Science building (completed in March) opened by Malcolm Fraser, federal minister for Education.
12 OCTOBER New College (completed in March) opened; the Reverend Noel A Pollard appointed as warden
13 OCTOBER JH Wootten QC appointed foundation professor of Law and first dean of the Faculty of Law (which was first approved in 1964).
31 OCTOBER Sir Robert Webster building officially named and its extensions opened.
8 NOVEMBER First Alumni Ball held.
14 NOVEMBER Electrical Engineering building final stage completed.

1970

University of New South Wales (Amendment) Act (NSW), 1970 — allows for increased student representation on Council (from one to three), and student participation at faculty level. • Sir Tyrone Guthrie directs *King Oedipus* at Clancy Auditorium • New chair of Traumatic and Orthopaedic Surgery endowed • Tyree chair of Electrical Engineering created • Compulsory science requirement removed for BA degree • Schools of Education and Librarianship transferred to Board of Vocational Studies • Board of Studies in General Education given a separate personnel and administrative budget • Indonesian university teachers' training program introduced in conjunction with federal Dept of Foreign Affairs • NEW DEGREE Optometry graduate course (MOptom).

RJL Hawke, as ACTU president, addresses Alumni Association 1972

Medical graduation — Dr Wilhelm and Dr Taylor 1970

MARCH Clancy Auditorium completed.

2 APRIL First PhD awarded at Broken Hill.

MAY Academic year changed into two sessions (formerly three terms) • PLB Oxley appointed foundation professor of Production Engineering.

JUNE Sir John Clancy retires as chancellor; Sir Robert Webster becomes chancellor • Commerce courtyard completed • Senior Common Room Club accommodation completed • New clinical school at St George Hospital completed.

13 JULY The vice-chancellor's designation changed to vice-chancellor and principal; the registrar's to registrar and deputy principal; the bursar's division is split: into Bursar and Property.

AUGUST Val Hodgson and Graeme Dunstan charged, in relation to *Tharunka*, with publishing, and assisting in publishing an obscene publication. The charges were dropped.

21 AUGUST New undergraduate teaching block — Frank Rundle House — opened at Royal Hospital for Women, Paddington.

OCTOBER Newton building completed and the School of Applied Physics and Optometry moves in — Optometry is the last unit of the university to move from Ultimo • Broken Hill Division's WS & LB Robinson University College stage II completed.

13 OCTOBER Senior Common Room Club (incorporated on 4 September) obtains liquor licence.

15 OCTOBER Hon. Sir John Clancy, the former chancellor, dies.

20 OCTOBER New ward teaching block opens at St Vincent's Hospital.

1971

1971

Special entry provisions authorised for Aboriginal students • JH Shaw appointed foundation professor of Town Planning • E Balint appointed foundation professor of Building • Faculty of Law: first enrolments — 219 students • Faculty of Commerce restructured into four schools • Department of Civil Engineering Materials created (in Civil Engineering school) • Library's IBM 357 mechanised loan system begins operation. • NEW DEGREE Master of Psychology, with two clinical specialisations.

MARCH Law Library opens.

MAY Construction of Central Lecture Block begun.

13 JUNE Warrane College opens.

JULY PERC opened (Physical Education Recreation Centre, completed in November 1970).

1 JULY School of Town Planning established.

AUGUST House at Pooh Corner, stage III completed.

4 AUGUST Alumni Award for Achievement inaugurated.

SEPTEMBER Morven Brown building gains an additional floor.

OCTOBER Wollongong University College Library building completed.

DECEMBER First graduation ceremony for Faculty of Military Studies, Royal Military College, Duntroon: 29 graduates.

1972

Australian combat troops gradually withdrawn from Vietnam by the end of the year • School of Applied Psychology renamed School of Psychology • School of Traffic Engineering renamed School of Transportation and Traffic • Continuous assessment in increasing use (vs end-of-year exams) • Overseas Students' Problems Committee set up by the vice-chancellor • 'Parent's Night' introduced as a feature of Orientation Week • A Bill to establish a new university in Wollongong announced, for introduction into State parliament — planning and preparation for autonomy in 1975 begins • Broken Hill Division building complex, stage III completed • Faculty of Military Studies, Royal Military College, Duntroon: first postgraduate students enrol. • NEW DEGREES Master of Librarianship (coursework) • DLitt, Master of Psychology, Master of Statistics — conferred for the first time

SELECTED EVENTS

Shelter for the Students' Union fruit and
veg coop market 1975

UNSW Cricket Club pennant
1980–81 season

MARCH Construction of
Shalom College begun.
APRIL Keith Burrows
Lecture Theatre (Physics)
completed.
MAY Dr RK Murphy dies
(one of the originators of the
idea that led to the creation
of the university) • Four
squash courts completed.
28 JULY EH Davis, the bursar,
retires.
1 SEPTEMBER ZH Amit
appointed master of Shalom
College.
5 DECEMBER EG Whitlam,
the newly elected prime
minister, announces the
abolition of peacetime conscription.

1973

Tuition fees abolished by the
federal government, and
TEAS (tertiary education
assistance scheme)
introduced — both effective
from 1974 • School of Civil
Engineering restructured into
four components: Civil
Engineering Materials,
Engineering Construction and
Management, Structural
Engineering, and Water
Engineering • Board of
Vocational Studies renamed
Board of Professional Studies
• Cobden Parkes Ward for
undergraduate teaching facili-
ties opened, Prince of Wales
Hospital. • Students' Union
establishes food and record
cooperatives on campus. •
Royal Military College,
Duntroon and UNSW hold
preliminary discussions aimed
at the college's eventual
academic autonomy. •
NEW DEGREES/DIPLOMAS
Master's degree by course-
work in School of Social
Work — the first of its kind
in Australia; (pass) MA in
School of Maths; Diploma in
Archives Administration •
Master of Chemistry, Master
of Applied Science, Master of
Physics, Bachelor of Town
Planning — conferred for
first time

29 MARCH Shalom College
opens
AUGUST A national
postgraduate school of
management education (to
become the AGSM)
announced by the federal
government for establishment
at UNSW, as recommended
by Cyert Report •
Construction of Library stack
tower begun • Mathews
building completed and fully
occupied.
NOVEMBER Dr LM Birt
takes office as vice-
chancellor-designate of the
future University of
Wollongong.

1974

P Spooner appointed founda-
tion professor of Landscape
Architecture • First year of
the new five-year medical
course • School of
Community Medicine estab-
lished • Department of
Theoretical and Applied
Mechanics established in the
School of Maths, Professor VT
Buchwald being appointed
head • Public Affairs Unit
created • New computer
network, CYBER 70 model
72, installed at the university
• NEW DEGREES/DIPLOMAS
Master of Engineering
Science, in Highway
Engineering; (pass) MComm
(for introduction in 1975);
Bachelor of Landscape
Architecture; graduate
diploma in Current Science
(to update Science degrees)
• Master of Social Work,
Bachelor of Jurisprudence —
conferred for first time •
CAMPUS IMPROVEMENTS upper
campus parking station begun;
Esme's coffee shop com-
pleted.

S E L E C T E D   E V E N T S

Clancy Auditorium opening —
Lady Clancy and Sir Robert Webster 1971

House at Pooh Corner
1970

MARCH Federal government announces its intention to establish a defence force academy — which would take over the academic activities of the Faculty of Military Studies at Duntroon — to begin in 1979 (the future ADFA) • GL Macauley retires as registrar, to be succeeded by C Plowman.
JULY Enquiry into Warrane College begins.
OCTOBER Tarban Creek boatshed opened.
NOVEMBER Warrane College enquiry findings exonerate the college and Opus Dei.
DECEMBER First PhD awarded by Faculty of Military Studies, Royal Military College, Duntroon • University Union acquires a liquor licence; lounge bar in Squarehouse completed.

1975

Vietnam war ends • Special admissions scheme for mature age, non-matriculated students introduced • P Brown appointed first director of the Australian Graduate School of Management (AGSM) • HL Davis appointed foundation professor of Pastoral Sciences • WJ O'Sullivan appointed foundation professor of Medical Biochemistry • New units established: Japanese Economic Studies Unit in School of Economics; Mass Spectrometer Unit in School of Physiology and Pharmacology. • School of Surveying's new sandwich course (intended to replace part-time courses by 1980) • Students' Union: first female president elected; two new executive positions created — an Education vice-president and an Overseas Student Services director • *Uniken* and *Quarterly* commence publication •

Unisearch purchases flats in High Street to provide interim accommodation for new staff •
NEW DEGREES BSc (Tech) replaced by Bachelor of Engineering; joint Science–Law degree •
CAMPUS IMPROVEMENTS upper campus parking station, stage I completed.

1 JANUARY Wollongong University College gains autonomy, to become the University of Wollongong — with Hon. Mr Justice RM Hope as chancellor and Dr LM Birt as vice-chancellor.
20 JANUARY Faculty of Professional Studies established.
APRIL Students' Union sets up Legal Aid Office for students and employs a full-time solicitor.
AUGUST RH Myers, the vice-chancellor, and Mrs Myers visit overseas alumni in Manila, Kuala Lumpur, and Hong Kong.
20 AUGUST All new capital commitments deferred by the federal government: hence, contracts for the medical building extension and the AGSM building are put on hold.
OCTOBER Family Planning Association opens Family Planning Clinic on campus for staff and students.
31 DECEMBER Sir Robert Webster retires as chancellor.

SELECTED EVENTS

Boom or bust? It was back again to bust, 'drastic steps to limit ... expenditure' as University Council verbiage had it. In the later part of 1969 the university was deferring appointments, not filling vacancies, imposing an overall cutback on all materials, including books. One of Baxter's many expansionist legacies was an accumulated deficit of $1.1 million, megabucks for those days. And the future looked very uncertain, if not downright bleak. The New South Wales government was reluctantly prepared to accept building commitments, but refused to endorse recurrent expenditure plans to 1973. Ominously, these would be determined 'later'. Meanwhile, the financial need was just to maintain viable cash liquidity — or, crudely, to have enough money to pay wages and salaries. To avert such a crisis, the State government provided, not a grant, but an advance of half a million dollars. It also took up with the Commonwealth the matter of supplementing the grant, to cover non-academic salary increases. It was not only that Baxter's chickens were coming home to roost: he had not been profligate, but his imperialism had been far from frugal, and things cost what they cost. There was also something which he could hardly have foreseen — inflation in the general economy on a scale which bit deep into university commitments.

But the university was not sympathetic to the plight of governments, only to its own, particularly as its authorities found themselves as having acted in good faith only to be let down by that instrument of federal government on which they relied — the Australian Universities Commission. The lesson bore learning — that governments could not always be trusted — but in fact the university had been proceeding by inference rather than explicit promise. The Universities Commission had stated that recurrent grants would include an allowance to achieve a minimum student-to-staff ratio of 11.0:1. But, on the funding provided, the best the university would hope for by 1972 was 11.7:1. (Within the university this ratio varied widely between faculties and schools. The small School of Wool Technology was very advantageously placed. Not so Arts. This had not only purely educational implications. Wool Technology was a happy place: staff and students knew each other and got on well. Arts did its best against the odds.) In 1969 the university's authorities felt themselves ignored. Supplementation was imperative and, they believed, justified. New South Wales University was atypical amongst Australian universities. It had a higher proportion of 'expensive' science-based students. Its main areas of expansion were new — clinical medicine, and law. It carried both Wollongong and Broken Hill. Financially, nothing was forthcoming to recognise and provide for these features. But nothing ever had been, and this was re-travelling old ground: the university's plaintive wails were for its own consumption. It did nothing to alleviate that 'feeling of grave concern' which pervaded the whole university atmosphere when it contemplated its future. Did it have one, at least as previously conceived?

There was another matter which called into question the Universities Commission's understanding of New South Wales University's special character. Its functioning required the backup of a strong force of laboratory and other technical assistants. The commission's report however, implied that the number of such persons should be reduced, or at least allowed to run down, a prospect which threatened both educational standards and teaching staff loads. Already overburdened teaching staff would have to carry such necessary non-academic tasks, vital, for instance, not only in laboratories, but in workshops and in the library. The university was already coping with what it could via automation, namely in the various processing functions of the Registrar's Division. The data system hired from IBM continued to be upgraded and expanded to deal with student records and financial activities. Automation was soon to become vital to the library. But all this was not enough.

By 1969 it was the fourth-largest university in Australia with 15,988 enrolments (14,000 people attended Open Day in that year), but size was not everything. There was still the feeling of misunderstood, impoverished outsider — which to some extent it still was. But where before there was dismissive contempt — Kenso Tech — such appellations were ringing increasingly hollow and reflecting more on the snobbery and stupidity of those guilty of making them: there was creeping in a tinge of grudging envy and even threatened fear. Here was a force to be reckoned with. Which is not to say the staff rejected all of the notions of inferiority thrust upon them: there remained a residue of insecurity and apology which lasted, perhaps, to the late 1980s when national performance indicators — and student choice — gave deficiency the lie.

Fairfax and Sons

Rupert Myers falls with style from an

elephant during Foundation Day

1971

∧

A student laboratory in the Chemistry department

ca 1961

From 1969 there was another factor. A change, a growth in style, to consolidate the extraordinary gains achieved under Baxter. That appearance of dictatorial approach and remote hauteur with which many superficial and hostile observers interpreted the Baxter years (there was more to them than that, far more complexity, far more the unavoidable costs of massive and quick achievement) had run its course. The university was less insecure, more democratic. And more 'Australian', though it had been that from the beginning — brash, self-willed, confident, to a degree. With Rupert Myers, Australianisation was firmly under way. True, he had been appointed as professor of Metallurgy (in 1952) from Harwell, Britain's famous centre for atomic research, but his birth and background were Australian. He was the first person to be awarded a doctorate by an Australian university (Melbourne) and his credentials were impeccable, according to the social mores of what is now 'old' Australia — honourable, courteous, decent. His prominence in the Victorian Boy Scouts movement said it all — archetypal Australian colonial British, with an Australian translation of Baden Powell's imperial virtues its standards and impetus. Humorists of the day might poke fun — Boy Scouts have pure knees — but it was without malice: it was recognised that such persons provided community service and espoused standards of personal behaviour, manners, and outdoor adventuring, which met general approval. Myers exemplified this at its most firm and admirable. He was an 'old' Australian of the best school (and schools — Melbourne High). He would listen and offer, most politely, a fair go. But he would not compromise on standards, professional or personal, and would not be messed about. Shirkers and trouble-makers beware. Frauds and fools also.

Tony Potter/UNSW Archives

The library catalogue system — the old and the new

(left) the old catalogue cards, January 1983

(right) the online system, with David Reeder and Georgina Brockley 1988

Two aspects of that character were of particular advantage to the university. His honesty. He was always open and honest with governments and bureaucrats, and was trusted by them. This had benefits in the general, but also in the particular: discretionary funds, when they emerged, tended to find their way to him. And he was non-political, taking pains not to be identified with governments of the day. As a result, all politicians of all persuasions respected him and the university which he led.

Yet, in a central sense it was business as usual. Myers shared Baxter's scientific view of the world and construed university priorities in that light. Indeed, Baxter intervened, in a way unprecedented for a retiree, to secure the selection of Myers as successor. The University Council was in the process of favouring the application of Professor Ronald Nyholm (later Sir Ronald), who had come through teaching at Sydney Technical College to be associate professor in Inorganic Chemistry at the University of New South Wales, 1952–55, going on to a distinguished international career in chemistry centred on University College, London. Nyholm had built a very positive reputation while a member of university staff: a gregarious man, it is said that he not so much entered a room as bubbled into it. He was credited with rejuvenating inorganic chemistry and bringing it up to date with the renaissance in the subject taking place overseas. And he was a great encourager of research, a difficult task given that most students were part-timers with full-time jobs. Intervening in discussion, Baxter declared his support for Myers. Most members 'went with the boss'. As did the Professorial Board, though not as easily. As it happened they were all very well-pleased with the outcome, but the Myers shoo-in was not so inevitable as it seemed.

∧

Students' Union Council BBQ hosted by Rupert and Io Myers

at Pindari, the vice-chancellor's residence

17 March 1974

The least-favoured faculty under the Myers regime was Arts, with Commerce running a close second. Perhaps Myers was more impatient with, and less under-standing of the Arts contribution and style. It was not so much that he opposed or distrusted the humanities and creative arts as such (witness his patronage of the uni-versity art collection and his wife's active role in cultural activities) as that he saw the Arts faculty as harbouring some of the less-desirable aspects of the academic environ-ment — pretence, licence, silly and fashionable radicalism, softness, marital infidelity and promiscuity, lack of personal discipline, perhaps even deficient personal hygiene: *mens sana*. He opened his own house for 'elevens' on Sunday mornings, in which a rota of invited staff met him and his family — the children acted as waiters — in what was obviously a secure and happy family environment. He must have known that some small-minded (and envious) staff would sneer, even at his taste in furniture. And as to Arts he had a point: my wife and I were cured of hospitality to students by the objectionable behaviour of honours students in our house in the 1970s: they were unable and unwilling to handle the conventions of polite society. Some staff as well.

The Myers's 'elevens', however, were highly productive. Staff met each other. Myers said of it: 'it created that sense of family. It sounds terribly corny — but it's a benign feeling that either permeates an institution or it doesn't.' It did. Still does. Myers extended his hospitality to students as well, at home, and at informal lunches in his rooms at the university. He was determined on presenting a human being rather than an authority. As a tactic for defusing student tension and confrontation — though it was much more than that — it was extremely successful even through the rigours of that period of student affairs when aggressive anarchy ruled.

Be that it cost him effort, and no small unease in that he was not naturally gregarious or convivial, in ways vital to university life in the 1970s, Myers was pre-eminent. It was not the social process he enjoyed, but its successful outcome — a relatively happy university when all around was conflict and destructive strife. He could relate to, and deal with students in a way in which the remote Baxter could not. Myers shared Baxter's traditional values and belief in the way that a university should work; but, given that it would not — and the late 1960s and early 1970s made that point confrontationally clear — he showed an extraordinary capacity to adapt positively to this, particularly to student restlessness and discontent, which often became ugly and disruptive in other universities. King Baxter's style and history were such that they could provoke only the response of serious revolution among dissatisfied student peasants; but Prince Rupert, as he was popularly known (his first day as vicechancellor was the day that Prince Charles was invested as Prince of Wales), was a figure of medieval Carnival — that period of merry-making and release in which the world of authority was briefly turned upside down, authority conniving in its own ridicule, knowing that tomorrow would see its re-establishment. Prince Rupert had that perception and willingness to allow himself, and the authority he represented, to be made a figure of fun — wheelchair throne, broom-handle sceptre, toilet-seat cope,

∇

The installation of Prince Rupert by students

July 1969

Allan West/UNSW Archives

pushed among the student throng — aware that this was a necessary sharing and safety valve and, fun over, most students wanted a return to roles as before, to authority administering the serfdom in its proper place. Thus, Prince Rupert became, not apart or distant, but part of the university commonality, his participation not demeaning him, but widening respect. The alternative of standing one's ground, and on dignity, was proved, in other universities, significantly unsuccessful: running scared did nobody any good. Neither did stand-up battles on principle.

At the end of his reign, Baxter had seen student problems looming, even the right way of dealing with them. But his own personality and the nature of his rule made it unlikely that he could have dealt with them himself. Certainly not as successfully as Myers, in this as in much else, the right man at the right time. Seen (but not too often), not heard, was Baxter's maxim in regard to students. They were a fact of vice-chancellor's life that would not go away. Obviously, the consequence of Baxter's empire-building was to attract more students; yet, it was almost as if they were an unwelcome nuisance. That Baxter was able to behave thus in the 1950s and into the 1960s reflected the nature of the student population, largely part-time and evening, their interests lying outside the university, and in any case small in number, well-behaved and docile in the manner of those days, and conscious of the newness (and reputed inferiority) of their institution. It reflected, too, the quiet of the Australia of that time, relatively free of big and divisive issues. Critics of the university would have added to this list the tyrannical nature of Baxter's regime, whose working discouraged any initiatives or participation from below, staff as well as students: students believed (without foundation) that troublesome staff were exiled to Broken Hill or Wollongong, Kensington's Siberias. There was more substance in the criticism of administrative structures. It was held that the appointment of deans by the vice-chancellor, rather than election by academic staff as in other universities, was indicative of an atmosphere of autocratic (if benevolently so) rule: the vice-chancellor decided; initiatives or protests were pointless. The vice-chancellor told the staff what the university (read himself) was doing from time to time, in general meetings which Baxter found increasingly irksome and intrusive, and the Staff Association regarded as closed to public and press, no doubt in an effort to protect from the consequences of reactive vice-chancellorial ire the small avenue of information the staff possessed.

This situation was one which only some kind of student pressure could disrupt: the staff felt insecure and powerless, and substantially at one with the Baxter success story, which had produced results and jobs, however autocratically achieved.

But, generally speaking, the students were contented enough. In the main their interest was getting their degrees. The playwright and novelist Alex Buzo, a student in the 1970s, left, in *The Search for Harry Allway* (1985), a less than exciting impression of campus denizens. 'NSW was a no-frills university, full of serious-minded lower-middle class types carrying briefcases [who] got their piece of paper, then left, never to return ... The only character the place had came from its fabulous jumble of buildings ... .' Harsh and partial, but not without its truth.

Richard Neville, in his reminiscence of the early 1960s, had a similar experience, though his was the view of a student activist. 'At Sydney Uni students marched to

Martin Place to protest apartheid; they mocked Anzac Day in *Honi Soit* [the student newspaper], and held wild public symposiums on free love. Meanwhile at Kenso High (as some called the new university), the big adventures were bible class, arms drill and finding a parking space. Here I was surrounded by a sea of metallurgy students in white Pelaco shirts and short back 'n' sides eating tinned spaghetti sandwiches. We arrived on campus with little to inherit, but much to invent.' Which Neville in his outrageous ways did — but his comment was also applicable to the attitudes and reactions of staff. Relations with staff were cordial — academic staff, that is. The administration was another matter — particularly students' view of the remote Baxter — though the registrar, Godfrey Macauley, did wonders in defusing potential tensions. As the administration's man on the Students' Union, Mac (he disliked his given name) was prepared to sit through long meetings until early morning in the pursuit of amicable solutions achieved helpfully and with good grace. A kind of father-figure, he won wide student respect, even affection: perhaps he served the vice-chancellor better than Baxter deserved. In another area than the formal, relations with staff were good. Professors Jock Salmon of History, Murray Kemp of Economics, and Harold Oliver of English played for the university cricket team; Professor Crawford Munro of Engineering was heavily involved with the rugby club and socialising. Generally, staff and students shared university sporting amenities, loyalties and interests, then as now. And less formal still, staff and students shared local watering holes — the Regent in Kingsford and the Doncaster in Kensington. The Regent was marginally more popular, perhaps because many staff used the Rural Bank branch in Kingsford, immediately opposite the hotel. There, in an age of a beer culture, convivial staff held court with colleagues and students in that male world uncomplicated by female admission. In those boozy early days, authority still reigned: the staff were older and many were excellent teachers and personally helpful; respect and gratitude permeated the student ethos, especially amongst those many who came from country backgrounds and who counted their blessings in the opportunity the university offered them. Moreover, staff and students inhabited in their different ways and degrees a common culture, that of beer-drinking, pub crawls, and rugby football. There was a shared set of social assumptions; the unthinking acceptance of the 1950s. And a shared university: the passing of knowledge, master and pupils; collars and ties.

As to staff wives, in that traditional, respectable, and male-dominated society? A vital dimension of the university's social operation was the formation of the Wives' Group, which dates from the foundation stone-laying ceremony for the main building on 25 February 1950. It arose from the need for companionship: five of the seven wives who initiated the group were newcomers to Sydney. They wanted to make new friends and embarked on a monthly program of visiting speakers and varied social occasions such as cooking demonstrations, its formal structure changing with the evolution of the university: it eschewed a fundraising function, being essentially a social organisation. Nevertheless, it acted in a profusion of ways helpful to the university: in basic practical ways — making curtains for early hostels — but above all in offering a warm, human face, welcoming new staff wives and students. In those innocent and

Wives' Group — (from left to right) Jean McMahon, Maureen Anderson,

Norah Astbury, Margaret Denning, Gladys Murphy,

Bessie Tainsh, Joyce Wood, Irene Reuter

ca 1950

uncomplicated times of the 1950s, the Wives' Group made 'paper leis in hundreds to help the cause of the Asian students'. It also offered such students hospitality, to an extent of making friendships, some of them lasting until the present day. And it acted, as a by-product, in bringing husbands together, across all schools and faculties.

There was, however, another less happy, aspect to the university wives' experience. Some wives hated the University of New South Wales and Australia generally. Some were county British and expected deference. Others were overawed by the fact that the wives tended to be those of professors, older, with big houses, older children, affluent, hierarchical — with husbands in the Sciences not Arts, engendering feelings of inadequacy. The dawning of the age of the career wife meant that many did not choose to devote themselves to their husband's career. The Wives' Group was eventually to be overtaken by the changing nature of the times.

In the early 1960s, viewed from the eminence of administration authority, student things began to fall apart. The commencement of the Faculty of Arts was the context rather than the cause, but that context was a powerful one, enabling the emergence of a new, disaffected student radicalism. Its mouthpiece — and weapon — was *Tharunka*, the student newspaper. Hitherto this had been essentially a house journal for predictable student trivia, with occasional Foundation Day incursions into the public arena — the street sale, for charity, of parody publications, the *Sydney*

Moaning Tharunka, for example. Harmless stuff. But in 1961 this changed, not only into the highly sexual, but also into full-frontal criticism of the university itself and of Baxter particularly and personally. The sexual issue was bad enough. Baxter, and after him Myers, when *Tharunka*'s content became sexual and blasphemous once again, ten years later, were bombarded by outraged parent protests, notably by fathers protective of their student daughters, based on the assumption that *Tharunka* was under some kind of official university control. Such protesters were unable to understand that the newspaper expressed the voice of the tiny group which controlled it within the autonomous Students' Union. The vice-chancellors were stuck with a public identification of *Tharunka* with the university's name and image. But that *Tharunka* should turn to savaging the university itself was totally intolerable: it demanded that the vice-chancellor resign and that the university be the subject of a royal commission of inquiry; the issue of 7 September 1961 declared the university was a wasteland.

This was too much for the Students' Union itself. Its director of publications (a student) suppressed the issue, and demanded that the editor resign. This demand was put in terms of breach of agreements and procedures within the Union and suggested that the criticisms of the university were — not wrong but — in 'bad taste'. The then president of the Students' Union, John Niland (the present vice-chancellor) called a special meeting to consider the situation — support suppression or oppose censorship. Niland emphatically denied he had been threatened by the administration. He was later to see the incident in light-hearted terms, the young, upright citizens of the Students' Union versus the apprentice bohemians of *Tharunka*, and no personal animus involved: just different types of people. But that was more true of *Tharunka*'s fun days, of such issues as the parody *Sydney Moaning Tharunka* with a photograph of the Harbour Bridge half-collapsed and people warned to stay off the streets — all of which the printers, John Fairfax, thought likely

<

Foundation Day

pranks — the

New South Wales

parliament building

in Macquarie Street

appropriately

labelled

1979

to cause public alarm, folding the paper inside out. Niland's view in the 1960s was more or less a student constant: *Tharunka* was seen as the mouthpiece of marginal oddballs and hobby-horse riders. A student wrote to *Tharunka* in March 1982 to the effect that she had endured it for three years, but its depiction — and that of various alternative handbooks — of university life as being free, feminist and liberal was a *Tharunka* pipe-dream. In reply, *Tharunka* denied it was a haven for sex and sin. The exchange was pleasant enough. The 1990s, however, saw the intrusion into *Tharunka* of militant gay and lesbian elements, who appeared to be ferociously intolerant of anything which might be interpreted as denigration or marginalising. No humour or light touch here. However, the outcome of the 1961 contretemps

UNSW Archives

UNSW Archives

John Niland and the Students' Union Council 1962 —

(from left to right: back row) I Hart, K Haylan, B Miller, I Pryer,

K Walker, A McKee, J Hilton, J Moran; (front row) Students'

Union Secretary, J Roebuck, D Baxter, J Niland, G Adams,

D Carlson, C Hume

◁

Tharunka office

1976

was that the Students' Union Council had it every which way. It supported the with-holding of the issue (22 votes to 2) but then released it with the insertion of a dis-claimer. Meanwhile, Professor AE Alexander of Sydney University had publicly linked the matter to the Ward case and the issue was clearly before the university administration, staff, and students: the university's own student newspaper was being used against it. This was one incident, but would there be others?

On this matter the administration and the overwhelming majority of students were at one: it could damage them both. Even those students who might agree with the substance of the *Tharunka* criticisms appreciated that such denigration of the university harmed the university's public reputation, and thus their own, as recipi-ents of its degrees. On the other hand, as the Students' Union contortions reveal, they were not going to be pushed around. John Kennedy (of Wool Technology and Animal Science), when Students' Union president, exemplified that balance of loy-alty and independence. On the occasion of the Duke of Edinburgh's visit in 1956, Macauley rang Kennedy, a friend, to ask if he would open the door of the duke's car on arrival. 'No way!' Kennedy responded, 'I'm not a boy scout. I'm president of the Students' Union; you haven't even invited me to the occasion ... so, no, I won't open the door for him.' Stung, Macauley yelled 'Alright!!! I'll open the bloody door myself!!!'. If the incident illustrates the assertion of responsible and strong student independence (perhaps also an expression of the days when wool commanded the status of national icon!), it also reveals the way in which the administration imagined the students — docile, submissive, disposable, with walk-on parts, part of the back-ground university scenery.

The rumpus over *Tharunka* in 1961 should have brought home to Baxter that here was an area over which he had little if any control but was reliant on student good (or ill) will. He was not invulnerable, a lesson he took to heart reluctantly and resentfully. It was pressed home by the 1963 *Orientation Handbook*, issued with another inserted disclaimer by the Students' Union. An article by Baxter and Bourke had been lifted from elsewhere, and printed with argumentative, derogatory foot-notes by the editor. Fortunately for it, the ire of the administration coincided with that of the Students' Union executive, itself lampooned, and annoyed by the gratu-itous inclusion of 'art' photographs of the editor's 'live-in lady love' and the finger paintings of her children. The outcome was fierce politics, resignations and new elec-tions in the Students' Union. But the university administration reacted — or rather, overreacted — to an extent which revealed the depth of Baxter's fury. It had been demonstrated again that maverick students could act in ways beyond control, and inimical, in Baxter's view, to the interests of the university. He played the heavy, and meant it, threatening the president of the Students' Union, Ian Lowe (now a profes-sor at Griffith University) with deprivation of his right to graduate — an absurdity, beyond Baxter's power. Much more real was another threat, that the university would discontinue collection of fees on behalf of the Students' Union. It would not require students to belong to the union, unless it ceased its objectionable activities. The uni-versity did not carry through this threat, which the wily Baxter sourced to public pres-sure — it would have destroyed the union's financial base — but the student editor of the *Orientation Handbook* appears to have been victimised in his effort to transfer from Medicine to Arts. The necessity for him to make a formal application allowed the university — obviously Baxter or someone of like mind — to impose onerous and submissive conditions the editor was unwilling to meet. He left the university. This smelt of being vindictive, and prompted questioning, not only by *Tharunka,* but also by the Staff Association, and the Professorial Board itself, as to victimisation and the abuse of power. Baxter was very powerful, but his limits had been reached, exceeded. So, too, in his use of 'grey men' (so named from their uniforms), university gate and ground attendants, to confiscate and destroy *Tharunka*: legal opinion had it that this was acting beyond his powers.

As to student representation in the university's counsels, essentially there was none. The student representative on the University Council was required to be a postgraduate, though Heinz Harant achieved a good deal in this role. Assessment, examinations, new courses — none of these had any student input. Baxter's low opinion of students constituted something of a self-fulfilling prophecy. His rule and practices encouraged that of which he publicly complained: he deplored, too, in the *Sydney Morning Herald* in 1963, 'their lack of purpose, ideals and driving aims'. This was untrue to the extent that students were the only element in the university willing and able to have him on, but true in that apathy was a predictable outcome of policies of exclusion. When students did become disruptively active in protest, as at the laying of the foundation stone of the medical school, and at the conferring of an honorary degree, the university's response, through the reaction of the Vice-Chancellor's Advisory Committee, was absurdly paternalistic. Give the students more responsibility through involvement — get them to wear academic gowns and act as ushers at university ceremonies. Baxter's relations with his own children were excellent. His son Denis was a member of the Students' Union executive in the conflict year of 1963.

And it was Baxter — though through intermediaries — who first made possible the position and facilities of the university clown, bridge between officialdom and student power, the Wizard, Ian Channell. Furthered, developed and used by Myers, the concept and person of the Wizard was crucial to the 'fun revolution' atmosphere which was to prevail in the student unrest of the 1970s, when other universities were experiencing violence and major disruption. For all his limitations, Baxter

∧

The Wizard — Ian Channell

December 1968

was alive to the imperative need to earth students' electric energies. Backing the Wizard was a stroke of genius, turning the serious and destructive into Mardi Gras.

It would be tempting, as a stylistic, polarising device, to point up pivotal differences, to use the Council Report for 1969, in which an elderly Baxter was farewelled, and a vibrant young Myers stressed the need to respond to student demands. This contrivance would be false. Baxter had pioneered the path with the Wizard. Channell had come from Britain (Leeds University), via adult education in Western Australia, to be a foundation tutor in the new School of Sociology in 1967.

The standard student flour-fight, library lawn

1970

The Wizard with Rupert Myers

February 1980

He was thirty-eight. Overloaded with teaching, unable to get on with his research or with his supervisor, Channell began to develop unusual performance modes of teaching, and of relating to the student confrontation movement generated from America. He supported consultation as reasonable, but saw the rest of the student power movement, with its call to take over the university and overthrow established hierarchies, as being silly and needlessly divisive, enslaved as it was to a boring and rigid left-wing bureaucratic socialism. Against this demand for serious confrontation and resort to violence, Channell posed the notion of 'fun revolution', entertaining students about the campus and in library lawn lunchtime meetings with his bizarre costume drama and games, and idiotic organisations, such as ALF, a Goon Show echo meaning 'Action for Love and Freedom'. Promoted erratically by a thoughtful *Tharunka*, the 'Fun Revolution' laughed the serious, doctrinaire socialists out of contention for student attention, to the left-wingers' rage and frustration, which they vented, not on the administration, but on Channell, as 'fascist pig' and vice-chancellor's stooge. The Wizard urged 'Soul Power and Fun Powder' against 'Will Power and Gun Powder'. Baxter, 'the Machiavellian Prince', the 'great master', as Channell later described him, watched from the wings. He might abhor the appearance of student mobilisation, but being stuck with it, how best to deal? Baxter saw the enormous advantages of the Wizard's way, backing him first with accommodation, then with half-funding, sharing a salary for Channell with the Students' Union. Sharing is the fact, but the word distorts the actuality. Baxter REQUIRED the Students' Union to share, coercion which made the Union ambivalent about the Wizard. Baxter and Channell did not differ greatly in their appraisal of academic stirrers: generals who never ventured into the revolution's front-line, or ego-tripping exhibitionists. Or of students — bored, prey to drugs, candidates for the fomenting of violence. Channell was later to complain of the authoritarianism of petty student politics, the ruling elites of the day, who were jealous of his influence over 'their' students and who tried to discredit him as 'a boring old fart'. He was anything but. He had organised his own tar-and-feathering to pursue his own agenda in making the whole university a theatre of the absurd. The Wizard saw himself, not as mad or silly, but playful, driving the left to fury, coaxing the administration into reform, avoiding conflict, generating fun.

Myers, the new vice-chancellor from 1 July 1969, entered into the spirit of this with apparent enthusiasm and, certainly, success. Here, in this absurd amalgam of Wizardry and administrative realism, lay the university's success in avoiding the polarising and dividing, not to say ugly and violent, experience of some universities elsewhere. Wizardry dissipated the destructive energies inherent in that international surge of student restlessness, for which he was hated by left-wing intellectuals, staff as well as students. And carried the cost. He was spat upon. The left took the lesson, moving to take over the Students' Union and *Tharunka*, eventually issuing in the attempt to assault society via pornography. In August 1970 the *Tharunka* editorial team appeared in court on obscenity charges. Some were dressed as nuns and priests, there was one in a gorilla suit, but the mood was not amusing: it sought to confront, shock, destroy, shake respectability at its foundation of decency.

But by then the revolutionary moment — if there had ever been one — had long passed. Myers had involved himself in the fun, appearing at outlandish ceremonies and capers. On one occasion he arranged with the Wizard to get an extension ladder to access one of the Chancellery balconies, to storm up to declare to the lunchtime crowd the independence of the university or something such, challenging Prince Rupert. Thereupon Myers would appear on the balcony in normal attire, only to pull open his shirt to reveal a bright yellow t-shirt emblazoned 'Dictatorship of the University of New South Wales'. Five minutes later, shirt buttoned, he welcomed formally to the university, the prime minister, Malcolm Fraser. What vice-chancellor would attempt, let alone bring off so successfully, such a spectacular performance? This on the grand scale. On the small, the Arts faculty students' newsletters congratulated the History staff: 'They smile a lot and never get obnoxious with uncomprehending students'. There was dissatisfaction with end-of-year examinations, but, all in all, the student revolt was 'a bit of a giggle'. To my recollection it was rather more: student pressure on staff was uncomfortable, at times even mildly threatening. The smile at times was hard to sustain. Nor were arts students the only ones affected. Late in 1968 chemistry students demanded immediate changes to syllabi, and threatened dire consequences if they were not met. The professors met with the students and agreed to set up a committee — which never met: students had lost interest. And despite the undoubted success Myers had at earthing student discontent, 'rent-a-crowd' elements created ugly invasions of the Chancellery, defused, Myers believed, only by a basic university commonality between himself and true students.

The 1960s saw the journey from student innocence to student awareness — which later grew into informed apathy. The university of the 1950s was a small, happy place, with students in awe of Baxter and respectful of their friend Macauley. Of the bursar, Joe Bourke, it used to be said around the university, harshly, albeit with humour, that the one unifying factor in this university was everybody's hatred of Joe Bourke: somebody had to be blamed for unpalatable decisions, often conveyed above the signature of that complete bureaucrat, and Bourke was a natural candidate for such odium.

In the 1950s there were virtually no girls and relatively few Asians. This male preserve exhibited a kind of friendly racism: classes at 'Taiwan Tech' (a University of Sydney jibe) could be convulsed by a lecturer's attempts to cope, in calling the roll, with the pronunciation of 'Ng' or lists of common Asian surnames. Asians were commonly dubbed *en masse* 'Arabs' and, with all freshers, subjected to college initiation practices they found incomprehensible — dumped in Martin Place at midnight in their underwear with no money to get home. Barbarous. Yet they were included and wished to be: they were to remember Kensington with affection. Memory has it — Chris Fell's memory — of Basser College dragooning into its football team a student named Yap, who had probably never seen the game before, let alone played. He could run like the wind and was put on the wing, and told to speed off when someone threw him the ball. He did, but seeing the opposition's forwards bearing down on him, panicked and threw the ball in the air, over his head. Through such primitive rituals — and drinking — Asian students of that Colombo Plan age were inducted into membership of the student clans of college life. For it was college life which was the main differential within student life of the 1950s. It was only college residents who had the collegiality, location and time to identify actively with the university: others were beset by Sydney's travel distances and involvement with local ties.

What, college or hostel fun aside, were the main student concerns of the 1950s? The absence of adequate facilities for eating, meeting and recreation; to be eventually met by the Roundhouse, situated to be near a south-eastern suburbs railway which never came. And fee increases, imposed lightly enough by the university, but experienced harshly by students uncushioned by scholarships. And the name and function change, from 'Technology' to 'New South Wales': students resented their

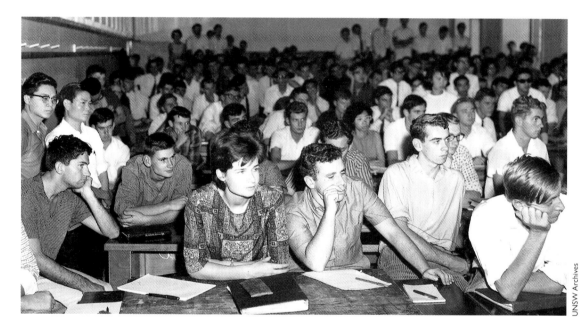

UNSW Archives

∧

Students listening to a lecture

1964

◁

International House residents

ca 1980s

UNSW Archives

not being consulted over this, and the implication that technology was not a sufficient base for a university: they were, after all, technologists themselves.

Character? A university of trams. The scattered nature of the campus, which could involve, at the beginning, not only Ultimo and Kensington, but East Sydney Tech, meant that the students (and some staff) were in a state of constant movement about the city. Spirit? Yes, but often akin to (as reminiscence puts it) that of being inmates of the same POW camp (there was, needlessly, originally even a barbed-wire perimeter fence at Kensington). And a weird sense of being thought second-rate, mixed with pride in creating something new, exciting and excellent, a bonding of outsiders. But outsiders with bridges. The most energetic student organisations of the 1950s, aside from the sporting, were religious — Evangelical Union, Newman Society, Student Christian Movement. And the Students' Union itself exhibited vigorous concern for overseas students, and their problems with immigration authorities, with housing, and welfare generally. The university pioneered the admission of Asian students and was to continue to attract far more than any other Australian university. In those early days it was the Australian students themselves, at the coal-face so to speak, who offered care and friendship, if at times crudely expressed, which made such admission real.

The importance of this Asian connection in the long term was to be immense. Their reception may have been a continuing generosity, reflecting well on an open-minded and big-hearted university, but it was also an investment which was to be amply repaid, both to the university itself and Australia generally. Asian students returned with an acquaintance of Australia which disposed them to an understanding and sympathy they might otherwise not have had. This was particularly important as they rose in their professions or came to exercise political power — a minister in the Malaysian cabinet, a minister in Indonesia, several Asian vice-chancellors. The same argument of offering Australia social awareness — as well as professional interaction — might be applied to the 250 Iranian PhD students introduced in the early 1990s: professional considerations apart, living and researching in the Australian environment was an endowment in trust to a happy future.

The 1960s provided ample entertainment, at home and abroad. In America campus agitation everywhere, in Europe students on the streets of Paris, Danny the Red, even Bernadette Devlin in Belfast. At home *Tharunka*, pornography, censorship, the challenge to the status quo; in Melbourne, Albert Langer. But also the dominance of rock-and-roll, the advent of big bands, new styles and fashions, sex, pot. All diversions for the young to swing their interests away from serious contentions such as might be beyond the translations of the Wizard. Besides, the university was moving to take more care, not only of its students, but of its graduates also. The first award for Alumni Achievement was made in 1971, recognising graduate involvement in the life of the community outside the university. The 1970s saw a marked student swing away from agitation towards concern with serious immediate problems, as evidenced in their 1971 submission to the Universities Commission: their wish that the university not become 'too big' and their urging that the building of the library-stack tower be a first priority. The library-stack tower was a self-interested practicality; the size matter was, also — if construed more diffusely. The feeling of unease in relation to growth was a new one, indicative of major change in the university's conception of itself. Big was good, but 'too big' — whatever that might mean — was worrisome. Whatever it meant, it suggested that students believed that a halt should be called. They were turning towards taking care of themselves rather than only the world. In 1974, 1000 students were caught by 'show cause' regulations, that is, required to prove to the university that they should be allowed to repeat subjects they had failed. By the early 1970s, 30 per cent of students were using student health and counselling services. More happily, from 1971 students were able to use the new Physical Education Recreation Centre, to which was added in 1980, with the aid of the U Committee, an indoor swimming pool: the weekly usage of the centre in 1974 was nearing 3000. And as to the much agitated matter of student consultation, when faculty elections were held, in 1973, students showed little interest. In Biological Science and Professional Studies, there were not even any nominations.

So had come, not to naught, for reasonable change had been brought about, but to something closely resembling it, the student extravagances of the mad 1960s. All Australian universities were, in the late 1960s, experiencing agitation for greater student representation in their government; Myers acted immediately, in 1969, in response. His initiatives were not stingy, and were at all levels but, most promptly, involved the setting up of staff–student committees in all schools. This — something of a pre-emptive master stroke — had the effect of localising and dispersing student agitation and focussing its diverse concerns on specific issues particular to the school experience. It placed responsible individual staff practices in the firing line of student criticism and complaint. It was a tactic (if it was that) which enfeebled and enraged student radicals, who much preferred a centralised authority they could denounce, confront and overthrow, according to the orthodox maxims of international socialist student power — infuriated, too, because it was so effective and successful. Students could talk directly to their own staff on both teaching and administrative issues. Students' Union officers of the 1960s and 1970s later testified that, to their surprise and gratitude, they had also found senior administrators approachable, friendly, and willing to discuss problems. Or simply, there was little basis for student frustration or unhappiness. With the university itself that is. In the wider context, the introduction of conscription and the highly contentious Vietnam War involvement from 1968 were issues which deeply agitated students generally and saw them acting in protest marches in the wider public arena.

By 1969, the Professorial Board was moving towards student representation on faculties, implemented in 1971. University Council was dragging its feet, partly because its members were isolated from daily pressure, but also because increasing student membership from one to three required amendment to the parliamentary Act. Baxter, and particularly Myers, had substantially forestalled the grievance base of student power by moving quickly to accommodate it; plus the magic of the Wizard. Disputes and abrasions occurred but lacked real steam. Hardly apathy; rather, no reason to support a tiny band of humourless revolutionaries. So, when in

∧

High-flying in the UNSW swimming pool

1988

July 1969 the *Bulletin* surveyed Australian university agitation, it saw the University of Sydney as running 'hot' but the University of New South Wales as 'cool'. And so it was to continue: the Students' Union devoted itself to helping clubs and child-care facilities — the House at Pooh Corner. At the Spartacist library lawn meeting in September 1971, students were urged to occupy the Chancellery: 20 voted yes, the remaining 1500 or so present dissolved into laughter.

Far from being disrupted, as militants sought, the business of the university continued as before. More autonomy for Wollongong and, most importantly, the appointment towards the end of 1969 of the barrister JH Wootten QC, as foundation professor and dean of Law, courses to begin in 1971. Building marched on, despite strikes and inflation, though inadequate to demands: many staff still shared rooms and thirty-four huts remained, relics of the First and Second World Wars. Hostel accommodation expanded, between 1968 and 1973: New, Warrane and Shalom. Nothing, it seemed, could halt the growth in students: 16,629 in 1970; in 1972, 18,085.

Quotas remained and were even extended: Arts, Commerce and Social Work from 1969. The Library had serious problems with space and staffing. Yet from outside the garden everything seemed rosy — and was. Drama was a continuing big success. The Parade Theatre was opened; the Old Tote Company, resident at the university, was nationally active — its audiences in 1970 were 106,000. Music, too, was an initiative

∧

Last night of the NIDA production, *The Man Who Came to Dinner* — final curtain for the Old Tote Theatre

31 October 1987

In happy voice — Patricia Brown conducts the Dowland Singers

1978

∨

which brought the university increasing public attention and repute. From its initial base as a service subject to General Studies, the Music department moved out first into performance programs for university lunchtime audiences, then to the wider public, this, by 1967, through the Grainger Consort, under the auspices of the U Committee. Through its Science Theatre, the university was becoming a frequent venue for outside artists. Increasingly, the Music department was becoming the generator of a wide range of musical initiatives, from electronic to early, focussing on the music of the seventeenth century in both performances and research. And opera. With the performance of Fauré's *Pénélope* in October 1997 University of New South Wales Opera achieved its forty-sixth production. These had begun in 1968 with Britten's *The Turn of the Screw* and had included many operas staged for the first time, or the first time in Australia. Still under the musical direction of Roger Covell, Baxter's appointment, who has been extraordinarily productive as a long-term investment both to the university's reputation and in Australian music.

However, one issue from the heydays of student discontent would not go away. It simmered on, powered by residual sectarianism, certainly by ideological considerations which went much deeper than those of crude student power. In 1966 *Tharunka*

The maestro himself —

Roger Covell

1977

The Australia Ensemble in foreign

parts — Red Square, Moscow

1985

162

had begun an attack on Opus Dei and its planned campus college, Warrane, opened in 1971, under the control of this Spanish-originated Roman Catholic organisation. Contention was to continue for almost a decade, until a University Council committee of inquiry vindicated the college and its practices in July 1974.

Various aspects of Warrane's character distinguished it from other colleges and affronted secular liberals. It was exclusively male. Its large staff of tutors, visits from public figures as lecturers, and studious atmosphere, together with strong sporting performances, were all in its favour, viewed neutrally. Viewed with hostility as against the prevailing student grain, Warrane was another matter. Its strict moral control — down to prohibition of women visitors in private rooms — gave it an ethos in contrast with other colleges and raised secular student protests against what was seen as petty and intrusive authoritarianism, but generally against the rigid and clericalist brand of Catholicism it was believed to represent. It was held to be un-Australian, fascist (it had links to, and a founder in Franco's Spain), was allegedly secretive and the enemy of freedom. In response, the college argued that it was conceived as much more than a place to live, but as offering the opportunity for Christian living, and a good study environment, friendship, and alertness to social responsibility. To provide this required not only a large staff of tutors, but a protective environment, free of the noise and the disruption of visitors, and the distraction of women, with regulations as to dress and closing times. In justification the college could point to its popularity with parents and the excellent academic and sporting results of its students.

There was a sense in which all this was a standing affront and challenge to emergent student mores, marked by anti-authoritarianism, anti-religion, and aggressive personal laxity. *Tharunka* led a venomous crusade against the college with a special anti-Warrane issue on 31 August 1971, following the college's expulsion of some of its tutors. 'Joe Must Go' was the slogan, referring to the master of the college, Dr

<|

Anti-Warrane graffiti

Science building

July 1974

RH Myers/UNSW Archives

Joe Martins. Invading students burnt him in effigy and defaced college buildings. Some forcibly entered the college. They demanded it be closed and Opus Dei banned. Martins's reasonable reply was ignored and protest continued, flaring up again in June 1972. Protests would simply not cease, eventually compelling the University Council to set up a committee of inquiry. Its report, exonerating the college from student charges, was itself the occasion of protest, with students occupying the Chancellery with the old demands — expel Opus Dei. But council's acceptance of the report, which concluded that the whole attack was unjustified and that any university interference would be wrong, effectively ended the Warrane affair. Thereafter, Warrane went its own way in peace. Those who did not like it, lumped it, with good enough grace. The issue had run out of steam.

Yet the matter was not trivial or irrelevant. It raised again the question of how a tiny group of students in *Tharunka* could sustain an agenda well past its use-by date: the era of student power had long ended and it was rationally and politically obvious that the anti-Warrane agitation could go nowhere, whatever the motions gone through. Why persevere with it then? Because there was nothing else. The Warrane hostilities raise the question of the role in such demonstrations of the rent-a-(very small)-crowd phenomenon: there was undoubtedly a number of 'revolutionaries' who appeared constantly at protests everywhere in Sydney. Yet, what of the home-grown group of militants grouped around *Tharunka*? Some were genuine radicals frustrated in their larger ambitions and seeing in Warrane a specifically local issue which they might champion with some hope of drawing on immediate and individual discontent — failing interest in overthrowing the world's repressive forces, at least Warrane was somewhere to begin, on the small scale. This was seen as the university's very own Achilles heel, appearing, as it was depicted, to jeopardise intellectual and personal freedoms. However, there was another contentious dimension, that of Warrane's Catholicism. To the anti-religious Warrane was Catholicism at its contemptible and brutishly deluded worst. But it was Catholics themselves who were more important in the *Tharunka* onslaught. This was in the aftermath of the Second Vatican Council, and liberal Catholics were sensitively anxious to rid the church, and themselves, of all that Opus Dei represented — clericalism, rigidity and conservatism in matters doctrinal and moral, apartness in society. Circumstances gave such sensitised Catholics a voice in *Tharunka*. Warrane's existence, and that of Opus Dei threatened their notion of what the Catholic Church should be, and they were prepared, indeed felt compelled, to push this matter, central to their own identity and self-regard, to its end, however futile and time-wasting for others. Curiously, in a university decidedly secular — apathy, distrust, and dissension had put paid to plans for a chapel — religion had entered the scene, through a back students' door.

Yes. But the place of religion on the University of New South Wales campus was a question much more complicated, subtle, more deeply divisive and long vexed than might be inferred from an eruption of student agitation. Anglican and Catholic chaplaincies — and student religious societies — were virtually coterminous with the beginnings of the university itself, carried over from the parishes embracing Ultimo.

In part, this was simply a reflection of the traditional assumptions then held about the nature of a university. It was anticipated unthinkingly that the new university would follow the pattern of the old: that is, associated with halls of residence conducted by various Christian denominations, as at the University of Sydney. But times, and expectations, had changed. Personalities and beliefs too. That early dynamic of New South Wales University, Philip Baxter, had no religious beliefs: the ideological progenitor of the university, the New South Wales Labor Party, was determinedly secular.

Baxter, and subsequent vice-chancellors, could see the use of religious chaplaincy in providing spiritual welfare for those students who wanted it, but his attitude towards the churches tended to be governed by what investment they might be prepared to bring to the university in terms of residential colleges. At this early stage, none. The major denominations, Anglican and Catholic, had neither money nor resources of manpower, and tended to see their university outreach as being sufficiently catered for by presence at the University of Sydney. Besides, their hierarchies were, to say the least, not notably intellectual — in the Catholic case, in Cardinal Gilroy, being uncomprehending if not hostile. Universities and intellectuals were trouble and likely to undermine faith. And anyhow, who was to know if this tiny and inferior Kensington outpost had any future? The post-war religious situation was one of increasing demands in servicing an exploding immigration population, particularly for a Catholicism already beset by the needs of financing its own schools. So, an acute shortage of both clergy and money — and imagination and disposition — interacted with a university disposed to ignore religion, to produce what? Nothing. Baxter's search for outside funds for residential accommodation took him to non-denominational sources, thus to the philanthropists Basser and Goldstein.

Nor was the subsequent Christian performance anything other than potentially alienating of university respect and trust — and destructive of the religion they affirmed in Christian common. The Anglicans were, and remained, riven by basic High Church/Low Church divisions, that is, between liberals and fundamentalists. A proposal to push for the introduction into the university of a Bachelor of Divinity course, surfacing originally in the 1960s but coming up again at various stages, always foundered on the hard rock of Low Church intransigencies — refusal to work with other churches, and unwillingness to water down or vary their dominance of the teaching in Moore College of the University of Sydney. Predictably, the idea of an ecumenical chapel in the university perished in essence on the same Anglican rock. Not only did the university have to cope with those who rejected the idea of a chapel as opposed to their form of worship — which it did by designating such a proposed building as a 'place' — it also had to deal with the rifts within Christians, notably those who would have no truck with ecumenism. Lest it be thought that the Warrane issue exhausted the supply of internal Christian division, division among Anglicans was no less intense, lacking only a public dimension. Report has it that this reached in the early 1980s a point at which Anglican New College and the Anglican chaplaincy had completely fallen out, to the extent that the college was unwilling to grant even the term 'Anglican' to a chaplaincy devoted to Bible fundamentalism so extreme and illiberal as to put the mission of the college under threat, and expose its own students to the

Fr King, Catholic chaplain, says Mass in the Roundhouse

1963

pressures of militant evangelism. This is not to trivialise the campus impact of Bible-oriented study groups, reaching somewhere about 2000–3000 students and staff. It is, however, to focus on the aggressive, missionary, confrontationist posture of some elements of the Bible movement, which some students of other belief or none regarded as an intrusive nuisance — for example, at library lawn lunch-hour relaxation.

Initially, and to this day, Catholic chaplaincy was extremely well-served by the Missionary Fathers of the Sacred Heart, the priests whose prominent head house was on the hill on the Kensington side, west of the university, and whose speciality was in Pacific missions. The university was very much in their physical proximity and, with the high number of Asian students, very much their spiritual territory as well. Very early, the third chaplain, John King, built up an extraordinary rapport with students, by way of the humanity and concern that illuminated his priesthood. The introduction of Opus Dei and Warrane caused him anguish rather than anger. He felt deeply worried, particularly after Opus Dei had made clear its wish to supplant him, that students and their spiritual life, must suffer, and the wider interests of religion at the university be placed in hazard.

Arguably, this is what occurred. The image of Opus Dei as a secret, conspiratorial society, potentially malevolent and corruptive of true Catholic life, a snare for the unwary, some kind of unknown and nameless threat, percolated into popular Catholic visions of 'the university' writ large. As late as 1987, nuns at a prominent Sydney Catholic girls' school warned their university-destined pupils against having anything to do with the Catholic chaplaincy at SYDNEY University, dominated as it allegedly was by the fearsome Opus Dei. The confusion compounds the ignorance and error, but points to the widespread misconceptions generated by what had happened in regard to Warrane.

At the time, within the university hierarchy, attitudes towards religion were hardly favourable. Myers became aware, very early in his vice-chancellorship, of the problems surrounding Warrane, specifically of a student meeting of about 3000 in the Roundhouse, to which it was proposed they march on Warrane *en masse*. Warned of this, and waiting in the Metallurgy building, Myers slipped in to the meeting, was spotted ('Rupert is here') and called on to speak. He spoke on the freedoms of a university, his willingness as a last resort to call police onto campus, the need for tolerance and acceptance of diversity. The students decided not to march. On returning home that evening, Myers was asked by his daughter if he had suffered any injury. Only that caused by his knees knocking together, he replied. It is easy to forget the psychological toll exacted by the tension of confronting and managing the ugly student aggression and menace of potential violence of those days. And in Myers's case the first such incident in his vice-chancellorship was generated in relation to matters associated with religion. He never forgot it. Not surprising that religion was a subject, or social area, which did not fill him with enthusiasm.

But the faults of neglect or rancour lay not only with religion. That dedicated, long-serving Catholic chaplain, John King, had made a special cause of the building of a non-denominational chapel at the university. He extracted an undertaking from a none-too-willing Baxter that this would proceed (it had been in the air since 1957), to the extent of commissioning an architect's report and site plan in 1963 — only to see the plan lapse, and, in 1966, the site given over to a car park. Distrusting the university's future intentions, King managed to get Baxter to accept $100 towards an eventual chapel appeal, with the idea of pinning him down. Baxter retired without honouring his agreement, though at one stage he came up with the idea of designing it himself, providing plans and sketches of what the chaplains agreed 'looked like an elephant house'. This left an unfilled commitment, which did not please his successor, Myers. He resorted to a proposal which the chaplains of all denominations thought to be an attempt to sabotage the idea by inflating it to absurd and financially impossibly proportions, an insincere temporising device. In 1976 King's successor, Michael Fallon was asking Myers to provide at least 'a quiet room' in the university's just announced Master Plan. He received in reply a vague assurance of general goodwill and was assured that his idea was 'interesting'. The Anglican Bishop Reid took up the matter with equal lack of success, though his letter made clear that churches other than the Catholic and Anglican and Methodist seemed little interested. All this was preceded by other schemes, and proposals, even from the Students' Union — all to no effect.

By the time of Michael Birt in 1982 the Anglican chaplaincy's militant Bible class and its refusal to cooperate with all other chaplains had united them by protest but rendered any 'chapel' idea out of the question. When it came to the pursuit of the enquiry, initiated and chaired by the deputy chancellor, Jessica Milner Davis — 'Campus Life and Environment', reporting in 1984 — the chaplains were asked their opinion on bettering spiritual life, but the report merely noted the absence, amongst a brief list of other things, of a chapel. Still, the chaplains, long-resident in the last of the remaining huts, were rewarded in the mid 1990s with an accommodation upgrade to rooms in the Union building, the Square House, and the designation 'The Religious Centre'. Most (including Buddhists and the Islamic Society) operated from there, though some (Jewish and Uniting Church and Greek Orthodox) had separate arrangements. This was a situation, it appears, with which they were all, more or less, happy. The university proclaimed its partnership with the rest of the community in pluralism. But it also, having a mind to the divisive potential of religion, issued the chaplains with firm and clear guidelines for behaviour. On all sides, the university's included, it had been an unhappy history: the University of New South Wales and religion did not mix. Though this, in some crucial ways, and not without some success, was not for lack of religions trying. All three religious colleges had public lecture programs seeking to bring together religion and secular university concerns. Bruce Kaye, in his mastership of New College (1983–93) was particularly energetic in his sponsorship of lectures and seminars on values and issues applying to matters of public interest. But Shalom and Warrane were also active in these religious-oriented and intellectual essays into the secular university and public domain.

By the mid-1970s the university's main problems continued to be buildings, delays and escalating costs, and the need to accommodate with appropriate services — food outlets, banking, a stationery shop — the growing move within the university's population to Upper Campus. Otherwise, things were as usual, more or less. The big success was Unisearch: in 1973, for instance, it investigated over a thousand projects. And good-bye to Wollongong, an independent university under Michael Birt, in 1975.

The real news was on funding. A revolution. The States bowed out. As from the beginning of 1974, the Australian federal government assumed responsibility for the full funding of tertiary education. The outcome was the ending of that special relationship with the State government which had so advantaged the earlier years of the university, and the beginning of the centralised federal control, which was to grow by the late 1980s into Canberra bureaucratic dictatorship. At the time few realised

The long-serving
Union hairdresser,
Louis the Barber —
Louis Solomon
1976

168

<|

Student regards

cashier with disbelief

and dismay

February 1980

just how intrusive and prescriptive this power would become. Indeed, many welcomed it, seeing it with the euphoria associated with the 'Whitlam Years', the period
of the Labor prime ministership of EG Whitlam from 1972 to 1975 and the range
of radical social reforms over which he presided. For the university this seemed an
incredible bonanza — the abolition of student fees, increases in staff numbers, pay
increases, library expansion, money everywhere. In those golden, halcyon days, the
view overwhelmingly held by staff was that at last the university, and themselves personally were entering into their just due, proper recognition of their true community value. Nobody paused to wonder if that community — or its parliamentary
representatives — might come to see this as unjustified prodigality. It seems to have
been assumed that things would be more or less unchanged, the book-keeping differently organised, but that under federal control universities would remain their
own separate and independent worlds. Who is to say that universities should be more
percipient and perceptive than others? Despite their dedication to things of the
mind? It was an obvious lesson of law and history that money meant power, and the

aggregation of financial responsibility to the Commonwealth signalled the beginning of a different ball game. No longer could one source of money be played against the other. Close relationships within State boundaries were out. The rule of the Canberra centraliser was on the way in. Although tempered by harsh experience by that time, the prime ministership of Labor's Paul Keating (1991–96) cast a Whitlamesque spell over university staff, a mesmerised anticipation that he would restore the Whitlam world and their rightful place within it. Sad, fruitless hope.

At virtually the same time, the university was beginning to experience its own internal revolution. Its atmosphere was changing. The extraordinary dynamic impetus which had driven the university helter-skelter through its first twenty-five years, was gearing down. Where, before, the dominant theme had been one of constant expansion, by 1975 the university authorities themselves conceded that the emphasis was shifting into consolidation, of maintaining what already existed. This was an unaccustomed role, and one to which it did not take readily. After a quarter of a century of hectic rushing ahead it must now stand still. This novelty was not altogether welcome. To keep the astonishing juggling act in the air called for qualities different from the skills required to get it there.

However, there was one last innovation of immense importance, Law, a faculty which would have major importance in contributing to the society of the future. Here the key figure was JH Wootten, first professor and dean of the faculty. Wootten, appointed in 1969, was no mere Sydney barrister. He had a diverse and restless legal experience. Initially a public service clerk, he had studied law part-time at the University of Sydney. He had become active in the University Union and Law Society; then a protégé of Professor Julius Stone, later influential in bringing Wootten to the University of New South Wales. But before that he had amassed a wide practical knowledge in aspects of the law involved in public life. John Kerr (later governor-general) sought him out to join the School of Pacific Administration to serve in New Guinea, lecturing to patrol officers. Then back to Sydney to work at the Bar with Kerr, mainly in advocacy for — and against — unions, and in matters

RH Myers/UNSW Archives

<|

Law and order —

prominent

student activist,

Peter Livesey (left),

and dean of Law,

Professor Garth Nettheim

March 1977

of industrial arbitration, drawing him into the world of governments, unions and large employers. Versatile, with an underlying disposition of radicalism, Wootten knew the movers and shakers. Formidable, brimming with ideas, he was anything but the dry-as-dust lawyer.

The move to establish Law dated from 1963 and Baxter's interest. It was also part of inter-university rivalry. Sydney decided that its law school would remain in the city rather than move on campus, as a device to prevent another university taking over its vacated city base. This was short-term thinking based on the erroneous assumption that law would remain a part-time degree. And in the competition for possession of a new Faculty of Law, Macquarie was no match for the older and wiser New South Wales.

Approached by Myers to found a school of law at the University of New South Wales, Wootten made his stance clear: 'Well, the only thing I know about legal education is how bad my own was'. This was to be the dynamic for what followed. He had sharp memories of courses and lectures at Sydney which were 'pathetic': silly rote learning of useless information — only Stone was exciting. There was far more to Wootten's vision than mere reaction against Sydney, but that was crucial. Central was his insistence on full-time staff for New South Wales University: part-time lecturing came from busy practitioners who had no time to devote to preparing lectures or relating to students.

But it was his experimental outlook, and that of those he employed (such as Garth Nettheim and Tony Blackshield from the University of Sydney Law school, and that young high-flyer, Ron Sackville, from Melbourne), that made the University of New South Wales Faculty of Law distinct, innovative, and increasingly highly regarded. It was Wootten's prestige and confidence which overcame the obstacles which any departure from the traditional and orthodox always encounters. It was he who piloted the new degree through the scepticism of a profession uncertain of whether it was law which was being taught, or sociology (and voiced the misgivings), and through a university system of authority resistant to Law's pushy and maverick ways. Behind this lay Wootten's belief in a wider role for law in society, building not only on his rejection of Sydney's narrow pedantries, but on the Monash experience of combined degrees — and on his own self-image of not being an academic.

So the Law degree came via the student's progression through Arts and Commerce in their first years, most of the law subjects later, a structure which, given the higher entry requirements for Law, had a spin-off of raising enrolment standards and student performance in those servicing faculties. Law injected a university-wide enhancement of student quality — and some understandable envy.

Law students? For them, halcyon days: the University of New South Wales experience maximised and transformed. Instant tradition: you made it yourself of Sydney concrete and high-rise, the freedom of the airport lounge, passengers passing through. Bands on the library lawn, a ramshackle Esme's, vending machines to abuse and plunder, the clientele a mixture of inner-city punks and Eastern suburbs new money; few from the North Shore; black, the prevailing dress code. Small classes and social facilities meant that everybody knew everybody; the ninth floor, set

aside for students, even billiard tables, seminal to the life of the place, coffee, ciga-
rette smoke everywhere, plans for this and that — debating, assignations, sport from
the orthodox to the ridiculous (frisbees, inner-tube water games), organising common intellectual activities (*Poetic Justice*, the student newsletter, and their *Annual*),
and talk, always talk. It was student nirvana, did they but know it. Most carried some
of it into later life, at least the wide acquaintance and the intellectual liberation.

To which the courses themselves made a vital contribution: what Law dispensed
was less a training than an education. Wootten and his cohorts saw law in relation to
society. This demanded a teaching program which assumed graduates going not
merely into private practice but also into corporations, governments, public affairs,
areas requiring flexible knowledge. Law's compulsory core would be as small as
possible, electives numerous and wide-ranging, content broad: so, criminology covered Foucault, Kafka, Truman Capote, even Pink Floyd's 'The Wall'. Students
would be active participants in their own courses and teaching. Class-time would be
interactive. It would presume prior reading and aim at enhancing understanding.
Therefore there must be small classes, dedicated and effective teachers and an end to
assessment via end-of-year examination. Small wonder the envy of others; but did
they have the Law staff's degree of commitment?

Conscious of the radical departure they were making from orthodoxy, the early
deans, Whitmont and Nettheim, were at pains to explain to law firms and regional
law societies the advantages of their graduates. They might not have narrow particular knowledge, but they had a wide grasp of law, could research it well, and were
skilled in argument. The performance of their graduates bore them out in the new
wider world of law dawning in the 1970s: by the 1990s Sydney's top ten law firms
preferred University of New South Wales graduates.

One of Law's manifestations was a direct Law faculty creation, the Aboriginal
Legal Service, established in 1970–71 by what Nettheim describes as a 'happy coa-
lescence' of academics, practitioners and Aboriginal people. Again, Wootten was
pivotal. He had been approached by two young tutors in touch with Aborigines concerned about police harassment in Redfern. Wootten, just back from the United
States, where the shopfront law movement had just begun, and with his New Guinea
experience, organised an interested group and wrote to every lawyer in the State,
seeking volunteer help. It was an initiative which drew federal government support,
and emulation in other States — and considerable public interest. It was he, too,
who persuaded the University Council to set up, in 1971, a special admission program for Aboriginal people.

Myers approved Wootten's vision, seeing in it what Law was to become — a
faculty internationally recognised as Australia's leading law school, distinctive, innovative, a presence in the Asia–Pacific area. The university (sometimes grudgingly)
gave it what it asked for — exemption from the General Studies requirement, three-
year deans when the practice was generally for permanence, six professors by 1972.
The only major thing it did not supply was a dedicated building: Law remained the
permanent house-guest of the Library. But then, in a spiritual sense, it was an
epitome of best practices, a shining example of the university's window on the world.

5

STEADY STATE
1976–87

1976

1976

Rhodes scholarships become available to women. • Board of Studies in Science and Mathematics established. • Department of Behavioural Science established as a separate unit. • Cornea and Contact Lens Research Unit established. • New research centres, for — Applied Economic Research; Biomedical Engineering; Study and Distribution of Electrical Energy • Solarch House Mk I constructed at Randwick Research Lab. • The journal *University of NSW Occasional Papers* launched. • Freislich Dam built at Fowler's Gap. • Rugby Union Club is first UNSW sports team to tour overseas. • First UNSW Fun Run. • At Broken Hill Division, WS & LB Robinson University College stage IV completed. •
NEW DEGREES Master of Health Planning (replacing Diploma in Health Administration). MBA and MPA courses approved for Australian Graduate School of Management (AGSM). •
CAMPUS IMPROVEMENTS Library stack tower completed.

JANUARY Mr Justice Gordon H Samuels becomes chancellor, and Dr FM Mathews,

deputy chancellor. • Department of Food Technology becomes a full school. • Fowler's Gap leased in perpetuity to UNSW as arid zone research centre.
AUGUST First Law students graduate. Pat O'Shane is the first Aboriginal person in Australia to graduate in law.
OCTOBER Science building and lecture theatres renamed the Mathews building and Mathews theatres, after the deputy chancellor. • Upper campus parking station, stage II begun.

1977

Redfern Legal Centre established. • Dowland Singers formed. • Optometry becomes a separate school and J Lederer appointed foundation professor of Optometry. • Schools of Highway Engineering and Transportation and Traffic form a single School of Transport and Highways. • Radiation and General Safety Unit established. • Construction of Solarch House at Fowler's Gap. • AGSM receives first student intake. • CYBER 171 computer acquired to augment the overloaded CYBER 72. • Electronic book security system and microfiche catalogues introduced to

campus libraries. • Social Sciences and Humanities Library set up as a separate entity from the Undergraduate Library. • *Focus* newsletter launched by Public Affairs Unit. • Sir Arthur George Loan Fund set up for students in need. • Students' Union acquires premises in Barker Street for a second child-care centre. •
NEW DEGREES Master of Science and Society; (pass) MA in History; Master of General Studies; BSc.DipEd. in School of Education, replaces BSc (Ed). •
CAMPUS IMPROVEMENTS Five all-weather tennis courts built and night-lighting installed. Asian food bar, self-service barbecue and health-food bar introduced.

MAY Upper campus parking station, stage II completed. • Kensington Lecture Series (lectures by academic staff to HSC students) begins, initiated by Io Myers with the U Committee.

1978

RJ Heffron dies (as Education minister, one of those originally instrumental in establishing the university). • U Committee endows annual UNSW Art Prize and Travelling Scholarship. •

AH Willis retires as pro-vice-chancellor. • Professor RM Golding appointed pro-vice-chancellor. • Graduate School of the Built Environment created (Faculty of Architecture). • New research centres, for — Biomedical Engineering (now constituted though founded in 1976); Energy Research and Information (ERDIC); Social Welfare Research. • Faculty of Commerce receives first wordprocessor in the university. • Committee on Experimental Procedures Involving Human Subjects established. • First mature age, special admission students graduate. • The University Academic Staff Association registers as a trade union and industrial organisation under the New South Wales Arbitration Act. • Students' Union appoints full-time Welfare/Research officer. •
NEW DEGREES Master of Biomedical Engineering; Master of Librarianship in Information Science; Master of Educational Administration; Bachelor of Medical Science; BA.DipEd; BComm.DipEd; joint Bachelor's degrees, in — Commerce (Marketing)–Laws; Science–Engineering (Civil Engineering). BA (Mil) and BSc (Mil) redesignated BA and BSc in the Faculty of Military Studies. • CAMPUS IMPROVEMENTS New fence constructed along Botany Street frontage; construction of swimming pool begun.

Michael Birt addressing students
1982

Orientation Week
1978

JULY Department of Industrial Arts transferred from Faculty of Professional Studies to Faculty of Architecture.

OCTOBER Medical building extension completed.

24 OCTOBER New wing opened of Institute of Administration's Derwent building at Little Bay.

DECEMBER Agreement signed with FACOM Aus. Ltd for the administration's existing data-processing equipment to be replaced (in mid-1979) by an M160S system.

12 DECEMBER Old Tote Theatre Company mounts its last production (having gone into liquidation on 23 August).

1979

A university invention — a separation membrane — wins a prize at the 4th Annual World Fair for Technology Exchange in Atlanta, USA. • Faculty of Arts contributes two conjoint editors and other staff to the Australian Bicentennial History Project • Professor AA Hukins appointed first dean of Professional Studies. • Health and safety measures adopted: an Occupational Health and Safety policy statement; an Emergency Preparedness Procedures program, with Zone Emergency Control officers appointed; a Biological Hazards Committee. • NEW DEGREES Master of Archives Administration (research); Master of Built Environment (research and coursework); Master of Paediatrics; Bachelor of Social Science. • CAMPUS IMPROVEMENTS new fences — brick on the High Street frontage and metal fencing along sections of Anzac Parade and High Street frontages; work commenced on Barker Street entrance.

JANUARY The Department of Behavioural Science (Faculty of Commerce) renamed Organisational Behaviour.

APRIL At the Australian Graduate School of Management (AGSM) 34 students, the first intake, complete their MBA and MPA courses.

JUNE AGSM building begun.

AUGUST Japanese Economic and Management Studies Centre established.

1980

University of New South Wales Ensemble formed (later called the Australia Ensemble). • JB Thornton retires as pro-vice-chancellor. • School of Electrical Engineering renamed Electrical Engineering and Computer Science. • New School of Chemical Engineering and Industrial Chemistry established. • Department of Ceramic Engineering transferred to the School of Metallurgy. • School of Transport and Highways renamed the Department of Transport Engineering and incorporated into the School of Civil Engineering. • University Oral History Project commenced. • Child Studies Unit established. • New centres, for — Industrial Relations Research; Social Welfare Research (opened). • Barraduc Field Station purchased. • First female president of UNSW Staff Association — Dr Jane Morrison. • CCTV converts to colour. • First students enrol in the combined Science–Medicine degree.

FEBRUARY University Archives established; LT Dillon appointed foundation university archivist.

1 MARCH Swimming pool opened (having been completed on 3 December 1979).

DECEMBER AGSM building completed.

1981

Collegium Musicum formed. • Dr Jessica Milner Davis becomes deputy chancellor — the first alumna and first woman to hold this position. • RE Vowels retires as pro-vice-chancellor. • Centre for Research in Finance established. • Department of Transport Engineering moves to Kensington campus. • Institute of Languages relocated to Randwick • Cornea and Contact Lens Research Unit set up at Randwick. • NEW DEGREES/DIPLOMAS MApplSc and graduate diploma, both in Arid Lands Management; Master of Architectural Design; Graduate Diploma in Surveying; Diploma in Information Management (in Librarianship or Archives Administration). • CAMPUS IMPROVEMENTS for the disabled, a ramp to the Civil Engineering building — the last building not to have one.

SELECTED EVENTS

Open-air tutorial
1979

Laboratory attire
1970s–80s

JANUARY Professor HR Vallentine appointed pro-vice-chancellor. • I Way appointed registrar.
FEBRUARY 50,000th degree awarded to Jane Ingham, MBBS.
23 APRIL Aboriginal Law Research Unit opened.
7 MAY Formal agreement made with federal government to establish a university college within the Australian Defence Force Academy (ADFA).
JULY Faculty of Law opens 'shopfront' legal clinic in Kingsford. • AGSM opened. • Dedication of the Rupert Myers Hall of Residence. • Kanga's House opened (completed in 1980).
31 JULY Sir Rupert Myers retires as vice-chancellor.
3 AUGUST LM Birt appointed vice-chancellor.
OCTOBER Centre for Remote Sensing established.
NOVEMBER Council decides to close the university's Broken Hill Division.

1982

University of New South Wales Ensemble releases its first recording and tours the United States. • Professor A Carrington appointed pro-vice-chancellor. • Professor G Wilson appointed rector, University College, ADFA. • New one-year course in the Faculty of Law for Aboriginal field officers, made available with funding from the Department of Aboriginal Affairs. • New research centres, for — Building Research; Study of Law and Technology. • Centre for Aboriginal students established. • Educational Testing Centre established as a body separate from TERC. • Grand-scale mass spectrometer installed in Faculty of Science. • New central processor for CYBER 171 and three new VAX 11/780 acquired. • Advisory committee on Equal Opportunity in Employment established. • Library cutbacks result in student protest 'sleep-in'.

MARCH New centres, for — Nerve-Muscle Research; Joint Micro-electronics Research
MAY Courses and Career Day held for the first time. • Report tabled of the federal government Committee of Inquiry into Management Education (Ralph Inquiry).
28 JUNE ADFA Interim Council holds its inaugural meeting.
I AUGUST New NIDA centre, to be erected on western campus, approved by federal government.
NOVEMBER Io Myers Studio opens. • Bicentennial History Project launched officially by the governor-general. • Biomedical Engineering Centre laboratory opened.

1983

The Baxter Years, a university history by Professor AH Willis, is published. • UNSW Ensemble renamed Australia Ensemble. • John T Waterhouse Herbarium Museum opens. • First university Corporate Plan. • New research centres, for — Immunology; Management Research and Development. • University enters into quantity-purchase arrangements for IBM and NEC personal computers. •
NEW DEGREES MApplSc (in Mining Geomechanics and Exploration Geochemistry); MSc (in Architecture); MSc (Industrial Design); MA (Hons) History; MA (Hons) Sociology; MSc (Psych); Master of Engineering Science (in Surveying); Master of Safety Science; Master of Health Personnel Education; Master of Science and Society (Hons) •
CAMPUS IMPROVEMENTS University Union opens the Blue Room cafeteria, Commerce courtyard; Dangerous Goods Stores constructed.

MAY Council agrees to the university affiliating with the Garvan Institute of Medical Research, St Vincent's Hospital (effective 1985).
AUGUST Ms R Squirchuk appointed director of EEO Unit.
19 NOVEMBER Professorial Board sponsors a seminar on the future of general education.
DECEMBER Council decides not to impose quotas on overseas student enrolments.

1984

High Street bus services introduced. • Professor J Ronayne and Professor M Chaikin both appointed pro-vice-chancellors. •. New research centres, for — Continuing Medical Education; Petroleum Engineering Studies; Study of Law and Technology. • *Alumni Papers* launched. • Oral History officer appointed, in Archives. • PABX telephone system

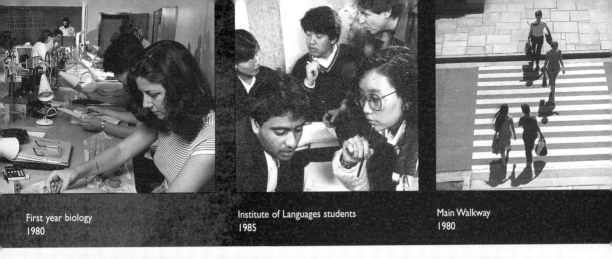

First year biology
1980

Institute of Languages students
1985

Main Walkway
1980

replaced. • Broken Hill Division — final year of teaching. •
NEW DEGREES/DIPLOMAS MApplSc Food Engineering; Master of Industrial Design; Master of Nursing Administration. BComm (in Accounting, Accounting & Finance, Accounting & Information Systems); Bachelor of Economics & Econometrics, of Economics & Finance, of Economics & Industrial Relations; BSc in Aeronautical Engineering, in Mining Geology, in Design Studies. Other Bachelor's degrees: of Information Systems, of Engineering, of Industrial Engineering, of Mechanical Engineering, of Naval Architecture. Graduate Diploma in Remote Sensing.

1985

The UNSW (Amendment) Act (NSW), 1985, provides for a 29-member council (formerly 44 members). • University of New South Wales Literary Fellowship established — believed to be the first such fellowship totally subsidised by a tertiary institution in Australia. • Exchange agreement established between UNSW and UCLA (University of California, Los Angeles) in all academic areas of mutual interest. • Pedestrian cross-

ings instituted in High Street. • I Way (formerly registrar) becomes deputy principal. J Gannon (formerly associate registrar) redesignated registrar. • Faculty of Applied Science regroups into six schools. • Council decides to impose quotas on overseas student enrolment in 7 of 78 undergraduate courses. • New research centres, for — Australasian Theatre Studies; Cardiovascular Research; Community Medicine in the Illawarra Region; French Australian Studies; Quantitative Research into Teaching and Learning; Safety Science. • FTICR Mass spectrometer and 500 MH NMR spectrometer acquired in the School of Chemistry. • Undergraduate library integrated into research libraries. • Broken Hill Division — last graduation ceremony. •
NEW DEGREE Master of Welfare Policy (in School of Social Work).

FEBRUARY U Committee launches new fundraising activity — the sale of memorabilia.
JULY Division of Postgraduate Extension Studies reconstituted as the Continuing Education Support Unit.
4 NOVEMBER Equal Opportunity advisers scheme begins.

1986

Federal Affirmative Action (Equal Opportunity for Women) Act, 1986. • School of History launches Local History Coordination Project (later renamed Community History Project). • Library introduces computerised Book Availability Terminals (BATs). • NSW Cancer Council transfers the Carcinogenesis Unit to UNSW. • Biomedical Lecture Theatre renamed the BJ Ralph Theatre as part of 30th anniversary of the School of Biological Sciences. • New research centres, for — Aboriginal Law (replacing the Research Unit); Contemporary Asia; Entomological Research and Insecticide Technology; Experimental Neurology; Human Rights; Industrial Laser Applications; Information Technology Research and Development; Manufacturing and Automation; Marine Science; National Drug and Alcohol Research; Taxation Business and Investment Law Research; Waste Management. • AM 500 Nuclear Magnetic Resonance spectrometer installed in School of Biological Sciences. • A special branch of the Property Division takes

specific responsibility for building and grounds maintenance. • Faculty of Military Studies staff and resources transfer to new University College at ADFA. •
NEW DEGREES/DIPLOMAS Doctor of Music and Master of Music; MComm (Hons) in Finance, in Information Systems; MComm program also revised to allow for greater specialisation in subject areas. Bachelor's degrees in Petroleum Engineering, in Metallurgical Engineering. Graduate diplomas in Materials Engineering, Textile Technology, Paediatrics.

9 DECEMBER Final event for the Faculty of Military Studies, at Royal Military College, Duntroon — the graduate parade and ceremony.
11 DECEMBER Inaugural graduation parade and opening ceremony of the Australian Defence Force Academy.

SELECTED EVENTS

Happy students on the library lawn 1983

teady in the sense of established, settled, stable, balanced in selfhood, such was the mood of the late 1970s and 1980s. Not in the sense of all being well, untroubled. The university was, with difficulty and some loss, maintaining its balance at the top of the university tree, threatened by the unsympathetic forces of Canberra bureaucratic parsimony, a famishment common to all Australian universities. At the top, because it was among Australia's largest and, in some faculties, best; vying with, and soon to overtake the University of Sydney, in a creative rivalry which always had a sharp edge. And always had its own atmosphere, ethos and style, and tenancy of time. Brash, pushy, a bit crude, drinkers of beer rather than dry sherry, something of a class thing, as in public versus private schools, so was the University of New South Wales. Yet, undeniably, and in the common perception, achieving excellence. To do this, it did little more than pursue the intrinsic demands of its subjects: reputation was a by-product, not deliberate puffery. Not for it this absurdity of Macquarie University's 1996 main roads billboards — 'Oxford in Sydney'. No: it was still Kenso at Kensington, wire-mesh perimeter fences and all. Very little gentrification, and what there was tended to be upgrading, reasonable refurbishment. That the University of New South Wales was able to carry this off, and prosper, was, given the way the world works, something more than excellence, though that, growing throughout the university, was the basic foundation. It was the quality of men at the top, Myers, Birt, later Niland, and a small group of chosen consuls.

Myers was the activist, man in a hurry, better the wrong decision than none at all, and him to make it. Birt was the ponderer, the consulter, slow but steady wins the race — if a race is what one is really engaged in. Baxter had seen the value of (and, by the limits of one man's energy, been compelled into using) able lieutenants, who would have specific areas of responsibility. In Baxter's case, these were David Phillips, Rupert Myers, John Clark, Al Willis — all men with their own individuality and talents, nevertheless all Baxter's men, implementing his policies, being, if independently, of one mind with him. Baxter permeated all, through his dominant persona, creating the illusion of vanquishment of all other authority levels. The Myers style was more that of a feudal king than a dictator, a hegemonic baron with his advisers, leading his Vice-Chancellor's Advisory Committee (VCAC) from the front. For deans, the VCAC was a command performance, not to be missed unless at death's door. Which was odd given the tedious nature of the meetings, and the fact that it was merely an advisory body: the vice-chancellor determined the agenda, and seeking advice did not necessarily mean taking it. Still, the perception was of decision-making power. Besides, no dean would absent himself when other deans were discussing matters of university importance.

That committee, in its enduring and present form, dated from April 1960, a development from an 'equipment and supplies' committee of 1950: the development makes clear its subsidiary role. The 1960 committee was a step further from changes made in 1957 to draw on the advice of deans of faculties, with the bursar and registrar in attendance, to meet weekly on Wednesday at 9:30 a.m. Given that deans were appointed by the vice-chancellor, the character of its general commonality was predictable. No major problems were expected; none came. The 1960 committee dealt not only with equipment but with everything else — buildings, personnel, appointments, the lot. Above all, the committee was a forum for exchange of views amongst the vice-chancellor (who chaired it), the bursar, registrar, and deans, the university's power-holders. Information and pronouncements from on high, in-fighting and horse-trading going on at the level below, with the deans' role, under Baxter, that of being informed and little consulted, the avenue down which university decisions and policy were conveyed to heads of schools and thence to staff. The committee was also a way of off-loading lesser decision-making onto tried and trusted senior staff. Nevertheless, it developed a very powerful life of its own and a club-like atmosphere, extending from its formal deliberations to the meeting table and lunch asides that accompanied it, and the telephone traffic that followed it. Weekly meetings made for close and effective administrative invigilance. Through the VCAC the autocracy was better informed and more immediate in operation, the deans more taken up in the whole university enterprise.

This system relied on the vice-chancellor's projection of mastery. Indeed, Baxter drew the idea from his industrial experience at ICI in Britain of senior management meetings, where decisions flowed from informed confidence. Myers generated this through his courtesy, willingness to listen, and the respect accorded to one so obviously in charge, so patently in command of the institution. In the reminiscence of others — and the image occurs more than once — not a sparrow could fall within the university but that he would know of it. Myers did not abuse his reputation for God-like omniscience. Much of his knowledge he kept to himself, or used discreetly — quiet admonition of errant staff, sympathetic concern in calamity: my wife gratefully remembers his telephoned kindness during my own illness. Much went into contriving that atmosphere of controlled consolidation that steadied a new exuberant university onto sure feet, in a world whose previous momentum had stopped.

That university sparrows could fly or fall was an omniscience not only of Myers himself but of his fellow reconnoitring aviators, viewing the scene from above. Bluff, honest, solid, long-serving (twenty-eight years) Al Willis was an admirable carry-over from Baxter's founding fathers, the subtitle of his book of history, *The Baxter Years* (1983) making clear his loyalties and the ground on which he stood. Legacy also, but only of Baxter's last year, was Rex Vowels, who was to become virtually Myers's other persona within the university—omnipresent, bland, hard-working, curious mixture of the apparently saturnine and the carefully caring, quiet power repository. Vowels suffered a heart problem. The stress and overwork associated with his position eventually killed him. One of Vowels's great achievements was that of getting the university to face the cost of the new technology in the 1970s. The early computers were big, required massive floor-space and, above all, needed expensive air conditioning — and astronomical sums of money, so much (several million) as to deprive everybody of any funds for research. Vowels sold this new and future-oriented idea to engineers and scientists much more taken up with immediate projects, on the basis of 'too bad, we've got to have it'. Certainly, it was an immediate and continuously expanding drain — but,

Movers and shakers — (from left to right) Registrar GL Macauley, Pro-Vice-Chancellor Rex Vowels,

Students' Union President John Green, Associate Registrar John Gannon, Deputy Registrar John Fitzgerald

1974

as Vowels saw, and eventually persuaded Myers, it was necessary, indeed obligatory.

Vowels's services to the university were immense. He had 'old-fashioned' standards of responsibility best summed up in the joke of the time — that he rang up the day after he retired to see if the university was still alright. The story points not only to his centrality in affairs but to his acceptance of a sense of real and personal commitment to what he did: a thoroughly decent man of unobtrusive power.

Other deputies — Wicken and Golding come to mind — coped only by commencing work every day at 6 a.m. Their duties went well beyond the merely onerous. Silly and uninformed university witticisms were generated even by that degree of dedication. Ray Golding was the butt of one such joke. He lived some small distance from the university. It was said of him, grossly unfairly, that he arrived in the dark, went home in the dark, and stayed in the dark all day. Golding, the nicest and most gentle of men, was an easy target for such cruel cleverness: it was simply impossible to deal with correspondence, decisions, and the like, in days crammed with meetings, without such a regimen. Slug-a-bed academics simply did not care or comprehend. They were probably ignorant also of Golding's vital role in bringing about crucial positive changes in the university's history.

Golding, a physical chemist of extraordinary breadth and energy, joined a school which was the largest in Australia: by the mid 1980s it had risen to about fifty-five staff. In 1998, with honorary associates, it was still well into the forties, and had long had a major international reputation. He had a brilliant talent for lateral organisation, a gift for being able to see more efficient and less troublesome ways of doing things. First he applied himself to his own faculty, ironing out needless duplication between Science and Applied Science. He soon rid himself of the cumbrous absurdity of having to sign every requisition himself, and delegated to responsible staff. Then he set up the Board of Studies in Science and Mathematics in 1976 as a coordinating body for science courses, construed very wide — maths, engineering, medicine, commerce, arts, and social sciences. It enabled students to plot their own path through the maze of subjects, to their own preference even into science and society, and to the enormous public advantage of the university's Science faculty; indeed, enhancing the reputation and image of the university in general. That genius for applying and encouraging staff initiatives and cooperative ventures, Golding then, in 1976, applied to the fostering of centres, of which there are currently seventy-two, ranging from the large to the very small. These enabled staff to pursue interdisciplinary interests across various fields.

But Golding's major innovation was budgetary, to give power and responsibility to deans of faculties. Up to 1979–80 the university had no budget, in the sense of a document presented to University Council: Myers carried it in his head, exhibiting that prodigious detailed knowledge of the university, its needs and possibilities, which was his hallmark. Golding saw that this was not a fruitful future course, and that devolution to deans of the allocation of faculty segments had immense advantages. He piloted this successfully with the Faculty of Military Studies and then proposed it to Myers. It represented a major abdication of the vice-chancellor's powers and Myers, after hearing the arguments, spent a night sleeping on it. To Golding's admiration of his selfless and realistic perception, Myers agreed. This in 1981.

The deans were not enthusiastic. Ron Sackville of Law objected that he could never do sums. He went on to prove not only that he could, but could use them to Law's advantage: other faculties, such as Engineering, had vast allocations to allow for purchase of equipment, why couldn't Law have an equivalence? And Sackville was a skilled and aggressive advocate. Three deans, Bob Walsh in Medicine, Malcolm Chaikin in Applied Science and Frank Crowley in Arts, believed that their budget allocations were merely notional and would not be enforced. They continued to spend as usual. Medicine and Applied Science were brought into line sharply by the university's refusal to pay travel costs when they had overstepped their budgets. Arts was more recalcitrant. Frank Crowley was personally a generous man, unwilling to say no to staff. His early popularity within the faculty rested on that disposition, which accorded with his own nature. If a proposal seemed reasonable he spent on. But the university — in the person of Golding — was insistent that this could not continue and demanded that Crowley keep within budget. His mild efforts to do so were highly unpopular within faculty — such is the nature of ingratitude — and, in any case, unavailing: the deficit moved towards an intolerable figure. Crisis was averted by Crowley's resignation in 1984, and his replacement by the hard-headed and unsympathetic Jarlath Ronayne.

As to that foolish joke that Golding remained in the dark, did not really know what was going on, nothing could be further from the truth: Golding WAS what was going on. It was the jokers, deceived by his mild manner and beaming smile, who were in the dark.

The appointment Myers himself immediately made, in 1969, was that of Jack Thornton. Thornton's experience of the university went back to its beginnings, but he was no swallower of official lines. Indeed, his long, central role in the Staff Association cast him necessarily in the role of critic and arbitrator, particularly given

K Doig/UNSW Archives

∧

Tom Daly in happy industrial mood passing through a student wake in the

Chancellery building for the so-called demise of the Library

9 May 1983

∧

Chancellor Samuels and his portrait by Clifton Pugh, Council Chamber
1979

his personal rationalising bent. His devising of the subject of History and Philosophy of Science, whereby arts students might fill their science requirement, points him up as a brilliant bridge-builder and span-seeker, seeking for that strange harmony that might be found in contrasts. And superbly good at achieving it in practice. The vast first-year lecture of these days could be housed only in the 800-person Science Theatre. (I took to referring to my own lectures there on Hitler as 'Nuremberg Rallies'.) Thornton's lectures on cosmology, which as professor and later dean he never delegated, became legendary with students: he could enthral and dominate gargantuan classes, a fact known to Myers from direct family experience — a daughter.

So, in 1969, in that year of beginning to live dangerously with students, Thornton was appointed pro-vice-chancellor, with special responsibility for dealing with students: Myers no doubt hoped that some of the magic might disperse generally. How much of the Myers student performance is attributable to the Thornton input is unclear. His appointment does clarify one general matter which must drift into the suspicious mind — jobs for the boys. He and Myers were never close. Myers, straight up and down, swift decisions; Thornton, considering all angles, testing Myers's patience with — on the one hand, this, but, on the other hand, there is … . None of the vice-chancellors proffered patronage. They sought men who could do a job, fill a need; hopefully congenial to work with. The appointments Myers made — few, Athol Carrington, Ray Golding, Rupert Vallentine, Jack Thornton — were of that kind, with Golding the most influential and warmly evident.

More important were powers behind the obvious throne — those long-servers as registrar and bursar. Macauley was registrar from 1950 to 1974, a continuity which protracted the Baxter years: neither of those who followed, Colin Plowman nor Keith Jennings, were there anything like as long, nor Ian Way and John Gannon, though Way had two stints, 1980–85 and 1987–92, which amounted to a decade. As bursar, the quiet Ted Davis followed the colourful Bourke, then came long term that able and charming operator, knower of all things, expert in industrial relations, Tom Daly, from 1972 to 1985. Birt's managerial manipulations reduced Daly's power and his successor, Alex Cicchinelli (1985–94), was not in a position to be anything as influential.

These were factors impinging on the detail of the day-to-day. So was the chancellor but his influence was also much more profound, general and continuous. Justice Gordon Samuels was chancellor from 1976 to 1994, University Council member from 1969, that is, from the end of Baxter, through Myers and Birt, to Niland. A man of extraordinary energy and broadness of interest — was it boring being a justice of the Supreme Court? — Samuels very actively involved himself in university affairs. No mere shaker of graduate hands at degree conferring ceremonies (though he was that, too), he was much taken up with matters of high university policy: appointments, reputation, power plays, on most of which he had strong and interventionist opinions. A similarly strong personality was his wife, the actress Jacqueline Kott. They made a formidable pair, with no bones about asserting their pre-eminent role. His predecessors Sir John Clancy and Sir Robert Webster, however excellent as chairmen of council, tended to be quiet, figurehead, formal figures;

but Samuels was a return to the Wurth mode — a finger in every university pie. In 1983 he began a Chancellor's Review in the university's *Annual Report*, in which he evaluated the major doings and problems of the year. In doing so he made clear the council's juridical base and his own conception of his role. The council was the university's supreme governing body, approving major decisions and ultimately responsible for what is taught and how. He was the chairman in charge of the body which was in charge. What this meant in reality depended, not only on the trenchancy of the chancellor, but on the strength of the vice-chancellor. With Myers, Samuels met his match; with Birt, less so, particularly given Birt's protracted absences overseas.

Birt? The university man, pondering what education meant; not the hard-nosed seeker of imperial power. Where Baxter and Myers were administrators, Birt was an educationalist. Even his outlining of developments within the university, for a regular feature in *Uniken*, tended to be philosophic reflections. He set his university position among a wide range of responsibilities and interests, Australian and overseas: Australian representative on the Association of Commonwealth Universities, the International Association of Universities, the Australian Vice-Chancellors' Committee, Police Board, Consumer Affairs, Health Services, acting vice-chancellor of Charles Sturt University (which New South Wales University sponsored), chair or member of this committee or that, overseas for a third of the year, to the extent of making the chancellor worried about these absences. Making lieutenants imperative — and powerful — and creating the impression within the university of his being never there. A Melbourne biochemist, Birt came to the University of New South Wales in 1981, having been foundation vice-chancellor of Wollongong from 1975. That was a much smaller task. He found the sheer size of the University of New South Wales daunting, did not like the impersonal relations necessarily consequent, and was not used to a university which had grown accustomed to its vice-chancellor's total involvement and dedication. Both he and his wife — she had strong cultural interests and painted for a hobby — gave themselves to the university, but he was much less visible than his predecessors, a matter for growing campus dissatisfaction. This interacted with external difficulties stemming from Commonwealth constrictions and interventions, to produce, in the 1980s, the feeling within that the university was experiencing, to quote a Law professor, 'a little bit of drift'. Particularly was this so from May 1990, when John Ward, vice-chancellor of Sydney University, was killed in a train disaster north of Sydney. Ward had been a vocal critic in the Sydney press of the policies of the federal minister responsible for Education, John Dawkins, who had entered the portfolio in July 1987. Ward had taken up the championing of the university cause reluctantly and late, but his was virtually the only Sydney public expression of anger widespread in universities themselves. (Dawkins was later to reveal, it was reported, that his proposals had been kite-flying, anticipating a fierce reaction from vice-chancellors, who in fact proved largely supine.) Birt's apparent inaction, particularly in contrast to Ward's outspokenness, made him seem weak and gutless, and perhaps in league with federal interventionists. None of which was true.

<|

A stern Michael Birt,

from his portrait by

Brian Dunlop in the

Council Chamber

1984

Vanessa King/50th Anniv. History Project

What he was, was an academic, a researcher, a scholar — as distinct from an administrator. An admirer of John Henry Newman, Birt saw in *The Idea of a University* a powerful and abiding influence. His oral history overview of his career is prefaced by a quotation from Proust's *Remembrance of Things Past*, a reference unthinkable in relation to Baxter or Myers. They were university men, but essentially managers, assertive doers rather than enquirers into the nature of things. Their achievements, in comparison with Birt's, raise the question of what constitutes appropriate vice-chancellorial disposition in a modern university, particularly one as ruthlessly pragmatic as the University of New South Wales. Birt's temperament and disposition tended to be with arts, one might even say 'religious'; whereas Baxter and Myers were men of science, secular, in tone with the whole character of that secular, scientific place. Birt was even otherworldly, unconcerned with matters of salary: 'we were paid — that was it'. No it wasn't, his Staff Association said. So too did a squeezing federal government. As to his Wollongong background? Hostile to being seen as a colonial outpost of the University of New South Wales, wary and suspicious of the scheming metropolis, warm in the closeness of its localised commitments. The University of New South Wales? Vast, its horizons the whole country and the entirety of human knowledge. Daunting indeed.

And what did one get in return for one's efforts to serve this giant imbroglio? Small thanks. Birt's efforts to correct what amounted to a scandalous financial imbalance in favour of applied sciences earned him the hatred and resentment of those adversely affected. His redistribution in favour of Arts won him few friends: the money was seen as too little, too long overdue, and nothing like what Arts really deserved. Moreover, Birt had taken over the university at a bad time: its very fabric was under threat. He had come at a stage when buildings were in need of major repair, or at least substantial refurbishment. It turned out that the university had been built on a series of white-ant nests: most buildings had been affected by infestations, which resisted all efforts to eradicate them — the Science Theatre, the Arts building, Commerce, the Library, Administration. In Electrical Engineering the white-ants had been known to travel up air ducts: it was a recurring and expensive problem. Of course, there was normal wear and tear, old age. In particular, flat roofs leaked, plumbing leaked, tiles fell off, things fell apart. Birt did what he could. He drew the attention of visiting groups of fund allocators, reporting to Canberra, to the grotty, run-down appearance of the university. He had the barbed-wire removed from perimeter fences — was it to keep people out or in? — and less repellent wire was substituted. It was still ugly, and about a quarter of the perimeter remains fenced in that way.

Birt's reign was also the context in which the traditional 'grey men', so detested by generations of students in particular, vanished. Gone went the drab grey, demob uniforms and the bus conductor caps (and something of the picturesque repressive Baxter regime). As new head of Patrol and Cleaning in 1989, Alan Egan saw 'grey men' as part of an image the university could well do without — elderly and cranky parking police set against all-comers. In came smarter blue, younger men and women and

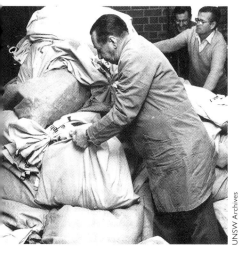

Λ

Mail-room staff — Ray Norman, Kevin Smith, and Frank Warban 1987

V

The first female gardener — Jill Merrin 1981

UNSW Archives

The ideal secretary —

Miss Joan Waghorn,

with Rupert Myers

1975

a major change to a high-profile security service, which became a model for others: it now has over 1500 alarm points on campus — and excellent relations with students, whom it now consults on initiatives. Much of this improvement came from an improved parking system. Unpleasant confrontations with 'grey men' had been part of the university parking situation in the 1980s, to the extent of cases of minor violence. An efficient, courteous and promptly accessible security system put an end to that. It was the demeanour of gate-persons which provided the first direct experience of the university for many members of the public. Positive encounters with pleasant, helpful gate-persons did much to enhance the image and reputation of the university on a down-to-earth, daily basis.

Here is as good a place as any to contemplate — and acknowledge — the legion of general staff which made the whole university enterprise possible and viable over the years. Secretaries, cleaners, groundsmen, support staff generally — a range of facilitating people who served the university on a practical day-to-day basis, who in many cases saw the university as the focus of their lives, and gave it their (often necessarily discreet) loyalty. The notion of secretaries knowing more about the inner operation of schools than their heads was particularly apposite in a work situation of dispersed and various staff involvement. As to focus and loyalty, the point is implicit in the continued existence and vitality of the Staff Social Club, whose Christmas parties for members and their children, with merry-go-rounds and fun entertainment, have long been legendary.

Birt's role in improving the university environs, as in other developments, tended to be that of initiating things which blossomed later. He did not have the money to do what he saw as necessary, and in the face of Commonwealth scrimping, tended to be easily discouraged. Few appreciated Birt's wider involvements in the external world, enhanced by his gentlemanly warmth and charm: selfishly, they only noticed his absences. Whereas the previous vice-chancellors had been strongly focussed on the university, hard men formidable in their emanations, Birt's impact was more dispersed, softer. His outreach, particularly into Asia via Hong Kong University, but also generally in the public domain, was of immense importance in locating the university outside itself, but it had a cost internally — those who felt neglected. Nor was what he instituted such as to produce any obvious, short-term results. Equally, his institutions were — as were his efforts to improve the university fabric — constricted by Commonwealth parsimony: grot continued to rule. It was left to Niland to identify himself with radical face-lifts.

Moreover, here were circumstances — long absences, other commitments — which, to deal with the day-to-day, demanded a retinue of lieutenants, indeed generals! Thornton, Vowels and Willis retired, each taking with them experience of the university from its beginnings. Rupert Vallentine was soon to go also, affable, easygoing; he whose smooth and friendly ways might have been expected to bridge change to a new regime and defuse possible tension. This is how Myers saw him, appointing him at sixty-four years of age. How Vallentine saw himself. Birt's replacements were of a different kind: young, energetic men of ambition, relatively transitory: three — Ray Golding, Alan Gilbert and Jarlath Ronayne — went on to vice-chancellorships elsewhere. Neither Athol Carrington nor Malcolm Chaikin stayed long. The fact that Birt was less visible around the university meant that his lieutenants were more so, with some consequent tensions between them, and others in the university power structure. Not that these did not exist under Myers. Thornton, who could see both and every side of a question, was slow deciding. This riled Golding as well as Myers, men of quick decisions.

Dispersion of power had effects both good and bad. The marked devolution Golding initiated in financial responsibility and power — towards faculty deans — was, in fact, little short of a contrived revolution in financial and administrative power. When the budget was controlled centrally, deans wanting to incur large expenditure had to go, cap in hand, to beg from the vice-chancellor. Now, under a devolved budget, they made their own decisions. But with that enormously enhanced power went responsibility, an avalanche of new work, in dealing with suppliant schools. The change transformed the role, power and workload of deans, and served the university generally in good stead, freeing up hierarchical log-jams, and bringing decision-making much closer to the actual workface. Golding's ample capacities, and those of Tony Wicken, appointed in 1990, provided control, continuity and stability, in periods of great, federal government-induced change. Jarlath Ronayne's elevation to deputy vice-chancellor in 1988 (the others remained pro-vice-chancellors) made that prickly, self-willed, engaging — and contradictory — Anglo-Irishman a major factor in power equations at the university's top. Indeed, it is often suggested that Ronayne virtually ran the day-to-day university in Birt's absences in his later years as vice-chancellor. Ran it in a style very different from that of the retiring, tolerant manner of Michael Birt. Birt's approach was to govern through consultation and open discussion. Ronayne was a superb lieutenant, efficient, effective. But his concept of executive authority was very different. Critics, even friendly ones, saw him as attempting to govern through edict, an approach not relished by academics, particularly when accustomed to Birt's mild, gentle, forbearing governance. On one occasion the VCAC was convulsed with laughter (in which Ronayne joined) by a dean's response to some such edict — 'Jawohl, mein Gruppenführer!'. This assertive, abrasive leadership irked some, but most — including Birt himself — accepted it as among the legitimate vagaries of human nature, and as nothing, set against Ronayne's excellence in administration. Given that others were steering the ship, the role of the captain was thereby reduced: Birt was substantially committed to the courses determined by these subordinates. However congenial and compliant they might be, they betokened a power dispersal which percolated down throughout the university. Those wedded to the idea of hierarchy might see this as abdication. Rather it was a necessary devolution, in tune with the general times. Traditional ideals on governance had first been challenged by students, but there was no reason why the process should stop there. Why should not deans be elected, as in other places? Or heads of schools? And why must these always be professors? University authority opposed all these steps. It had a point, in that tight control from the top had advantaged the university's progress in the past. But when it came to submitting, reluctantly, to proletarian pressure, it found that this outcome had advantages. Now, cynics rejoiced, blame might fall, and power struggles be fought out, at faculty and school level, rather than be sheeted home to an administration above. User pays.

To all this, the different styles and personalities of Myers and Birt were central. Myers had much of the Baxter disposition in him. He did not delegate easily. Even while on family holiday he might return (from Terrigal) to crucial meetings, although his acting vice-chancellor, Rex Vowels, was extremely competent. And placid. Had Vowels been less tolerant he might have construed the actions of Myers as reflecting lack of trust. He didn't and it wasn't. Myers took an attitude of 'the buck stops here'. Seeing himself as ultimately responsible, he was determined that all decisions be his. The king in his council, but his barons were just, and only, that.

Birt was of a different cast, believing in dispersing executive tasks (and, in consequence, power); far less anxious to exert authority personally.

Back to 1975. Where stood we then? At the top of a wave, at the peak of a long, gathering surge of change. The surfing analogy applies. Paddling, pushing, thrusting, all energy straining to catch the mounting swell of forwardness, discerning the best, most promising, currents, then riding the wave of dynamic change in society. Initially and throughout a product of, and in tune with profound social change, we were swept along, students, staff, curriculum, in waves much larger, deeper, wider, than the university's mere self. Forced into, reflecting, expressing, the encounter with Asia, pop culture, the emergence of women in social and economic life, the collapse of religion into a mindless secularism — all part of the cultural environment of those days. Product of its times. The wave breaks. The early 1970s saw the

University of New South Wales transformed from a 'new' to a 'modern' university.

And the cost of modernity was self-reflection. Who gave a thought to introspection when the wave was being ridden? In the heady excitement of surfing across a changing world, who gave a thought to a distant shore, to the calm of mere ebb and flow? Ebb? Inconceivable.

But so — the images and analogies crowd in — came, in the 1970s, steady state, a university beginning to look in at itself, rather than constantly directed by imperium and the demands of seeking and servicing the new. Now the mood was to be one of consolidation, refining, the process of cut and polish, cultivation. A strong settlement had been hacked from the wilderness. Now was time to concentrate on smoothing the rough, pioneering edges and establishing a civilisation.

This process was symbolised by the commencement of publication of *Uniken* in March 1975. Intended as 'a potentially vital channel of communication within the University' by the Public Affairs Unit under Peter Pockley, a leading science adviser, it sought to meet staff needs for publicity. Carrying news and opinion within the university, house journal so to speak, *Uniken* had a circulation of an initial 3600 among staff. Though bland in tone, its general effect was radical, that of making the university aware of itself, its diversity, its achievements. It carried correspondence but never lived up to its candid possibilities. This was not the fault of Pockley, a very forthright and opinionated Public Affairs adviser, who was eventually to fall victim in 1988 to a reorganisation of Public Affairs, which abolished his position and transferred its duties from within the vice-chancellor's inner sanctum to more conventional parts of administration: this falling out was spectacular, contentious and very public. Yet it remains the case that Pockley's role had been vital to publicising the university, particularly in allowing, through *Uniken*, an avenue for staff keen to report 'science' developments they had made, to the general public. Pockley's high reputation among science reporters led to *Uniken*'s becoming a regular source for *Sydney Morning Herald* and ABC coverage of University of New South Wales stories. Scuttle-butt had it that he went simply because he was too powerful—influential—outside the university, but the fact is that the whole matter of the Public Affairs function was the subject of a protracted university committee review, open to response from within the university. Certainly, Pockley's was a strong personality and he enlisted the support of the Staff Association in a way which annoyed some of the committee, but matters of personal abrasion, always present in human dealings, seem nothing untoward on this occasion, although the protagonists saw it otherwise. No. *Uniken*'s mild tone was a function of the prevailing diffidence (and apathy) of staff, perhaps distrustful of an administration-sponsored publication, more likely taken up with their own professional concerns, happy when they were the stars, oblivious to others. Down the years the photographed visages of the beaming staff of this project or that smiled out together with vice-chancellorial benedictions so standard as to be virtually interchangeable, like the meaningless repetition of men with beards in books of Victorian illustrations. All these activities had their particular and narrow interest, and a wider one in general, in promoting a feeling, warm and proud, of being part of an important and illustrious organisation. Neither *Uniken* nor its sibling, *Quarterly* (also begun in 1975), moved past the level of information, valuable in itself in fostering coherence and self-regard, but not venturing into the world of thought, or intellectual contention. Their nature was on a par with the face-lifts administered to the annual reports and faculty handbooks about this time — colour, illustrations, more user-friendly style.

This institution in 1975, served 17,061 students, with over 5000 more in various graduate extension courses. In 1976 the university became the biggest in Australia—18,378 enrolments, an extraordinary achievement in twenty-seven years of growth, and given that eschewing of the empire-building opportunities offered by amalgamations. Along the way it had established first Australian chairs in Drama, Landscape Architecture, Librarianship, Marketing, Optometry, Sociology, Transport Engineering, and so on, with consequent interaction with the professions these represented. The public impact and involvement was enormous. The university granted over 4000 degrees in 1977. The staff was nearly 4000, with 1400 of them academics. It was a very large-scale enterprise. Its schools of Architecture and Engineering were among the largest and strongest of their kind. Several schools were unique in Australia—in chemical and textile technologies, wool and pastoral sciences. Progress was being made towards the Australian Graduate School of Management. The two-session system, replacing the three-term year in 1970, was firmly in place. Admission of mature age students, that is for those without matriculation, was established procedure. New staff were offered a three-day introductory conference. And the process of building a campus community, and civilising it, was continued by the U Committee (a voluntary group of women formed in 1963, and still continuing, to raise funds for the university) and the Monomeeth Association (a society of parents and friends formed in 1963, existing until 1996) — Art show and Faculty nights. Above all, in terms of harmonious relations among staff and between staff, students, and the local community, was the substantial settlement of that most vexing of questions — parking: a multi-storey car park capable of accommodating 416 cars was opened on upper campus in 1975, a second stage in 1977. This removed much of the space pressure which had been the source of tension and discord. Much, but not all. Staff competed for the places nearest their own rooms, and agitated against reserved parking sites: the privileged lived in aggressive fear of dispossession. Rational reorganisation of parking space in 1996 encountered sensitivities and resistance to any change. The whole parking matter generated emotions of astonishing intensity: the car as private, felt extension of personal space, and its accommodation, was capable of begetting passions well beyond any other staff discontents.

So much for happy car-owners. The plight of those reliant on public transport offers a much more vexing story with elements of long-running high farce — were it not for its seriously inconvenient and frustrative aspects. Here the villain of the piece was the State Department of Motor Transport, latterly the Urban Transport Authority, uncomprehending and impervious to needs, or tardy and mean in recognising them. There was the promise, constantly renewed into the 1970s of a south-eastern suburbs railway, panacea (which never eventuated) for all university transport ills. Trams along Anzac Parade were being replaced by buses — the last

∧

A small group of Anzac Parade bus-catchers on a dry day

1960s

∨

Students try their luck in High Street, before the crossing is marked

early 1980s

tram passing the university was in February 1961. In the 1950s buses would not set down in front of the university, but carried passengers on to a stop which entailed a third of a mile walk back to the university, by students and staff. Timetables ensured late arrival of students (and staff) for 9 a.m. work commencement as well as protracted delays for evening students going home. Services were grossly inadequate to meet demand. Students were left stranded at city bus stops as full buses went by, and departing often involved a scrum, which left the faint-hearted to the next bus, whenever that might turn up. Transport authorities seemed unable to cope with the bi-location of teaching — Ultimo and Kensington — or the gradual move to the Kensington campus. Whereas in the 1970s most buses went to Circular Quay, not to Central Railway, now the position is reversed — but not before major trauma and time-lags. Medical students were particularly disadvantaged. Most elected to use Randwick-Coogee buses as their long walk — either to the Prince of Wales Hospital, or the faculty building on campus — was downhill. Getting to the other teaching hospital — Prince Henry at Little Bay, to the south — was a complex, time-consuming expedition. But so was the whole bus-travelling enterprise — long waits, buses late, or full and not stopping, drivers changing shifts or taking meal breaks, dumping passengers in heavy rain at stops without shelters.

In all this, students, staff, and higher administration were united in complaints and representations to urban transport authorities. They were met by lame explanations and excuses of insufficient funds. Thus, when a particularly rainy winter in 1963 further agitated drenched students to press for bus shelters, the Students' Union was compelled to meet the cost itself, the transport authority pleading penury. A similar saga awaited the 1963 request that the university's move in locational emphasis from lower to upper campus be recognised by provision of service in High Street to meet demand at both gates eight and nine. This time the excuse was staff shortage. When eventually, twenty years later, in 1984, High Street services were provided, the transport authority refused to re-route them to drop passengers on the university side of the road. The result was that, lacking marked pedestrian crossings, alighting students crossed the road haphazardly under threat of death or injury. It took the efforts of the vice-chancellor directly contacting the minister for Transport to get provision of crossings in 1985. Express buses were a similar matter of difficulty, the transport authority maintaining there was not sufficient demand. When they began in the 1980s, the university appealed to students to patronise them. To great effect. In 1988 there were 71 expresses; ten years later there were 252, carrying 29,000 people per week. In a letter to the registrar in February 1980 Peter Pockley described the bus services to and from the university as 'appallingly inadequate', an umbrella remark which covered the details above and had its own general validity. That the daily experience of coming and going could be so fraught with nightmare difficulties obviously conditioned many students' university experience. Not that university authorities did not strive strenuously on their behalf. It was simply that the university was powerless to effect change in that area — at least quickly. The Department of Motor Transport was a master of the arts of run-around, bureaucratic gymnastics, and resistance to change. Herein lies the stimulus to the proliferation of old student bombs which, when parked, clogged the streets adjacent to the university.

The developments of the mid 1970s were in the context of severe financial stringency and uncertainty, most particularly in view of the federal government's decision not to accept the University Grants Committee's recommendations for 1976–78. No new building contracts could be let, affecting plans for extensions to Medicine, the Australian Graduate School of Management, and a building for Law. These were eventually to proceed, save for a Law building. It was the end of the golden age of construction, a halt from which some projects, such as Law, were not to recover. So, too, vanished plans for the replacement of that ancient pioneering feature — huts: they still endure, if soon to go. Yet, despite funding cuts and the government's abandonment of triennial funding AND the inroads of that rampant inflation that began to grip the Australian economy and erode public funding from about this time, some things were done in what was now, in 1976, the largest university in Australia.

GM Downie/UNSW Archives

∧

Vestiges of things past—huts

still there on campus

October 1979

A target date for the Australian Defence Force Academy (ADFA) was set for 1982. And a consolidated plan for campus development — landscaping, better walkways, and the like — was put to staff for comment in 1975. Hard times, but never say die.

One feature of the campus which was to continue to prosper, wax important, was the library lawn. A popular place for student sociability at lunchtime or whenever, venue for addresses by politicians, university or otherwise, in the 1980s it became the auditorium for pop music bands, sponsored by the Students' Union. Many of Sydney's top bands performed there in lunchtime, making the buildings that enclosed it — Library, Arts, Chancellery, lecture block — uninhabitable under the assault of sheer sound.

As to the student body, it was of a mood more serious, less carefree than before: the swinging 1960s and 1970s had left a sour mark. Not that students were not there to learn, and rebel, but that their mode of doing so was with a tinge of disillusionment and truculence. The happy days had gone.

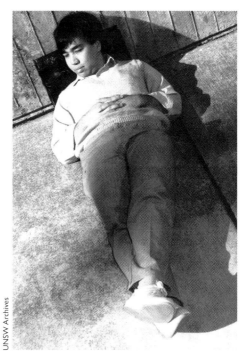

UNSW Archives

A typical student attitude

1988

Yet who is to rest easy with such a conclusion? Each student was an individual personality, and the student body had a multiplicity of family backgrounds and expectations, coming to twelve faculties and over a hundred schools, themselves with internal options. Their encounter with the university was the context for growing up, for meeting wider worlds, for relationships with people of other kinds, for love, sex, self-discovery, for becoming young adults. To generalise about such subject matter is hazardous indeed. Or to disentangle what was training in some profession, from that which was education, higher learning: the University of New South Wales aspired to both.

Yet, yet. The student atmosphere had changed, become more serious. Economic conditions always impacted on student attitudes, and the downturn and uncertainties of the late 1970s and 1980s took their toll. So did the increasing number of Asian students, not only culturally distant, but reliant on good results to sustain their continued presence and family pride. A degree was a serious matter. Even those habitual denizens of the Science Cafeteria (famed centre for coffee drinking, substance smoking, exchange of trivia and intellectuality in protracted conversations, all-day skipping of classes) were not immune, victims of that dubious, student-sought reform of the 1970s — continuous assessment. Gone were the days of first-term frivolity, third-term slavery: it was a case of a form of continuous, low-level slavery. In

Professor Rupert
Myers at the Forum
on Assessment
October 1974

UNSW Archives

Student views of
typical lecture material
— on the library lawn
1983

K Doig/UNSW Archives

the face of continuous assessment student ingenuity devoted itself to ways of coping with it: narrow reading, clever contentiousness, or at tiny minority of worst behaviour, purchasing ready made cribs from previous students via a known grapevine.

Pressures to achieve and perform continuously were one thing, but the University of New South Wales offered something valuable and unique, which students saw — freedom, the chance not to be dominated by the past, ancient tradition, the opportunity not to be BOUND to do this or that. Those students saw things true. Staff who joined the university in the late 1970s, early 1980s, shared common perspectives on what they encountered. Big and strong, unpretentious, pragmatic, no standing on ceremony, open in disposition, a strangely CBD atmosphere, committed, a commuter university which prepared people for professional engagement,

Geoff Swinburn/UNSW Archives

devoid of romance and even style, a strikingly ugly place, where the quality of the people and their achievements were the redemptive saving grace. To translate to the student experience, the ideal place to escape the bonds of school, to meet new people and places. But gone, forever gone, was the 'hippie' approach to study, casualty to economic constraint. Gone were the times of sleeping in the Library's bean bags. The bean bags have their own history and symbolism — symbols of that leisured, relaxed age when students and their social comfort were king. Predating the bean bags was 'the talking room', a glassed-in area, with desks and typewriters, an undergraduate area which often degenerated into paper fights and various rowdy behaviour, annoying other, serious, library users. Librarian Pat Howard introduced bean bags in 1975, ten of them in various colours, orange, lime green, brown, in a 'casual seating area' on level three of the Library. This area was also equipped with a supply of uncatalogued paperbacks and journals. It remained so until a refurbishment of the Library in 1984, in which the undergraduate library disappeared. Keeping the bean bags 'topped up' with beans was a constant problem — money to buy them and the chore of collection. Besides, sometimes they were used for what a senior librarian politely described as 'horizontal dancing', activity at which (given this public location) the mind boggles. So passeth the bean bag, doughy, smiling flaccidity: the age of the hard, upright chair had arrived.

The Library itself, of course, seemed immutable, even into the 1990s. There was a Library building (opened by Sir

The A to Z of Academia
by Phil Schofield **B is for Brain**

GIRLS
BOOZE
GROG
FOOTY
MORE GROG
MORE BOOZE
STUDY

ACADEMIC VIEW OF THE STUDENT BRAIN

ACADEMIC VIEW OF THE STUDENT BRAIN

ANTIQUATED JOKES

GOOD LECTURES

STUDENT VIEW OF THE ACADEMIC BRAIN

P Schofield

Phil Schofield

caricature series

Uniken 24 March 1979

Robert Menzies) and there was the library lawn, both central to the student experience and the whole notion of university life. But the Library as official entity was to vanish in 1995, subsumed into the Client Services Unit (together with the Library Strategic Planning and Policy Unit and the Collection Services Unit) of the Division of the Director of Information Services and Deputy Principal. Librarians there still were, but could they survive the attritions of corporatist jargon as well as the declining book and periodical purchasing power of the Australian dollar?

The Library had always had a centrally separatist life and history. Initially carried over from the Sydney Technical College to a room in the old Main Building at Kensington with two librarians, it grew by 1958 to occupy the first floor of the

Homage to the distant past — student

adaptation of library lawn wall-materials

1966

Dalton Chemistry building. John Metcalfe, a prize Baxter had inveigled from the State Library, where he was principal, was appointed librarian in 1959. The Library moved in 1962 to the top floor of the Heffron building, then, in 1966 to the present site. The year 1960 saw a library of about 75,000 books, five staff. In the early 1960s its policy for the future was to build up an undergraduate library, concentrate on periodicals, improve service to readers, establish, in 1960 the first library school in Australia — and not duplicate the holdings of other libraries, the State Library and University of Sydney. And to look at automation. It was soon to develop specialist offshoots — the Biomedical Library in 1960, the Law Library in 1970, the Physical Sciences Library in 1976. Social Sciences in the same year. Over this presided, first, John Metcalfe, whose first interest was in the School of Librarianship and the extraordinary service that provided to the Australian profession; then, from 1966, that skilled university politician in the Library's interests, until 1988 — Allan Horton.

Max Franklin/UNSW Archives collection

Allan Horton, librarian

and library advocate

1966

The Library and its staff tended to have an existence which seemed to other staff, stable and unchanging. The reality was less placid, but certainly less exposed to the questionings and social turmoil of the 1970s.

Gone then were the happy days of student respect for, and trust in, academic staff. Staff were obliged to earn that against a background of suspicion, even hostility. An anecdote from Law in the early 1980s illustrates. A student, speeding along Anzac Parade in his prehistoric Honda 360 cc panel van (the one with the dashboard-mounted gearshift) espied his lecturer, obviously distressed, due to lecture in ten minutes, at the roadside lacking transport. He pulled over and offered a lift. He took the lecturer to a place nearest Law but inconvenient to his own parking plans. Consequently, he was a few minutes late arriving at the class. The lecturer stopped, and said: 'Mr ——, it is ten minutes past nine. I will not tolerate lateness in my students. Please leave the room.' The story has a sequel. Some years later the student's younger brother found himself unfairly hassled by the same lecturer. Eventually he responded by saying, 'I know a story about you', and recounted his brother's experience. The class fell about laughing, 'pissing themselves' as the crudities of student parlance had it, in that mixture of outrage and astonishment the incident engenders. The lecturer, discomforted and confused, attempted to justify its weird logic, explain it away.

This was an unpleasant but relatively harmless oddity, as was, perhaps, the behaviour of the lecturer in the Faculty of Medicine who lectured in the nude, to avoid his clothes becoming bloodied: in deference to his female students he wore an apron.

And there were the cross-dressers, or the eccentric staff member who would never recognise even close colleagues if he encountered them on public transport. Complaints — and there were some from students and parents — were dealt with discreetly by the administration. But complaints were few. Some subjects were unique, indeed a whole raft of them in technology and science: the whole university was peppered with new, unusual, and unique subject explorations, often with staff of acknowledged eminence. Even in Arts aspects of pioneering obtrude. History and Philosophy of Science one of only two such schools in Australia; others, for instance French, were among the best in Australia — adventurous, radical, wide-ranging, full of new angles and ideas. And taught by young staff: the stereotype of socially inept, untidily bearded middle-aged men wearing sandals did not apply. Although that youth had its pitfalls. In Arts, liaisons by some staff with female students created a diversity of problems and gossip allegations, which seldom surfaced publicly — grades for favours, and the like. Marriages became unstuck. Staff foibles (or worse) were a central element in the student conversations that bubbled on endlessly in the Science Cafeteria, library lawn and other student resorts — the Blue Room, with banks of vending machines, blue carpet, and no furniture, and Esme's, named (then unofficially) after the middle-aged woman who served cappuccinos there — a motherly, human touch that warmed lonely student hearts. These places had their distinctive clientele — the Science Cafeteria, everybody, cosmopolitan; Blue Room, dope smokers; Esme's, showy language students conversing in foreign tongues; the Commerce

K Doig/UNSW Archives

∧

Enthusiasm for learning — receiving free ice-creams on the library lawn

March 1984

quadrangle, Asian students; the library lawn, also everybody, plus an infestation of Christian fundamentalists, Spartacists, various oddballs, brought in for the occasion.

Certainly, staff behaviour provided ample material for student education, diversion and discussion, some schools more than others. The School of French, for instance. One lecturer possessed and made much of the complete works of the Marquis de Sade, prompting endless student speculation; another was president of the Gay Association. Various of the tutors had very bohemian lifestyles. First-year French exposed students to cult film classics such as the shocking, anarchist *Themroc*, with its scenes of incest, cannibalism and regression to cave-dwelling.

Some students protested at being shown such material. Others were too innocent to comprehend it: convent school education — or any other — did not prepare students for this. The professor, Judith Robinson, was the daughter of the librarian of the National Library of Australia, and brilliantly qualified. Charming, but very formidable, she dressed in Paris chic and was to marry into the French intellectual aristocracy: she had built up a superb modern French library at the University of New South Wales. Few schools could match French for colour and panache, but many had a similar dedication and enthusiasm, winning student involvement and respect.

In matters less intellectual, student culture was sustained by an extraordinary proliferation of clubs and societies, ranging from the standard (rugby, cricket, every known sport) to religious and cultural associations, to activities more exotic — kung fu, tai chi. There was even beneath all this, a mildly scatological dimension — the graffiti behind lavatory doors. Much of this was predictable, but some was serious critical comment of a kind which could not be elsewhere expressed, about courses and people. One, close to home, repeated to me, was 'X is the worst lecturer in the university', to which someone had added 'I agree'. So did I, in that case. The university cleaning staff made valiant efforts to remove this offensive material, obliterate this expression of the basic student mind, but to clean the doors was to invite they be filled again, a warfare captured in the legendary doggerel response: 'Though the grey men try in vain/ The —— house poet strikes again'.

Of all the student social activities, that centred around the Rugby Club was the most outrageous. Denied access to the Village Green — for cricket only: Baxter is reputed to have said it was improper for physical contact of male human bodies to take place in Anzac

UNSW Archives

∧

Better luck next time —

a malfunction in the

Archery Club

late 1970s

Parade, which was a memorial parade — the club took matters into its own hands, purchased a surplus army hut as clubhouse and had it transported to their allocated home ground, to the great indignation of the university administration. This clubhouse became the centre for wild and noisy parties, drinking, even strip shows — the club had in the 1960s a couple of girl groupies specialising in the chant:

> Here we are in New South Wales
> Shearing sheep as big as whales
> Of golden fleece and pearly tails
> You can all go and get ——

And other ditties of similar cultural, literary and moral worth.

The Rugby Club was the core of antics, harmless and otherwise, which marked the Foundation Day scavenger hunts, and sported legendary characters such as the student driver so defective in eyesight as to need passengers to tell him whether traffic lights were red or green. Club members were prominent in the wild larrikinism of Bacchus Recovery and Foundation Day Balls, including one in which the Roundhouse toilets were smashed. Camaraderie yes, and a feeling, in those smaller days, of identifying with the totality of the institution, and of competing with Sydney University. But this hooliganism — outdoing Sydney pranks, going one better in

∇

Rugger persons —

NSW University of Technology *vs* Western Suburbs

1952

Rugby Union Club UNSW Archives collection

everything — was not appreciated by those who valued dignity and good behaviour. University authorities came down hard on destructive or riotous goings on, with disciplinary committees, even expulsions. Various factors curbed the outrageous 1960s, but not least was sporting success, the demands of discipline and responsibility which went with public acceptance and recognition.

That the quirks of staff should be a matter of student conversation could be expected: they were the medium by which university education reached them. Most of it was gossip and its stimulus small. Not so in the case of English, whose vagaries — to call them that — went to the heart of the university's operation. Given his fanatical addiction to horse racing, and his smooth, Brylcreemed appearance, Harold Oliver, professor of English from 1956 to 1981, should have been a university 'character'. He was; but not, some thought, in a benign way. Oliver had a substantial international intellectual reputation, and publication, as a leading Shakespearian scholar, but he also had a virtually obsessive belief in the necessity for the highest standards, had a narrow view of what was literature and what should be taught —

nothing Australian for instance — and ran his own school as an autocracy, in which he insisted on determining all matters of syllabus, examinations and admissions, holding all power in decision-making, major and trivial. He had succeeded in building a highly gifted staff — testimony to his own distinguished talent — but many of them found his policies alienating and frustrative: it was an unhappy school. Most important for the university generally was a student avoidance of English. They reacted to narrow course structures, and to high failure rates in the name of preservation of standards, and to Oliver's personal autocracy. No doubt the university contained other schools in which the personality of the professor produced problems. Indeed, it would be amazing if tensions and conflicts did not exist among highly intelligent and opinionated people engaged in a hierarchically controlled, common cause. But English was an extreme, or at least very obvious, case. Outside the school, abrasions occurred as other schools were confronted at faculty meetings with Oliver's undisguised contempt for their allegedly lower standards — Sociology most of all. And in university committees generally, Harold Oliver became known for his strenuous insistence on unyielding standards, and protocols, to the great annoyance of manipulators and compromisers. Above all, in terms of the university's general health, this produced a skewed

The A to Z of Academia

by Phil Schofield

L is for lectures

P. Schofield

Phil Schofield caricature series

Uniken 25 August 1979

Arts faculty, as students avoided English. History's prosperity, for instance, rode on English poverty for the long length of Oliver's reign, its student numbers inflated by the off-putting reputation of English.

The excellent English staff? — three to professorships elsewhere; Leonie Kramer to Sydney, Peter Elkin to New England, Harry Heseltine eventually to Duntroon. It is said that Oliver had few friends but some people got on well with him. He was rigidly honest, had the highest possible (even higher!) standards and was a scholar of international distinction. In the faculty he took a consistent stand against the soft options offered by Sociology, which bestowed high distinctions and first-class honours lavishly. His opposition became something of a predictable joke, but it had an effective biting edge, which warred against slackness and ill-discipline in the faculty and university generally. Oliver's wrath was terrible to encounter, therapeutic to others more easy-going. He edited three of Shakespeare's plays for the Penguin edition, no small achievement in a heavily populated international scholarly area. This was a distinction neglected by those who fell foul of his view of what the scholarly world should be.

One other student thing. From the 1960s to the 1980s students were increasingly taking on part-time employment — in hotels, as shop assistants, child-minders, waitressing, as night fillers for supermarkets, service stations, whatever. In some cases this was in order to survive, but in most it related to lifestyle — old cars, nice clothes, hi-fis — those things a previous generation of students never had or needed. The Op Shop or St Vincent de Paul became the sources of the student wardrobe. Radical female make-up, startling hair-styles, bizarre friends (often from the Sydney band scene) confounded and confronted parents unused to such aberrations. Even strange cults and religions and trips to that Beatles-flavoured fashion — country of the mystic East — India. The sitar was too difficult but a guitar could crudely approximate. Musically, the revolution found its earlier mild and pleasant voices in Peter, Paul and Mary. Pete Seeger sang in the Roundhouse. And the — to parents — incomprehensible moans of Bob Dylan and his legion of imitators wailed down from the 1960s to

The A to Z of Academia

by Phil Schofield

J is for jeans

SPECIAL! TOP QUALITY PRE-STAINED PRE-BLEACHED PRE-RIPPED PRE-PATCHED PRE-SCUNGIED STUDENT JEANS

P Schofield

Phil Schofield caricature series

Uniken 28 July 1979

the 1980s, Iggy Pop, David Bowie, U2: is that what university is about? Full-time ceased to mean exactly that. The wheel had come full — or part — circle since the 1950s. Here were full-time students with part-time jobs. Some of which were vast fun and outlets for tomfoolery. A favourite employment opportunity was waitering for the University Union at the frequent, large social functions held at the Roundhouse. (The invariable menu was rubber chicken, small potatoes and green peas, followed by tinned fruit salad and ice cream.) This allowed — in the sense of enabled; management prohibitions were in vain — free eating and, on one famous occasion, drinking. Being locked 'accidentally' in the Roundhouse liquor store, students resorted to predictable behaviour, spreading their sampling across the whole range of bottles — rum, vodka, gin, bourbon, Bailey's Irish Cream, and so on — in order to disguise the impact of their depredations. This was justified as being to make sure none of the guests were poisoned: such was the wit of university hoons — to use their word. Few part-time jobs were as entertaining as this, but many had their mischief-making moments.

By 1977 incremental creep was becoming a major problem, reflecting the university's aging and growth. Of an annual budget which now exceeded $90 million, 86 per cent was spent on salaries, on a staff which was more expensive, but not commensurately more numerous; age meant promotions and superannuation, costs necessary but unproductive. Furthermore, the Commonwealth policy of supplementation for cost increases was being cut back. The brake on capital works remained, with no prospect of being removed. And the Staff Association was seeking better pay and conditions.

The first intake for the Australian Graduate School of Management (AGSM), a nationally funded centre for graduates in business and public administration, went forward without a designated home. For what was to become such an important — and image-promoting — aspect of the university's activities, the beginnings of the AGSM were hardly auspicious. The brainchild of the Cyert Report to the federal government in March 1970, the aim was to enhance the effectiveness of Australian management; the school was to be 'semi-autonomous' and situated at the University of New South Wales, which Myers regarded as a major coup. Over three years later, the government set aside $2.3 million, but delayed paying it, until overtaken by the funding freeze. Thus, it was not until June 1979 that building began. In fact, the university already had a perfectly — or at least adequately — good Graduate School of Business Management within the Faculty of Commerce. But Myers had little respect for the then dean, Bryan Smyth, and had other, political, reasons for advancing the AGSM idea. The result was essentially two graduate schools of business, and considerable tension and rivalry between them, existing to the present. This to add to another tension within the faculty itself. Economics perceived itself as the intellectually dominant partner within the Faculty of Commerce and acted accordingly, meeting the resistance of the first two deans, Smyth and Athol Carrington — both accountants. Commerce had also sprouted Marketing, under Roger Layton, with a Japanese dimension from 1973, recognising the facts of Australia's trade. Under John Hewson, Economics was running a rearguard action to preserve itself within the faculty.

Meanwhile, the university in 1975 began advertising for staff (eleven positions) for the AGSM, and set up a Board of Management, and appointed a foundation director, Professor Philip Brown. This proceeded, not without professorial objection or at least dissatisfaction. Not only was the AGSM not a faculty and thus not accountable to the Professorial Board, its staff were paid what others saw as outrageously large salary loadings in order to compensate them for not being in the business world. The whole thing was seen as a Myers jack-up, an executive bypass of all normal procedures. In 1977 teaching began (forty-seven students, twelve from Asia) in Master of Business Administration (MBA) and Master of Public Administration. In 1979 Jeremy Davis was appointed director, firm on American models; Fred Hilmer, from 1989 to 1997, then Peter Dodd. Over this period courses have become more diverse, shorter, and with more Asian students — now about half. Moreover, the school has expanded into a distance-learning dimension Australia-wide, where students can remain at the workplace and pursue an MBA. Its various programs attract (in 1998) around a thousand students, with (in 1997) a Hong Kong intensive course service, and a multiplicity of in-house programs and special lectures. Hilmer wanted the AGSM to be one of the Global Top Twenty, a disposition very in tune with John Niland's 'world class' ambitions for the university generally, but diminished by international size factors — and the proliferation of lucrative management schools in other Australian universities. Most full-time MBAs were not sponsored; rather, they were private students seeking a career change — an expensive qualification ensuring high-levels of commitment, often of people who

▽

Business as usual — the AGSM building

1981

K Doig/UNSW Archives

wished to start their own business. They often remained in contact with the school through its own very active alumni association. The school itself had strong links to the corporate business community, to the extent of raising a good proportion of the cost of its 1994–96 building extensions from donations, and of making itself a model for university funding in the vice-chancellor's eyes: the majority of its costs it raised itself. (It was a misleading model: few other university areas had similar sources of outside funds.)

But this is a future success story. Looking back on the dark and homeless days of 1977, when AGSM teaching began, then penury ruled all university enterprises. The late 1970s saw problems generated by government initiatives, federal and State: with the Commonwealth, on account of its Tertiary Education Commission, reorganising university finance and power to suit itself; with the State, on account of its intention to set up an education commission, seen as a threat to the university's academic and administrative autonomy. The new 1976 Higher School Certificate led to intense public debate in 1977: new introductory programs had to be introduced in maths, physics, and chemistry.

Difficult and stressful times, worsening in 1978. Fewer staff, more work. But one positive outcome did accrue — some cooperation between universities. It was no consolation that the whole community was sharing the same squeeze. In 1977 Myers was elected as chairman of the Australian Vice-Chancellors' Committee. In that year, the University of New South Wales in concert with the other eighteen Australian universities protested to the Commonwealth against the freezes on building and other funding constrictions. Admission of the University of New South Wales to the university family had occurred under circumstances of shared financial bereavement. Normal growth, budgets and funding on an annual basis, meant that long-term planning was not possible. Nor was commitment in major areas of traditional academic investment or preferred development. The funding realities increasingly dictated flexibility, readiness and willingness to respond to the swings and fashions of student demands and popular preference, interacting with the pragmatism of political and bureaucratic decision-making. (A good illustration is that of the teaching of Indian history, built up to meet that swamified, sari-ed facet of Beatlemania that gripped the late 1960s. Staff to teach Indian history rose in the 1970s to four, including a professor. But the fascination with India vanished as rapidly as it had emerged, leaving that staff without students. In contrast with other universities, where India-oriented staff refused to teach anything else, to their gross under-employment and the hostility of their colleagues, those affected at New South Wales University re-deployed themselves voluntarily into other courses or devised new teaching initiatives of their own.) The University of New South Wales, less up itself, less hallucinated by false protections of traditional independence, proved to be good at the adapting required, adept at the hard game of fiscal challenge and response. As university management generally became increasingly such an exercise into the 1990s, in matters of dealing with the Canberra bureaucracy and politicians, this university's survival capacities were put to the test — and found, very painfully, to be adequate. That this should be so reflects the quality of management and its willingness to take harsh and internally unpopular decisions, but it also attests to the realism of staff, under no illusions as to their vulnerability in hostile and uncomprehending economic climes.

In 1978 triennial funding came back — emaciated: real money continued to reduce by about 1 per cent annually into the 1980s. In 1979 the response seemed obvious — fewer staff: over a hundred went in that year; more to follow. The full impact of this (it eroded staff morale) was disguised by not filling vacancies, and a device of ominous utility — non-tenured, fixed term staff contracts. Myers put the best light on this, as preserving flexibility, and promising opportunity for the brightest graduates, whatever the cuts. He also declaimed that such was not to be a major feature of staffing policy. But his good intentions depended on the return of good times. They never did return.

Or if they did, in this form of less bad times, such disposable appointments were too useful, and too expensive to upgrade. Schools were thereafter stuck with a substratum of junior tutor labour, often over-worked, used as dogsbodies for this chore or that — an embarrassing and divisive element in school life. Exploited and

K. Doig/UNSW Archives

∧

Jane Morrison, president of the Staff Association, addresses academic staff

13 October 1981

expendable. Blame administrative policy if you will, but its implementation fell to those at the workplace — to their corruption and diminishment as people. It was not enough that some schools were able to do well in major research (Australian Research Council grants in 1976 and 1978, and thereafter, were the largest of any university). More to the point of academic morale was the fact that academic study leave was under investigation in 1978 by the Tertiary Education Commission (no perk but the lifeblood of excellence in teaching and research). That it should be questioned beto-

kened that incomprehension that bedevilled the body public in university matters. Closer to home was the program for energy-saving in university buildings. Lights off, money saved. Sure: but at what cost? Their morale was high, the vice-chancellor told staff. Nor was it particularly exciting to get concessions in areas of old news. In 1979 construction was to begin of the AGSM, and extensions to Medicine were to be completed. For everybody else — nothing.

Given dearth, the university turned to making good with what it had, a policy with which it became remarkably proficient. Research centres became flavour of the year in 1978, with cross-disciplinary research groups working in three major areas: biomedical engineering, energy, and social welfare. All of these used existing resources in ways which were innovative, internally stimulating, and often generating outreach services to government and community, productive of extra funding. Other initiatives warred against stagnation — the six-year medical course was reduced to five, new degree programs sprouted with the aid of computers, the Library upped its act, staff developed overseas schemes particularly in Asia and the Pacific, Law imported distinguished barristers as visitors; also, in a university traditionally known for its atomic research, it developed, in response to

Pioneer U Committee members gathered at the committee's 200th meeting — Mrs Jenny Birt (centre), and (clockwise from left) Mrs Vimy Wilhelm, Lady Myers, Mrs Kath Freeland, Mrs Helga Angyal and Lady Webster November 1983

UNSW Archives

the growing public unease of the late 1970s over radiation hazards and uranium mining, a Safety Unit to investigate that area. Similar response to public sensitivities may be seen in university guidelines covering research involving humans, and animals.

Stir itself up and push itself out. Press advertisements listed campus activities open to the public. Here, music and the university's voluntary helpers set an energetic scene. The pioneering Old Tote Theatre, having moved to the Opera House, came to an end with the withdrawal of Australia Council funding in 1978. But music was on a roll: two opera productions by that unique venture the University of New South Wales Opera in 1978; in 1980 the founding of the University of New South Wales Ensemble for chamber music, a name which was soon to be changed, in 1983 to its present, internationally known form — the Australia Ensemble, half-funded by the university and carrying the university's name nationally and overseas. (The name change reflected its larger reputation, but also the ignorance of critics and audiences overseas who had assumed that the Ensemble had its origins in Wales, a mistake also often made by ignorant overseas academics.) In other public-oriented activities, the U Committee achieved extraordinary success — the Book Fair, and the Kensington Lectures for Higher School Certificate students. (At one of these the English lecturer dropped dead on stage. 'A hard act to follow', a wag remarked to me, as next in the series.) The U Committee profits enabled it to endow a University of New South Wales Art Prize and Travelling Scholarship. The Monomeeth Association donated a John Coburn tapestry for the Science Theatre. Of a parcel with all this outreach, university promotion took pride in the increasing number of its staff involved in prestigious public activities, and receiving various honours and distinctions.

By 1980 steady state had indeed been reached: 50,000 degrees had been awarded, the Library held a million items. Student numbers were virtually static around 18,000, staff was slowly declining in numbers as vacancies were not filled. Nothing unusual in this, as funding constriction hit all public institutions; quoting favourable figures was government-speak: in real terms, the same money meant less. Steady state? Declining state, argued Myers, given the university's inability to keep up-to-date with equipment demands in the sciences. In such reduced circumstances, funds derived from sources other than direct Commonwealth grants became increasingly important — 15 per cent of income in 1979, but climbing. Gifts, bequests and donations reached $3 million in that year. Here was an aspect of university financing under its own control, and thus of growing attractive power. What the university could earn for itself offered unfettered freedom as Commonwealth stringency tightened in the late 1970s. By the mid 1990s this element of self-generated income had grown to 40 per cent — in 1995, 41.07 per cent. It was an avenue which the university had pursued vigorously through the 1980s. Although such a large element of the budget could hardly be viewed as luxury funding — most of it went on bread and butter, day-to-day — there was a little for cake. In 1979 vice-chancellor's discretionary funds made it possible to foster major faculty initiatives, such as the establishment of a Japan Economic and Management Studies Centre, association with the United Nations University, and location of a major part of the Bicentennial History Project within the Faculty of Arts.

What was not 'steady state' (whatever that is, in human affairs?) was the radical change occurring within the character of student enrolments: the university was producing more arts/commerce graduates than those in science or technology. Of almost 3000 (2982) bachelor degrees awarded in 1979, 53 per cent were in arts, commerce, and related courses, 47 per cent in science, engineering, medicine and law — with law substantially arts-based. This reflected a wider community swing from science-based certainties (and faith in science's job-generating capacities) towards interest in social issues — and education as employment: teachers' college scholarships were attractive. Of course, the Whitlam government's abolition of fees was central to the whole process of university education. This fundamentally altered, not only practicalities for students, but the way university education was regarded as a possible option, not seen so before by some of the less affluent sections of the population. But when graduate employment surveys revealed a community acceptance above that of other universities, the vice-chancellor was prone to take pride in this as proclaiming 'the relevance of its courses to the needs of the nation' in the old ways: his mind-set thought science. He read relevance, the buzz word and fashionable notion of that day (and, sadly, of the educational 1990s), as science. After all, this was the cause the university had always espoused and constantly urged from its beginnings. Indeed, it was built into its very nature, this stress on applied knowledge. Yet this was not the only way of viewing knowledge, or conceiving its communication. More traditional ways centred on essences and contemplation rather than practicality. In the matter of useable information, the University of New South Wales had profound advantages over other universities: it thought that way, not only on specific subjects, but as a general intellectual disposition. It had come into its own, though not in or through the areas it thought strongest and valued most. Relevance yes, but to what? And how?

As the general public outlook gradually swung from the traditional foci with their emphasis on British models, the university's appraisal of itself became more assured, more acceptable. It was a swing generated not only by the favourable community experience of graduates (notably in medicine and law) but also by that curious mood of excitement and self-awareness that peaked in the bicentennial celebrations of 1988. The University of New South Wales fitted the active mood and expectations of the 1980s. Would the era of contemplation ever come again, the circle turn? Unanswerable question. If it did the university, at last at one with itself, would be in a strong position to respond.

Steady state in the 1980s meant what it said. Around the same number of students: some movement, particularly from full-time to part-time study, 1 per cent overall, up to 4 per cent in arts and science, higher Higher School Certificate requirements, fewer first year acceptances. Staff numbers about the same; 132 courses. Research productivity: over 2000 publications. Outside support: $4 million. All good signs. But, on the negative, fewer postgraduates, particularly in engineering and applied science; fewer Commonwealth student awards, of declining value; and a crisis situation in funding for equipment. Not much new, save in finalising plans for the Australian Defence Force Academy (ADFA), and initiatives in computer programs and built environment.

What was new was bad — significant shrinkage of funds for salaries. For the first time major problems surfaced in industrial difficulties with general staff, to become endemic. Academic staff salaries were in the hands of a Commonwealth tribunal, which awarded a 4 per cent increase in 1980, entrenching a decline in relativities against the professions, managers, and the bureaucracy, which contrived to accelerate and widen their own salaries. This led, not only to major dissatisfaction and drop in morale, but to a significant diminishing of the attractive power of university positions into the 1990s. This decline had complex outcomes. Some of the best students chose careers elsewhere, in private enterprise or well-paid bureaucracy. It could be argued that the consequence was to reduce the quality of such new staff — few — as might be employed. Against this, it could be contended that staff competition for positions raised standards. This interacted with the general community, feminist push for equal opportunity. In all university areas female staff became increasingly evident, partly because of legislative and bureaucratic pressure from Canberra, but also because of male desertion. The university had been classed as 'exempt' from the 1977 Anti-Discrimination Act, but was, so to speak, on notice, moving towards the Equal Employment Opportunity and Affirmative Action Policy Unit in 1983. In 1980 women comprised 32 per cent total staff; in 1995, 43 per cent: in the same period the proportion of women academic staff rose from 14 per cent to 26 per cent.

Staff already employed in highly marketable areas of public demand were given salary loadings, or permitted to engage in private practice, as those in Medicine had long been. In such areas as commerce, management and computer science the university was competing for teaching staff from a position of totally inadequate financial resources. The Commerce car park demonstrated this in a graphic way: during the day older, ordinary vehicles; the evening flooded with BMWs, cars of the month. Students at the AGSM drew salaries from their employers far exceeding those of the staff that taught them. Yet it was also the era of make-believe, of university pretence that all was getting better in the best of Commonwealth-dictated worlds. It was the era of TERC (Tertiary Education Research Centre); the university held thirty workshops for staff in 1980, as well as sponsoring a general staff conference. Teaching the teachers was a good idea. But in the context of shrinking Commonwealth funding? Getting more quality from the dwindling teaching dollar? Or trying to placate hostile Canberra bureaucrats? They could point to a $6.9 million increase in funding in 1980. What they chose to ignore were costs not covered — superannuation, promotion, price rises, that incremental creep. The university's financial state was precarious: 'finely balanced stability', Myers described it. Optimistically. In fact, equipment in science was becoming seriously outmoded: extended a little longer, dearth would mean permanent damage to standards.

In July 1981 Rupert Myers retired. Nearly thirty years at the university, twelve as vice-chancellor. He departed with predictable words of thanks for 'an exciting and happy experience', and some personal observations far from clichéd — his 'heartfelt thanks' to his wife and family, and an appeal that penny-pinching governments see the national error of their ways. Io Myers deserved every thanks. Her remarkable poise and devoted energy in a whole range of cultural activities gave to the university a dimension of civilisation and refinement (via strenuous, volunteer money-making by wives) it might otherwise have lacked. And it pointed up a lesson which equal opportunity zealots were prone to ignore: the imperative need, in this position of high-level public demand on the vice-chancellor, of the involvement of his wife in her husband's career — two commitments for the price of one. As to governments, the remarks Myers made were both a plea and a polite rebuke. He urged that it 'would be a pity, and incompatible with national needs, if they [universities] were to fall victims to the current drive on the part of governments to reduce public-sector expenditure'. That drive was to continue — and accelerate — up to the present, whatever university protests. The Myers line was that universities took a long time to develop and flourish, a short time to render ineffective, at national cost. This was a lesson he had learnt from the mid 1970s onwards. Perhaps he offered it too mildly to have any impact: who could be bothered by the maunderings of a retiring vice-chancellor? More likely governments were impervious to his reasoning and long-term overview. Then, as now, governments regarded such criticism (if they noticed it at all) as self-interested, vain, and void of realism. That universities were beyond mere training schools for the professions to be guardians of this national interest, went beyond the comprehension of vote-constricted politicians. Then, as now.

Myers retired at sixty years of age. He could have continued for another five years. But did he have the taste to do so, in a mean and obstructive age? He was the last significant legacy of Baxter's imperial age: all the other builders had gone. Gentleman, with a core of steel. His successor, Michael Birt, was a gentle man, his steel of much milder cast. But Birt was not a leader of the Myers kind. Anything but. His was the mode of dispersed decision-making: his was the time of the pro-vice-chancellors. At his own — and the university's — risk. Risk of their being unequal to their delegated tasks, or contrary-wise, to their reputation growing, risk of the fragmentation of power. Risk, too, of compounding inertia and stagnancy from the absence of the chief executive from the day-to-day. To a staff long accustomed to the interventionist, ever-present style of the Baxter/Myers years (a style which served to define what a vice-chancellor was), Birt acquired an image of weakness, of being insufficient. His personality radiated warmth and charm, but not confidence, of being in charge. He did not satisfy the expectations of a combative past, of that sense of battle, difference. He fell victim to that strange conviction of strength through joy, triumph of the will, motif that imbued the university's character. It was a very odd, aggressive, place, and Birt did not fit in. This was sensed, rather than seen. Birt sensed it too. Nobody's fault. The way things were.

The 1980s begin with steady state. How to interpret and present this situation? Birt announced in his first University of New South Wales report in 1981: 'After some 22 years of growth, it now enters a period of contraction'. If brave, not an auspicious way to begin his vice-chancellorship, nor a good note to strike, however true. Myers had been presiding over constriction for some time without admitting it so baldly, always finding positive compensations. At the start Birt spelt it out starkly, without redemption, indeed indicating that the university was planning for it: offering fewer student places in future, drastic cuts in some areas in order to preserve others, closing down the Broken Hill college — all to the effect of raising staff jealousies, suspicions, fears and resentment. The Broken Hill college experiment dated from the late 1950s — the first graduation (of seven students) was in 1966, the last in 1985. Its impetus came from the university's founding mandate, to take technical education to the country areas of the State — in Broken Hill's case, 1100 km from Sydney, a mining town on the edge of the great Australian desert. The initiative had always been under financial threat. In 1963 the Universities Commission refused to fund it, as expenditure disproportionate to the location. It survived only through the substantial support of the mining companies that owned both mines

Tony Long/UNSW Archives collection

∧

University College, Broken Hill

1980

and town. In 1967 it had thirteen academic staff, in science and engineering, servicing the mining industry, mainly of harder drinking men who thus coped with the arid environment — successfully: they produced over 200 graduates and 168 diplomates over its twenty-year history. But its financial viability was always in question. So was its relationship with Kensington. In 1967 the syllabus for third year physical chemistry was changed substantially. No one thought of informing Broken Hill. At the final examinations in November, students were aghast at the sight of the examination paper, set to the new syllabus. All passed, whether by wit or management. At its closure Birt revealed that the cost per student at Broken Hill was four times what it was at Kensington. This was simply unsustainable in the then climate. No consolation that this would leave room, so he said, for imponderables, entirely new ventures which might become desirable. No joy in any of this, or respect for a vice-chancellor who identified with it. Silly or unjustified these human reactions may have been, but they conditioned the way in which staff viewed Birt. His message was gloom and doom — or so it seemed. Even his democratic intentions were so tainted. His intentions were to disperse power, by involving those most affected by decision-making, the deans, in allocating faculty budgets. Fine. But, overall, faculty funding remained centrally determined and deans saw each other as fighting among themselves to carve up a shrinking cake, and being held accountable by their aggrieved schools.

Still, all in all, Birt remained culturally committed, an admirer of the university's enormous diversity (beyond anything conceivable at Wollongong), identifying not only with its core work of teaching and research, but with its humane cultural achievements. When he said, in 1982, that he had no doubt that 'the University is giving effective expression to John Henry Newman's noble definition of a University's fundamental role in the community "a university training is this great ordinary means to a great but ordinary end; it aims at raising the intellectual tone of society"', he was using words (and a source) which neither Myers nor Baxter would have used. And he meant them seriously, deeply. Too seriously. Birt came across as essentially a sad man, witness to the insufficiency of mankind.

There was room for sadness enough: in 1982 a 3 per cent fall in Commonwealth funding, a drop in numbers of sixty-five in academic staff, thirty-nine in general. The federal government was laying down the financial law to all universities: increasingly they were its creatures, or rather that of the growing horde of public servants intent on translating university work into a bureaucratic image and likeness. Financial promulgations on an annual basis made forward planning impossible. There was strong student demand, but the university met this with even tighter entry requirements and the promise of more to come. Staff vacancies were left unfilled; the student-to-staff ratio increased from 11.8 in 1981 to 12.6 in 1982. The number of lecturers on contract increased. A Senate Committee of Inquiry into Academic Tenure (brazen intrusion into university independence) recommended that 10 per cent of lecturing positions be on contract. From control of the purse strings the federal government had extended its power by saying in effect whom universities should employ and on what terms. This drew a mild demur from

Birt, on matters of practical implementation. But where, from any university, were the cries of outrage, protests against incursions into their independence, and rejection of what such government dictation might in future presage?

The general ground conceded, whether from lack of courage or of perception, the best Birt could promise was to think more about flexibility in staff deployment and to stress improvement in staff development, that is, in teaching existing staff to be better at it. Lest this be construed out of context, other universities were even more supine. There seems to have been a belief within universities that they were indeed wasteful institutions, needing reform, together with a polite assumption that their traditional independence would be respected and a decent deferral by politicians made to the proper nature of things.

Not so. It was the fate of that nice man Birt to encounter the age of the pirate politician, thuggish, ignorant, no respecter of the past. And the pressure of the Ministry of Science and Technology, playing on the university's traditional strength, pushed arts to the bottom of every barrel.

So driven, Birt entered upon a general review of the university's work. In 1982 he began a round of visits to the university's eleven faculties and fifty-five schools, then withdrawing himself and his pro-vice-chancellors from day-to-day affairs so that they could best appraise goals, achievements — and consider economies. None of this investigation and distancing endeared itself to the academic body. Moreover, Birt stressed that the university had a specific charter to foster science and technology; good-bye to all else. He threatened that the review policy must issue in 'a long period of adaptation'. All this seemed bad news, particularly when conveyed in unwinning words. 'Those who serve universities', declared Birt — and then comes the prescriptive phrase — 'must get used to this fact' — now wait for the painful truth — 'that the most significant outcomes of their own contributions will bear fruit, not today, but in a distant tomorrow!' But we knew that already. Banal. What's the fuss? Some hidden agenda? Again, needless alienation.

Sure there was deterioration, but not in student numbers, of whom 33 per cent were female, 3 per cent of mature age. True, a continued drift to part-time, but postgraduate numbers were growing. Staff? Ah, yes, problem there. A drop of eighty-nine, mainly lecturers: thirty-nine vacant chairs. And the usual bubbling of the internal brew. In 1983 the university established a policy of equal opportunity of employment and affirmative action — no more appointments committees asking about age, marital status, anything remotely discriminatory: hardly revolutionary in relation to previous good practice. Progress was made on developing the Australian Defence Force Academy into a university college. Locals asserted their independent intentions to Sydney 'strangers' (led by Professor of Mechanical Engineering Noel Svensson), who flew to Canberra on a monthly basis to help. The Sydneyites had no managerial ambitions, and recoiled in the face of combat needlessly offered.

The normal round of cultural activity continued and expanded. The University of New South Wales Ensemble toured the United States of America. The National Institute of Dramatic Art got a new home, courtesy of major Commonwealth funding. The U Committee's Book Fair raised $78,000, distributed to cultural and recreational causes on campus. With $190,000 profit from the 1996 Book Fair, the U Committee had suffi-cient to make a handsome donation — $250,000 — to the construction of the Scientia. But its membership was dwindling, toll to social change. Female employment and demanding careers were much more common. Time had eroded the institution of mar-riage. The day of staff wives with time they could devote to such voluntary work was pass-ing and there were insufficient younger replacements for those subject to the normal attritions of age. In 1997 the committee opened its membership to men. Still, that is itself an expression of the adaptability central to its survival as a volunteer fundraising organi-sation, providing money to improve the university's amenities and enhance the environ-ment of the campus. Its seventeen Kensington lectures for Higher School Certificate students had attracted an average attendance of 500, and introduced them gently to the idea of enrolling at the university when they matriculated.

The big questions of 1983 were general education and overseas students — old problems revisited. The matter of the general education requirement had rumbled below the surface since the university's beginnings, erupting for whatever reason, from time to time: 1983 was such a year. Everyone agreed with the principle that general education was a good thing. Nobody could agree, at least for any time, on how best to pursue it in practice. And there were always pressures this way and that. Law argued successfully to be allowed to opt out. Resistant students awoke many years later to being glad of the compulsion. Sniffy Arts staff rubbed along with mad zealots to do the teaching — or some of it: the numbers involved led to the massive recruitment of part-time tutors, some excellent postgraduates, others lazy or super-annuated money-grubbers. There were other repercussions, given that the General Studies requirement applied to Arts students as well. Psychology acquired the repu-tation of easy option, and became the burdensome target of lazy or indifferent Arts students in the 1960s and 1970s, to the unhappiness of Psychology staff.

All this went under the lens in 1983 to issue in a revamped version in 1987 — the Centre for Liberal and General Studies. This presided over fifty-six teaching hours per student, in courses drawn from the entire university, in each of three areas — environmental studies, the cultural bases of knowledge and belief, and the devel-opment of political, legal, economic, and social systems. It was essentially a tarted-up version of the original 1948 plan with fashionable language and presentation. Plus a contextual course to fit eventual professional activity into wider demands of critical ethics and communication skills. The student was to be taught to think and write clearly across the entire world of knowledge. Grand designs, whatever the inevitable practical shortfall. General Studies continued to be a vexed and vexing question as the economy of universities came under increasing pressure in the 1980s. It was an obvious target for cuts, even abolition. Its staff fell under siege. They saw their golden age as being in the 1970s, followed by a halving of staff into the 1980s. They were the constant subject of inconclusive university committees of review, con-tinually required to justify themselves, never sure of their future, eroded by the leav-ing of staff who saw better opportunities elsewhere. It was a staff who believed that most of the professoriate was opposed to the whole notion of General Studies and that its engagement of student time was too limited and peripheral. Its mood was that of feeling unwanted, cheated, unhappy — something the various changes and tinkering left unmoved. Nor could it be otherwise. General Studies did not see itself as an adornment, a luxury, but as a professional and social necessity. A major element within the university did not. The administration had the task of balancing these opposites, the outcome being bound to leave both positions disgruntled. It was not until Niland that some kind of a workable solution was reached.

Why so mysterious that General Studies be not a success? That other Australian universities did not have it is part — possibly a large part — of an answer: it was a path of New South Wales University pioneering that other universities refused to follow. Was this a reaction engendered by its American look, its departure from English models, which other Australian universities preferred? And, once being rejected by all others, leaving University of New South Wales staff with a sense of isolated difference and competitive liability many of them felt they could well do without.

As to government intervention; at last some spirited resistance, some assertion of, albeit careful, independence. The occasion was the parliamentary Committee to Review Private Overseas Student Policy. The university, apart from restriction on entry to medicine, had never imposed any limitation on overseas students. In 1982 it had 1770 such students, 12.1 per cent of the student body: only Monash came close. The situation had already raised questions at the University of New South Wales, mainly prompted by uneven faculty spread. Arts had few, but in 1983 the proportion of overseas students in some courses was over 40 per cent. The obvious questions were — did these displace local students, and was it an unacceptable drain on university finances? There was also the matter of the impact of these students on the university climate. They tended to congregate very visibly around general university facilities, library, food outlets — meeting points where they spoke their own language to each other. The easy intermix of Colombo Plan days increasingly changed to isolation, demarcated by separate social groups, foreign language, and distancing from the university society. Local students became resentful of what seemed to them a dominance of, and exclusion from their own university, even to the point of physical occupancy of university walkways and outdoor seating by large groups of Asians — 'packs of Chongers' in the student parlance of the day. This balance of student attitudes changed as overseas students increased in such numbers — in 1984, 2767, or 15 per cent of all students, sufficient to make ethnic enclaves possible and assimilation unnecessary. But also raising questions of tolerance. All of this was in the context of wider public debate over Asian immigration; in 1983 over Vietnamese at Fairfield, and in 1984, over remarks made by Professor Geoffrey Blainey of Melbourne University.

Of which the university was aware. Birt had met representatives of People Against Racism, an organisation formed in response to assertions that the neo-Nazi National Action was active on campus. It was not a happy encounter: they found Birt aloof and imperious; for whatever reason (probably because he could not bring himself to believe it), for he was entirely opposed to racism. In 1984, both the chancellor and vice-chancellor deplored the appearance of racial intolerance on campus. Their remarks were general, indicating the difficulty of finding a target to identify. And they offered the best corrective, as fostering an intellectual environment in which irrational hostility towards other races could not survive. Improbable pieties, as was the vice-chancellor's call for tolerance, friendship, and mix, working together. The chancellor's view was that Australia's controls over entry were in no way racist, merely open to misrepresentation as such. The government had increased visa charges, and laid down that no tertiary institution have more than 10 per cent overseas students, and no course more than 20 per cent. So much for this university's unrestricted open-hearted hospitality to what, in Birt's generous but inapposite words, was the latter-day version of the medieval 'wandering scholars'. Whatever the government decided, the University Council proclaimed it would do what it needed in pursuit of the national good. It was not until 1985 that the university fell partly into line with government by imposing course quotas. Birt hailed this as in accord with both government and council policies, though how it was this — reconciling open door with one partly closed — was a prodigy of mental gymnastics. The government also announced a policy to admit full fee-paying students, which had the university worrying about how it might respond. It tried to affirm its own policies of independence, but the pretence was thin.

Still, a stand had been made. If it accepted the government's dictates politely, even generously, council stuck to its guns. It was in Australia's interests to accept overseas students, even at some expense of excluding Australian residents: not often was a government flatly contradicted on its view of Australian needs. Council affirmed that academic criteria was the measure; local students should not be advantaged. It saw no need to alter its policy of no quotas. But the wider questions on cohesion and community character remained unasked. How would overseas students in such numbers relate to the ethos of the university? Would it simply be providing an off-shore university service for various Asian countries for students who had no real interaction with their Australian environment? In student enclaves whose only life was their own? If so, did it matter; was not generosity enough? Should the university foster assimilation? Was this a desirable aim, an appropriate consideration? Nobody bothered to ask, let alone think these things through.

Meanwhile, the vice-chancellor was about his business of internal review, demanding self-justification, and stressful to staff. After it was all over nothing much had happened. What had happened was the advent of a federal Labor government in 1983. This was welcomed as the dawning of a new age of brightness and light by those many academics committed to the Labor cause. They underestimated the commonality of politicians on the university question. Worse, not better, was to come. Labor announced immediately a Commonwealth Tertiary Education Commission, whose first priority was to be equity. There was to be a greater participation in higher education by disadvantaged groups — women, children of ordinary working people, and some ethnic groups, rural youth, and Aboriginal people. In all these categories the university was already performing reasonably well. In ten years from 1972, the proportion of female undergraduates had increased from 23.7 to 35.7 per cent. In particular, women had made up most of the mature age entry, particularly in Arts. Their presence, highly motivated, articulate — mature — did much to enhance student tutorial involvement. As to ethnic groups, the presence of a large number of Greek Australian students — notably women — was a feature of the late

1970s, early 1980s. In 1971 Aboriginal students were exempted from quotas: sixty-one students so exempted had enrolled by 1983, five had graduated. Economic pressure on farmers made the rural growth policy very difficult to implement. The government had no patience with such excuses as a depressed economy. Birt was anxious to cooperate, frustrated only by the realities of the economy and the impossibilities of following ideological political dreaming. He was at pains throughout the 1980s to adapt the university to government imperatives made in the name of service to the community. Such presumption was hard to endure from governments — of all complexions — which did little to disguise the fact that they regarded universities as peopled by an irrelevant bunch of highly paid poseurs. Whitlam was lordly, knew it all better and beforehand (on introduction as expert on the Irish in Australia, I was treated to a dogmatic, potted history of that area). Universities were for engineering social change. Birt found Fraser dead hostile and boorish with it. Despite his university background, Hawke was simply not interested. Such was Birt's experience of the prime ministers: Education ministers were in some cases better; but, from Dawkins to Vanstone to Kemp, they tended to be products of university teaching — a fact not easy to believe.

The basic fact was that politicians had no comprehension, let alone sympathy with what universities were, or were on about. Those few who did — Barry Jones comes to mind — were swiftly sidelined in the power game. Nevertheless, Birt tried to work in with their wishes, however time-consuming or trivial. Indeed, he had little choice in the face of bully-boys whose maxim was 'jump or I'll —— ', a threat never stated but constantly implied. The university turned in on itself and its own resources — the Alumni Association with a potential membership of 50,000, pushed by a new pro-vice-chancellor, Malcolm Chaikin. Keeping its own house in order was the main university priority. A small cut — 175 — was made in first year enrolments, to balance reduced funding, but most effort, much of it necessarily non-productive, went into the matter of disadvantaged students, which the government was pursuing, to the degree of unrealistic obsession, in 1984. To help cope with a pressure situation, Jarlath Ronayne together with Chaikin and Golding joined the vice-chancellor as a core group.

Nor was the Commonwealth the only level of government to treat the university with contempt. Without any consultation whatever of the university, or affected parties, in 1985 the New South Wales minister for Education, Rodney Cavalier, reduced the membership of the University Council from forty-four to twenty-nine. He explained the reduction as mainly a move to ensure uniformity among universities: Chancellor Samuels declared it motivated by 'doctrinaire compulsion'. Its effect was to increase the proportion of positions within the minister's own gift and significantly enhance government power. It also severed the university's traditional links with manufacturing industry. And the minister's failure to consult with the university was construed as an insult. It was probably more a reflection of the standard politician's view of things. Universities were to be disposed of as suited politics. Courtesies were irrelevant.

In speaking to the Bill in April 1985 Cavalier urged efficiency and cost-effectiveness as prompters. He also made clear his anti-hierarchical intentions: sub-professorial staff must outnumber the professorial staff on council. Arguing that the university had out-grown its business and industrial beginnings, he said that the old order would forfeit its monopoly place: the minister would consult whom he wished. He announced, 'the first generation of the University of New South Wales is over', had been for some years.

At a sessional meeting with staff, Birt made clear that he was less concerned over the matter than many staff: he thought the reduction in size 'useful'. He thought the prospect of more sub-professorial staff on council not 'necessarily appropriate' — mild words — and had nothing to say in response to Neil Harpley of the Staff Association, who was critical of increased government intrusion into university affairs. Harpley expressed disappointment with the vice-chancellor and declared it time for a more vigorous response to government.

In fact, both chancellor and vice-chancellor had been informed generally before-hand by the minister, pledged to the strictest confidence, and given to understand that he was not prepared to negotiate. Samuels was quietly furious at such treatment, but all that the council could do was to deplore what had been done, in terms of failure to consult, and to worry about such precedent.

Birt soldiered on into the late 1980s to prove that the university could change, could do what the Commonwealth government demanded, could review its own inter-nal functions, could assist the halt and the lame, the outsiders and the disadvantaged. Could dance to the government tune, whatever that was, but — this was Birt's soul-saving imperative — at the same time advance that with which he had been entrusted, service to an institution dedicated to the cause of the entire body of human knowledge.

The year 1986 saw more students, 639 more, but 268 of these belonged to the Australian Defence Force Academy, opened in that year. The rest were mainly in the Faculty of Arts, and mainly women. Up too were Higher School Certificate aggre-gates. Down? Funding, 1 per cent in real terms; constriction continued. The University College of the Defence Force Academy replaced the Faculty of Military Studies established in 1968. The evolution had not been without difficulties and tensions, but never anything serious, and its outcome was an educated officer class, aware of community backgrounds and expectations.

The vice-chancellor pondered the thirteen years which had passed since the Commonwealth took over responsibility for funding. He saw clearly the increasing push to increase and broaden the base for participation in higher education and for immediately employable products — all within government budgetary austerity. Though he did not say so, it was a policy of wanting more, for less. A 1986 gov-ernment review indicated that, in real terms, total government outlay on universities had remained unchanged for a decade while student numbers had increased by a third. The government recognised this in very practical terms with a charge of $250 per student. Birt's response was to wonder if the university was doing enough to meet government demands that it be more relevant to national economic needs. His 1986 report stressed the implementation of government policies. Overseas enrol-ments had been reduced to meet the guidelines. The Commonwealth would even fund initiatives to help disadvantaged students. Birt introduced a 'Corporate Planning Process' to better relate to industry and commerce. Commonwealth dog wagged university tail, a process which the university rewarded by conferring in April 1987 an honorary Doctor of Laws on Bob Hawke.

Nevertheless, in 1987 the university had woken up to the vital importance of private money for the future: it was likely the Commonwealth stringency would continue, probably intensify. The raising of private money was imperative if university operations were to continue at 'an acceptable level'.

Lacking private benefactors of the American kind — the general public view was that governments should fund universities — the university decided to establish a foundation to raise money: the Alumni Association would have a leading role in that. Further, as the chancellor pointed out, the matter was not only that of maintaining standards, but 'will also protect our academic independence and our institutional autonomy' in the interests of a free society. That these had been under increasing threat, must surely have been seen for some time — the incursions and dictates of state power were constantly increasing. When would they become quite intolerable? Perhaps such encroachments were of such a kind — smallish, not unreasonable, gradual — as to arrest major disquiet, but the cumulative effect and inherent trend were patently clear by 1987: academic independence and autonomy were at stake. Worse, much worse, was to come. In July of that year John Dawkins became minister for, not Education, but Employment, Education and Training, a label which proclaimed the government's scheme of things. Certainly, universities were polite places, not used to public disputation and its barbarous ways. Nor did they see it as their function to contend with government. And, as always, there was apathy and the disposition to leave things to others: if vice-chancellors did not protest, all must be relatively well. For all their vaunted dedication to free inquiry, universities are extremely hierarchical structures. There was also a widespread — indeed dominant — faith, particularly in the Arts faculty (where criticism might have been expected), in the beneficence of the Labor government: fear of the malevolent intentions of the Coalition parties produced blindness to the damage being inflicted by Labor.

This was in the future. By 1987 something of a equilibrium had been again achieved and confidence was returning. The soul-searching, internal reviews of the previous four years had been concluded, a corporate plan for mission and strategic direction had been adopted, and the vice-chancellor felt the university had responded as much as it could to the challenge of government (and allegedly community) demands. It had done so willingly and successfully. It had measured itself and found itself not wanting. It had responded to insistence that it give demonstrable value for public money. At what cost to itself? A 'corporate plan'? Was the university merely another corporation, to be appraised and evaluated as such? Was its function and character thus diminished? Changed, yes, but also sustained, by an academic staff which went about its traditional business.

The government's demands fell on all Australian universities. Birt isolated two areas of particular New South Wales University responsibility. First, a coherent program of liberal studies to suit the demands of a modern culture and economy in South-East Asia. It now had that, in the revamping that began in 1983. The second imperative was to preserve its stress on science and technology, that is, to maintain its authentic original character, to make special provision for teaching and research in science, technology, and such adjuncts as commerce and management. So, Applied Science in particular was to receive more than its due share of university rations. And Arts was skewed towards the vocational with the introduction of a Bachelor of Social Science degree in 1987. Arts would not only serve itself but provide useful interdisciplinary services and service various bureaucracies. Even more to the utilitarian point was the Bachelor of Science in Business Information Technology, with students on scholarships funded by such organisations as AMP, Westpac, and IBM. The Japanese computer company NEC outfitted a computing room (cost $80,000) for Marketing. Joint ventures proliferated, notably with St Vincent's Hospital on AIDS funding by government ($2.5 million) and private sources — $1 million from the Australian Cancer Foundation. There was massive, publicly funded work in health, water, drugs. The accounting firm Price Waterhouse sponsored a chair of Accounting. University centres and special units shot up to deal with, and attract, such activity — from thirty-six in 1986 to fifty-six in 1988. It was the old university of 1949 in new guise: sponsorships, scholarships, out-working with other authorities and institutions. It was without the vice-chancellorial dynamic that had created a university around Baxter. Birt presided rather than drove. But he had allowed and encouraged an entrepreneurial staff to have its head in a way and to a degree that ensured the university's survival in a hostile world.

No question that the university was recovering and regrouping, pulling in outside money and reorganising its internal resources. Indeed, the 1980s were years of considerable success for the university in attracting grants. It played that game well, overseen particularly by Birt and Alan Gilbert. Thus, the University of New South Wales was in a position to deal with, and survive — with morale intact — the Dawkins tertiary assault and its consequences. Yet, not before doubt and major travail, before the existence of the university in its present form had been called into most serious question.

6

TRANSFORMATION
1987–92

1987

1987

Board of Studies in General Education and Department of General Studies dissolved and replaced by the Centre for Liberal and General Studies. • New research centres, for — Australian Defence Studies; Chemical Analysis; Children's Leukaemia and Cancer Research; Cognitive Science; Export Marketing; Groundwater Management and Hydrogeology; Membrane and Separation Technology; South Pacific Studies; Studies in Management and Logistics; Wastewater Treatment; Urban Water Policy; Women's Studies. • Introduction of ACCESS scheme to assist entry of disadvantaged students. • Aboriginal Student Support Program begins. • NEW DEGREES/DIPLOMAS Master of Project Management; Bachelor of Social Science; BSc in Business Information Technology; Diploma of Education (merit)

MAY Archives relocated from Chancellery to Library building.
11 JUNE Link building (sport and recreation centre) opened by the chancellor.
1 JULY J Dawkins appointed minister for Education, and his Green Paper 'Higher Education — a Policy Discussion Paper' is subsequently released. • UNSW receives a self-insurance licence for worker's compensation (Unicare Insurance P/L) — the first New South Wales university to do so.
SEPTEMBER Centre for Manufacturing and Automation opened. • Computer Aided Design and Computer Integrated Manufacturing laboratories opened in the Faculty of Engineering. • IBM 4381 mainframe computer donated by IBM.
DECEMBER NIDA building completed. • IBM 3090 computer installed in Library Tower (replacing the CYBER 172 unit).
14 DECEMBER University of New South Wales Foundation Ltd established to raise money for the purposes of the university and reduce reliance on government funding.

1988

1988

Professor J Ronayne appointed deputy vice-chancellor. • Professor A Gilbert appointed pro-vice-chancellor. • Professorial Board replaced by Academic Board. • Six-year medical course reintroduced. • New research centres, for — Acoustics and Vibration; Asia Pacific Institute for Nuclear Science; Cross Cultural Social Work Education; Food Industry Development; Information Technology Research; Key Centre for Mines; Public Health. • Faculty of Commerce renamed Faculty of Commerce and Economics, three new schools being established within it. • Institute of Languages establishes a special unit for the teaching of English for academic purposes (EAP) to overseas students. • Media Liaison Office established, separating publications and public relations (previously carried out by the Public Affairs Unit). • News Service Unit established within Administrative Services Branch. • UNSW HIV-AIDS

policy statement issued. • Safety Unit imposes smoking restrictions in various buildings on campus. • Introduction of online public access computer catalogues (OPAC) to library. • Campus-wide fibre optic network becomes fully operational, providing for the interconnection of all computers on campus. • NEW DEGREES Master of Public Health; BSc in Business Information Technology; joint Social Work–Law degree.

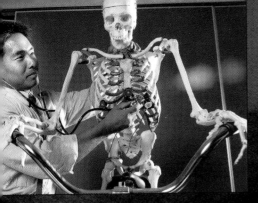

Physiology and Pharmacology
1987

Interment of the School of Botany
1987

Library lawn clock
unveiled 1993

FEBRUARY University Archives launches a series of published oral history interviews.

1 MARCH UNSW joins Superannuation Scheme for Australian Universities (compulsory) for academic appointees.

1 APRIL State Authorities Superannuation Scheme (noncompulsory) begins for new appointees to general staff.

JULY White Paper 'Higher Education — a Policy Statement' issued by J Dawkins.

SEPTEMBER A Horton retires as university librarian; Dr C Henderson replaces him.

OCTOBER Discussion paper 'The Future Structure of Higher Education in NSW — a position paper' launched by Dr T Metherell, New South Wales minister for Education.

DECEMBER Intake of subsidised overseas students to cease (from 1 January 1990).

1989

Binary higher education system replaced by a unified national system. • HECS (Higher Education Contribution Scheme) introduced. • Assisted Overseas Student Scheme replaced by full-fee programs — private students now provide up to 15 per cent of UNSW's revenues. • UNSW agrees to act as academic sponsor for new Charles Sturt University. • UNSW–State Transit Authority Liaison Committee formed. • UNSW Orchestra formed. • Faculty decision-making devolution introduced by Pro-Vice-Chancellor RM Golding. • Full-fee-paying, overseas students allowed to enrol in Medicine. • A position of Overseas Student Recruitment Officer created. • New research centres, for — Bioengineering; Postgraduate Studies in Civil Engineering; Communications Security Research (ADFA). • Inaugural Alumni Scholarships awarded. • Freedom From

Harassment policy statement issued. • Senior Common Room Club renamed UNSW Club. • Museum of the History of Science officially opened in Heffron building. • New degrees Master of Laws (coursework); Bachelor of Economics; BComm in Marketing and Hospitality Management; Bachelor of Computer Engineering. • Master of Construction Management — a one-year full-time course available only to full fee-paying, overseas students. • Campus improvements David Phillips Field clubhouse commenced; Undercroft Cafeteria opens.

1 JANUARY TERC and Staff Development Unit become the Professional Development Centre.

24 JANUARY UNSW Sports Association Scholarship Endowment Fund Ltd established (later called UNSW Ben Lexcen Endowment Fund).

APRIL Professor J Niland appointed dean of the Faculty of Commerce and Economics.

JULY The International Professional and Continuing Education Institute (IPACE) formed, as a division of Unisearch.

1 JULY Freedom of Information legislation introduced in New South Wales.

SEPTEMBER Sir Philip Baxter dies.

NOVEMBER Specific pathogen-free (SPF) rodent facility commissioned at Little Bay.

SELECTED EVENTS

Cuban band Los Noveles,
library lawn 1987

Graduation
1987

1990

Cooperative Research
Centres initiative announced
by the prime minister. •
Fast-track MComm program
linked with Dept of Extra-
Mural Studies, University of
Hong Kong. • Faculty of Arts
renamed Faculty of Arts and
Social Sciences. • School of
Electrical Engineering and
Computer Science splits into
two (effective 1 January
1991). • New research
centres, for — Business
Econometrics and Forecasting
Group; Corporate Change;
Fujitsu Centre for Managing
Information Technology in
Organisations; Management
Accounting Development;
Photovoltaic Systems and
Devices; Vision Education. •
Campus-wide paper recycling
program introduced. •
Faculty of Science institutes
pilot remedial summer ses-
sions for undergraduates. •
NEW DEGREES BSc in Earth and
Environmental Science; joint
Bachelor of Music–Education.
Other Bachelor's degrees: of
Bioprocess Engineering, of
Environmental Engineering, of
Japanese Studies, of
Marketing, of Materials
Engineering, of Sports
Science, of Taxation (effective

1991). At College of Fine
Arts former graduate diploma
courses become Master's
degrees — of Art Education,
of Art, Arts Administration. •
CAMPUS IMPROVEMENTS Campus
refurbishment program
begins; David Phillips Field
clubhouse completed. • New
building begun at the College
of Fine Arts.

1 JANUARY College of Fine
Arts (COFA) and St George
campus — formerly the City
Art Institute and the Institute
of Education, parts of the
now dissolved Sydney CAE
— formally become part of
UNSW.
MARCH Between UNSW
and Joint Coal Board negotiations take place for establishment of Mines Health and
Safety Trust.
MAY John Ward, vice-chan-
cellor of the University of
Sydney, dies in train crash.
28 JUNE Graduate manage-
ment qualification launched at
AGSM.
1 JULY Newly constituted
University Council takes
office (under the recent
UNSW Act, with its membership limited to 21 members).
SEPTEMBER Professor AJ
Wicken appointed pro-vice-
chancellor.
OCTOBER EEO guidelines
issued, for recruitment and
selection of staff.
19 OCTOBER Asia–Australia
Institute opened.
17 NOVEMBER UNSW signs
agreement with the Australian
Tax Office to establish distance courses in Australian
taxation studies.

1991

Cooperative Research
Centres established, for —
Aerospace Structures; Eye
Research and Technology;
Waste Management and
Pollution Control. • Record
over-enrolment — 1600
EFTSUs (Effective Full-Time
Student Units). • Code of
practice developed for
research. • New research
centres, for — Aboriginal
Research and Resource;
Hospital Management and
Information Systems
Research; Munro Centre for
Civil and Environmental
Engineering; National Centre
for Banking and Capital
Markets; Prince of Wales
Medical Research Institute. •
In the Library: resource centre established for users with
disabilities; RAPID launched
(information search and document delivery service). •
Students' Union establishes a
child-care cooperative in
Arthur Street, Randwick. •
External Affairs Directorate
established (to improve
advice and support received
from alumni, employers, and
so on). • Computer Support
and Sales Centre introduced
to provide user-support
for UNSW computing

SELECTED EVENTS

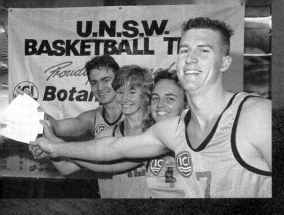

UNSW basketball team sponsorships
1992

Iwan Sujono, designer of the library lawn clock
1992

environment. •
NEW DEGREES/DIPLOMAS
Master of Sports Science;
Master of Welfare Studies and
Practice; MEd in Creative
Arts; MApplSc in
Construction Management, in
Engineering Materials, in
Geological Data Processing, in
Mineral and Mining
Engineering; Master in
Environmental Engineering;
Master in Taxation. Bachelor
of Leisure Studies; Bachelor
of Design; Bachelor of Art
Theory. Graduate diplomas in
Commerce, Economics,
Advanced Taxation, Taxation
Studies, Defence Studies,
Technology Management. •
CAMPUS IMPROVEMENTS
Property & Works
Department develop Space
Planning and Management
System (SPAM); Barker Street
parking station begun; COFA's
art and design complex com-
pleted — Flinders St and
Paddington campuses consoli-
dated into one campus, at
Paddington. • UNSW
Campus-Wide Network
(CWN) connected to
Australian Academic and
Research Network (AARnet)
and FACOM computer sys-
tem; two new microwave
communication links extend
CWN facilities to COFA and
Randwick campuses.

MARCH Publication of
University Safety Manual.
1 MARCH Professor C Fell
appointed pro-vice-chancellor.
JUNE University of
Technology, Sydney and
UNSW sign agreement for
pilot library reciprocal-bor-
rowing scheme.
AUGUST Students' Union
security shuttle bus service
begins.
SEPTEMBER J Ronayne
resigns as deputy vice-chancellor.
4 NOVEMBER APPOINTMENTS
C Fell, deputy vice-chancellor
(Academic Affairs); AJ Wicken,
deputy vice-chancellor
(Research and Development).

1992

UNIMAIL network service
provides e-mail facility. •
Burraduc Field Station sold. •
New research centres, for —
Australian Maritime
Engineering; Cardiac
Technology; Optical Fibre and
Photonic Technology. • A
learning and communications
skills centre is set up — the
Learning Centre. •
Introduction of 'Yellow Shirts'
— senior students helping
enrolling students in
Orientation Week. •
UNIBEAT launched — a cam-
pus community security
scheme. • Basser College
adopts a 'responsible use of
alcohol' policy. •
NEW DEGREES/DIPLOMAS
Applied Science programs in
Food Microbiology and
Materials Engineering. Joint
degrees, in — Mining
Engineering–Civil Engineering;
Arts–Medicine; Arts–Science.
Graduate diplomas in Asian
and European Studies (Faculty
of Arts). In Education —
Doctor of Education; MEd in
Teaching; Bachelor of Teaching
(Hons); graduate diplomas in
Education Studies, Gifted
Education. • CAMPUS
IMPROVEMENTS Samuels building
(completed 1991) opened;

Barker Street parking station
completed; Quadrangle building, and substantial upgrading
of upper campus begun; covered arcade constructed over
Mathews plaza; glass-houses
removed from Biological
Sciences–Medicine precinct.

13 MAY Library launches LIB-
LINK system — access to
online catalogues of all New
South Wales libraries.
JUNE Institute for
Environmental Studies estab-
lished. • Centre for
Advanced Numerical
Computation in Engineering
established.

SELECTED EVENTS

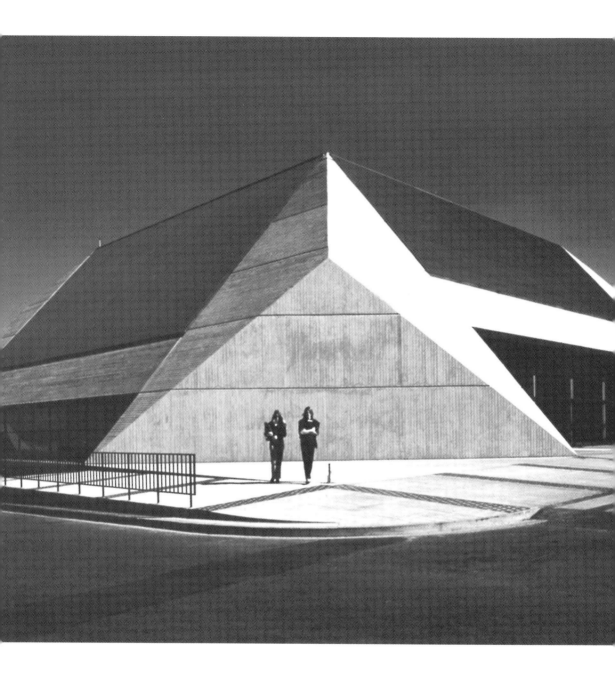

∧

The Clancy Auditorium

1970

It has been said that universities never suited Australia, its ethos, style, the way things were here. Not in the way that Oxford was integral to Britain. Sure, Australia needed professionals — doctors, lawyers, dentists, vets, scientists, some others — but they could be provided by top-level training schools. Universities, in the sense of institutions dedicated to the life and development of the intellect, were viewed as essentially superfluous, if not wasteful and incomprehensible, luxuries. That this pragmatism should become the dominant fashion of the Bicentennial (and thereafter) mind-frame was not surprising, particularly given its harmony with emergent economic rationalism. This chimed in with the traditional distrust of — even contempt for — the university and the intellect, to place them under increasing question. The Bicentennial was the occasion for what seemed to be a liberation of identity, which made Australia more itself, a repudiation of 'colonialism', of dependence on things past, towards a growth which had its happy gains—but also its sad debilitation and losses. One such was decreasing care for the life of the intellect; never great, now less.

In that regard, the University of New South Wales was significantly less ill-advantaged (the negative phrase applies) than other Australian universities. Its science and technology basis, together with medicine and law, and Birt's careful management with an eye to keeping in touch with the governmental and bureaucratic demands of the day (however intrusive), plus its strong orientation towards Asia, to say nothing of its sheer size and increasing public reputation — matters close to politicians' hearts — made it less unpopular than others, in the view from Canberra. So, too, did its successful efforts, first under Birt, then, spectacularly, under Niland, to take on the appurtenances of a public corporation, complete with strategic planning, mission statements, goals and priorities, and a public face to go with them: the refurbishment of the Chancellery building commencing in February 1993 both symbolised and expressed that upbeat, new approach to image which was to be a feature of the university's self-promotion thereafter. Those cosmetics, so important in a world of appearances, were purchased in a financial environment freed, in 1993 by the Department of Employment, Education and Training (DEET), of the former requirement to argue all capital expenses with an ill-disposed Commonwealth. From 1993 funding was made available in a lump sum, which allowed the vice-chancellor discretionary power over its disposal.

The trick was to sustain the corporate act while still maintaining integrity and pre-eminence as a higher educational institution — a true university. It was a balancing and illusionist performance not easy to bring off successfully, and subject to wax and wane. Of necessity the vice-chancellor carried the corporate weight, the day-to-day interaction with business, government, national and international affairs. But the pyramid of which he was the apex depended on the quality of its ground-level, intellectual base. Without excellence there, he would have nothing to sell. So, a staff of the highest university calibre was imperative to establishing their positions at the international top of their disciplines. If the corporation was to be successful in its field, its daily achievements and representatives would have to make it so.

230

Given that the field was university education, and that the corporate mode was not only novel but, arguably, in some degree of conflict with its nature, cohabitation was sometimes tense, never particularly comfortable. Academics reluctantly accepted the realities of government constriction and dogmatism and the dictates of a corporate world — but they did not enjoy them. Particularly was this so at the University of New South Wales, because the staff was long disposed to generate its own changes naturally, from its own internal dynamics, its own appraisal of the demands of the needs of its subjects, and community requirements. Staff felt — with justification — that it did not need a Canberra ginger-up, indeed that this was an arrogant imposition of bureaucratic time-wasting: it betokened both ignorance and interference. The imperatives whereby science subjects kept up with the times are obvious. Indeed, internationally, science and technology MADE those times. A university founded on the notion that the community needed such practical skills, hardly needed Canberra to galvanise it. And at the University of New South Wales Arts was formed in the same socially responsive mode.

The School of History illustrates this sensitivity. First, under Jock Salmon as professor, broad courses on British and European history; then under Frank Crowley, strong emphasis on Australian history with Indian, American and Asian introduced (Indian to lapse after popular support fell away). Then to follow, under the subsequent elected, sub-professorial heads of school a situation of anything goes, as courses followed the interests of individual members of staff — so women, sport, the environment, and so on. It was the history of the social directions of Australia, reflected in the phases of teaching of the School of History — British colonial, Australian home-grown, concern for Asia, then smorgasbord without cohesion or direction. Logical progression this, even down to the dominant personalities: Salmon, a traditionalist man of the army and military, the antipodean Raj; Crowley, the gifted Australian larrikin, vastly engaging and entertaining, colourful to outrageous lengths, serious teacher and champion of Australian history; then, as authority passed away from the 'god-professor', a procession of diverse, elected heads of school. Crowley? Higher things. To be dean of Arts: prodigally great and

The A to Z of Academia

by Phil Schofield

H is for Head of School

SCHOFIELD

∧

Phil Schofield caricature series

Uniken 16 June 1979

P Schofield

generous when university money was waxing, far less popular when it waned. Eater of crisp apples during solemn university meetings. Big man in himself, whatever faults and shortcomings. Deans came in all sorts and sizes, none more spectacular than Frank Crowley. As to heads of school, all trying — largely successfully — to manage what Crowley described as a pack of prima donnas: trying to organise academics is like trying to herd cats.

These heads, as in all schools, were increasingly burdened by the consequences of what might be termed a managerial revolution, the devolution of power and the percolation of authority, which occurred in the university in the 1980s. Increasing internal reviews and the demands of Canberra bureaucracy impacted on heads of school, generating an exponential growth in paper-work, committee attendances, and staff liaison. Thus, middle and lower management carried the bureaucratic weight (much of it superfluous) that went into building the new university. Moreover, the swing to elected heads of school, from the early 1980s, meant that each staff member became increasingly king in his or her own specialist castle, each little known beyond their own intellectual fiefdom, heirs to the post-professorial dispersion of authority. True, as the then prevalent wisdom had it, professors were not necessarily good managers, but neither were many of those elected. Particularly was this so when the headship was revealed as being time-consuming and personally thankless, and thus increasingly repellent to those perhaps best-fitted for the task. Further, although promotion to full professor became available in 1990, heads often lacked the intangible authority and self-confidence necessary to govern colleagues. The out-

The A to Z
of Academia

by Phil Schofield

D is for Dean

P Schofield

Phil Schofield caricature series

Uniken 21 April 1979

come was often one of inertia and drift: school policies became reactive rather than innovatory. Cliques, interest groups, strong personalities called the tune, often to be drowned out in passive disharmony. But this is to stress the Arts scene. It was the exception rather than the rule. Most heads of schools in the university as a whole, remained appointed by deans, who did so after consultation of staff. They made a conscious decision to appoint what in their view was the best person, not necessarily the most popular. Indeed, in some faculties deans chose too well, in the sense of appointing heads of independent ability — and challenging strength. Tom Daly told me a story of such a situation. A dean (who shall be nameless) generated such widespread opposition and intense hostility within his faculty, particularly over his use of the budget to advantage his own projects, that he feared the vice-chancellor would act to remove him. Returning to his office from some meeting, his secretary informed him that the vice-chancellor wanted to see him immediately. Determined to forestall the ignominy of being fired, he wrote his resignation and handed it to the vice-chancellor on arrival. The vice-chancellor accepted it with some surprise and regret: he had wanted to discuss with the dean some matter of general university policy. Tom related this with glee and relish, such was the disarming hubris of that particular dean.

The wonder of it was the system worked and survived, and that so remarkably well — not least because individual staff members devoted their talents to the demands of personal responsibilities. While these had their modern twist — that of being market-driven or -dominated — they had a ring of the unreconstructed 1950s and 1960s: large, impersonal classes; how to adapt traditional and unfashionable skills to an uncomprehending student world. Each school, each faculty had its multitude of variant characters — those who impinged most on student consciousness and reminiscence. Say the warm and scholarly Stones — Julius and Margaret — or the dry Don Harding, or that champion of Aborigines, Garth Nettheim, in Law. Or that dour Northern Ireland man, Darty Glover, in Medicine and, at the other remove there, that constant university gadfly, Jack Carmody. The gregarious Crawford Munro in Civil Engineering. Many of these identities had public impacts and reputations well beyond the university: Roger Covell in music, Tony Vinson in prison reform, Max Freeland as Australia's foremost architectural historian, Ross Blunden in traffic management, Donald Horne as public intellectual, Alex Carey as rebel in many causes. This is to say nothing of the prodigies of the internal builders: BJ Ralph, for instance, who established, in 1956, the first Australian School of Biological Sciences, and stayed with it until distinguished retirement in 1980. On and on it goes. It was not vice-chancellors students knew, it was the teachers they encountered. With 126,326 degrees awarded by 1996, almost 30,000 students in that year, with 1641 academic staff, it is impossible to do anything resembling justice to the student–staff interaction involved. The diversity of student experience is obvious beyond any comprehensible depiction. Yet it is those individual experiences — the workface of the university — which make it up as an institution and give it life and zest. And locate it in an immediate community.

Of course, this is the rosy side. There is also the reverse of the coin. There are also those staff who came across to students as shonky, hot-air balloonists, the lazy and incompetent. And vice versa. Of their nature, universities are peopled by the highly intelligent, those who are sensitive to, aware of the quality and characteristics of the minds they encounter. Falsity is soon detected in the teaching situation — which is, after all, what universities are about, their reason for existence. The best students are keenly aware of which of the staff open and extend their minds, of who are the indifferent, who the duds. The university was among the first to formalise student evaluation of teaching, opinions and reactions which fed back into staff promotion procedures. Birt stressed teaching.

What complexity could be more in tune both with the times and its own necessary nature? Who needed Canberra bureaucracy and uncomprehending politicians to tell it its own business? Who needed shaking up by Canberra suit-heads, on a campus where, by the 1980s, the vice-chancellor was regarded, by students, as a distant irrelevance, seen occasionally around the place in blue blazer, silver buttons, and grey bags — uniform of that hostile, foreign place, the University of Sydney? (Strange how this matter of dress could be so important and carry such heavy implied meaning. Some staff thought it enough to say of Birt, 'he wore cardigans' as if that was sufficient summation of character.) Since the 1970s, indeed from the beginning, students were quite able to fend for themselves. Unsatisfactory lecturers got the heat, even to the extent of being locked out of lecture rooms by rowdy students within. Dissatisfied students took their grievances as far as Baxter, which that advocate of hierarchy and good order did not at all like. In response he instituted an inquiry into teaching. Students did not need Canberra to protect them, in the name of some righteous public good. Indeed, Canberra was increasingly to emerge as their enemy, beginning with the Higher Education Contribution Scheme in 1989.

The bicentennial year, 1988, brought the university little to celebrate. The Dawkins White Paper on Tertiary Education abolished the division between colleges

UNSW Archives

The Clancy Auditorium meeting opposing amalgamation proposals —

with Michel Birt (standing), and (from left to right) Tony Wicken, John Milfull,

Gordon Samuels, Gavin Brown, John Nevile, Jessica Milner Davis

22 March 1989

of advanced education (CAEs) and universities, entailing open competition for funds (in which some colleges faced the prospect of extinction). It was to be noted — later — that the Dawkins 'reforms', which had profound consequences for universities, had passed without perceptible opposition from vice-chancellors. (Stalinist is how Joseph Forgas described these reforms animated by the idea that the Canberra bureaucracy best knew how to run universities.) This is hardly fair to Birt privately, even officially, if it might seem so in the public arena. In April 1988 in response to an invitation by Dawkins to comment on the minister's Green Paper on Higher Education, he put his differing views clearly but very mildly to Dawkins, in a spirit of gentlemanly and pondered exchange: University Council was to advance a similar, somewhat more combative view, at a special meeting. The problem was that Dawkins was not interested in civilised discussion or exchange of views, but only in announcing his intentions. He was acting politically; Birt and the University Council were responding academically. Perhaps if Birt (and other vice-chancellors) had jumped up and down in rage, and screamed objections which engaged the electorate, Dawkins might have been given pause. But ideology was in play; so was the numbers game, as the parliamentary debates reveal. Criticism was met by declarations of central bureaucratic necessity, fiscal responsibility, and sheer assertions of heedless power. Consultation was paraded as agreement. Protest was ignored. Much was said at the time about the pursuit of excellence, but in fact the reforms were animated by the spirit of egalitarianism and equal opportunity. Quantity counted more than quality and thereafter for the University of New South Wales defence of quality was the issue of the day — and every day. However, at the university, this was obscured by two major factors: Birt's pacificatory and accepting disposition, and the serious disruption caused by the response to the Dawkins initiatives of the New South Wales minister for Education, Dr Terry Metherell. So far as the University of New South Wales is concerned, had this not been the context, serious discussion of the nature of universities, and the potentially deleterious nature of the Dawkins agenda might have taken place.

Metherell added to Dawkins his own gloss, with a radical plan of amalgamation between the university and the former colleges of advanced education in New South Wales. He sought (and was supported in principle by the university), as did Dawkins, to achieve equity in access to tertiary institutions of recognised quality, bearing in mind particularly country areas and disadvantaged groups. However, the means he proposed to bring this about were highly contentious and divisive, provoking vigorous opposition within the university, led formidably by the chancellor, Justice Samuels. But not by the vice-chancellor, Michael Birt, who took a different view of the situation. It was a matter which divided the two men and, given the fact that most of the university community sided with the Samuels position, weakened — permanently — the power and respect accorded Birt. Birt's ways of quietude and acceptance were not in accord with Samuels's — and the university's — disposition to resist, fight.

The New South Wales minister for Education, known for his strongly interventionist approach to other education areas — came up with 'a network system', designed to place the University of New South Wales at the centre of a federation of certain of the former regional colleges of advanced education — Riverina-Murray Institute of Advanced Education, Mitchell CAE at Bathurst, and other, small colleges. The system was to rest its reputation on the university's.

This alarmed some people within the university, as fraught with serious problems for the future. A number of staff, at various early stages, perceived the threat and eventually the matter was taken up with the chancellor, who was persuaded to act to oppose the proposal. Above all was the matter of integrity of the university's degrees, hard-won in reputation, and seen as under threat from courses in institutions of different background and aspirations. To put it politely, it seemed to offer the certainty of the cheapening of the university's degrees. How would standards be maintained? The university would have to retain dominant supervisory rights over the lesser elements of such a federation. Did the university have the resources, in time, energy, and money, to hold together such a State-wide mega-university? Discussions with the colleges got nowhere on the vital matter — from the university's viewpoint — of its overriding supervisory power. The colleges were determined on their individual autonomy.

The University Council rejected the plan, but the parliamentary discussion paper was nevertheless put forward. It sought to abolish the existing university, and its senior governance, from chancellor down: in writing his 1988 annual report Samuels saw it as being possibly his last, 'a letter from the tomb'. It was to be succeeded — in a style in keeping with Dr Metherell's radical and dictatorial educational disposition — by an interim board of governors of eighteen members, fifteen of whom would be appointed by the minister: it was hard to conceive of a political intervention and control more thoroughgoing than this. The university's name was to remain the same.

All this prompted a swift and formidable public denunciation by Samuels, not a person to be trifled with or held in coercion. He deplored the minister's board as open to great abuse, entirely contrary to any legislative precedent in university governance and to the principle of universities being governed by elected persons with staff participation. Its provision for accommodating staff viewpoints was so tiny as to destroy it. And ministerial appointment rather than election was reprehensible, retrograde, and essentially absurd, ludicrous, given an institution of 24,000 students, with staff to match. Besides, all of this was unnecessary. The minister could achieve his purpose simply by making the CAEs colleges of the university under existing 1968 legislation: the university had long and successful experience with colleges. Such a course would avoid 'repugnant devices', and reconcile the university's wishes with those of colleges insistent on local autonomy.

As Samuels saw them, the Metherell proposals spelt the death of the university as hitherto known and understood, a fundamental challenge. The vice-chancellor did not share this perspective: Michael Birt was taken up with internal matters of corporate plans and mission statements. As he appraised the university's evolving situation, it was part of a worldwide movement towards a corporate approach in universities. The university was moving from a general statement of mission to a specific set of goals to implement it, over the next six years. These goals, in essence, amounted to concentration on what Birt saw as the university's strengths, dressed up by him in the meaningless, high-flown verbiage of the day.

Birt viewed the Dawkins changes in government policy generally as having 'complemented our planning process', a curious exemplar of the tail wagging the dog perspective. Whatever, chicken or egg, the situation allowed a well-prepared university to respond to the change in government policy 'with alacrity and coherence'. The government had required all educational institutions to negotiate an educational profile with DEET to define their role and act as a basis for funding, and to put that funding on a more commercial basis. Birt accepted this demand as a positive stimulus to document the university's research and teaching activities in more detail. The outcome of the consequent discussions with DEET was, Birt judged, 'mutually satisfactory'. Student intake was maintained at the 1988 levels until 1991, but there was some decrease in master's courses, and increased student load. The university undertook to expand its intake of Aboriginal and disadvantaged students and took pride in its attraction of the highest number of Australian Research Council (ARC) grants.

Indeed, Birt was taking particular interest in developing the university's research potential, appointing serious-minded Alan Gilbert as pro-vice-chancellor with special responsibility for research; with a plan highlighted in 1988 to maximise the university's research potential, with a special office designed to provide staff with stimulus and practical help in formulating and forwarding projects — building on strength, Birt called it. This strategy was extraordinarily successful, first under Alan Gilbert's direction, then Chris Fell's. From 1991 to the present the university led all others in ARC Large Grants. Taking note of the ARC's offering of funds for collaborative research, it made something of an art form of applying for such funding, consistently gaining a third of such grants, Australia-wide. That major continuing bias in the university's character was well under way from 1988. Or is it correct to call it bias? More, redressing balance. On joining Psychology from Oxford in 1977, Joseph Forgas found a very applied, non-academically oriented, and non-research productive department, akin to what one might expect of Technical and Further Education — a situation which the then newish professor, Syd Lovibond, was determined to change. As late as the 1970s, the university contained pockets of practical, non-scholarly endeavour which harked back to technical college beginnings.

However, the major internal development of 1988 was the termination of the Professorial Board in July, and its replacement by a new, largely elective, Academic Board. The Professorial Board, although enormously powerful, had become ineffective and unwieldy: the university had 138 professors in 1987 (225 by 1996), with an increasingly small attendance at the board, often less than a quorum, and there were the variations in attendance associated with specific issues and interest groups. Nevertheless, there was major and intense opposition to any change, the conservatives led by the long-serving and power-insider chairman, Doug McCallum, whose tenure had become so protracted as to make him virtually irremovable. Besides, many professors who seldom if ever attended meetings saw the end of the board as a diminishment of their rights and privileges. Replacement by an Academic Board of fifty-four members, elective and to some extent non-professorial, met strenuous opposition: the patriarchal system enshrined in the board's formality and its dominance by McCallum, died hard, despite the fact that it had reached a point where lack of quorum was paralysing its conducting of necessary business. It 'was like one of those machines that got so large that it couldn't move anymore' — so it was described by one of those urging reform. And the democratic temper of the times was against it — as were the younger members of the board itself, such as Jeremy Davis, who chaired the reform committee.

The end of the Professorial Board and the creation of the Academic Board passed by a very small majority at an intensely emotional meeting. Continuity was maintained in the person of Derek Anderson, mild, pleasant, popular, vice-chairman of the old Professorial Board, chairman of the new Academic Board, able to change happily to fit the new environment of managerialism. To follow him, came Jane Morrison, from 1992 to 1994; first female president, in 1980, of the University of New South Wales Staff Association, powerful university facilitator but warm and urbane with it. Her chairmanship formed a bridge from a soft person to a hard — Davis himself, aware, astute, no sufferer of fools, strong-viewed, in ways and in manners not to everyone's liking.

As to planning, 1989–93? Improved accommodation in Applied Science, Engineering, and Commerce; modernising equipment in Engineering; upgrading teaching; completing the introduction of Liberal and General Studies; all graduates to be computer literate. Specifically, a range of initiatives: among them, a Bachelor of Social Science; a Bachelor of Science in Business Information Technology, a chair in Genetics, an Asian Language Unit in Arts; and the University of New South Wales Coop Program from 1987, in which over eighty companies provided 150 scholarships (of $8000 each) in engineering, applied science and business information in 1989. Here was industry-linked and corporate sponsorship, in which Birt took particular pride and which he promoted in the university community. As well he should. And all this — together with internal corporate reviews, mission statements, practical implementation thereof — Birt saw as positively and responsibly meeting Commonwealth objectives in 1989 and beyond, in seeking to develop the general economy.

So there it was: Samuels standing up for a university under perceived basic threat, Birt presuming government goodwill and the university working harmoniously with necessary change. Not a happy conjunction, given the disparity of attitudes and principles involved. It dented the easy friendship that had existed between the two men and split the university community: in large part, it did not share the Birt position.

The end of the world as we had known it. What Samuels had feared did not come to pass. The proposed amalgamation did not proceed. The Bill was abandoned. Instead, the university agreed to sponsor a new university at Bathurst — Charles Sturt. Samuels was delighted. As he saw it, the win against amalgamation represented a victory for a large majority within the university and a supportive alumni group, who had campaigned against it. The minister had been inundated with protests. More, the university and its graduates had emerged from the testing ground of this controversy more united than ever before.

But, to borrow the chancellor's words, 'although one dragon had been slain, there remained another to contend with' — the matter of the University Council's size. Here the Samuels view had not prevailed. The government, after some polite wrangling, decided that all universities in the State have twenty-one council members, a reduction, in New South Wales University's case, of eight. It was the thinking behind this that most worried Samuels and, perhaps, gave him cause to consider his continuance as chancellor, although he was to remain there until 1994. The government's belief was, and there were those in the university who shared it, that university governance should follow the model of corporate boards. Administration and decision-making would be greatly improved, as Samuels sarcastically put it, if universities could be run by 'governing bodies variously called "lean" "spare" "tight" and "hardnosed". A board or committee displaying all these characteristics would be wonder indeed!'.

However, such wonders were to be in contemplation and Samuels was swimming against the tide. He was willing to concede that there were some principles of corporate management which might be usefully applied, but 'the business of a university is so different from that of a trading corporation that it is hardly sensible to imagine that the style and composition of their governing bodies ought to be the same — or even similar'. Moreover, that universities should be governed by outside appointees, was 'to misconceive entirely the essential functions to be carried out' — and to increase the undesirable likelihood that such councils would stray from policy determination into management matters. Worse still, they denied necessary representation. As Samuels saw things, councils were designed partly to make policy decisions, but also to act as a forum, in which the diverse views of all elements within the university could be heard. He held strongly to the proposition that 'a university fundamentally consists of those who work in it, that is to say, the general staff, the students and the academic staff' (a listing whose unusual order itself made a point). They must have a voice in their own institution. And his view was that the new council, from July 1990, was less widely drawn than desirable. It was a healthy and percipient view. Samuels must have been aware that some within the university disagreed. They saw council meetings as a time-wasting chore, in which the idiots had to have simple things explained, the talkers went on forever, and the argumentative were difficult and frustrating. The real work of the university could be fast-forwarded without them and the fewer of such persons the better: so thought thoughtless men or women, those in a hurry. But Samuels saw universities and their councils, not as efficient corporate entities, but as voices, talking-shops, forums for discussion and debate. These had their inherent costs, in what some might see as needless time-wasting. The alternative was some kind of tyranny, something less free. The price of liberty? Eternal vigilance — and time, lots of time.

When it came to the crunch — in the new University of New South Wales in July 1990 — the outcome was, in Samuels's view, acceptable if not ideal. Council was reduced from twenty-nine to twenty-one; but, after protracted discussions with the government, twelve were elected representatives, thus preserving, as he saw it, its 'broadly representative character'. The whole exercise entailed considerable reorganisation of council committees, but this was an internal university matter, as were other consequent administrative power-shifts, delegations to the vice-chancellor, time-wasting reportage. Small cost to pay.

What was the vice-chancellor's role in this? It was to be suggested afterwards by critics that the plan of a consolidated State-wide university had been 'cooked up' by Metherell and Birt for their own specific interests, in Birt's case that of getting away from besetment by academics and students to the quietude of a city office, a compliant bureaucracy and congenial company. Birt was reputed to be reclusive. The story is told of he and his wife remaining seated during the intermissions at Ensemble concerts in order to avoid being accosted by suppliants and complaint-mongers. Stories abound of his delays — assisted by a protective secretary — in providing signatures or in seeing staff who wished to discuss matters with him. Whatever of these allegations, it was certainly the case that the university opposition to Metherell's plans came to be led by the chancellor, not Birt, though even Samuels had to be alerted by concerned staff to the potentially serious implications of the proposals. And while Samuels put his public opposition in terms of principles, a cynical view might see it in terms of a diminution of personal chancellorial power. Eventually, Birt identified himself with the weight of university opinion, but only reluctantly it seems. As to the Metherell plan, Birt's explanation was that the minister insisted that he be sworn to secrecy. That the discussion paper had been withdrawn was due to the New South Wales premier, Nick Greiner. Apprised of university opposition and the content of the Bill, Greiner simply summoned Metherell and told him it was not on. It vanished. But the whole affair, and Birt's role, increased that inherent tension between academics and administrators. Administrators were distrusted, seen as lackeys of Canberra — a corrosive, damaging and demoralising division, which ate deeply into any collegiality.

The chancellor's annual report to the university in 1988 had been entirely given over to criticism of the government's discussion paper; Birt's report made no reference to it. It was not until his 1989 report, when the fuss was over, that he adverted to it. (Fair enough — if one is interested only in outcomes and not in attempting to influence them beforehand.) That of 1989 referred to 'dramatic structural changes', the end of the two-fold division between universities and colleges of advanced education, and its replacement by one national system (that of the Commonwealth), and the State government's discussion paper. He did not mention the rumpus (he called them 'negotiations') that had led to the government's withdrawal, only (true to his concern with outcomes) what had eventually happened — the university to take over the St George Institute of Education, and the City Art Institute; and to act as 'academic sponsor' for a multi-campus regional Charles Sturt University, which included the colleges at Bathurst and Wagga.

St George specialised in teacher education and health and recreational science, with some arts and computing. These were absorbed into existing faculties in the university: they brought 940 students, 48 academics and 32 general staff. Birt remarked that the incorporation of the City Art Institute might seem anomalous given the university's special science and technology (and business and management) character. But this was to ignore its long history of involvement in the performing arts — theatre and music, the School of Performing Arts. And there was the Australia Ensemble, choirs, opera, even an orchestra. To say nothing of involvement across its history in the National Institute of Dramatic Art, the Old Tote, with the Elizabethan Trust and ABC. The College of Fine Arts merely added a new, extra dimension to this. The college had been established in 1975 as the School of Arts within the Alexander Mackie CAE, evolving, in 1982, into the City Art Institute (emphasising the visual arts) of the Sydney CAE. It became a faculty of the university on 1 January 1990, with Ken Reinhard as foundation professor of Art and Design Education. From 1992 it consolidated its activities on one campus at Albion Avenue in Paddington. Despite their removed location, college staff soon became active figures in general university concerns. As to sponsorship of the three Charles Sturt campuses, Riverina (Albury), Mitchell (Bathurst) and Murray (Wagga), the university agreed to act for an initial period of six years, in collaboration with them in academic programs. In that, the university's involvement was not in teaching itself, but on selection and promotion committees and some membership on governing and academic boards — remote and very partial invigilation, so to speak. Plus encouragement (not direction) of university staff to help out Charles Sturt staff, with postgraduate supervision. Generally, both administration and academic staff undertook to be sensitively helpful and friendly to Charles Sturt.

In November 1989, for obvious reasons of self-explanation, Michael Birt set out his views of The Changing University Scene. As he saw it, since the mid-1960s Australian tertiary education had been governed by a dual system of universities (devoted both to teaching and research) and colleges of advanced education (given to teaching, particularly of a practical kind). In theory, the two were to be equal in esteem but different in role; in practice, the colleges were initially widely regarded as being so inferior as to hardly bear comparison. Nevertheless, for various reasons, not least for what Birt called the 'blurring' of the distinction, the government decided to abolish the then division in favour of a single national system, in which institutions were to be distinguished (and funded) by their differing educational profiles, based on student numbers and extent and character of research. This funding was to be supplemented by what the institution could itself raise from other, non-government, sources — a new, and marked, swing away from revenue reliance on the Commonwealth.

Birt noted that 1989 'has seen most of these changes put into effect' — a form of mild words for what others regarded as a revolution. Nineteen universities and forty-four colleges had been transformed into between thirty-five and forty institutions, of which most would be universities. He also observed that government intervention had become more 'direct and intense, and will probably remain so for a time'. (O hopeful dream!) Government demands for information from these tertiary institutions had 'expanded dramatically' 'to a point where they consume enormous amounts of time and effort'. Staff morale had suffered. Yet, despite this, Birt could see some advantages. The new arrangements facilitated planning, funding, research, better use of resources generally. He saw things positively in terms of 'more efficient', 'better' this, 'clearer' that, 'improved' and 'extended' the other.

Acknowledging the 'many different views' (again that very mild construction of what had involved anger and outrage) of the positive and negative aspects of the new system, Birt set out his own position. His major, and continuing concern was not for the universities such as his own, but the effects on the old CAEs. He thought the abolition of the binary system would produce a narrowing of educational opportunities by removing separate, explicit recognition of applied and vocational courses. Those whose talents were not for scholarly academic and professional work would be disadvantaged. Thus, he believed a rare opportunity to restructure post-secondary education had been lost. A single American-style system of broad university-level education (humanities-oriented colleges) could stop there, or lead onto specialised studies in universities. He foresaw what was to occur, only more quickly and intensely than he had imagined, that there would be pressure on ALL institutions to become 'university-like' — intense and probably irresistible. He so predicted, only too accurately.

In his November 1989 remarks Birt went on to a substantial sketch of his vision, based on the American model: of how best to meet Australia's educational needs: colleges and universities, the colleges avoiding that disease of Australian post-secondary education — excessive specialisation. It was a pondered and insightful sketch, but (in many ways sadly, particularly given its educational worth and human value) it lacked reality and relevance. Birt seems to have been under the impression that such matters were still open to discussion. In fact, the government had decided its course and that was the end of the matter. In keeping with his general educational concern, Birt saw the matter broad. He underrated the selfishness of the CAEs: they were determined on being universities, at least in name (and salaries). And his own university was not interested in the wider educational issues: its concern was for itself. Who was to say it should not be? Indeed, unfair critics of Birt were impatient of his theorising and generalities: 'He could talk under wet cement'.

It was in wider educational and social contexts that Birt continued to view the university into the 1990s and with a disposition to make the best of the changes — the new national system — that government had foisted upon it. He saw no point in lamentation or complaint, indeed every reason to see change as a valuable stimulus encouraging a university response of flexibility, imagination, and innovation. After all, one had to live, like it or not, with the new regime of around thirty-seven universities, plus, from 1990, three private ones — Bond, Notre Dame in Western Australia, and the multi-campus Catholic University of Australia. Birt believed that the main danger of the changes was diminution of educational opportunities available to school-leavers, and saw his own pre-eminent role as that of ensuring that this did not happen at the University of New South Wales: its 'varied provision for student admission' would be maintained.

As to the government's funding approach, emphasising outside sources and charging fees for courses given, Birt saw this as largely beneficial, 'one of the striking innovations', as one by which 'the universities have acquired a freedom, and indeed, are now encouraged to generate funds for themselves'. This, and the ability to offer salary supplements to staff working in high-demand areas, was to take a very roseate view of things, to choose flattering words for processes which might be much more harshly described — economising, anti-intellectual, perform or perish. But he was certainly aware of the repercussions for staff salaries, already much fallen in relativity. This needed 'urgent and sympathetic' attention from government, universities and staff unions — which it was not to get. The government was increasingly adamant that it would do nothing. It was left to restructuring in 1991 to do most justice to those in junior positions; it was only then that universities — and that also within their own resources — moved to address this problem, and only at internal cost: more money equals fewer staff.

Generally, Birt's stance in 1990 was that changes which had been radical and difficult had become more familiar and less fearsome than they had seemed. DEET's incursions and demands 'ensure that the University as a whole considers its priorities. It makes us clarify our aspirations in a corporate [dreaded word] process which is salutary and informative.' Which, looked at from that corporate perspective, is dandy. Besides, the university did well — very well — from the new arrangements for research funding: competitive allocation.

Reviewing the university's position in 1990, Birt took justified pride. From 18,800 students in 1981, the number had expanded to 22,400 — 18,700 at Kensington, 1900 at the Defence Force Academy in Canberra, and 1800 in the newly acquired College of Fine Arts and at the St George campus. There were 1470 academic staff, 2800 general staff. Expenditure was about $300 million, of which the university, in one way or another, raised about a third. Birt pointed out that the university was an operation bigger than many non-metropolitan cities or most Australian commercial enterprises. Its student base was wide-ranging, its Asian contacts long-established and growing: 2737 Asian students in 1990, with about one in three Asian graduates of Australian universities coming from the University of New South Wales. Within the student body, the disadvantaged were increasingly catered for: there had been 196 Aboriginal admissions. (Equity was being achieved within the staff: the percentage of females had grown from 34 per cent in 1983 to 43 per cent in 1995.) Student entry had become increasingly demanding. Only in science was recruitment difficult, an Australia-wide problem, but one particularly vexing for this university, given its traditional science emphasis. Various efforts were being made to combat this, not least a 'Cooperative Education Program' of general university application, which amounted to a revamped return to the university's origins — scholarships based on work involvement. The 1990 version was enormously successful: 375 scholarships were funded, at a cost to sponsors of $3 million per annum. And Unisearch continued to be a money-spinner. Its gross turnover was $10 million, with about 2500 consultancies annually: in 1997 it reached the million dollar profit mark.

Everywhere there was outreach and diversification. An Asia–Australia Institute under the direction of Dr Stephen Fitzgerald (former Australian ambassador to China) was established to provide Australian and Asian business executives with high-level management courses — wider and more ambitious still, to involve political and government leaders and interests — and to conduct seminars. An arrange-ment was made with the Coal Board to house the School of Mines, and sponsor research on safety. The university agreed with the Australian Taxation Office to establish new courses in tax law in return for full funding to 1996. In cooperation with the State govern-ment, a feasibility study for an Advanced Technology Park, to be sited at the former railway repair yards at Eveleigh, in Redfern, was completed in 1990. This did not proceed then, but Birt regarded it as valuable experi-ence, and it was to come good eventually.

Birt had expressly disavowed his intention of wishing to sound like Candide — that of holding that all things were for the best in the best of possible worlds. Yet, increasingly, he did. His picture of the university in 1990 was that of 'a productive and exciting year', one of strengthening in all areas, 'a vibrant and stim-ulating place'. Which it was. All he said was true. Yet, weirdly, it seemed not to be so: Birt's words rang strangely hollow. Not in fact. Who could gainsay them? But in the atmosphere of his saying them. It would not be fair or accurate to speak of any malaise at the top, but since the Metherell mega-univer-sity affair, the university felt distant from its vice-chancellor and he from it. He emanated remoteness, unease, the sense of being tired. So what that he could point out undoubted achievements, many to the credit of his per-sonal vision and encouragement? 'The University' — if such a putative commonality existed — had ceased to believe in him. Birt gave notice that he would retire in 1992. Samuels said of him that he had been able to maintain the proper notion of what a univer-sity should be, together with a pragmatic per-ception of what was possible. Above all, he

John Niland as a young professor

1974

UNSW Archives

PROFESSOR NILAND

244

had pursued academic excellence. It was a fair summation, but a low-key recognition of what Birt had done — set the university early on a corporate path, which prepared it for an even more arduous and corporate-oriented future.

In the leaving of it, Birt bequeathed to his successor, John Niland, a legacy of plans, initiatives and achievements, intellectual and physical, that had the potential and momentum to mould the immediate hereafter (and redound in their implementation to his successor's reputation). Some of the main features with which Niland came to be identified had already been sketched or begun. Implementation was one thing — and obviously a vital one — but ideas and intentions were already in the air.

The A to Z of Academia
by Phil Schofield

R is for Research

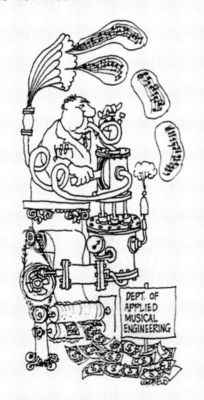

Phil Schofield caricature series

Uniken 17 November 1979

And it was Birt who carried the can for major negative developments outside the university's control — the trauma of government-imposed, educational revolution, and the impact of national recession in 1990–91. Favoured indeed is the leader blessed with auspicious times.

Looking back on his last year of office — 1991 — Birt viewed even the difficulties positively: the university was living in the future. Faced with a revolution in education — enrolments rising to 27,000; staff, from 4000 up to 5000; an annual budget jumping to $400 million — the university had responded with self-funding and an element of fee-paying; and a swing towards emphasis on research. All this amounted to a 'shock', as the 'public responsibility of Australian universities and of their individual staff members has been redefined'. Birt-speak. And close to academic jargon. Far more down to earth was a record over-enrolment, amounting to 1600 full-time students, without the staff or accommodation to deal with them. No consolation that this was part of a nationwide trend caused by recession. A depressed job-market impacted on school-leavers, more of whom entered university instead of seeking employment. School retention rates had climbed. As Birt discerned, the very nature of university education had changed, away from that of being an elite avocation towards having a wider social base. (What he did not note was that this trend affected this particular university more quickly and more extensively than others: it had always drawn on, and appealed to the less affluent, not least because its catchment was in the less-favoured suburbs and within upwardly mobile ethnic groups.) Thus, the university, with its vocational orientation historically, was traditionally well-placed to take advantage of government training levies, and of diverse continuing education programs (1991 saw the university receiving more of this kind of money — $17 million — than any other university). And its very history advantaged it in dealing with industry, with which its contacts had been long, wide, and various. Recession bit in other ways. What had seemed, even the previous year, to be big steps forward, fell through, stopped or faltered. The Advanced Technology Park project wound towards what seemed to be a halt, the Asia–Australia Institute was effectively on hold, the proposed arrangement with the Joint Coal Board had fallen through.

∧

The Quadrangle courtyard

1998

Still, Birt took pride in what were undoubtedly positive developments in 1991 — the establishment of cooperative research centres funded by the federal government to the tune of about $2 million each annually. The centres were in waste management and pollution control, contact lens technology, the petroleum industry, and bio-pharmaceutical research. The university also had a share in other research centres — aerospace, optical fibres, food industry, wool, intelligent manufacturing systems, and photonic technology. In addition to all this were the funds attracted by individual researchers, totalling $13 million in 1992 from the ARC (13 per cent of the national total) and $5 million (up a million from 1991) from the National Health and Medical Research Council (NH&MRC). The number of research publications had skyrocketed also — from 2800 in 1987 to 3600 in 1990. In all, an astounding research explosion marked Birt's final years, but he was anxious, given the government's expectations in relation to the teaching role of the universities, to balance this with encouragement of teaching. He did this by stressing teaching as a criterion for staff promotions and setting up Vice-Chancellor's Awards for Teaching Excellence. In theory, these were an important redressing of pro-research bias in the university's ethos, but that bias was, in practice, difficult to shift, at least to any substantial degree.

Birt was to leave marks much more enduring, which had their appearance and outcome long after his official time. Most striking was his building and landscaping program. At his leaving in 1992, refurbishment of buildings was well under way, with such improvements as carpets in place of vinyl floors in corridors. These made for much quieter passage and environment generally; and for making much more comfortable that feature of student life — sitting on floors. Substantial landscaping had been completed and was to continue; the outdoor environment was improving. But beyond all else, as physical legacy, was the planning of the Quadrangle project. This dated back to DEET approval of a Commerce/Law building in 1989 — 'a crucial first step in achieving the sort of development we would like to see on campus'. This had become the Quadrangle project in 1991, completed in 1993, with $18.3 million of the total cost of $32.5 million being provided by the government. He was thus to leave, as a legacy of immense reputational value to John Niland, not only an enhancement of accommodation, but an enduring structure of architectural note. Still, this is perhaps to exaggerate the debt. As dean of Commerce Niland did much himself to further the project.

Something less tangible but no less far-reaching in implication was Birt's opening the university's own administration to the inspection of outside evaluation. In mid 1991 he asked the State government's Office of Public Management to examine the university's administration. As a consequence he made a range and series of changes to improve efficiency, flexibility, and — that main requirement of a university administration, as Birt saw it — responsiveness. For a man so devoted to corporate planning, Birt's notion of an administration is surprisingly free of corporate jargon and keenly to the point of stressing the unique nature of a university. He saw administration, not as crudely directive, but as subtle service — as being responsive to the needs of various elements with a view to reconciling them — students, staff, governments, clients. Birt's order of priorities reflects a traditional view asserted in a new guise.

It is within that framework that Birt put forward his corporate plan, seeing it as forestalling Commonwealth imposition. He saw the university as acting in ways which prepared it to meet government requirements before they were made, thus advantaging it in the face of the inevitable. He even had his own precursor to what Niland was to develop as that fulcrum of planning: UNSW 2000. Birt sought not to make predictions, but to perceive the desirable with realism, to ask what the university wants from the future; 'to answer the question why are we doing this?', to recognise success — and enjoy it.

So left Birt, much of his future behind him. So, too, left Gilbert to the University of Tasmania, later Melbourne, leaving a reputation for mildness, intelligence, clarity and directness: no petty politician, he took things on merit, though his driving ambition is self-evident. Geoff Wilson of the Australian Defence Force Academy went to Deakin University; Ronayne, to the Victoria University of Technology; soon, Derek Anderson of the Academic Board, to Sydney; the registrar, Ian Way, retired; Gavin Brown, dean of Science, to Adelaide, then to the University of Sydney. The list is Birt's. Not a clean sweep of senior management, but a deck-clearing nonetheless. Clean sweep? Hardly appropriate words to convey the flavour of what were the results of the personal decisions of the individuals concerned and of the fact that they were moving to key places in other institutions. Its effect was deck-clearing at the University of New South Wales; but if the university's top team was dispersed to higher things in other places, it suggests the compliment of flattery. The process, in total, implies what amounted to a raid by other institutions, seeking to capture the secret of New South Wales University's success.

7

WORLD PLAYERS
1992–

1992

JULY LM Birt resigns as vice-chancellor; J Niland appointed vice-chancellor.
24 AUGUST C Condous appointed registrar and deputy principal — the first woman to hold these positions.
DECEMBER UNSW becomes a partner in Cooperative Research Centres for — Biopharmaceutical Research; Food Industry Innovation; Intelligent Manufacturing Systems; Premium Quality Wool.

1993

UNSW joins with University of Sydney and University of Technology, Sydney, in establishment of Advanced Technology Park at Eveleigh site, Redfern. • Michael Birt Gardens dedicated. • UNSW wins national Affirmative Action Noteworthy Award for its *Merit Based Selection Manual.* •
NEW DEGREES/DIPLOMAS Bachelor of Applied Arts; Graduate Diploma in Couple and Family Therapy; Graduate Certificate in Health Services Management (for International Students).

1 JANUARY UNSW Students' Union changes its name and constitution, becoming the Guild of Postgraduate and Undergraduate Students.
20 APRIL 100,000th degree awarded, to Paul Gompels, BComm.
JUNE First overseas graduation ceremony, held at Kuala Lumpur, Malaysia. • Mathews forecourt development completed.
DECEMBER Quadrangle building, stage I completed.

1994

The first Report of the Committee for Quality Assurance in Higher Education ranks UNSW in the top of six tiers of Australian universities. • UNSW formally begins sponsorship of Southern Cross University. • Hon. Gordon Samuels retires as chancellor; Sir Anthony Mason succeeds him. • The Division of Information Services established, incorporating the university Library; C Page-Hanify appointed director and deputy principal. • J Morrison appointed pro-vice-chancellor (1 January). • Centre of Liberal and General Studies abolished. • Department of Aviation established, with a degree — Bachelor of Aviation. • 'UNSW' lettering erected on the library tower.

1995

UNSW agrees to act as academic sponsor for the first private English language university in China — the Beijing New Asia University. • First 60 students enrol in a UNSW MComm program in Guangzhou, China. •
Act Now Against Racism Campaign 1995. • Anthony Mason Fellowship scheme inaugurated. •
NEW DEGREE Doctor of Juridical Science. • CAMPUS IMPROVEMENTS Quadrangle building, stage II completed.

1996

Quadrangle Project wins Australian Design Award. • Establishment of a Postgraduate Medical School approved. • New General Education program implemented — all general education subjects offered through the faculties for the first time. • CAMPUS IMPROVEMENTS Science precinct development (later known as the Red Centre) begun; Barker Street student housing, stage I begun.

24 JULY UNSW wins the Good Universities Guide University of the Year Award for undergraduate teaching.
9 AUGUST Higher Education Budget statement issued.
2 DECEMBER University Council votes 15 to 4 for UNSW 2000 program.

SELECTED EVENTS

Applied Science building clock
1992

Bim Hinder's Union crest
1992

Mathews plaza
1993

1997

Vice-Chancellor John Niland elected president of the Australian Vice-Chancellors' Committee. • UNSW placed first of all Australian universities and sixth overall in *Asiaweek's* ranking of the top 50 universities in the Asia-Pacific region. • Professor Merilyn Sleigh appointed dean of the Faculty of Life Sciences — the first woman to be appointed dean. • Equity and Diversity Unit incorporates previous EEO and Student Equity Units and begins operation. • UNSW Charity Week instituted. • First 16 students graduate with the UNSW MComm in Guangzhou. • NEW DEGREE BA (Media and Communication). • CAMPUS IMPROVEMENTS The Red Centre/Science precinct development, stage I completed; The Scientia building construction begun (stage I due for completion in March 1999). •

I JANUARY Faculty of Professional Studies disestablished.
JULY Following the Working Party's Report on Future of St George Campus, Council requests that negotiation continue 'to finalise an arrangement for the future use of the campus with benefits to the University, the higher education sector, and the community, including the St George community'. • Following the Working Party's recommendation on Fees and Revenue Generation, Council decides to admit fee-paying, local, undergraduate students. • 'World Class University' advertising campaign launched.
I JULY Faculties of Applied Science, Biological and Behavioural Science and Science disestablished, being replaced by two new faculties — Life Sciences, and Science and Technology.
AUGUST Faculty of Law widens to include the Board of Studies in Taxation. • Admissions cease at St George campus, but teaching continues there until January 1999.
OCTOBER New category of visiting and full-time professors approved — 'Scientia professors'.
NOVEMBER UNSW 2000 home page on World Wide Web launched.

1998

Radiation Protection Program offered to all postgrads and other persons using radioactive materials. • Composting program launched, to capture recyclable waste from food outlets and gardens on campus. • CAMPUS IMPROVEMENTS Rupert Myers building begun (due for completion, in May 1999); Webster building renovations (due for completion, February 1999).

FEBRUARY Barker Street student housing, stage II completed.
I MARCH Professor M Wainwright appointed pro-vice-chancellor (research) to assist C Fell when he is acting vice-chancellor (following J Niland's appointment as AVCC president).
16 MARCH Java@Java internet cafe opened in Mathews building — the largest internet cafe in the Southern hemisphere.
22 MARCH Inaugural 'Back to UNSW Day'.
APRIL Red Centre/Science precinct building, stage II completed.
2 JUNE Merger of the AGSM and the Graduate School of Business, University of Sydney.
JULY Sir Gerard Brennan (retired chief justice) joins UNSW as Foundation Visiting Scientia Professor. • 50th Anniversary website launched.

1999

MARCH The first week of university and Alumni events celebrating the 50th Anniversary, with the theme 'Our Earned Reputation'.
19 MARCH Press Conference and Launch of the official history — *UNSW A Portrait: The University of New South Wales 1949–1999*, by Patrick O'Farrell.
JUNE–JULY The second week of university and Alumni events celebrating the 50th Anniversary, with the theme 'Our Physical and Intellectual Legacy'.
24 JUNE Official opening of The Scientia.
I JULY Fiftieth Anniversary of founding of the university — a Foundation dinner.
SEPTEMBER The third week of university and Alumni events celebrating the 50th Anniversary, with the theme: 'Our Community'.
3 SEPTEMBER Aboriginal Reconciliation Ceremony, on campus.
4 SEPTEMBER UNSW Expo

SELECTED EVENTS

Different angle
furnished by
UNSW

The University of New South Wales
is not the same.

Our outlook is inventive, our thinking is original
and our track record of achievement is unique.

In fact the only things predictable about us are
our advanced facilities, our friendly environment
and our international reputation.

If you want life to start looking up, join the World Class. UNSW.

For further information call us on (02) 9385 1844,
email studentrecruitment@unsw.edu.au
or visit our WWW site at http://www.unsw.edu.au
Visit UNSW's Courses & Careers Day on 6 Sep 1997.

UNSW

THE UNIVERSITY OF NEW SOUTH WALES

PAD UNSW

World visions — university promotion to the general public

August 1997

In came Niland, the new broom. Broom? Hardly. More the gentle but firm — granulated — cleaning device, fluid, computer-compatible, with name and sales ambitions worldwide, corporate to the extent required by its furtherance. Whereas previous vice-chancellors had been narrowly concerned with growth, and dogged in defence of gains, Niland's outlook and designs were much more grand, radically so — and directed at international eminence. His ambition and desire was to exalt the university. In this his measure was not the University of Sydney, or Melbourne (though bettering them was a pleasant step along the way), but Harvard, Oxford. Niland had an eye, a determination, to join the big league. That this ambition would carry him up personally in the process met little of the usual cynical criticism, given that this was patently largely selfless, evidently without hubris. His personality and leadership style were unpretentious and open. Besides which, he soon revealed abilities conceded by both friend and foe — a mover and shaker who knew the top end of town, with good connections across the political spectrum, willingness to listen and learn, the capacity to decide. And the wide use of established university consultative structures and systems: even enemies (and there were to be few) were involved in what happened. He had a winning personality and the personality of a winner. And again besides, after Birt, Niland's aggressive promotion of the university was widely welcomed: both staff and students enjoyed their university being in the news.

On his appointment, the university hardly knew what it was getting — one never does. Nor perhaps, did Niland himself: he was to grow with the job. Appointment was not before hoop jumping, peer inspection of the most intrusive kind. Birt had been invited to apply and had been interviewed by a committee chaired by Samuels. (He remarked later that such was the atmosphere of secrecy that he felt he should wear a paper bag on his head while visiting Kensington.) No such privacy attended the Niland appointment. The short-list was well-known and each person on it was grilled (politely) by the Academic Board, in what amounted to a public session if theoretically in camera. Some remember candidates' answers to that most interesting of questions — what will you do if appointed? The conditions of appointment were corporate — a five-year contract, renewable (and subsequently renewed), with substantial salary to match the responsibilities; one confidential in keeping with corporate practice, but generally believed to be around $250,000 (increased to $350,000 in 1997). Put baldly like that, the figure excites parched academic dreams — and less creditable reactions. The fact is less dramatic in that the package had to meet costs and superannuation provisions (normally met in part by the university). Besides, as a University Council member put it, Niland was worth that and more.

Niland looked nothing. In 1992. Stocky, thin and straggly on top, possessed of suits which seemed of the kind purveyed by the two for the price of one outfitters. (Confronted by this comment, Niland's wit was equal to that jokery. He quipped 'I got only one. Who got the other?'.) A bit shy, diffident, unsure of his reception in unfamiliar circles. A lop-sided larrikin grin. All of this now gone, and that quickly, in a transformation of grooming — decent, young man's haircut, a tailor with an eye for cut and colour. And in the intangibles of confidence generated by success, the emanations of authority and accomplishment, at ease with colleagues, obviously dedicated.

With a wife very much her own person, though very different from the vice-chancellors' wives that had preceded her. With two children, Carmel Niland built a career for herself to become Anti-Discrimination commissioner for New South Wales and deputy chancellor of the university, a position she relinquished following her husband's appointment. She was to pursue her work as a consultant. And continue her membership of council. No deferrer, she. She voted against her husband's motion of 2 June 1997 to introduce fees. Niland put his motion as 'not a motion for fees but a vote for survival'. His wife opposed it as a 'threshold issue'. She said that the University of New South Wales had a long and proud tradition of offering a quality education to students from disadvantaged families, many of whom were women or the first in their families to go to university: she might have cited her own husband. In keeping with this egalitarian disposition, it is hardly surprising that she should seek selection, in August 1997, as a candidate for the New South Wales Labor Party. In May 1998 she was appointed director-general of the New South Wales Department of Community Services, an onerous and publicly exposed position.

At the time of his appointment, Niland had been professor of Industrial Relations and dean of Commerce at the University of New South Wales. He put his political experience and toughening, and familiarity with the ways of the media — and public profile — down to his chairmanship of the State Environment Protection Authority 1990–95, a responsible and newsworthy position. His association with the university went back long before this — to 1960 when he had come, on a BHP scholarship, as a boy from the bush, Lismore. Basser College, president of the Students' Union and the University Union, wide acquaintanceship, freedom, football, a gamut of Commerce friends, Rugby. A footballing man, still at fifty-seven years old playing in the International Golden Oldies tournament — Dublin 1993, Vancouver 1997 — in it for the culture, not the biffo. Yet at the same time a university debater and patron of that art from then to now, all enjoyed immensely and conducive to a strong loyalty to the university. He was perfectly capable, as vice-chancellor, of taking immense pleasure in the dynamic history he had lived through, been part of, savouring the discomfiture and pursed lips of those of the old one-city, one-university brigade. He loved the idea of being involved in a place that represented and asserted major dislocation in the stolid higher education cosmos. Niland saw his university as, from the 1940s, breaking the ancient mould, thereafter sustained by that momentum and internal dynamism. Himself? Buoyed by the excitement of the upstart successful new. A PhD at the University of Illinois, teaching at Cornell (hence the American dimension in his orientation), then back to a senior lectureship, then readership at the Australian National University (ANU), then the University of New South Wales, as the first graduate of this university to hold a chair. Then the chance both to move up and to demonstrate that loyalty in the boldest manner.

John Niland in the Michael Birt Gardens

22 June 1995

First task? Attend to appearances. With audacity. Niland the assertive image-maker. Enhancer of environment for both inside and outside consumption. Gardens. The Quadrangle project. Down to guidelines for university paperwork. The giant letters, 4.3 m high, around the top of the library tower, visible on the skyline from adjacent suburbs. (Student wit had it that only two features on earth were visible from outer space — the Great Wall of China, and the UNSW tower.) Such was the potential thereof, that the Randwick Council attempted to impose advertising fees — unsuccessfully, but sufficient, given protracted correspondence, to delay erection until 1994. The letters were there for themselves but also to affirm the promoted shortened version of the university's name (given its cumbrous title) — UNSW. Students resorted to 'New South' even 'Kenso'. Niland wanted to encourage a common usage to suit all circumstances, Asian and Australian. Staid annual reports and the like took on corporate gloss. The plush foyer and ante-room refurbishment of the Chancellery — the better to impress, sedate, or overawe visitors. And the casual atmospherics: nothing pleased Niland more than hearing on national radio commentators at the Sydney Cricket Ground (admittedly one — Geoff Lawson — was a UNSW graduate) refer to what had been the Randwick end as 'the university end'. Yet Niland also saw the importance of remaining in touch with staff, the bright and chirpy family doctor on his school rounds, listener for aches and pains.

In 1993, shortly after his appointment, Niland set up an image project, which led to a working party and eventual report in 1995. He was initially hesitant about this: it could turn out to be a prodigious generator of flam. (To some extent it was.) But Niland reasoned that while image was nothing without substance, substance was not its own reward. As distinct from those purists who held that the university's excellences should speak for themselves, Niland saw that they never do: lights hidden under bushels stay hidden. So, proclaim one's presence and achievements from the roof tops — or above them in the case of the 4.3 m-high UNSW. Which the image committee did, down to small university print. All on the proposition that image, public relations, is not gloss but serves a vital academic purpose, which was to ensure that the university be taken seriously by Canberra, and all those in the impressionable corporate world. That went, too, for his own high media profile, a tremendous public asset, but prone to internal misunderstanding: it could lead to the assumption that its manufacture was all that was going on in the Chancellery. Or concocting budgets as some corporate exercise or servile appendage of government: Niland lived in some dread of his efforts to create a functional, modern university, preserving core values, being misunderstood by his own staff. This was a salutary fear, as there were indeed staff who saw (and suffered) the particular implementations, but did not appreciate Niland's grand plan, which operated in the general, seeking to retain university values in scholarship, autonomy and freedom. Seeing the whole was Niland's job, but it was a big ask to expect academics, each about their own specialities and careers, to have similar wide-ranging perceptions. The extent to which they did was a tribute to the quality of those who inhabited that institution. One of the image committee's manifestations was a set of identity standards — symbols, typeface, layout, colours.

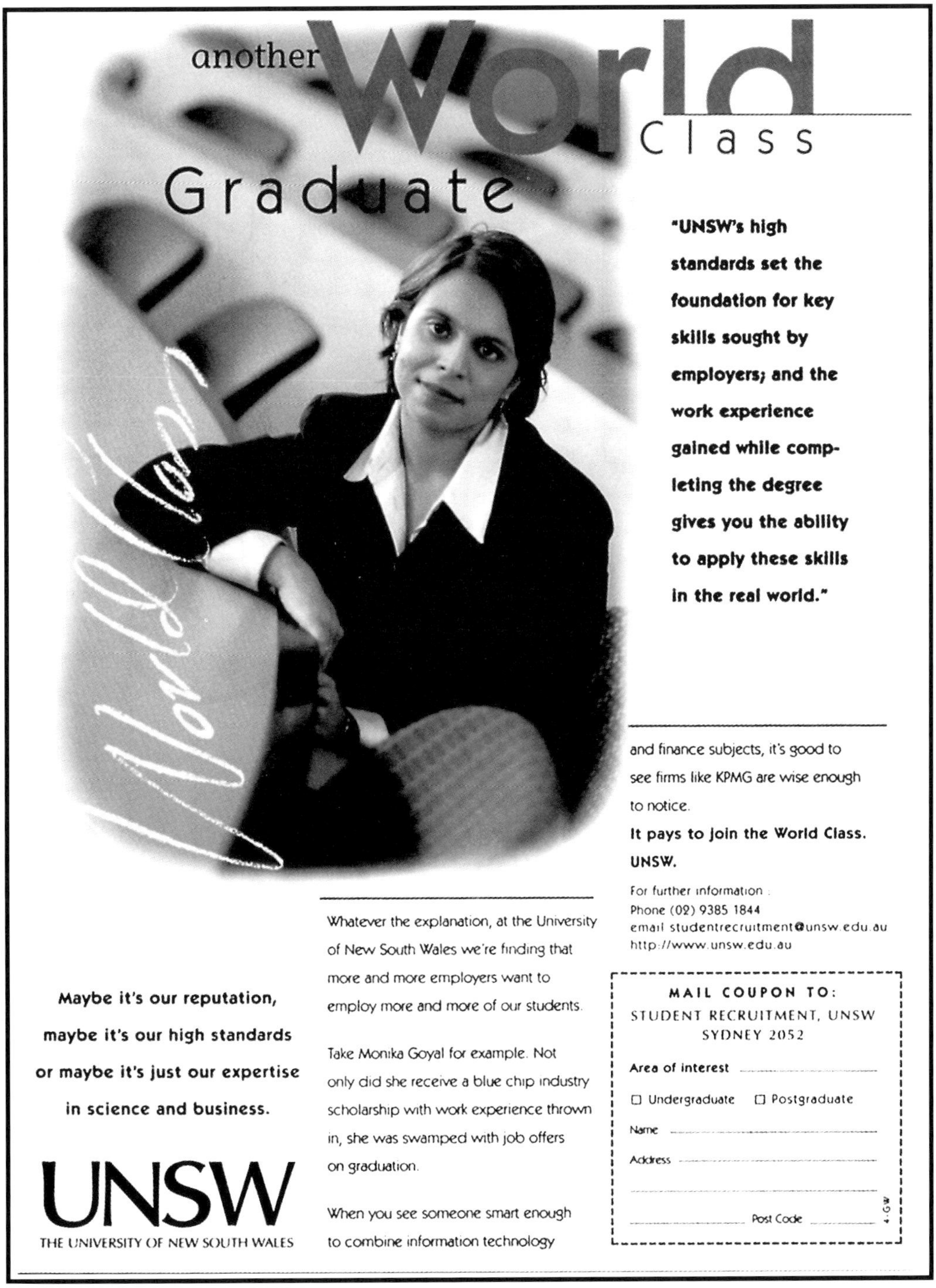

another **World** Class

Graduate

"UNSW's high
standards set the
foundation for key
skills sought by
employers; and the
work experience
gained while comp-
leting the degree
gives you the ability
to apply these skills
in the real world."

and finance subjects, it's good to
see firms like KPMG are wise enough
to notice.

**It pays to join the World Class.
UNSW.**

For further information :
Phone (02) 9385 1844
email studentrecruitment@unsw.edu.au
http://www.unsw.edu.au

Whatever the explanation, at the University
of New South Wales we're finding that
more and more employers want to
employ more and more of our students.

Take Monika Goyal for example. Not
only did she receive a blue chip industry
scholarship with work experience thrown
in, she was swamped with job offers
on graduation.

When you see someone smart enough
to combine information technology

**Maybe it's our reputation,
maybe it's our high standards
or maybe it's just our expertise
in science and business.**

UNSW
THE UNIVERSITY OF NEW SOUTH WALES

```
MAIL COUPON TO:
STUDENT RECRUITMENT, UNSW
SYDNEY 2052

Area of interest ...........................

☐ Undergraduate    ☐ Postgraduate

Name ...........................

Address ...........................

...................... Post Code ..........
```

PAD UNSW

World Class? The claim to fame press advertisement

1997

These betrayed American modes — if only those of the (contract) designer. So the university set down 'Corporate' and 'Equity' colours (meaning 'official' and 'letter-head') adjectives accepted unthinkingly until questioned in 1997. The jargon of American corporatism was gradually seeping into the official university usage in an involuntary way — until brought up short by the vigilant.

Whatever the misgivings of conservative academics, the tide of corporatism, and its attendant apparatus of technocracy, computer-speak, and de-personalisation, was too powerful to resist. Too pervasive. Too necessary in an international, internet, e-mail world. The very word 'image' was anathema to academics of the old school, who were scandalised by the series of full-page advertisements for UNSW The World Class University, which appeared in the *Sydney Morning Herald Good Weekend* in July 1997 — at $10,000 a pop. Useless extravagance? Or necessary in a media-driven age? Some of these media ideas had Niland's personal spin. The newspaper photograph of an assemblage of top Higher School Certificate (HSC) students indicated inter alia the large number destined for courses at UNSW. Soft sell to succeeding HSC students and parents, confirmation of choice to those who

◁

Inside the refurbished AGSM

1998

Rosemary Allan/50th Anniv. History Project

The Red Centre

1998

had already made it. On the international stage it was Niland's wide personal contacts that paved the university's way.

As to 'world class', an ambition much vaunted in the 1990s, some staff regarded the term as embarrassing, tasteless, parvenu. Perhaps more to the point was that it was needless internally, however appropriate it might be to vulgar public promotion. The observation of a university medallist in Medicine in the 1970s that he could not have been better taught anywhere (it was the time of McCloskey and Lance) — a judgement confirmed by subsequent overseas experience — put me in mind of my own comparative recollection of the 1960s. In that year I first visited Britain and Ireland. Tutored in the role of assumed colonial inferiority and deference, I was taken aback by the indifferent (at best) performances of conference paper-givers, many of great reputation in the discipline. I concluded that Australian standards, in both teaching and research, were equal, if not superior. But it would be a fool who would not concede that Australia generally lacks the resources to compete in scale, with the major universities of the United States of America, Britain and Europe: the University of New South Wales lacked, in particular, major bequests and a vastly wealthy alumni. World class in some areas, less than that in others?

At the top, Niland the Energiser, the managerial entrepreneur, his reports to University Council meetings instructive and beneficial, interesting and entertaining. Samuels had been a council member since 1969: it was the first occasion on which he had heard a vice-chancellor applauded. Why? Because Niland was so committed, an enthusiast for the university. And obviously so dedicated. So much master of the enterprise. All of this he patently enjoyed: duty was a pleasure. Irresistible to those engaged in common cause, a source of delight to those associated with it. But, in sharing this, Samuels issued an implied warning. He made it clear — as he had done on previous occasions — that the university was a unique institution, whose understanding was best advanced by studying other universities: 'other corporate activities are only limited exemplars'. Perhaps this advice was of a generalised kind. Perhaps he had Niland specifically in mind, for certainly the leaning towards corporate models was a disposition Niland obviously shared.

Corporate models? Management? These had a piquant taste of déjà-vu in the university's history: we had been there before in other times and ways: '... why are you always questioning Baxter's proposals? You should think of him as being managing director of a large firm. He gives the orders and our responsibility is to carry them out' — this from conversations following a Professorial Board meeting in the early 1950s.

Or was it that Niland's study of other universities left him with the conclusion that theirs, with their in some cases plastic or incompetent vice-chancellors, was not the way to go? That the inertia, blindness, in-fighting and lack of engagement with the realities of wider power and policy, offered lessons in what not to do, or paths not to follow?

How did Niland view things on his incumbency? His overall objective was nothing limited or small — nothing less than a world-class university. Which he

∧

The environment upgraded — John Niland checks one of the seedlings being distributed

at the environment policy launch, on library lawn, as Registrar and Deputy Principal

Crystal Condous (centre), and Pro-Vice-Chancellor Jane Morrison look on

3 April 1995

obviously conceived in the singular in this comparison — a world-class cricket team. Not the Sheffield Shield of States and Clubs, but the one team. In universities, UNSW was to be it. Given that UNSW could expect no further numerical growth (the previous generator of life and energy), the university would have to change internally to maintain its pursuit of the new, would have to adjust its endeavours to respond to relevant new demands — perhaps at the cost of reducing the old. It anticipated the expanded reign of 'verifiers' (jargon for performance indicators) as a newly prevailing university practice was taken up by the Commonwealth Department of Employment, Education and Training (DEET, later DEETYA) nationwide. This would raise problems but might also offer enormous opportunities for transformation and improvement. Niland also anticipated major changes consequent on a move away from a contrived award system to enterprise bargaining — a more localised and flexible negotiation of wages and conditions: this, he believed also offered 'great opportunities' — if also difficulties. He did not mention cuts and redundancy, but they were implicit in his choice of words: increasing staff costs would entail staff economies. In this process he — the former professor of Industrial Relations — saw UNSW at the forefront. Not, however, the Staff Association.

In the domain of bricks and mortar, Niland was, perhaps, even more radical and interested: a cast of mind integrated with the physical context and presentation of his wider, international ambitions. A drab run-down environment would not proclaim or carry the weight of world pretensions. Upgrading the campus had been one of Birt's areas of planning: indeed, much of what was identified with Niland when it came to pass, had been Birt's in inception. But Niland's vision was much more grand, and infused with his own determination and dynamic. This was the obvious Niland, open to view. It was behind the scenes that he himself saw as more important — restructuring budgets so as to better facilitate teaching and research, money to further main purposes. And restructuring faculty anticipations and mind-sets — such as the laager mentality and cargo cultism of Applied Science (long the university's most favoured nation, bitterly resistant to all change). Certainly, what work was undertaken in the early 1990s was in large part necessary refurbishment and maintenance of buildings put up twenty or more years before. But Niland went well beyond this in setting out 'to provide our staff and students with accommodation befitting the status of the University'. Befitting the status? Think large, be large; be humble, be nothing. Niland himself was humble, in that he was not inflated by personal affectation, but his ambitions for the university were vaulting enough — Australia's only world-class university.

So the summer semester breaks were given over to repaving courtyards, building facilities for eateries and walkways, getting rid of worn-out aspects of this and that, better provision for student seating. Larger works included an Upper Campus facelift — the Mathews Plaza given a covered mall, a remodelled Chancellery. The idea was to create eventually an attractive and dignified university front door, not only for students and staff, but having in view its location as a venue for major international conferences and professional exhibitions. Then there was the Quadrangle project, the university's largest development for many years, due to be in use for 1994. This was a transformation of the Lower Campus, to include not only a Commerce building, but computer-teaching space, a 100-seat theatre, a range of staff and student facilities, a cafeteria, shops, landscaping — even 'a grand colonnade and gallery' to be part of the University Walk, that all-weather route to the Union Roundhouse and bus stops. 'Grand Colonnade'. Huh! When it became accessible, in 1996, the development received warm professional approbation from architects and an Australian Design Award. The *Sydney Morning Herald*'s architecture correspondent was in raptures: order had returned to campus. This was significant urban design, giving dignity and coherence, expressive of classic principles of order stretching back to the Gothic. A welcoming, memorable unity had returned to the university after nearly fifty years of 'dead-eye Modernist megastructures', godless monuments strewn randomly.

The same correspondent, EM Farrelly, took a similar view of the remodelling of the Australian Graduate School of Management (AGSM) building in 1996: 'God, as well as the money, is in the details', a transformation centred on a big idea, a unifying courtyard. Her enthusiasm carried through to September 1997 and the Science precinct — a joy to the world, magic, buildings filled with light. Praise from the university community as well. Even those critics who had criticised the construction on the basis that university resources could be better used, conceded the style and value of what had been done. There had been a mind-frame conditioned by the dingy and depressing condition of the existing buildings to believe that improvement was impossible, and that anything to be proud of was out of the question and folly to attempt. Niland, with his experience of a university wasteland stretching back to *Tharunka*'s onslaught of 1961, proved this wrong. More, similar projects were envisioned. Other things, too, of a major kind, which a change in the structure of government funding made possible: a roll-in of capital funds guaranteed this works program in future. So had the coincidence of Commonwealth policy change advantaged Niland. Thus, luck (to the extent that such a change was 'luck') was a friend which freed Niland of the framework of financial constrictions which had bound Birt.

But Samuels had been right. Niland was a corporate man, addicted to the rituals of the corporate world. So, internal reviews of effectiveness were back in, as 'part of the university's on-going commitment to modern management philosophy and practices'. On-going since when? asked those not sharing this view. Since the last five years, implied the vice-chancellor, listing half the faculties and a team of assorted university oddments. Vital centralities also. The central administration had also been reviewed in July 1992. To Deputy Vice-Chancellor Tony Wicken fell Academic Affairs; to Deputy Vice-Chancellor Chris Fell went Research: Niland implemented and augmented his plans for massive delegations with a pro-vice-chancellor, Jane Morrison, appointed in 1994. An inner cabinet extending to the new registrar, Crystal Condous (the university's first female executive administrator, appointed in August 1992), and including the head of finance and the director of Information Services, with the prime minister very much in charge, dealing direct, and separately, with deputies. An enthusiast, too, for other corporate devices — PR (the initials are sufficient jargon), through Open Day and a revitalised Alumni Association, with graduates now reaching prominence and top management in banks and major private companies: Niland's list was commercial, innocent of achievers in the arts and politics. And as to the world stage, in 1993 UNSW would conduct, for the first time, graduation ceremonies overseas. UNSW, the corporation university. Yet, fortunately, here was a tolerant, culture-seeking, cultivated man, open to the wider world of arts and humanity and of encountering the human condition and the ways it might be experienced. For all the corporate hype, the humanities could live easily with him. Live, too, because of his generally open disposition, with the Academic Board's heavy involvement with the corporate

262

planning process. Nor did he have to work hard at the task of being capitalist. Coming from a font of commercial and managerial know-how — the Commerce faculty — Niland was at home with corporatism, and able to swim in those (and other) deep waters with easy confidence. In times when others floundered in unfamiliar tides, he was a successful natural. The Academic Board oversaw, in 1993, a diversity of changes — to teaching strategy and degree structures, and the like — which amply justified Niland's hopes for the move to the new.

The figures backed up this bullishness. Australian Research Council (ARC) grants in 1993 were the largest ($12.5 million over 430 projects) of any institution in Australia and associated schemes and grants brought the ARC funding up to $20 million. National Health and Medical Research Council (NH&MRC) grants were $5 million, the university in fifth place nationally. All up, research funds awarded in 1992 were $71 million, big bikkies indeed. Then there was private sector support, as much as $1.6 million in the case of the Optometric Vision Research Foundation. And, as always, profits from Unisearch. Virtually from its beginnings in 1959 Unisearch possessed a business ethos: its company board was composed of people who were mainly not from the university. (Its less successful imitations at other universities were dominated by academics.) Particularly in the 1980s, its efforts to attract investors to take up university-generated projects had proved successful — and lucrative. Unisearch also worked for the university in other ways — for instance, devising a program for screening overseas student entry, which is still in place, to ensure high standards. Unisearch also provided consulting, contractual advice and expert consultancies — using university staff resources — on a commercial basis: it has worked for 10,000 companies, has 12,000 experts on call. Its dividends are not merely financial but, importantly, reputational, for the university. And its benefits are also protective. Unisearch knows the fields of commerce and industry, and how to avoid litigation. And it is big — or at least biggish — business in its own right, with 130 staff in 1997. Innovative, enthusiastic, pioneering in business and education projects, Unisearch was a major success story, providing gainful and prestigious university outreach in the world of commerce and industry. Exposure to market forces, however, had a downside. Losses could be incurred as well as gains, and 1997 was a less happy year for some aspects of Unisearch activities. Faculty decision-making devolution, established in 1989, was maintained, but new factors were introduced to take account of changes in the Commonwealth funding emphasis towards industry and the emergence of the post-1987 universities as significant bidders for funds. The Research Office was reviewed and the Research Plan updated.

Research? From its founding the university had aspired to be research-intensive: Baxter had brought from Britain a keen and experienced sensitivity to its importance. And the demands of the Cold War situation internationally, and of development nationally, pressed home, in his view, the imperative need for his university to provide research leadership. In this he was initially hampered by the nature of the early institution, so substantially drawing its staff from Sydney Technical College, where research was of little consequence and teaching the main concern. His own professorial appointments had a strong research dimension and this swiftly became the pattern for staff selection at all levels. So, when I joined the university in 1959, it was well-known that appointment, and promotion within and between grades, was dependent on research performance, which was vigorously encouraged — and rewarded — by promotion, thereby offering tangible recognition of research initiatives and publication. By the 1960s research in chemistry, physics, various branches of engineering, and applied sciences had gained significant international reputations. In all this Baxter was interested, not only in the notion of research per se, but in enhancing the reputation of the university through this means. However, the 1960s were less a time of research development than a period of new courses and of new buildings. It was the 1970s which saw the convergence of nationally significant research groups and in the 1980s research came spectacularly into its own, buoyed by increasing ARC funds. This is the era of the photovoltaic cell, membrane technology, the Garvan Institute for Medical Research, a host of areas of other innovations, developments, and commercial applications too various and numerous to detail. And, from 1989, UNSW led nationally for eight years in the award of ARC Large Grants and collaborative grants with industry. The 1990s saw further projects of astonishing diversity, many of them associated with a profusion of university centres — over sixty — established by the university. All this in response to the federal government placing a much greater emphasis and requirements on university research. These smaller generalities add up to a whole situation in 1998 where research at UNSW receives over $100 million annually — 20 per cent of its yearly budget. Teaching and research? The research element in the university's performance has become beyond the merely spectacular to be vital to its continuing life. Baxter's ambition realised beyond any expectation — even any individual comprehension.

All this is to stress revenue, the economics of research. It neglects what could be called the culture of research: the disposition to value and respect research that placed UNSW, despite distance and inadequate resourcing, among the best in the world — that mainly among those areas central to the university's long-term character. The sciences and engineering, plus the life sciences and medicine — it is these research achievements which have been, in large part, what UNSW has drawn on to establish its international reputation. Invidious though it is to select from a remarkable diversity of research talent — across all faculties are those staff with international reputations — Martin Green in Electrical Engineering and Michael Paddon-Row in Organic Chemistry come to mind as exemplars. Then there is George Paxinos in Psychology, whose *Atlas of the Rat Brain* is said to be one of the most highly cited references in modern biological science. In Medicine John Dwyer, Ian McCloskey. The list is partial, selective and subjective: every member of the university would have his or her own — and ample reasons for having so.

In keeping with Niland's hopes, internationalisation was on the march, and that rapidly. In 1992 the university had 3211 international (the term for non-Australian, foreign) overseas students, 1177 of whom were studying for higher degrees. This exceeded planning estimates by a massive 36 per cent from 1989. Most were fee-paying, to an extent where they contributed significantly to the university's budget.

264

The *Tharunka* view

of senior management

1995

They were, in 1993, 12 per cent of student load and provided fees of over \$31 million. The first overseas graduation was held in Kuala Lumpur in June 1993: there were eighty-six graduands. More generally, the university supported Community Aid Abroad by facilitating staff payroll deductions. Fee-paying was established practice with overseas students and had been introduced quietly as a matter of course: the agitation in May–June 1997 which had accompanied the application of fee payment to Australian undergraduate students had construed that issue as very different, which of course it was, but it did have points of similarity, not least the aspect of revenue production for the university. In its international ambitions the university widened its dialogue to include the United States. The Study Abroad Program, which enabled American and eventually European students to study at the university for one or two semesters, had initially 250 students; 500, by 1996. This arrangement had a distinctive impact on the Faculty of Arts, mainly to take advantage of Australian emphases: other international students tended to Science, Engineering, and Commerce. Of course, there were student exchanges as well: by 1992 agreements were in place with thirty universities abroad. Internationalisation was well under way and more was to come. Within the university itself, the major emphasis was on structures to enhance and reorganise excellence in teaching and learning — as distinct from research.

Corporatisation continued apace, building on the first Corporate Plan of 1983, with jargon run amok. In 1993 the vice-chancellor, announcing a new mission statement, laid it down to the perplexed multitude that 'the emphasis to the end of the decade is on strategic initiatives in five key areas: demand for quality; stakeholder involvement; competitive pressures; advanced technology and internationalisation'. Please translate. But no. 'In this context priorities being addressed include the development of facilities, international educational initiatives, quality assurance and community involvement' — some of which verbiage is intelligible, if trite, the rest mystification or gobbledygook. Or did all this simply mean business more or less as usual? Thank God, yes, with a nip here, a tuck there, and more of everything.

Certainly, the silly rhetoric was that of American business evangelism, sitting ill with Birt's attempt to preserve Newman's idea of the university, and illustrating the swing, under John Niland, towards the notion of corporate identity and its attendant postures and unmeaning: where now was the true religion of academe, buried under the gloss and flummery? The possibilities of serious laughing-stock and black farce were waiting in the wings. Thus, the Niland-Crystal Condous (Viceman-Crystal Avenger) comic in *Tharunka* October 1995 carries in its final box: 'These are the voyages of the starship UNSW Enterprise, on a 6 year corporate plan to seek new ways of saying "World Class University" and "International Standing" and to boldly use the word "Quality" in contexts where no one has gone before'.

Beautification in other than linguistic ways was another matter. The Quadrangle building, completed in 1993, was a disciplined joy to the astringent eye. The Clancy precinct and Chancellery forecourt had been 'converted into a pleasant environment for passive recreations by the campus community' (more jargon, somnolent this time) and named the Michael Birt Gardens. (The name produced some criticism from those unhappy with such naming in relation to the contemporary, or unwilling to concede Birt's status. It also produced an extraordinary and unfortunate error: the plaque read Michael Burt Gardens, a misspelling left in place for an unconscionable time.) Upgrading of the university's 200 teaching rooms had commenced. All was directed to ensuring that, by 1999, on the fiftieth anniversary of its founding, all building facilities would have been renovated and re-configured to provide 'quality space' to meet the objective of being a university of 'eminent world class'. Locally friendly, too, providing the Randwick region — so it reported in 'Profitable Neighbours' — with employment of 1600 indirect jobs additional to the university's direct employees.

The year 1994 saw the release, by the federal government, of the first report of the Committee for Quality Assurance in Higher Education. UNSW was ranked (with five other universities) in the highest category, a cause of growing pride and confidence — and increasing student first preferences in enrolment. Reviews continued, creating a new Division of Information Services, and placing both Aboriginal Education and Education itself under scrutiny. The hard-working Jane Morrison from Spanish and Latin American Studies, former president of the Academic Board, was appointed as pro-vice-chancellor with responsibility for a variety of academic operations — the first time the university had appointed a female academic to its top executive group. The Review of General Studies had major repercussions. The Centre of Liberal and General Studies was abolished and its subject areas devolved to the faculties. The idea was to thus integrate such subjects into the undergraduate program and to tailor them in the most appropriate ways to professional requirements and relevance. The actuality, by involving faculty members, was to enhance quality for students, and to — hopefully — achieve permanence in solving the humanities problem, an achievement for which Niland took credit.

Corporate planning continued as before, with a 1994–99 Six-Year Plan — the term was worrying: had nobody heard of Stalin's Five-Year Plan? (and surely six was worse) — approved, extending and refining directions already taken, in all directions, but particularly in information, management, function: everything was to operate more efficiently. The university environment had been enhanced not only by the Quadrangle project, but by that new arcade under the Mathews Plaza, and extensions to the Botany Street car park. The AGSM had its activities centralised. As well, the Science precinct development (commonly called the Red Centre) had commenced — a major new building housing the Faculty of Science, the Faculty of the Built Environment, and services for international students. That overseas dimension was recognised by a graduation ceremony not only in Kuala Lumpur but in Hong Kong, Jakarta and mainland China. Asian alumni groups proliferated.

Internally, in matters close to bread and butter rather than the intellect, things were changing in employment conditions — hardly notable at first, but potentially of fundamental importance. Framework agreements for enterprise bargaining were reached in late 1993 and early 1994: the Commonwealth agreed to fund a minor salary increase — 2.9 per cent. Negotiations between the Staff Association and university administration proceeded on enterprise bargaining, to issue eventually in

1997, in a general academic salary rise of 13.9 per cent to be phased-in over two years. General staff secured an increase as well — 12.5 per cent. But not before strikes and threats of strikes, situations involving considerable heat among staff and even some minor violence, during a clash with pickets. And not before there were ominous harbingers of radical change — proposals for weekend lectures, an extra summer semester, easier dismissal procedures and, in response, resort to confrontationist and nasty trade union tactics. The pay increase was to be funded by the university from its own resources. What did these emollient words entail in practice? Surely, even if crudely, more money, fewer staff. The increase was little enough — if the highest in the country — and held little prospect of protracted contentment. Particularly worrying was the feeling abroad among some distinguished leaders of their fields across the university, members of the various learned academies — to the extent of having meetings across 1996–97 to discuss their disquiet among themselves — that the institution did not value their contributions sufficiently. High-achievers felt resentful of the remuneration packages and perks they saw in administration. Saw as unjust and little merited in an institution which, of its nature, rested for its meaning and reputation on internationally recognised scholarship.

The path of enterprise bargaining, on which the university had perforce embarked, held future hazards, in which success for some was at the expense of those who were moving close to the wall. In 1995 Niland put the whole salary situation in a peculiar way. 'Despite', he said, 'the testing challenges' — what an absurd choice of words — 'posed by Commonwealth reluctance' — again, *refusal* is the correct word — 'to fund long overdue salary increases for academic and general staff in universities, we are building on great and increasing recognised strengths in the skills, creativity, knowledge and dedication and the sophistication of our administrative systems which allow us to pursue our mission with confidence.' Undoubtedly this was the case in fact, but this blah pays no heed to the widespread resentment, frustration, and sense of injustice experienced by staff: it was only the fact that other universities were in the same boat that sustained UNSW. 'We continue to build up our reputational capital by performing our core functions with distinction.' Indeed. And it was the fact also that the emphases in 1995 were on the international context and the physical environment of the campus, and these were outgoing matters which took academic minds off their internal personal grievances.

Those grievances, as affecting the non-professorial academic staff, had an important internal dimension, a cutting internal edge. This element of staff — by far the greatest section — had borne the heat of the day. They had long endured rigorous promotion procedures. Promotion from lecturer was difficult; above senior lecturer, excruciatingly hard until the 1990s: the Staff Association had done comparative statistical work which demonstrated the significantly higher standards of achievement for promotion required of UNSW staff. Similar expectations applied to initial appointments: it was harder to get in. This was generally accepted by incumbent staff as the cost of ensuring quality, and by the 1980s that staff enjoyed the impression that its quality overall — nebulous and elusive though such a judgement might be — was superior to that of other universities. And on this, it was assumed, the university's reputation rested. How DID this university get its leading reputation, its high research funds attraction, its extraordinary publication statistics, its increasing student popularity, if, on the whole, it had not picked well for all its academic ranks in the 1960s, 1970s and 1980s. Baxter was constrained to some extent in his staff choice — with the legacy of Sydney Technical College and the imperatives of filling new positions. Myers, however, was determined to have only the best. He personally chaired every professorial selection committee, acting according to his maxim, 'when in doubt, leave them out', a principle which paid rich dividends. It seemed obvious to the staff itself that the university's reputation was built on and by them. They were a well-qualified lot, early in the piece — young, modern, relatively efficient. Frank Crowley was looked on, from outside the university, as being insufferably vulgar in his insistence in the 1960s that a PhD was a requirement for appointees in History. That degree was seen at the time — by older universities — as a new-fangled American affectation: few of their

The A to Z of Academia
by Phil Schofield

F is for Funding

WIFe, FaMiLY aND UNiVERSiTY To SuppoRt

scнoтials

P Schofield

∧

Phil Schofield caricature series

Uniken 19 May 1979

professors had more than master's degrees. UNSW was in the van of requiring higher qualification of its staff. They all worked harder and were expected to be more productive than colleagues elsewhere.

That being so, when it came to the enterprise agreement salary negotiations of early 1996, such staff were driven to a jaundiced view of proceedings. For the first time, among this broad staff constituency, a distinction came to be made between 'the university' and 'the management'. Perhaps such a realisation was no new discovery, having long been the property of cynics — or realists? — or could be described as naive, but the fact seems to have been the widespread abandonment of the age of innocence. There had long been an assumption, among the mass of academics wedded to teaching and research, that 'the university', conceived perhaps in some beneficent, otherworldly fashion, would take good care of them. Disillusionment brought an element of rage. How could the management, on its fat packages, boast of UNSW's achievements and simultaneously appear to be so disdainful of the staff's ability? And how could that management demand such demeaning trade-offs for any pay increase; such smart-ass, corporatist trade-offs? Were they blind to the vast adaptability, forbearance and goodwill shown by the staff all along? So, it now seemed to many staff, formerly used to an atmosphere of trust, and the even tenor of their ways, that they had been badly treated, and their virtues unappreciated. This was an unfortunate conclusion and not justified. But it pointed to the consequences of continuous and radical government cost-cutting: leave it to the universities to carve up their shrinking cake and let them devour themselves in the process. The salary matter could be largely left to the operations of time and residual goodwill. But operating more widely, among senior and committed staff, was a growing conviction that not only was the administration running the university in the sense of aggregating all power to itself, tail wagging dog, but that the administration did not understand the intellectual life nor comprehend what a university should be. Superb managers and administrators they might be, the best in Australia's universities, but academics felt they were increasingly demeaned by that administration into the role of productive ciphers: they felt — and it was due to their own dereliction — that they had lost their way. Was this being ruled all academic life was? Was there not some better accommodation? Nobody had thought this through in realistic, future-oriented terms.

Running as a thread through all of this was the distinctive nature of the staff ethos. Elusive, subtle, there was a difference between UNSW staff and that of other Australian universities. Was it a legacy of those remote technical college origins? Or was it the conditioning inseparable from making their way up in an uncaring, fault-finding world? Perhaps, as some have suggested, the cause is more specific — the diversity of staff recruited in the 1980s and thereafter. UNSW has a higher proportion of staff with American qualifications and experience than any other Australian university. It is these who have given the university a different approach, less inclined to indulge in in-fighting and internal politics, healthily cynical about boards and committees, the belief that such things are not worthwhile, a waste of valuable time. Get on with the job of teaching and research. Whatever of such speculative theorising, staff at UNSW seem to have been slow to adopt the culture of complaint. Perhaps their history had inured them into making the most of hard times, for times were ever hard, in one way or another. But, for whatever reason, even, strangely, some kind of natural common disposition, the dominant staff mood was one of optimism, more than mere belief in survival, but a cheerful conviction that all would be well — even in the worst of possible worlds.

Some problems were too large and pressing to be avoided. Foremost in 1996 were reductions in federal operating grants, continuing the trend of shrinkage — 9 per cent per student — which had been eroding university income since the early 1980s. The new minister, Senator Vanstone, offered little consolation, attacking everything and everybody within universities. They should seek the best in everybody, not just in the brightest. She damned student politicians, incompetent vice-chancellors, lazy lecturers. Nothing escaped her strictures: universities lacked the barbarity to deal with this intemperate onslaught.

In the face of Commonwealth constriction, the university had to resort to 'rationalisation' — faculty and course restructuring — which resulted in redundancies in 1997. Deep regret was little consolation to offer 'loyal and dedicated' staff. This was an overarching concern. However, there were positive developments, the establishment of a postgraduate medical school for instance, and the extension of the sponsorship of Southern Cross University for another two years from 1997. No money but ample awards. In 1996 the Quadrangle project's design award. In 1997 UNSW topped Australian universities in a list in the prestigious *Asiaweek*. The university was again in the top band of Commonwealth quality assurance awards and was chosen by the Good Universities Guide as 1996 University of the Year: it produced 'an able, cosmopolitan, intellectually-engaged, open-minded, successful body of students'. Praise indeed. Almost too much to be believable.

At the same time a good deal of what was described as budgeting reform and administrative enhancement was taking place. The particular focus was UNSW 2000, the reviews and reforms designed to respond to the federal budget cuts and refusal to supplement urgent salary increases. These were first fielded as an assemblage of 'hypotheticals' and 'options', circulated widely for critical comment and exposed to public forums. Universities had developed various modes of dealing with the funding cuts imposed by the federal government. Some had brought in overseas consultants. Others had resorted to severe horizontal cuts, operative across the whole university. UNSW 2000 was the Kensington answer, put forward as the whole university thinking aloud, a program which consulted staff and students on the way ahead. There were six working parties — on integrating measures, research policy and strategy, education technology, chancellery services, fees, and the St George campus. The process was time intensive but it had the merit of involving everybody in hard decisions, an initiative both democratic and spreading of responsibility. Thus, divisive criticism was kept to a minimum, as everybody took their share of blame for unpalatable outcomes. The upshot was eventually to decide on the necessity for staff cuts, determined vertically and strategically, that is, cutting out whole faculties deemed less important, including the St George campus: 'it had never fitted in' said Jeremy Davis. His remark found agreement, in the broad, from the *Sydney Morning Herald*. It held that, given the university's elitist aspirations, its pursuit of an international reputation, it needed to move out of primary teacher training. The ideal of universities being all things to all interest groups was no longer valid. The *Herald* foresaw a small group of elite universities — of which UNSW was one — and a large group of vocationally oriented ones.

A range of courses in Professional Studies and Applied Science were purged. The entire Faculty of Professional Studies was abolished and the remnants dispersed. The same treatment was applied, from mid-1997, to Applied Science, Biological and Behavioural Science, and Science. Two newly established faculties — Science and Technology, and Life Sciences — mopped up some of the residue. It was a radical spring-clean, very painful to those who experienced it. The only positive aspect of the consequent, and otherwise generated, redundancies (particularly in general staff) was the comparatively attractive packages offered —

up to seventy weeks' pay in contrast with the private sector's twenty weeks.

Despite the internal airing, the measures prompted the predictable response — that they were merely slash and burn, that cuts should have been horizontal and better considered, that there was no necessity for cuts, that the vice-chancellor should resign. (Niland responded 'Our 1998 budget is some $9 million less than it would have been by 1991 standards ... we face the task of finding a further $18 to $20 million each year'.) There was also a vehement and angry response from the State and federal parliamentary members, and mayors of the St George area (mainly Labor politicians) alleging indecent haste and lack of community consultation, as lacking logical or moral justification; the closure was seen as a slap in the face for courses recently acquired in trust, obligations dishonoured. All to suit the convenience of 'old guard' schools. So ran the criticism: it was held a shoddy attempt to solve the university's fund shortage in one convenient grab: 1500 students would have their courses phased out. (Actually it was 980, full-time.) The university should either reverse its decision, or give the campus to the University of Wollongong. More, as baseless media coverage in June 1997 suggested, the university proposed to sell — for sums of up to $60 million, a site it had acquired for a token dollar ($1). This in particular enraged critics, who saw the university, not only as treating the people of southern Sydney with contempt, but as engaging in massive profiteering in the process. Such an intention was denied by Niland. However, by October 1997, the university was considering sale or long-term lease, after international advertisement. It did not have the money to sustain the School of Teacher Education beyond 1998, believed there were adequate alternative facilities, deemed its consultative process 'exemplary', and saw no reason why it should not dispose of the site at a profit. Besides, as the university pointed out, a condition of disposal was that its new purpose remain broadly educational.

Spring-cleaning continued into winter. By June 1997 the Staff Association was cataloguing the on-going loss of academic and general staff which had occurred or was in train — about 100 at the St George campus and a sprinkle (in some areas heavy drizzle) across Kensington: Engineering, Physics, Chemistry, Fibre Science, Community Medicine, cleaning staff, technical workshop closures. Two here, five there: how did academics expect their salary increases would be funded? If not from building funds, obviously by not only vague rationalisation but also decreasing the number of staff in vulnerable areas — that is, in those areas experiencing decreasing student demand, or traditionally overpopulated. These were the hard facts. Yet there was abroad something of an uncaring feeling of unreality, an unthinking assumption that things should remain the same: that this should rebound on morale is not surprising. Each man or woman for themselves.

Yet, on the other hand, cheerful, expansive business as usual: a virtual boom of goings-on. The 1995 bonanza of $45 million from Pacific Power to develop and commercialise solar-cell technology highlighted the fact that by 1996 university funding was 40 per cent privatised. A Working Party on Intellectual Property was a sign of the times. New courses sprouted — interior architecture, biomedical engineering, aviation. And old disciplines adapted to new circumstances, old principles of serving the pragmatic and changing needs of industry applied to new confluences. Mechatronics in the Engineering faculty brought together mechanics, electronics and computing to produce an immediately employable hybrid to meet the demands of industries operating in the new electronic machine world. But empires were falling too. Under Malcolm Chaikin as dean, Applied Science had been the darling of the 1970s and 1980s, recipient of substantial outside grants, from the Wool Board for instance, and lavish internal funding, which made it the envy of other faculties whose budgets suffered, and who saw Applied Science profiting at their expense. Wool Science had been shrinking by the late 1980s, but the situation of Textile Technology had become so disastrous by the late 1990s that enrolments were discontinued in 1998: there were not enough students for its viability. What had happened? Despite vigorous promotion to schools, and new programs and subject consolidations, student interest had dwindled to almost nil. This reflected major changes in the Australian textile industry. It had moved to Victoria: New South Wales was left with only 20 per cent of the country's textile manufacturing. The lesson was simple — no demand meant no supply, a situation of change to which technological services to a changing world would always be painfully vulnerable.

On the positive side, other less tangible things. Former prime minister Paul Keating accepted a visiting professorship. Mark Taylor, as captain, and Michael Slater were in the Australian cricket team. Bob Carr was premier of New South

The Scientia

Λ

John Niland explains the case for the St George campus closure,

by video relay to university staff

December 1996

Wales. UNSW graduates everywhere. And their university cried it abroad. A new advertising campaign from May 1997 was, in effect, directed against other universities, closely aligned with 'its position in the marketplace'. UNSW sought to stand 'out from the crowd'. The competition was fierce in Asia, where most universities had agents. UNSW had representatives everywhere from India to Fiji, usually shared, avoiding private agents where it could. Niland was determined that UNSW be top of the perceived hierarchy of Australian universities. Doing it tough but doing it smart.

Building was on the move. Dear to Niland's heart. To implement these designs — home to, and of a piece with, his world-class university — a Facilities Planning Workshop was established to identify greatest building needs: a university centre building (the Scientia, costing $25 million) to be a venue for major ceremonies and for enrolment and examinations, and to provide performance space for music and theatre studies (part-funded by alumni for the Fiftieth Anniversary), then the Sciences precinct to house Mathematics and various other activities, and the Barker Street housing for students, of 130 beds. A campus to enjoy rather than endure.

Driving into the future

1997

Above all came the university centre, both signature and symbol, a physical message proclaiming world class and cultural affirmation, performance area, legacy of fifty years of achievement, a proclamation of status to the wider world.

All else in 1996–97 seemed positive or innocuous planning save in two respects — the future of St George campus, and the possibility of charging fees to Australian students. The government had legislated to allow this. Access and equity seemed to the vice-chancellor the only next considerations. However, in both cases — St George and fees — the matters were both contentious and divisive, splitting the university community. In both the outcomes were close-run things.

Fees? Ah that was a matter fraught: 'it is without doubt the most difficult issue I have faced in more than 30 years in higher education' Niland told University Council in a crucial meeting on 2 June 1997. Sophie's Choice, he called it, the lesser of two evils: 260 fee-paying Australian students were to be admitted to UNSW from 1998, worth $3 million. By ten Council votes to eight. What if it had been nine all? Or gone the other way? The decision was preceded and accompanied by intense politicking: within the university on matters mainly of principle; within council on matters of principle, yes, but spilling over into wider divisions of political ideology, and involving the whole matter of the vice-chancellor's future and power. The vote was taken to the chants of a small number of students outside. For the second time in 1997 — the first was in relation to the St George campus — Niland had put his job on the line. And was this time, by the narrowest of margins, victorious. Not a desirable way to govern: risk-taking could misfire. Yet the outcome was not seriously divisive, because the university community conceded (however cynical its view of power) that Niland was fundamentally honest, trying his best (however he saw it) to deal with an impossible situation, imposed by a government determined to reduce public spending to the absolute minimum politically tolerable. However academics might rage, the public did not care. The university's failure to educate the public, the inertia, stupidity, the lack of any foresight, long predated Niland, and went back at least to the time when the Commonwealth took over university funding.

It was also a dereliction common to all Australian universities: they had all long-failed to win hearts and minds — and pockets. Niland was the first Australian vice-chancellor to consistently attempt to redeem the ground. From early in 1996 he was increasingly prominent in the media — both television and newspapers — in defence of universities and in criticism of savage government funding cuts. This drew a positive, Australia-wide, academic expression of satisfaction, delight even, that someone was providing leadership. And, in an article in the *Sydney Morning Herald* in May 1996, he extended reasoned argument for the university case. This was not a stance — or person — to be ignored. On the one side it inhibited a clear government intention to further slash and burn and led on, in a general cabinet reshuffle in October 1997, to the replacement of Senator Vanstone as Education minister by the more sympathetic Dr David Kemp. Within academe it led on to Niland's election as Australian Vice-Chancellors' Committee (AVCC) president in August 1997. He had proved himself adept, indeed pre-eminent, in exploiting the new situation to this university's advantage. Moreover, as newly elected president of the AVCC, he came out with fighting words: promising to turn up the heat on the federal government — a simmering long overdue. He made it clear that the AVCC, in the past regarded as a 'gentleman's club', would have to bestir itself politically, and become active in the next federal election. It would have to abandon neutrality and passivity and scrutinise the political parties' higher education policies. Particularly in regard to funding. So, politicians be warned. Niland saw Australia slipping in relation to other universities in the Asian region. He declared that universities would have to educate and win over public opinion to recognition of their vital social importance. All this signalled the end of the 'ivory tower', that phrase of dismissive contempt which had caught the essence of universities' public stance — remote, polite, superior, to which the real world owed a living. Gone. The new university's job was realist, competitive, combative. Such was Niland's view. As to tactics, certainly one can give in too soon, but it is fatal to hang on too long. It is a matter of responsible judgement as to when it was time to survive so as to live, and fight again another day. Many agreed with him, and with his ability to lead a charge into the new age.

After winning the support of the Academic Board (thirty votes to seventeen) Niland put his case for undergraduate fees payment to the University Council. He argued that the matter was one of survival, avoidance of becoming second-rate. To admit about 260 undergraduates in 1998 was to raise $3 million, with a pipeline of $9 million, but the financial context was a shortfall of $20 million by 1999. Moreover, he forewarned of staff cuts as devastating and extensive as those which had terminated St George. As it was, the majority of schools would not be able to appoint a professor until 2005.

Those who opposed fees did so on grounds of ethics and equity. They held that it would downgrade merit, adversely affect disadvantaged groups, privilege the wealthy. The university was bartering social conscience for a quick fix. The federal government must be resisted. Fine. But how? Those who urged fees had an unanswerable response. They accepted the points raised by critics. They agreed with them. But they were irrelevant to the dollar facts, and they, not the critics, were in charge of the books. As for resisting the federal government? The power realities were as they were.

Where did students stand on fees? Predictable but politely opposed. Since the introduction of HECS (Higher Education Contribution Scheme) in 1989, students had revealed themselves as less interested and more acquiescent than might have been anticipated, to government impost. HECS, and government economic contraction generally, changed the student climate. Being a student had become a much more serious affair in an economic environment difficult, resistant, even hostile. Protest against fees, for instance, was narrowly based: demonstrations were small in size and substantially taken over by groups (ideologues and militants) external to campus. Yet, there was ample evidence of student vitality, albeit in restructuring their own affairs. The old Students' Union was wound up and replaced by student initiative, with an Australian first, a Guild of Postgraduate and Undergraduate Students, on 1 January 1993. Its internal departments were much more autonomous than before in disposing of a budget close to a million dollars,

courtesy *Tharunka*

∧

The student response to the introduction of

full fee-paying for local students

1997

and in giving postgraduates a much larger role. It was more representational, more open to vigorous student electioneering, and much more conscious of the university's social and economic role in fitting students for that resistant and demanding 'real' world. The students' Guild fees-protest video was mild and inoffensive: it was shown, with staff support, to lecture classes passively silent, or disposed to be critical of the Guild — a contrary stance of some antiquity. Students were for ever claiming that the Guild which they had elected did not represent them. And there were other enduring themes: in *Tharunka*, for instance, correspondence directed 'to the [only the obscenities varied over time] who stole my bike last week' — on this occasion a bike bought from a small bequest from his grandmother as a memento. Cycle theft was an enduring campus problem — from the 1970s at least, to the extent of loading motor bikes on utes. But *Tharunka* itself had changed, had become internalised, apologetic. The sexual ground had shifted. When the Wizard revisited the campus in 1996, he circulated a flyer — Save the Males. Gay and lesbian students extracted a prominent apology in June 1997: offence had been caused and grovelling ensued. Days when *Tharunka* offended everybody had gone. If *Tharunka* be any guide, political correctness ruled within the student body —

and, as usual, unfunny scatology and sexual depravity. Politics of the traditional kind ranked thin: reviews of the fringe and oddball (films, CDs, gigs) waxed large. As did, mercifully from time to time, genuine talented humour — Viceman and the Crystal Avenger were clever and not unkindly comics in 1995, as was the emendation of the university's public sign — UNSW to UN$W — in the fee protest of June 1997. Comment on campus features was amusing — library lawn types (the Wog Pit), the clock thereon (If I met God, I would ... Get Him to fix the clock on the Library Lawn, because if anyone can fix it, it's him ... maybe.) The clock had been vandalised and remained unrepaired, a kind of Oxbridge echo of Rupert Brooke's 'Grantchester' 'Stands the clock at ten to three? And is there honey still for tea?'.

Affirmation of high principle and pre-eminence of academic ability came too late. Or did it? From 1996, elements in the academic staff became increasingly critical of the pains taken by the university administration and management. The Professional Development Centre came under fire for the way it introduced new staff to UNSW. Whereas in the past stress had been on values and commitment necessary to bind the academic community together, by 1997 the emphasis on scholarship and excellence and collegiality had given way to discussing financial imperatives, income and salary issues, greater output and efficiency. To put it in the words of Joseph Forgas in March 1997, 'some sections of our institution have lost their way ... a university is different from a commercial corporation'. This was an overall view held by some in the highest quarters — Sir Anthony Mason, the chancellor.

In a University Council meeting of 12 August 1996 in the course of a mid-term review by the pro-vice-chancellor of the UNSW Corporate Plan in relation to student enrolment a 'Client Impact Cluster' was presented to be 'evaluated during the next Triennium with particular emphasis on client satisfaction'. Following protest, the vice-chancellor noted that it was the view of some members (they included Mason) 'that "client" was not an appropriate word to use for a student' and directed it not be used again. (A cynical observer remarked 'Strike out "clients", substitute "customers"' — a term used by some parliamentarians.) The word implied views of what the university was, and the preservation of 'student' was an important affirmation of the traditional character of university life and purpose against the drift towards consumerism and corporation-speak gradually eroding university life as conceived by its managers: indeed, the word 'manager', as implying and indicating the function of what a university 'administration' did and sought to do, gave the game away. Academics were no longer a community of scholars, but workers being managed — for profit in a service industry. Note the change from 'Academic Staff Office' to 'Human Resources'. The university was increasingly accepting the tame and passive, intellectually vacant, role being set for it by the federal parliament, where the word 'client' was increasingly being used, from 1996 to describe students. In fact, the cause had already been lost to managerialism in the 1995 restructuring of the Library, which emerged as the Client Services Unit. That restructuring was necessitated by the proliferation of modern information services — computing, the web, audio-visual, and the like — all sections headed by persons titled 'manager'. The Library as traditionally understood, now holding 2 million items, had a principal librarian — Marian Bate — but only after intense and heated debate on the Library Advisory Committee of the Academic Board: the argument that the university should retain a university librarian was lost. The principal librarian and all other unit managers, reported to the director and deputy principal of Information Services, Christine Page-Hanify. 'The Library' remained common usage, and, fortunately for the realities of university operation, there remained, in ledgers, a distinct 'library budget', but in terms of the formality of the *University Calendar*, the Library had ceased to exist.

And, looking backwards to the achievements of former students, the character of what the university was providing was — to its justified pride — prominent in the commercial world. Of eight 'big-ticketed' directors listed in the *Australian Financial Review* in June 1998, two were UNSW BSc graduates.

Small wonder (as the cliché has it) that some disenchanted staff, some at professorial level, looked askance at this, and other instances of the encroachments of managerialism. They were impervious to arguments of efficiency and economy, indeed contemptuous of management as practised at UNSW — and hostile (sometimes unrestrainedly so in private) to all they regarded as its practitioners. Allegations of anti-intellectualism, failure to comprehend the true university spirit, governance at all levels by power-hungry third-raters, even the sectarian absurdity (when will such bigotry end?) of control by the Catholic Right, were the charges uttered by a few extremists: more widespread was a sense of unease at what seemed to be happening. The extremists, in particular, seemed to have no comprehension that these pressures towards managerialism were Australia-wide, induced as both a consequence of, and response to radical, federal government cost-cutting applicable to all universities. Indeed, it could be argued that UNSW strategies protected the university from an even worse situation. The question remained for critics, how could purist notions of their ideal academic and professional life be maintained in the face of extreme financial stringency? Could they do it better? Of course they could, in a make-believe world. So did the duress of economics make some few academics lose their powers of reason and conjure up monstrous and oppressive mythologies of evil and darkness. But, not so fast and furious or so high-principled. What of students themselves?

Unaided, except for the prevailing notions of individual protection, and full value for money, students were intent on their own self-destruction. As a distinctive class, historical genus that is. They were determined to be 'consumers', with consumer rights. After a (small) student survey, the students' Guild announced in October 1997 this would be its policy: 'students are no longer willing to accept poor quality teaching or inadequate resources'. They paid HECS or full fees and would no longer tolerate 'overcrowded classrooms where students were forced to sit on the floor'. The analogy offered was not at a high level of academic intellectualism: 'If you buy a washing machine and it doesn't work, you're entitled to your money back'. Education as consumer-durable white goods? Perhaps some better analogy might have to be found in the world of, say, operatic or gig performance, but in any case the Guild solicitor was available to handle consumer dissatisfaction, and the media made much of the UNSW initiative. And was the student practice of calling John

Niland, not vice-chancellor but 'chairman' of UNSW another acceptance of the language of corporatism, another instance of students themselves selling the pass? So what is to be made of the *Tharunka* spread of 19 May 1998, in which various interviewed students, some from the Guild, were at one in agreeing that UNSW lacked any 'university spirit', was aimed to produce the best marketable product (no quarrel with that), and was populated by apathetic students, 81 per cent of whom had paid work? The answer is confusion — and unwillingness to accept that the dream world of the traditionalist freedom, leisure and intellectual exploration, must fall casualty to the demands of the guaranteed washing-machine.

But 1996 saw this process of abdication moving towards hesitation, even some halt. Traditional questions of character, purpose, nature were beginning to obtrude. Academics, always slow and reluctant to act, always about their own scholarly business, as they should be, had become painfully conscious of their need to bestir themselves in a harsh and uncomprehending world: the price of liberty. The vice-chancellor himself, sovereign in his roles of management, realised that his very existence and rationale were under threat if his mission became hollow, if the medium overwhelmed the message. If, in pursuit of 'excellence' and 'quality' as a corporation, he lost sight of the meaning of the enterprise, its integrity and pre-eminence as an educational institution, its nature as a humane, intellectual endeavour, an academic community, he would lose the confidence of the members of the institution itself. After all, at the workface, the university was populated by intelligent and dedicated men and women who loved their subjects and were perfectly willing to endure the cost of unfilled vacancies in pursuit of the best, and not merely any, candidate — the cost being increased teaching loads for themselves. Well, willing enough, if their sacrifice was recognised within their own institution. Vice-chancellorial authority was a concessional convenience, rather than something arising from agreed, scholarly pre-eminence. With the community, too. He would become the nominal leader of a sham confidence-trick. The very being and meaning of the whole enterprise would evaporate: he would be vice-chancellor — of what? A nothing.

Niland was too intelligent to permit this to happen, to allow too wide a gap to open between corporate and traditional values. Taxed with precisely this, implicitly and directly, in 1997 he averred his future intention of affirming publicly and outspokenly his belief in the essence of the 'old' university. His response was to concede that UNSW, more than others, had moved down the 'modern' road. He saw this as a position of strength, from which to affirm the continued validity of 'tradition', in which he firmly believed. He could see the need, evident within the university, for restoring balance; otherwise, he would lose the basic elements of his constituency. If he lost or weakened that, the whole edifice would quickly crumble.

The future of UNSW had elements of a serious family argument: John Niland the pragmatic, the hard-headed bean-counter, ambitious to be biggest and best; Carmel Niland stressing the sense and value of history, the human, the character of equalities and liberations had been achieved. A family matter, each conceding the other's viewpoint, the difference being one of balance, emphasis: the facts seen in the same light, the difference lying in the differing perceptions of gender and assessment of priorities. But nonetheless a family matter, the cohesion greater than the disagreements: the common enterprise must be maintained. (Yet who could doubt that the fees matter marked a stage in the death of the old order. Things could never be the same again.)

More to it than that. Where was the university going? Certainly towards different balance and character of students. Some things different. Some accentuated. Different, the mix from 1988, the fee-paying element. If initially it was not large (and only about half in number of those expected), the theory was what counted for the future. And the impact of differences in changes between universities, as yet unknown. What effect would it have on enrolments that arts at UNSW (at $10,000 per annum) was $500 less than the University of Sydney or law more? Or on morale? And joint university arrangements: as with University of Technology, Sydney (UTS), research on provincial China; or, much more domestically revolutionary, with the University of Sydney in a merger of management education — the mega-business school? Imponderables. Or more revolutionary and imponderable still — major initiatives and developments in Asia, a course beloved of Chris Fell, building on initiatives already in train there and taking advantage of the university's long-developed mentoring skills, which went back to its foundation. Changed, too, would be the balance of the university's character, as Asian demand drew on the university's expertise in management and accounting.

Accentuations? A student body already conservative, becoming more so. More conscious of economic pressures as costs and changes increased. The need to do well, and quickly, get out fast and get a job. Impatience with both student capers and shoddy teaching. Less time, less fun. The golden years of student leisure and liberty, freedom and thought, perhaps sadly gone: paying meant taking things more seriously.

What of the essences of the institution? With high-flyer Niland in charge, not only of the university but of the AVCC, there was that determination that Australian universities not fall behind in world comparisons; that a mean and short-sighted government not be allowed to short-change society, that it be pushed to provide the means to foster intellectual leadership. The university, under Niland, had become the leading impetus behind the Group of Eight, the major Australian research universities — ANU, Monash, Adelaide, Melbourne, UNSW, Queensland, Sydney, Western Australia — which had banded themselves together to protect the interests of these top institutions. Initially an informal group during the Dawkins period, it met strong criticism of elitism and of being an effort to undermine the uniform national system, criticism which came in large part from institutions not in the eight. However, this feeling of commonality firmed up to become a cohesive group in the Vanstone years, to the extent of making, through Niland, a joint submission to the West Review of Higher Education Financing and Policy in 1997, set up to advise the Howard government elected in March 1996. The emphasis of this submission was on research funding. Niland's own submission was to argue for a social contract which would ensure that an agreed, higher, proportion of GDP (gross domestic product) be devoted to higher education, given that Australia was increasingly falling behind the proportion spent in comparable Western countries. A world-class system was impossible without world-class funding. In keeping with its new political orientation and initiatives, the AVCC had taken action to pre-empt government cost-cutting. A survey, conducted by a major polling company, was released in November 1997 indicating that most voters (and that is how respondents were represented) wanted expenditure on universities increased or, at worst, maintained: only 4 per cent favoured further cuts. Of those polled, 92 per cent regarded research as important to Australia's future.

Interesting — and important. But were there not questions about the role of universities which ought to have been in the public domain but were not? Basic problems about meaning and function? The public expectation of university education was both too much and too little — too much in that it wanted provision of some kind of social cure-all; too little in terms of being content with an intellectual status quo. These were problems common to the public position of all Australian universities, but in one area the University of New South Wales had unique dimensions of experience. More than that of any other university, UNSW was grounded in science and technology, that is, in those areas productive of a public sense of well-being — the accumulation of wealth and its consequences, new dimensions of consumerism and comfort. But it had from its beginnings, in its humanities and social sciences programs, faced the proposition that science was not enough. In part, this was a utilitarian acceptance of the needs of effective citizenship, but it was also a recognition that bread, gadgets, and circuses were not sufficient for the truly human life. This university had, throughout its history, faced the question of the role of arts within the responsibilities of university education, and had tried, with whatever shortcomings, to blend them with the pursuits of science and technology. It was a remarkable attempt, no less necessary now than it was at its inception. How will human values and the life of the soul survive, be encouraged, in an educational environment dedicated to practical, material things?

Academic leadership? That, Niland could provide, in the role of encouraging others, and did. But the essence of the institution? Increasingly the corporation? Not to be encouraged, said the West Report. Indeed, Roderick West stated that he regarded mere vocational training as 'education for servitude'. Universities should implant a general sense of confidence and exhilaration adaptable to any career. He saw academics as feeling threatened by the inroads of commercial orientation and in themselves both conscientious and over-worked, compliments which seldom came their way. West held the pass against the university conceived as corporation. Rather, everything which had been in the minds of men since the thirteenth century, everything conveyed by the phrase 'the idea of the university', the disciplined, vigorous, searching life of the intellect. Complicating all this was the row which broke out in New South Wales in November 1997 over the government-proposed reforms to the Higher School Certificate. Niland led criticism of them as discouraging bright students from taking the most demanding subjects: universities would have to consider how to deal with this, in order to ensure their students were adequately prepared. This drew a predictable anti-elitist response; it also made clear that Niland took the high ground on the university's function and character.

But human things are subject to unpredictable flux and change, and unexpected repercussions, whatever the good intentions involved. The Asian economic crisis of 1997–98 entailed obvious immediate student consequences, but what of outcomes in the longer term? Faced with a downturn of Asian enrolments, which might be as great as 30 per cent, the university anticipated that 1998 in that area of outreach might be 'a rough year', a crisis which had to be weathered. Two strategies were applied. One was to manage the situation in such a way that the university's Asian good name be preserved for better times to come. So, various measures were taken to ease the fees burden and help Asian students already here. And hopes turned to India, as a future customer. From where should students come? The general question remained, breathing uncertainty back from an unknown future. It was a question which bore on the long-term character of a university, which had seen itself as serving Asian needs — and was significantly dependent on that.

Will the number of fee-paying Asian students drop significantly? To an extent where local fee-payers may be called on to meet the shortfall? And in any case, 1998 figures indicate a poor local response to that dimension of university activity and financing. Is it totally absurd to think of the ultimate commercial-induced betrayal — will it be cheaper to teach in Asia rather than Kensington? The logic of viewing education as a commodity leads to conclusions similar to those that have operated on — and destroyed — the Australian garment industry. If economic forces drive raiment for the body off-shore, why not raiment of the mind? Unthinkable scenario.

So, which? Corporation or thirteenth century? In this day and at this time, probably a bit of both, but the essentials of the old and civilised held firm. At least in the mind, where it mattered. Firm and fast was loyalty still, to concepts and values of the scholarly intellectual life, and to the belief that, whatever the apostasies, the *trahison des clercs*, their vocation remained intact and their institution committed to it.

For gone were the golden days, buried distant in the lecture halls of time. Perhaps there were never such days, but only fond illusion. Only struggle and contention, the pains of growing up, the stress and anxieties of building; awkward, tangled dancing to the music of time.

Who can deny a little poetry in the meaning of academic lives, be they ever so grumble? Or gainsay a little grandeur to the institution that gave them place and space? Whatever of that, the present environment was uneasy, troubled, uncertain — and the future more problematic than futures usually are. The whole idea of university, beyond mere professional preparatory school, was under threat; academics feared the end of civilisation as they had known it, and administrators were strangled by government's financial constrictions, enforcing the need for unpopular internal economies and compelling resort to redundancies.

It would be nice to report that a heroic UNSW triumphed over all these inflicted adversities: with one bound it was free! Not so. But the university had much going for it, in past experience and present disposition, to enable it to confront bad times with resolve and ingenuity. It brought to that task optimism, a 'can do' presumption, and a confident blend of realism and scholarship.

Per ardua ad astra — telescope for Geomatic Engineering,

Geography and Surveying building

1998

It is more than this one book can do to do justice to those who make up, and have made up, the University of New South Wales. Far too few of those whose abilities and energies, and great gifts and benefactions, have created the whole astonishing intellectual enterprise, have entered these pages. It must be a matter of wistful regret that this is so; so many names and faces of colleagues and students, known and partly known, valued and human. Still, set against this is a story of uncommon achievement, of something new and exciting, something successful and worthwhile. For all the neglects and negligences, here at least is some of the context, a glimpse of the stage on which these talented actors performed.

So much then for fifty years of time, not just elapsed time, but packed, crowded time, informed by a dominant 'give it a go' philosophy, ultimate Australian affirmation of practical faith. Affirmation, too, of the freedom of trusting people and hoping for their independent and committed best. And with the laconic 'give it a go' mentality went the confident 'can do'. No doubts. Just get on with the job. In the midst of all this busyness — sometimes in spite of it, always in tension with it — the search went on for a new university growing out of the old. However forgotten, beset, betrayed, and in jeopardy, the hungry hunt remained on for the ever-elusive, universal knowledge and community of scholars.

BIBLIOGRAPHY

GOVERNMENT AND PARLIAMENTARY MATERIALS

Australia. House of Representatives 1987–88; 1996–97. *Debates*.

——. Parliament 1954. *First Annual Report of the Australian Atomic Energy Commission 1953*.

——. Senate 1987–88; 1996–97. *Debates*.

Baldwin, P. *Higher Education: Quality and Diversity in the 1990s*. Australian Government Publishing Service, Canberra, October 1991.

Dawkins, JS. *The Challenge for Higher Education in Australia* (Green Paper). Australian Government Publishing Service, Canberra, 1987.

——. *Higher Education: A Policy Statement* (White Paper). Australian Government Publishing Service, Canberra, July 1988.

New South Wales. Government. Developmental Council. Minutes 1947–49.

——. Legislative Assembly 1948–50; 1984–86. *Debates*.

——. Legislative Council 1948–50; 1984–86. *Debates*.

Parry, R. *The Future Structure of Higher Education in NSW*. position paper prepared by the Office of Higher Education, October 1988 (the Parry Report).

UNIVERSITY OF NEW SOUTH WALES MATERIALS

[This covers material in various forms originated within the university, for either general or internal circulation.]

1 UNIVERSITY PUBLICATIONS

OFFICIAL PUBLICATIONS
Annual Reports 1950–97.
Calendars 1950–98.

Focus 1977–98.
Origins (UNSW Archives newsletter) 1995–98.
Technology 1956–69.
Uniken 1975–98.
University News 1962–74.
UNSW Quarterly 1975–82.
UNSW Research and Publications Reports. 1949–98.

OTHER PUBLICATIONS, INCLUDING BY STUDENT GROUPS

Bounders 1983–87.
Newswatch (University Staff Association newsletter) 1971–98.
Poetic Justice (Law student publication) 1984–98.
Tharunka 1953–98.
Unilogic (University of Technology Society of Students publication) 1951.
University of Technology Students' Revue programs 1950s.

2 INTERNAL MINUTES, PAPERS AND REPORTS
[This includes material whose circulation was primarily confined to within the university.]

'Campus Life and Environment'. 1984.
Committee of Enquiry into Warrane College. Report. November 1974.
Committee to review the Public Affairs Function of UNSW. Background Paper to the Issues
    Sheet prepared by the Committee. September 1986.
——. Report. December 1987.
Gray, GA & Short, LN. *Student Progress in the University: The Report of the Investigation of
    Student Failure and Wastage and Related Matters.* June 1958 – July 1960. University
    of New South Wales 1961.
Identity Standards Manual. UNSW. December 1995.
Kenny, D. 'General Education Policy and Development Document 1986–93'. Centre for
    Liberal and General Studies, UNSW.
Niland, J. Vice-Chancellor's Statement of Goals and Priorities 1997–98. January 1997.
Property and Works Department. Capital Projects 1992: Progress Report.
Standing Committee on General Education. General Education University Seminar.
    November 1983.
Tribute to Long-serving Personnel. Publications Section. July 1994.
University Council. Minutes (selected dates).
——. National Institute of Dramatic Art (NIDA). Annual Reports 1975–96.
——. Vice-Chancellor's Reports (selected dates).
University 2000 Project. Various Reports of Working Parties. 1997.

3 RESPONSES AND SUBMISSIONS TO EXTERNAL INQUIRIES OR PUBLICATIONS

Birt, M. Personal Response to the Green Paper. April 1988.
Response to 'Higher Education - A Policy Discussion paper'. April 1988.
Submission to the Committee of Inquiry into Education and Training from the University
    of NSW. April 1977.

University of NSW Network Consultative Group. The Shape of Things To Come: Student Response to the NSW Office of Higher Education Position Paper on the Future Structure of Higher Education in NSW. December 1988.

4 HISTORIES OF FACULTIES AND UNIVERSITY ORGANISATIONS

Broun, M & Reuter, FH. 'The University Co-operative Bookshop Limited', unpublished paper. (nd) [UNSW Archives collection].

Daniels, EC. 'A History of the Faculty of Architecture'. Faculty of Architecture, UNSW. 1988.

Deasey, DJ. *The History of the UNSW Regiment*. Haldane Publishing Company, Sydney 1978.

Douglas, J. 'A Brief History of the Department of Statistics: The University of New South Wales 1948–83', unpublished typescript. March 1996 [UNSW Archives collection].

Franki, G (ed.). *The University of NSW Library 1959–84: An Informal Record*. UNSW Printing Section, March 1985.

Hall, S. 'Civil Engineering - the Early Days', unpublished typescript. 1997 [UNSW Archives collection].

Horne, J and McCarthy, L. *Unique Providers: Money Raising and the University of New South Wales U Committee 1963–1993*. Oral History Project, UNSW Archives 1994.

Hughes, A. 'A Soccer Fan's Forgotten Dream: The William Kennard Cup'. *ASSH Bulletin* No 24, June 1996.

——. 'The UNSW Soccer Club's Early Years 1956–60', unpublished manuscript. 1998 [UNSW Archives collection].

Ingleson, J (ed.). *A Decade in Grade Cricket: The University of NSW Cricket Club*. The University Cricket Club, Kensington. April 1983.

Livingstone, S. 'A History of the School of Chemistry at the University of NSW 1879–1985'. June 1991 [UNSW Archives collection].

——. 'Highlights in the History of the School of Chemistry 1879–1979', talk. August 1979 [UNSW Archives collection].

McLintock, R. 'The development of the Buildings and Grounds of the University of NSW', unpublished typescript. March 1993 [UNSW Archives collection].

O'Farrell, PJ. 'The History of History ... 1959–65', seminar paper, School of History. 2 August 1995 [private circulation].

Powell, JP and Barrett, EM. *TERC 1961–1982: A Brief History of a Higher Education Research and Development Centre*. Occasional Publication no 20, UNSW 1982.

Reuter, FH. 'Food Technology Education in Sydney 1952–70', unpublished manuscript [author's copy].

Rickwood, PC. 'UNSW Club History: The Early Years 1965–70', unpublished manuscript, May 1998 [UNSW Archives collection].

University of New South Wales. *The University of New South Wales*. Verity Press, Sydney 1961.

UNSW Press website research material. 1998.

Winton, R. 'With Hand, Mind and Heart: A Look Back at the First Quarter Century of the Faculty of Medicine UNSW', unpublished manuscript. (nd) [Faculty of Medicine].

ARCHIVAL MATERIALS

[Unless otherwise stated, all archival material is held in the collection of the UNSW Archives. Material specifically held by, or originating in the Oral History Project of the UNSW Archives is designated OHP.]

MATERIAL COLLECTED AND COMPILED BY FIFTIETH ANNIVERSARY HISTORY PROJECT

Correspondence 1994–98 [author's collection].

Fell, C. Typescript and research reports. 1998.

Hutchings, K. 'Idealism and a radical perspective — the student movement at UNSW 1960s–80': research report. February 1996.

——. 'Press Coverage of the Tharunka Pornography Trial 1970–72': research report. 1997.

——. 'Students in the 1950s': research report summarising the responses to the survey questionnaire conducted by the Oral History Project, UNSW Archives. 1997.

——. 'Students in the 1960s': research report summarising the responses to the survey questionnaire conducted by the Oral History Project, UNSW Archives. 1998.

——. 'The Tie': research report. February 1996.

——. 'Women in the University': research report summarising the responses to the survey questionnaire conducted by the Oral History Project, UNSW Archives. February 1998.

Hutchings, K (compiler). Materials from Sydney University Archives on foundation of University of Technology. 1995.

MATERIAL COLLECTED AND COMPILED BY ORAL HISTORY PROJECT, UNSW ARCHIVES

Campbell, R. Index to the University Oral History Project.

Horne, J. Students in the 1950s: A Survey of Student Experience at UNSW. And survey responses. 1996.

——. Students in the 1960s: A Survey of Student Experience at UNSW. And survey responses. 1997.

——. Women in the Archives: A Survey of Women's Experience to assist in writing the recent history of women at UNSW for its fiftieth anniversary. And survey responses. 1997.

PERSONAL, PRIVATE OR OFFICIAL PAPERS OF INDIVIDUALS

Baxter papers 1956–67.

Baxter, JP. 'The Day the Sun Rose in the West', unpublished play (nd).

Birt, LM. Personal papers.

Chappell, J (student 1960s). Typescript January 1998.

Fraser, JS. 'The University of NSW: Its History and Progress' (roneoed format). December 1962.

History, School of. Syllabi and course outlines 1960s–1990s [author's collection].

Howie, DS. Correspondence [author's collection].

Kaye, Rev Dr BN (Anglican Synod). Correspondence 1998 [author's collection].

Lawrence, J. Selected personal materials on Social Work.

McMahon, J and Reuter, I. 'The Host Family Scheme: Overseas Students in Australia'. [Reuter collection].

Milner, CJ. Personal papers.

Myers, RH. Personal papers.

Newman Society. Material 1960s–1980s.

Niland, J. Papers and correspondence.

O'Farrell, C (Arts student 1975–79). Recollections 1997.

O'Farrell, G (Arts/Law student 1978–82). Typescript 1996.

O'Farrell, P. Selected correspondence, various papers [author's collection].

O'Farrell, V (Arts student and PhD student 1979–95). Typescript 1997.

Reuter, I. Personal correspondence and press clippings re U Committee and Host Family Scheme, 1960s–1980 [Reuter collection].

Sacred Heart Monastery. Material on UNSW chapel and chaplaincy [Sacred Heart Monastery collection].

Smith, R (Associate Professor, Surgery, Royal North Shore Hospital). Notes and Reminiscences of 1968. 1998.

Thornton, JB. Correspondence and phone conversations 1996–98 [author's collection].

Woods, LC. Unpublished memoirs (nd) [Woods collection].

UNSW Archives holdings, by subject

AGSM

Alexander, AE

Amalgamation — press clippings December 1988 – March 1989

ANZAAS

Asian overseas student enrolment figures at UNSW 1963–95

Baxter, JP

Broken Hill University College campus

Buzo, A

Campus refurbishment

Charles Sturt University amalgamation and sponsorship by UNSW

College of Fine Arts (COFA)

Commerce Society,

Conatus

Dawkins & Metherell — articles on 1987–89

Denning, A

Development of UNSW — press clippings 1967

Freeland, M

General Staff Enterprise Agreement 1997

General Studies

Hartwell, RM 1956–80s

Heffron, RJ

ORAL HISTORY INTERVIEWS AND PHONE CONVERSATIONS

Interviews conducted by the Fiftieth Anniversary History Project were given on the basis of confidentiality. Unless this has been waived, these, while held by the University Archives, will not be available without the written permission of the interviewee. Telephone conversation notes remain in the possession of the author.

For the availability of access to those interviews carried out by the Oral History Project (signified below by [OHP]), consult UNSW Archives.

Alexander, C (School of English). July 1995.

Alexander, P (School of English). July 1995.

Allen, J (School of English). October 1995.

Allen, N (School of Science and Technology Studies). October 1995.

Atkins, R (School of Political Science). May 1983 [OHP].

Bell, R (School of History). September 1995.

Birt, LM (Vice-Chancellor). 1994 [OHP].

Black, Dr I (School of History). August 1995.

Blunden, R (School of Traffic Engineering). May 1985 [OHP].

Bosson, G (School of Maths). September 1983 [OHP].

Brookes, C (School of Information Systems). October 1997.

Brown, HJ (School of Electrical Engineering). May 1998; and March 1982 [OHP].

Butcher, E (NIDA). June 1996.

Carmody, J (School of Physiology and Pharmacology). May 1997.

Cavill, K (School of Chemistry). August 1996.

Chaikin, M (Pro-Vice-Chancellor). September 1989 [OHP].

Channell, I (School of Sociology). March 1996.

Clark, J (Director, NIDA). October 1996.

Coffey, C (Vice-Chancellor's Division). May 1997.

Condous, C (Registrar). April 1997.

Crouch, M (School of Sociology). September 1997.

Crowley, F (Dean, Faculty of Arts). February 1996; and National Library of Australia Oral History Section, October 1986.

Cuningham, AT (Warden, University Union). April 1980 [OHP].

Davis, J (President of the Academic Board). March 1996.

Douglas, J (Department of Statistics). May 1998.

Earle, T (Secretary, ADFA University College). September 1995.

Evans J (Secretary, Faculty of Arts & Social Sciences). October 1996.

Fell, C (Deputy Vice-Chancellor). March 1996 and January 1998.

Forgas, J (School of Psychology). August 1997.

Gannon, J (Bursar). June 1995.

Garrick, J (Director, Institute of Languages). November 1981 [OHP].

Gascoigne, J (School of History). September 1995.

Gascoigne, RM (Schools of Chemistry and General Studies). tape recording, March 1994.

Glover, D (Dean, Faculty of Medicine). February 1996.

Golding, RM (Pro-Vice-Chancellor). telephone conversation notes April 1998; and June 1986 [OHP].

Grace, M (Commerce student 1960s). June 1996.

Harcourt, M (School of History). September 1995.

Harpley, N (School of Philosophy). September 1995.

Hartwell, RM (Dean, Faculty of Humanities and Social Sciences). 1982 [OHP].

Haymet, T (University medallist and eye specialist). March 1998.

Hornby, S (Librarian, AGSM). November 1997.

Horton, A (University Librarian). 1988 [OHP].

Howie, DS (Managing-Director, UNSW Press). August 1996.

Hundt, K (Coordinator, Laboratory Services, School of Mechanical and Manufacturing Engineering). May 1997.

Ingleson, J (Dean, Faculty of Arts and Social Sciences). August 1995.

Kaan, R (Director, Unisearch). September 1997.

Kennedy, J (School of Wool Technology). January 1996; and August 1997 [OHP].

Lawrence, J (School of Social Work). April 1998.

Layton, R (Department of Marketing). March 1996.

Levy, Dr J (School of Spanish and Latin American Studies). February 1996.

Lowe, I (president UNSW Students' Union; Professor, Griffith University). October 1996.

Lumbers, E (School of Physiology and Pharmacology). July 1997.

Macauley, GL (Registrar). March 1984 [OHP].

McBrearty, K (Human Resources). May 1997.

McNamara, T (Executive Officer, Faculty of Commerce and Economics). April 1996.

Milfull, J (Dean, Faculty of Arts). November 1995.

Milner, CJ (School of Applied Physics). December 1984 [OHP].

Milner Davis, J (Deputy Chancellor). August 1996.

Morrison, I (School of Electrical Engineering). January 1996.

Morrison, J (Pro-Vice-Chancellor). March 1996.

Myers, RH (Vice-Chancellor). August 1996.

Nairn, B (National Dictionary of Biography, ANU). telephone conversation notes May 1995.

Nettheim, G (Law). November 1995.

Nightingale, P (Director, Professional Development Centre). June 1997.

Niland, J (Vice-Chancellor). interview March 1995; and notes of informal chat October 1997.

Oliver, H (School of English). December 1981 [OHP].

Pearson, M (School of History). November 1995.

Pert, RE (Assistant Registrar). February 1984 [OHP].

Pont, Dr G (School of General Studies). October 1995.

Pusey, M (Sociology). March 1998.

Radcliffe, J (School of Chemical Engineering). September 1995.

Rigby, B (Campus optical technician). July 1997.

Ronayne, J (Deputy Vice-Chancellor). April 1998.

Rosen, Dr R (School of Nuclear Engineering). telephone conversation notes May 1995.

Samways, C (Safety Officer, School of Nuclear Engineering). March 1996.

Smith, FB (History ANU). telephone conversation notes May 1995.

Smyth, B (Dean, Faculty of Commerce and Economics). October 1983 [OHP].

Somervaille, I (School of Civil Engineering). 1996.

Spooner, P (School of Landscape Architecture). January 1981 [OHP].

Stewart, L (Secretary, University Council). July 1996.

Thompson, E (School of Political Science). July 1996.

Vinson, T (School of Social Work). May 1997.

Webb, J (School of Mining Engineering). November 1983 [OHP].

Whiffen, N (School of Chemical Engineering). June 1993 [OHP]; and telephone conversation notes 1994.

Wicken, T (Deputy Vice-Chancellor). September 1997.

Willis, AH (Pro-Vice-Chancellor). January 1996; and March–May 1984 [OHP].

Windsor, G (Novelist, School of English). June 1995.

Wood, J (Schools of Mechanical Engineering and General Studies). September 1983 [OHP].

Wootten, JH (Law). April 1988 [OHP].

Wyse, N (Medical student 1960s). December 1997.

OTHER PUBLISHED MATERIAL

BOOKS AND PAMPHLETS

Allen, B. *Art at UNSW: collecting from a university's perspective—selected acquisitions 1991–95.* University Publications, January 1996.

Australian Council for Educational Research. *Review of Education in Australia 1955–62,* Hawthorn, Victoria 1964.

Ayres, P. *Malcolm Fraser: A Biography.* Heinemann, Richmond, Victoria 1987.

Baker, AJ. *Anderson's Social Philosophy.* Angus & Robertson, London 1979.

Barcan, A. *A History of Australian Education.* Oxford University Press, Melbourne 1980.

——. *Two Centuries of Education in NSW.* UNSW Press, Kensington 1988.

Barker, V (ed.). *Phyllis Margaret Rountree: Honorary Research Associate in the School of Microbiology the University of NSW 1971–.* University Interviews Project, UNSW Archives 1991.

Barlow, A. *Scientific Manpower* [Barlow Report]. HMSO 1946.

Birrell, PC & Martins, JF (eds). *Newman and the Nature of a University.* Warrane College, UNSW, 1990.

Bowman, L (ed.). *John Philip Baxter: Vice Chancellor of UNSW 1955–69,* University Interviews Project, UNSW Archives 1987.

Bowman, L and Barker, V (eds). *Rupert Horace Myers: Vice-Chancellor of the University of NSW 1969–81,* University Interviews Project, UNSW Archives 1990.

Brown, N. *Governing Prosperity: Social Change and Social Analysis in Australia in the 1950s.* Cambridge University Press, Cambridge 1995.

Buzo, Alex. *The Search for Harry Allway.* Angus & Robertson, North Ryde 1985.

Caine, B *et al* (eds). *History at Sydney 1891–91: Centenary Reflections.* Highland Press, Canberra, 1992.

Carey, G. *In My Father's House*. Picador, Chippendale, 1992.

Castle, J. *University of Wollongong: An Illustrated History*. University of Wollongong Press, Wollongong 1991.

Chapman, P (ed.). *Forty Years of FAUSA 1952–92: Proceedings of the 40th Anniversary Conference of the Federation of Australian University Staff, September 1992*. NTEU, Melbourne 1993.

Cockburn, S & Ellyard, D. *Oliphant: The Life and Times of Sir Mark Oliphant*. Axiom Books, Australia 1981.

Connell, WF *et al*. *Australia's First: A History of the University of Sydney 1850–1990* (2 vols). Hale & Iremonger, Sydney 1995.

Crowley, F. *Degrees Galore: Australia's Academic Teller Machines*. privately published 1997.

Dudman, M. *Images of the University of NSW*. Ebeling Publications, Maroubra 1989.

Foster, SG and Varghese, MM. *The Making of the Australian National University 1946–96*. Allen & Unwin, St Leonards 1996.

Fox, J and Wright, P. *Thinking Ahead: Planning Growth in Australian Higher Education*. FAUSA and FCA, June 1988.

Garis, B de. *Campus in the Community: the University of Western Australia 1963–87*. University of Western Australia Press 1988.

Harman, G and Meek, V Lynn. *Australian Higher Education Reconstructed? Analysis of the Proposals and Assumptions of the Dawkins Green Paper*. Department of Administration and Higher Education Studies, University of New England 1988.

Harries, O (ed.). *Liberty and Politics: Studies in Social Theory*. Pergamon Press, Rushcutters Bay 1976.

Harrison, B (ed.). *The History of the University of Oxford: Volume 8 The Twentieth Century*. Clarendon Press, Oxford 1994.

Haskell, J. *Haskell's Sydney*. Hale and Iremonger, Marrickville 1983.

Hollows, F and Corris, P. *Fred Hollows: An Autobiography*. Kerr Publishing, Balmain 1992.

Horne, J (ed.). *Not an Ivory Tower: The Making of an Australian Vice-Chancellor. Based on Interviews with Jenny and Michael Birt*, UNSW Archives 1997.

Kennedy, B. *A Passion To Oppose: John Anderson, Philosopher*, Melbourne University Press, Carlton South, Victoria 1995.

Lumby, C. *Bad Girls: The Media, Sex and Feminism in the 90s*. Allen & Unwin, St Leonards 1997.

Mansfield, B & Hutchinson, M. *Liberality of Opportunity: A History of Macquarie University 1964–89*, Hale & Iremonger, Sydney 1992.

Murphy, JA. *The College: A History of Queen's University College Cork 1845–1995*, Cork University Press, Cork 1995.

Neill, N. *Technically and Further: Sydney Technical College 1891–1991*. Hale & Iremonger, Marrickville 1991.

Neville, R. *Hippie Hippie Shake: the dreams, the trips, the trials, the love-ins, the screw ups ... the sixties*. William Heinemann Australia, Melbourne 1995.

Percy, Lord Eustace. *Higher Technological Education in Great Britain* [Percy Report]. HMSO 1945.

Poynter, J & Rasmussen, C. *A Place Apart: The University of Melbourne: Decades of Change*. Melbourne University Press, Melbourne 1996.

Quirke, N. *Preparing for the Future: A History of Griffith University 1971–96.* Boolarong Press, Nathan 1996.

Rumley, K. *The University of NSW Collection: Integrating Art on Campus.* UNSW, Kensington 1992.

Snow, CP. *The Two Cultures and a Second Look.* Cambridge University Press, Cambridge [1959] 1988.

Star, L. *Julius Stone: An Intellectual Life.* Oxford University Press, South Melbourne 1992.

University of Melbourne. *Change and Tradition: A Portrait of the University of Melbourne.* University of Melbourne Press, Brunswick 1993.

Vickers, M. *Universities and the National Interest: the Dawkins Plan for Higher Education in Australia: A Case Study in Policy Development and Implementation.* Public Policy Program ANU, Canberra, July 1989.

Ward, R. *A Radical Life: The Autobiography of Russel Ward.* Macmillan, South Melbourne 1988.

Willis, AH. *The University of NSW: The Baxter Years.* New South Wales University Press, Kensington 1983.

Wright, D. *Looking Back: A History of the University of Newcastle.* Newcastle University Press. 1992.

ARTICLES, SPEECHES AND EPHEMERAL PUBLICATIONS

Angyal, SJ. 'Sir Philip Baxter 1905–89'. *Historical Records of Australian Science* vol. 8 no. 3: 183–97.

Australian (selected issues).

Baxter, JP. 'A Short History of the University of NSW to 1964'. *The Australian University* vol. 3 no. 1, May 1965.

——. 'Some Comments on Ann Moyal's *The Australian Atomic Energy Commission: A Case Study*'. *Search* vol. 6 no. 11–12, November–December 1975, pp456–59.

Brown, HJ. 'Trends in Higher Technological Education and Developments in NSW'. *The Journal* vol. 21, September 1949.

Clarke, AM and Birt, LM. 'Evaluative Reviews in Universities: the influence of public policies'. *Higher Education* vol. 11, 1982, 1–26.

Croker, G. 'The Samuels Curtain Falls on a Twenty-five year Run'. *Uniken* 10 June 1994.

'ELW'. 'Political Tests for university appointments — the Russel Ward case'. *Vestes*, vol. 4 no. 1, March 1961.

Haynes, M & Haynes, M. 'My Perspective'. Alumni Association Speech 1998 [UNSW Archives collection].

Kaye, BN. 'Cardinal Newman at the University of NSW'. *Australasian Catholic Record*, lxviii, one, January 1991.

Metherell, T. Address to the University of Sydney Convocation Graduate Annual Dinner. July 1988.

Myers, RH. 'Toast to Sir Philip and Lady Baxter'. *Technology*, vol. 14 no. 2, August 1969.

Oliphant, M. 'University or Institute of Technology?'. *Universities Quarterly*, vol. 4 no. 1, 1949, pp19–23.

Pont, G. 'Don Laycock: Collector and Creator of Dirty Songs'. In T Dutton, M Ross and

D Tryon (eds), 'The Language Game: Papers in Memory of Donald C Laycock', *Pacific Linguistics* c-110, 1992, pp635–44.

——. 'General Education in the 21st Century: Planning for a Clever Country'. *Alumni Papers* September–November 1991.

Public Relations Officer (ed.). 'Humanities and Social Sciences'. *Technology*, UNSW Kensington, vol. 4 no. 2, July 1959, pp58–60.

Ratcliffe, J. 'A Short History of the University: reading from the other book of Genesis'. speech at 40-year reunion of graduates, August 1992.

Stretton, H. 'Life After Dawkins: Teaching and Research with Diminishing Resources'. Sixth Wallace Wurth Memorial Lecture, September 1989.

Sydney Morning Herald (selected issues).

Willgoss, R. 'Mechatronics: Australia's Future is in Synergistic Engineering'. talk given 22 May 1997 on Radio National, Australian Broadcasting Corporation.

Windsor, G. 'The Professor and the Trumpeter'. In G Windsor, *Harlots Enter First*, Hale & Iremonger, Sydney, 1982.

INDEX

Illustrations are shown in this index by page numbers in **bold** type.